HARLEY QUINN

HARLEY DESTROYS THE UNIVERSE

VOL. 2

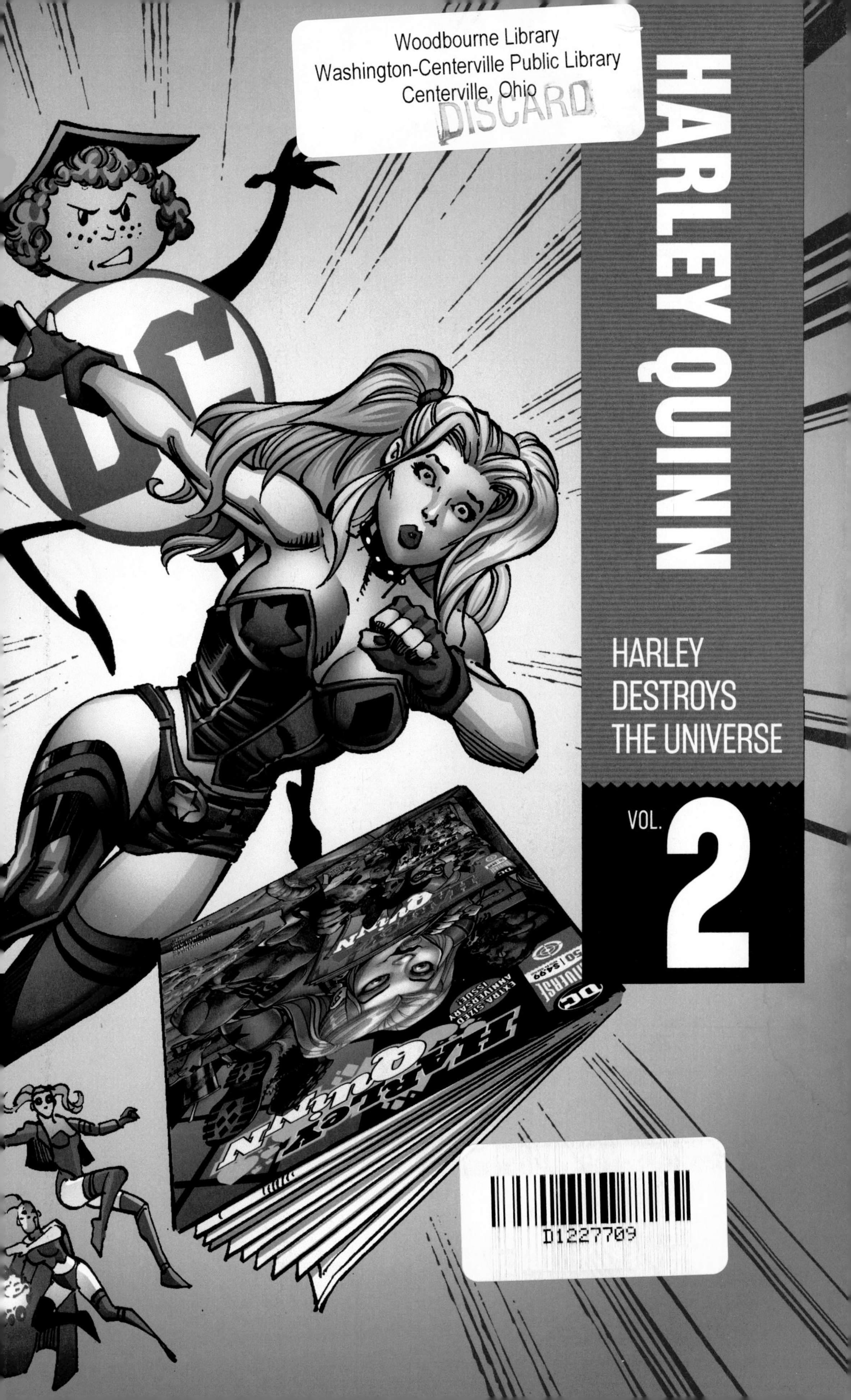
HARLEY QUINN
EXTRA-SIZED ANNIVERSARY ISSUE!

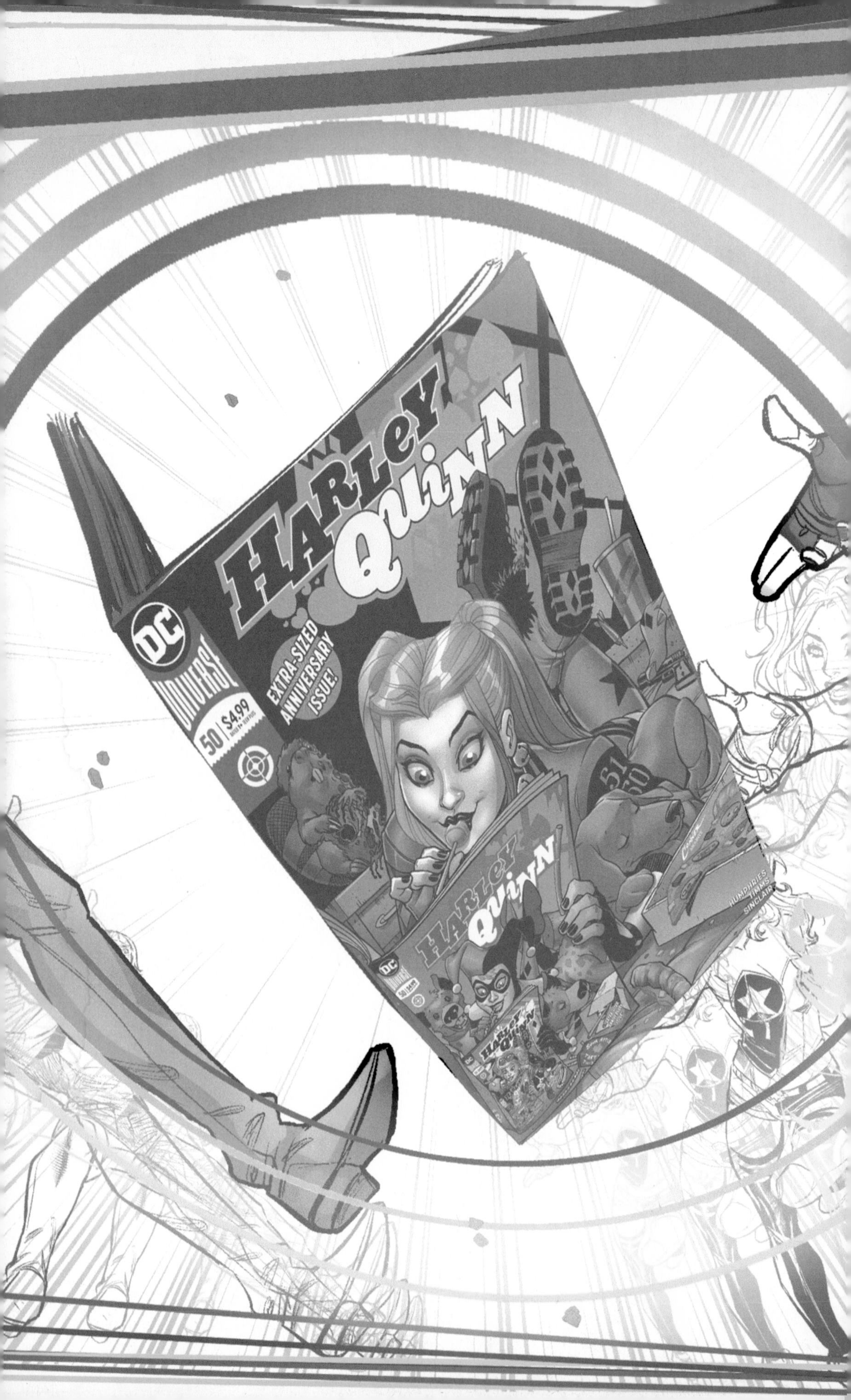
HARLEY QUINN
DC UNIVERSE
50 $4.99
EXTRA-SIZED ANNIVERSARY ISSUE!
HUMPHRIES
TIMMS
SINCLAIR

HARLEY QUINN
HARLEY DESTROYS
THE UNIVERSE

writers

SAM HUMPHRIES
MARK RUSSELL

artists

SAMI BASRI \ LUCAS WERNECK
MIRKA ANDOLFO
JOHN TIMMS \ WHILCE PORTACIO
AGNES GARBOWSKA \ JOHN McCREA
KELLEY JONES \ JON DAVIS-HUNT
BRETT BOOTH \ NORM RAPMUND
SCOTT KOLINS \ DAN JURGENS
GUILLEM MARCH \ BABS TARR
TOM GRUMMETT \ CAM SMITH

colorists

ALEX SINCLAIR
GABE ELTAEB \ ARIF PRIANTO
JOHN KALISZ \ MICHELLE MADSEN
ANDREW DALHOUSE \ ROMULO FAJARDO JR.

letterer

DAVE SHARPE

collection cover artist

JULIAN TOTINO TEDESCO

HARLEY QUINN created by PAUL DINI and BRUCE TIMM
SUPERMAN created by JERRY SIEGEL and JOE SHUSTER
By special arrangement with the Jerry Siegel family

VOL. **2**

ALEX ANTONE Editor – Original Series
ANDREA SHEA Assistant Editor – Original Series
JEB WOODARD Group Editor – Collected Editions
ROBIN WILDMAN Editor – Collected Edition
STEVE COOK Design Director – Books
CURTIS KING JR. Publication Design

BOB HARRAS Senior VP – Editor-in-Chief, DC Comics
PAT McCALLUM Executive Editor, DC Comics

DAN DiDIO Publisher
JIM LEE Publisher & Chief Creative Officer
AMIT DESAI Executive VP – Business & Marketing Strategy, Direct to
                  Consumer & Global Franchise Management
BOBBIE CHASE VP & Executive Editor, Young Reader & Talent Development
MARK CHIARELLO Senior VP – Art, Design & Collected Editions
JOHN CUNNINGHAM Senior VP – Sales & Trade Marketing
BRIAR DARDEN VP – Business Affairs
ANNE DePIES Senior VP – Business Strategy, Finance & Administration
DON FALLETTI VP – Manufacturing Operations
LAWRENCE GANEM VP – Editorial Administration & Talent Relations
ALISON GILL Senior VP – Manufacturing & Operations
JASON GREENBERG VP – Business Strategy & Finance
HANK KANALZ Senior VP – Editorial Strategy & Administration
JAY KOGAN Senior VP – Legal Affairs
NICK J. NAPOLITANO VP – Manufacturing Administration
LISETTE OSTERLOH VP – Digital Marketing & Events
EDDIE SCANNELL VP – Consumer Marketing
COURTNEY SIMMONS Senior VP – Publicity & Communications
JIM (SKI) SOKOLOWSKI VP – Comic Book Specialty Sales & Trade Marketing
NANCY SPEARS VP – Mass, Book, Digital Sales & Trade Marketing
MICHELE R. WELLS VP – Content Strategy

HARLEY QUINN VOL. 2: HARLEY DESTROYS THE UNIVERSE

DC Comics, 2900 West Alameda Ave., Burbank, CA 91505
Printed by LSC Communications, Owensville, MO, USA. 2/22/19. First Printing.
ISBN: 978-1-4012-8809-9

Library of Congress Cataloging-in-Publication Data is available.

PEFC Certified
This product is from
sustainably managed
forests and controlled
sources
PEFC/29-31-337   www.pefc.org

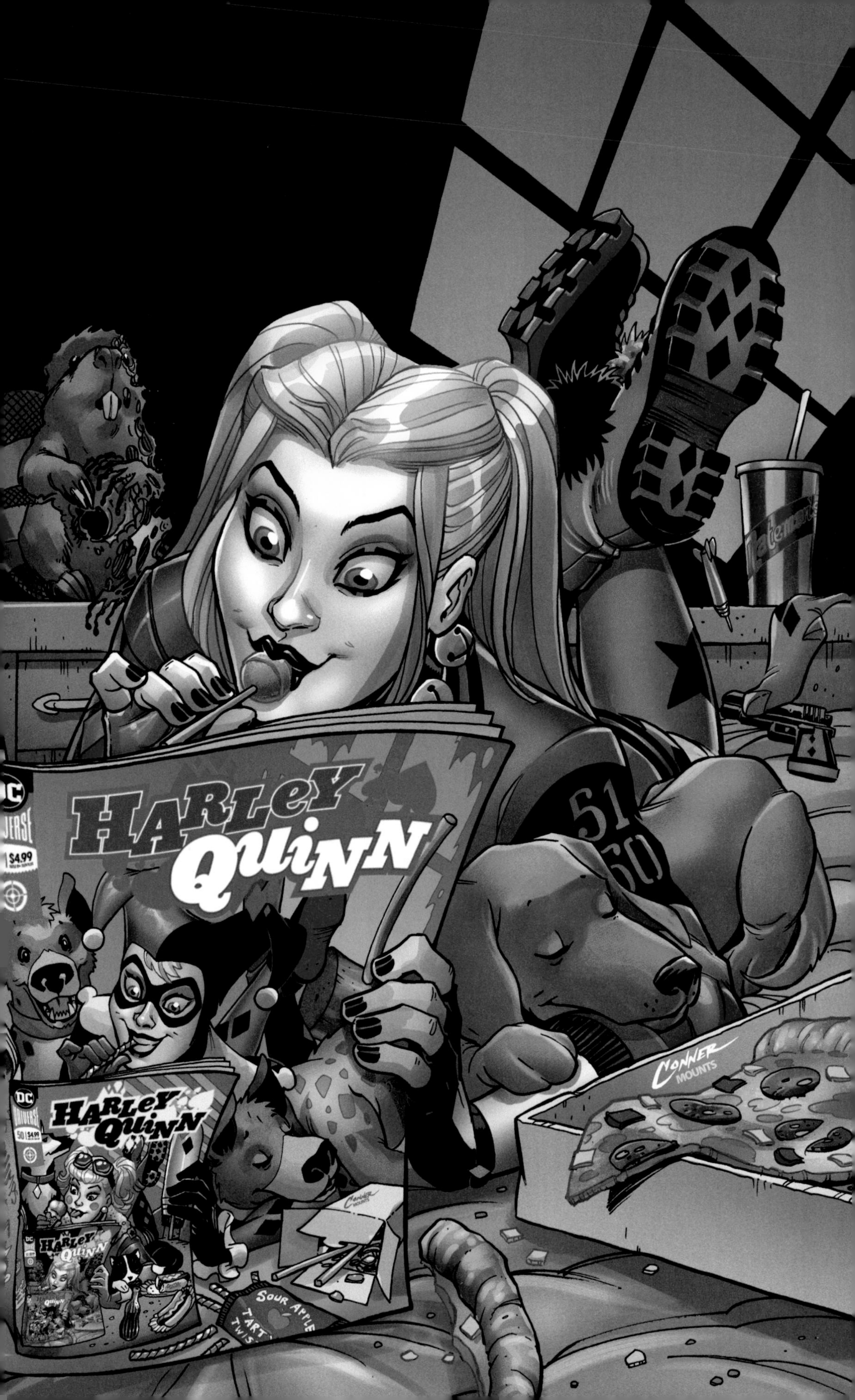

HARLEY QUINN
$4.99
51
60
CONNER MOUNTS
HARLEY QUINN
50 $4.99
SOUR APPLE

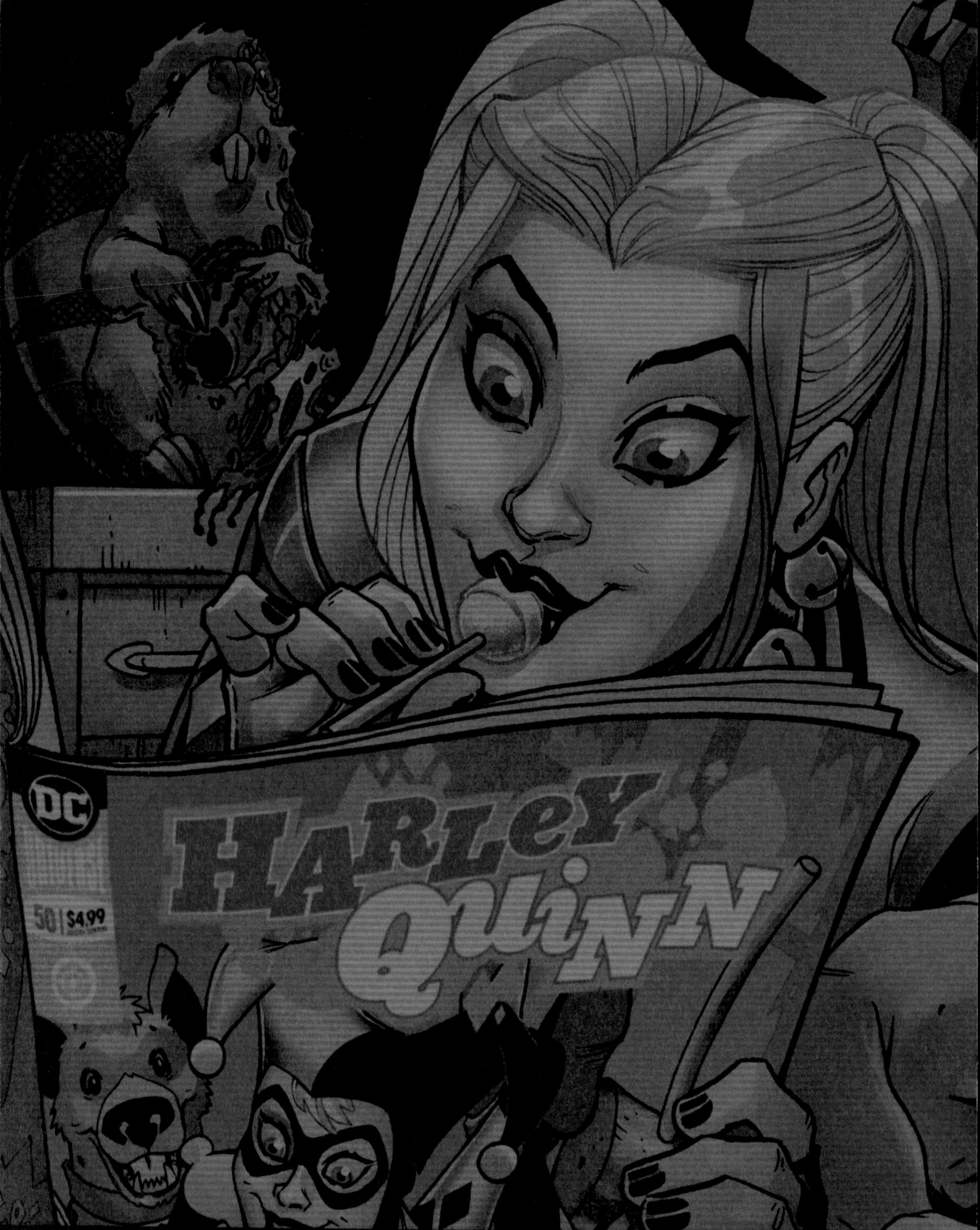
DC
HARLEY QUINN
50 | $4.99

HARLEY QUINN
#50

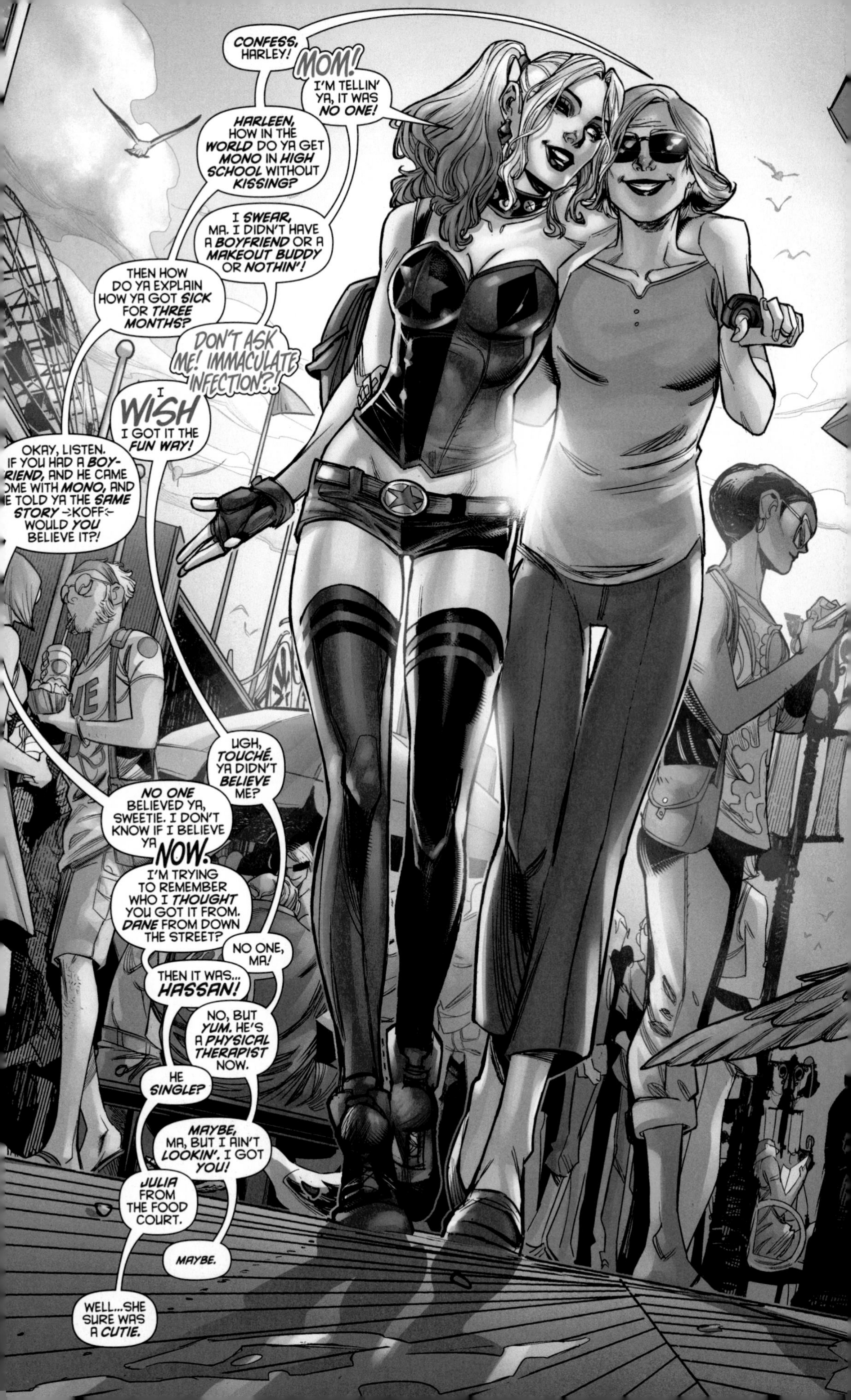
CONFESS, HARLEY!
MOM!
I'M TELLIN' YA, IT WAS NO ONE!
HARLEEN, HOW IN THE WORLD DO YA GET MONO IN HIGH SCHOOL WITHOUT KISSING?
I SWEAR, MA. I DIDN'T HAVE A BOYFRIEND OR A MAKEOUT BUDDY OR NOTHIN'!
THEN HOW DO YA EXPLAIN HOW YA GOT SICK FOR THREE MONTHS?
DON'T ASK ME! IMMACULATE INFECTION?!
I WISH I GOT IT THE FUN WAY!
OKAY, LISTEN. IF YOU HAD A BOY-FRIEND, AND HE CAME HOME WITH MONO, AND HE TOLD YA THE SAME STORY -KOFF- WOULD YOU BELIEVE IT?!
UGH, TOUCHÉ. YA DIDN'T BELIEVE ME?
NO ONE BELIEVED YA, SWEETIE. I DON'T KNOW IF I BELIEVE YA NOW.
I'M TRYING TO REMEMBER WHO I THOUGHT YOU GOT IT FROM. DANE FROM DOWN THE STREET?
NO ONE, MA!
THEN IT WAS... HASSAN!
NO, BUT YUM. HE'S A PHYSICAL THERAPIST NOW.
HE SINGLE?
MAYBE, MA, BUT I AIN'T LOOKIN'. I GOT YOU!
JULIA FROM THE FOOD COURT.
MAYBE.
WELL...SHE SURE WAS A CUTIE.

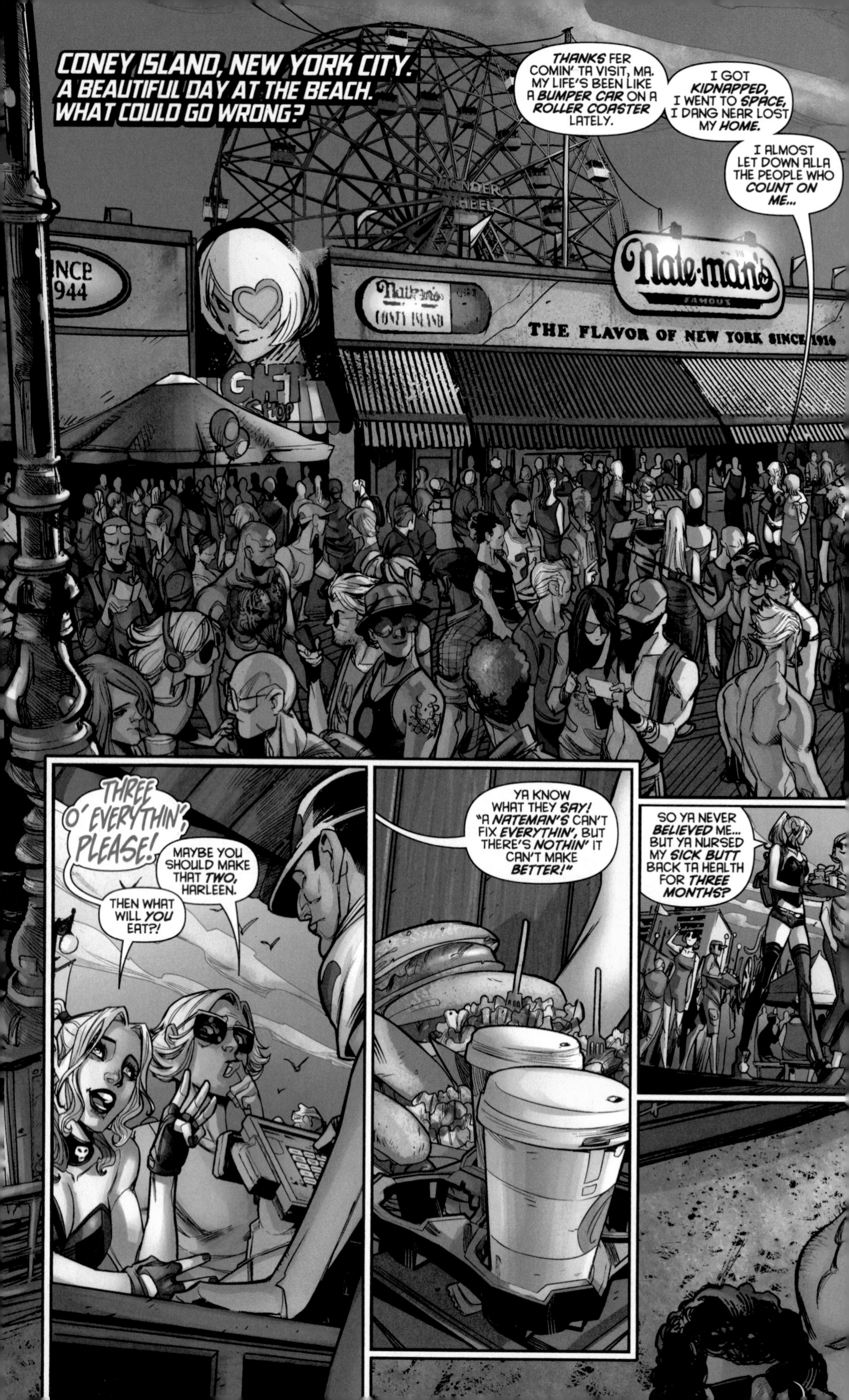
CONEY ISLAND, NEW YORK CITY.
A BEAUTIFUL DAY AT THE BEACH.
WHAT COULD GO WRONG?
THANKS FER COMIN' TA VISIT, MA. MY LIFE'S BEEN LIKE A BUMPER CAR ON A ROLLER COASTER LATELY.
I GOT KIDNAPPED, I WENT TO SPACE, I DANG NEAR LOST MY HOME.
I ALMOST LET DOWN ALLA THE PEOPLE WHO COUNT ON ME...
SINCE 1944
WONDER WHEEL
Nate-man's
FAMOUS
Nate-man's
CONEY ISLAND
THE FLAVOR OF NEW YORK SINCE 1916
GIFT SHOP
THREE O' EVERYTHIN', PLEASE!
MAYBE YOU SHOULD MAKE THAT TWO, HARLEEN.
THEN WHAT WILL YOU EAT?!
YA KNOW WHAT THEY SAY! "A NATEMAN'S CAN'T FIX EVERYTHIN', BUT THERE'S NOTHIN' IT CAN'T MAKE BETTER!"
SO YA NEVER BELIEVED ME... BUT YA NURSED MY SICK BUTT BACK TA HEALTH FOR THREE MONTHS?

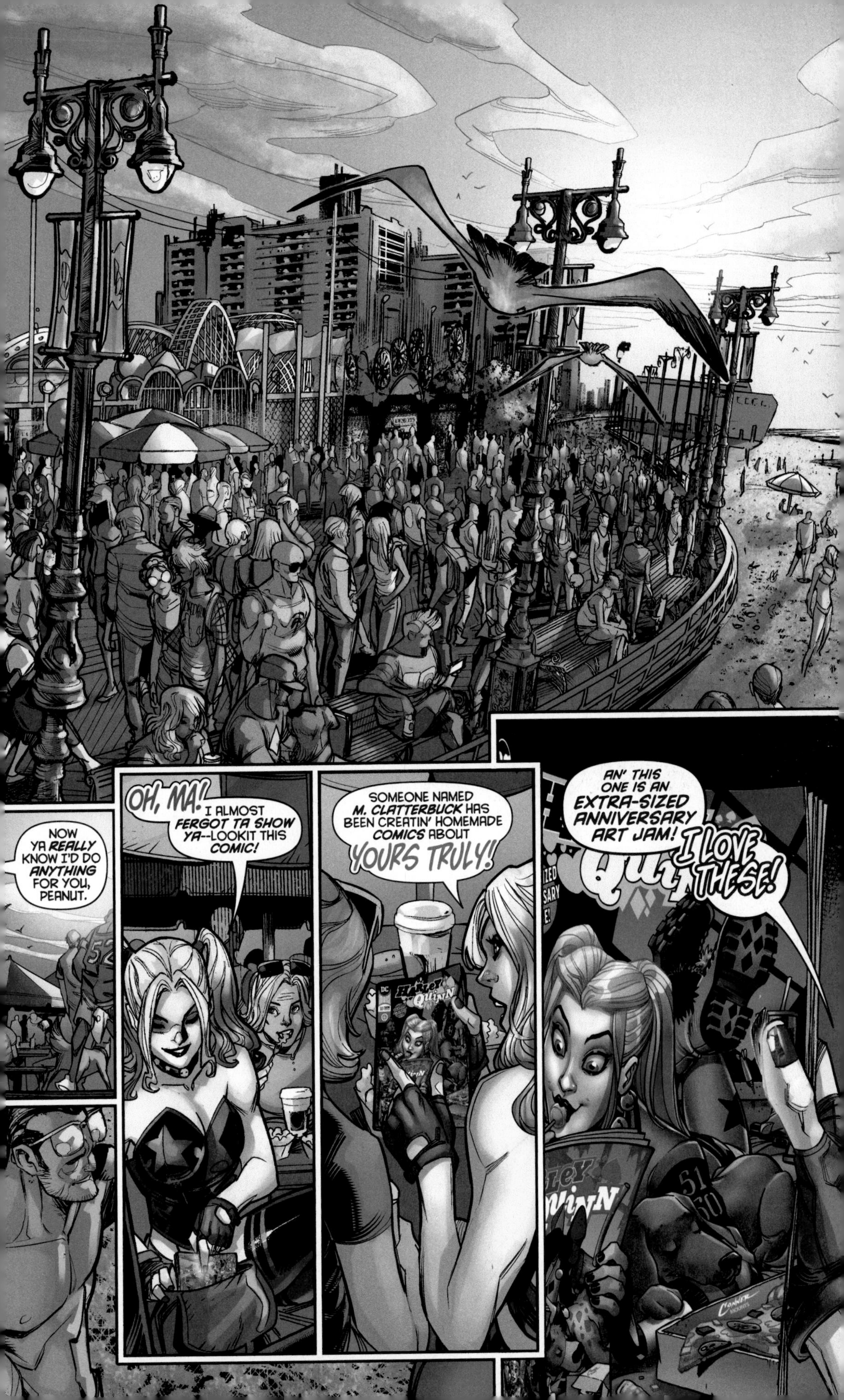
NOW YA REALLY KNOW I'D DO ANYTHING FOR YOU, PEANUT.
OH, MA! I ALMOST FERGOT TA SHOW YA--LOOKIT THIS COMIC!
SOMEONE NAMED M. CLATTERBUCK HAS BEEN CREATIN' HOMEMADE COMICS ABOUT YOURS TRULY!
AN' THIS ONE IS AN EXTRA-SIZED ANNIVERSARY ART JAM!
I LOVE THESE!

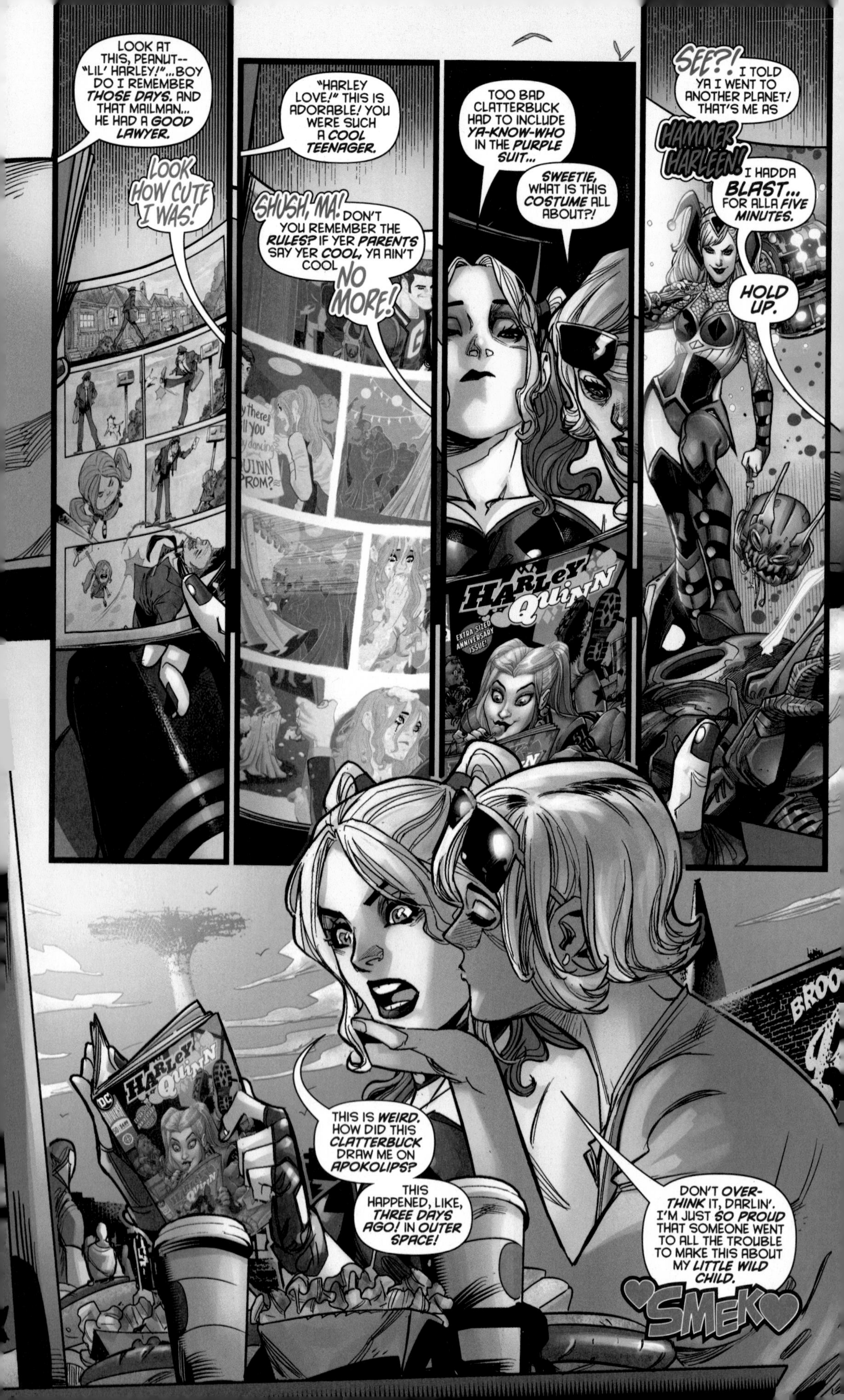
LOOK AT THIS, PEANUT-- "LIL' HARLEY!"...BOY DO I REMEMBER THOSE DAYS. AND THAT MAILMAN... HE HAD A GOOD LAWYER.
LOOK HOW CUTE I WAS!
"HARLEY LOVE!" THIS IS ADORABLE! YOU WERE SUCH A COOL TEENAGER.
SHUSH, MA! DON'T YOU REMEMBER THE RULES? IF YER PARENTS SAY YER COOL, YA AIN'T COOL NO MORE!
TOO BAD CLATTERBUCK HAD TO INCLUDE YA-KNOW-WHO IN THE PURPLE SUIT...
SWEETIE, WHAT IS THIS COSTUME ALL ABOUT?!
HARLEY QUINN
EXTRA-SIZED ANNIVERSARY ISSUE!
SEE?! I TOLD YA I WENT TO ANOTHER PLANET! THAT'S ME AS HAMMER HARLEEN! I HADDA BLAST... FOR ALLA FIVE MINUTES.
HOLD UP.
THIS IS WEIRD. HOW DID THIS CLATTERBUCK DRAW ME ON APOKOLIPS?
THIS HAPPENED, LIKE, THREE DAYS AGO! IN OUTER SPACE!
DON'T OVER-THINK IT, DARLIN'. I'M JUST SO PROUD THAT SOMEONE WENT TO ALL THE TROUBLE TO MAKE THIS ABOUT MY LITTLE WILD CHILD.
SMEK

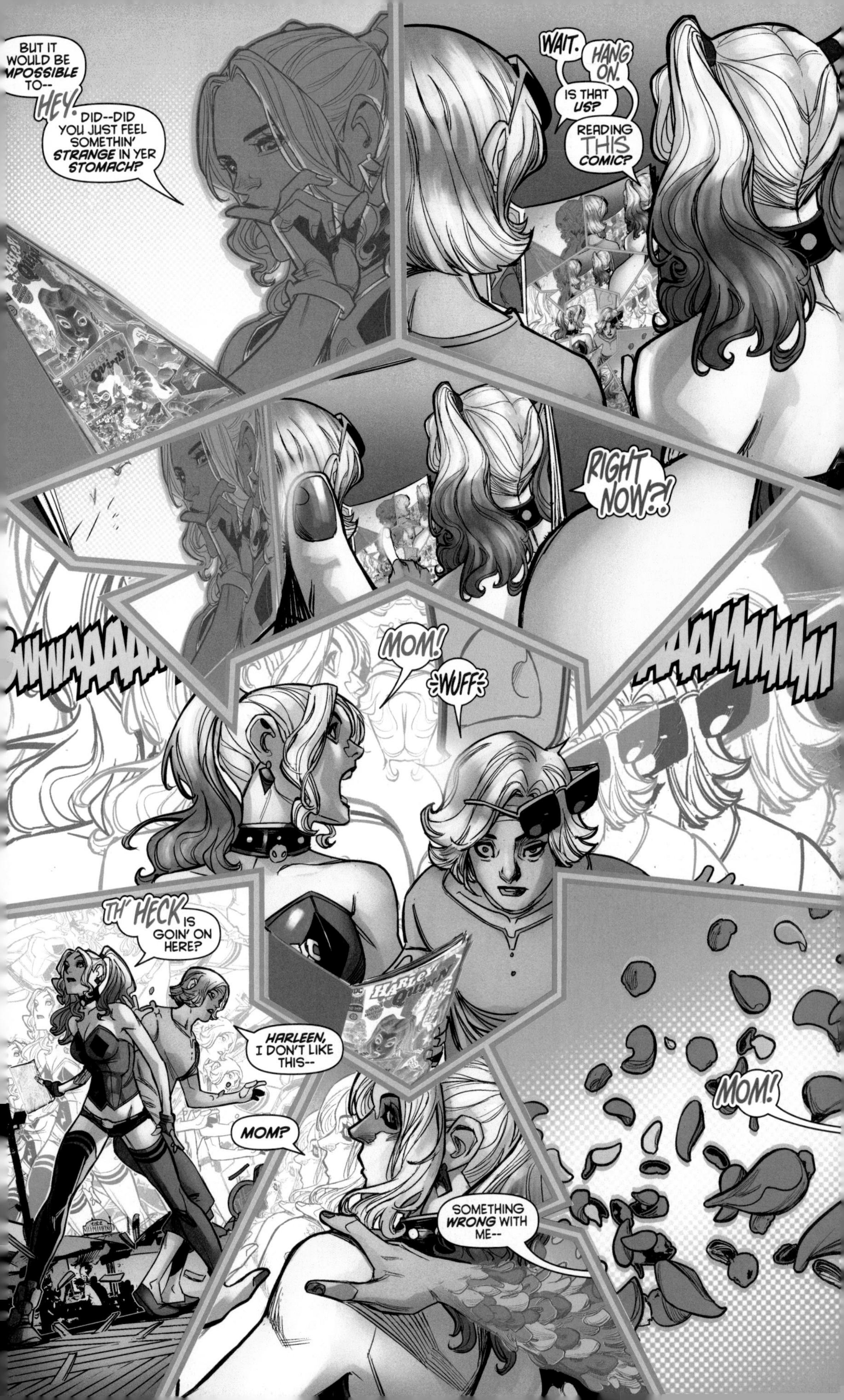
BUT IT WOULD BE IMPOSSIBLE TO--
HEY.
DID--DID YOU JUST FEEL SOMETHIN' STRANGE IN YER STOMACH?
WAIT.
HANG ON.
IS THAT US?
READING THIS COMIC?
RIGHT NOW?!
WWAAAAA
AAMMMMM
MOM!
WUFF
TH' HECK IS GOIN' ON HERE?
HARLEEN, I DON'T LIKE THIS--
MOM?
SOMETHING WRONG WITH ME--
MOM!

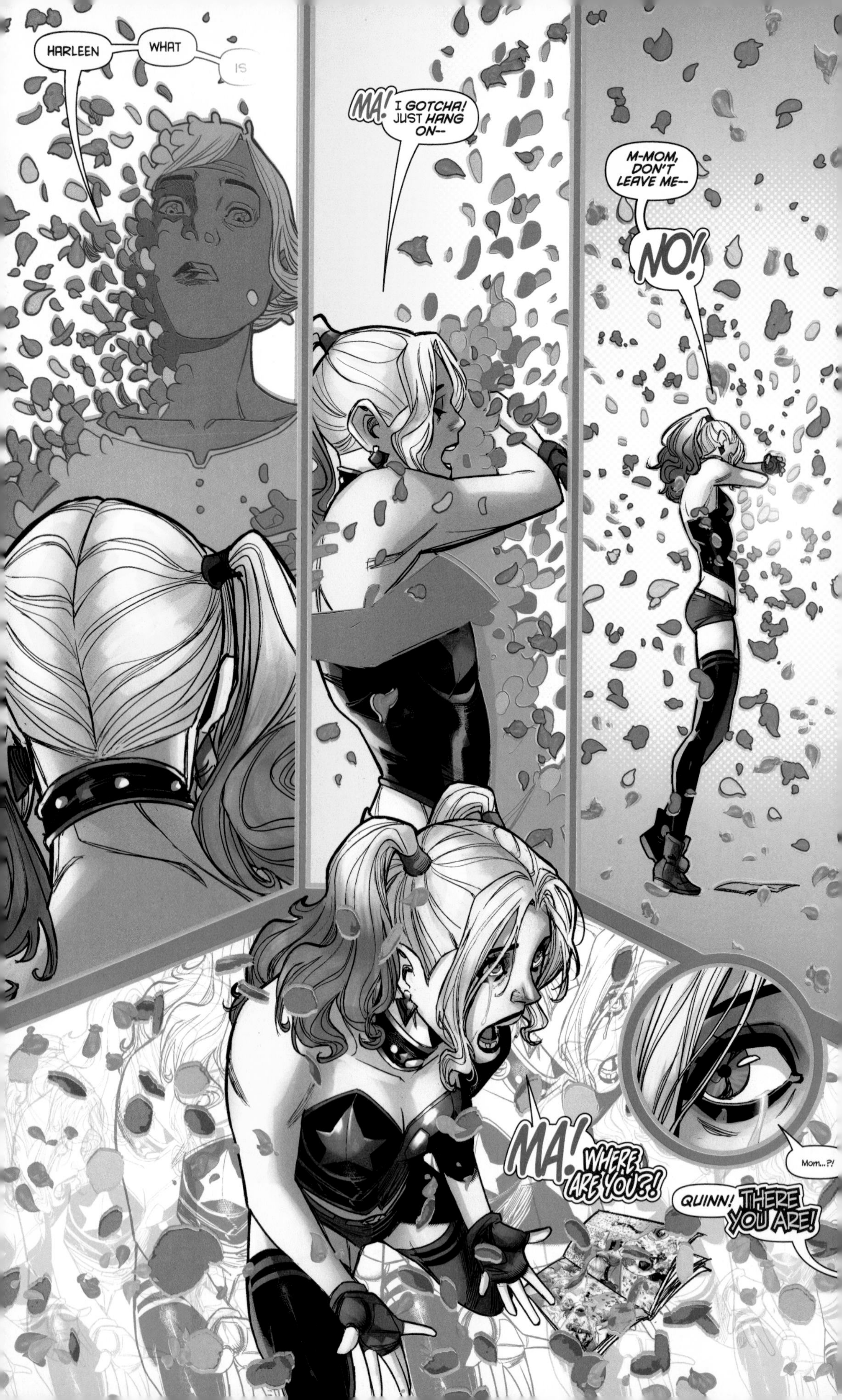
HARLEEN
WHAT
IS
MA! I GOTCHA! JUST HANG ON--
M-MOM, DON'T LEAVE ME--
NO!
MA! WHERE ARE YOU?!
Mom...?!
QUINN! THERE YOU ARE!

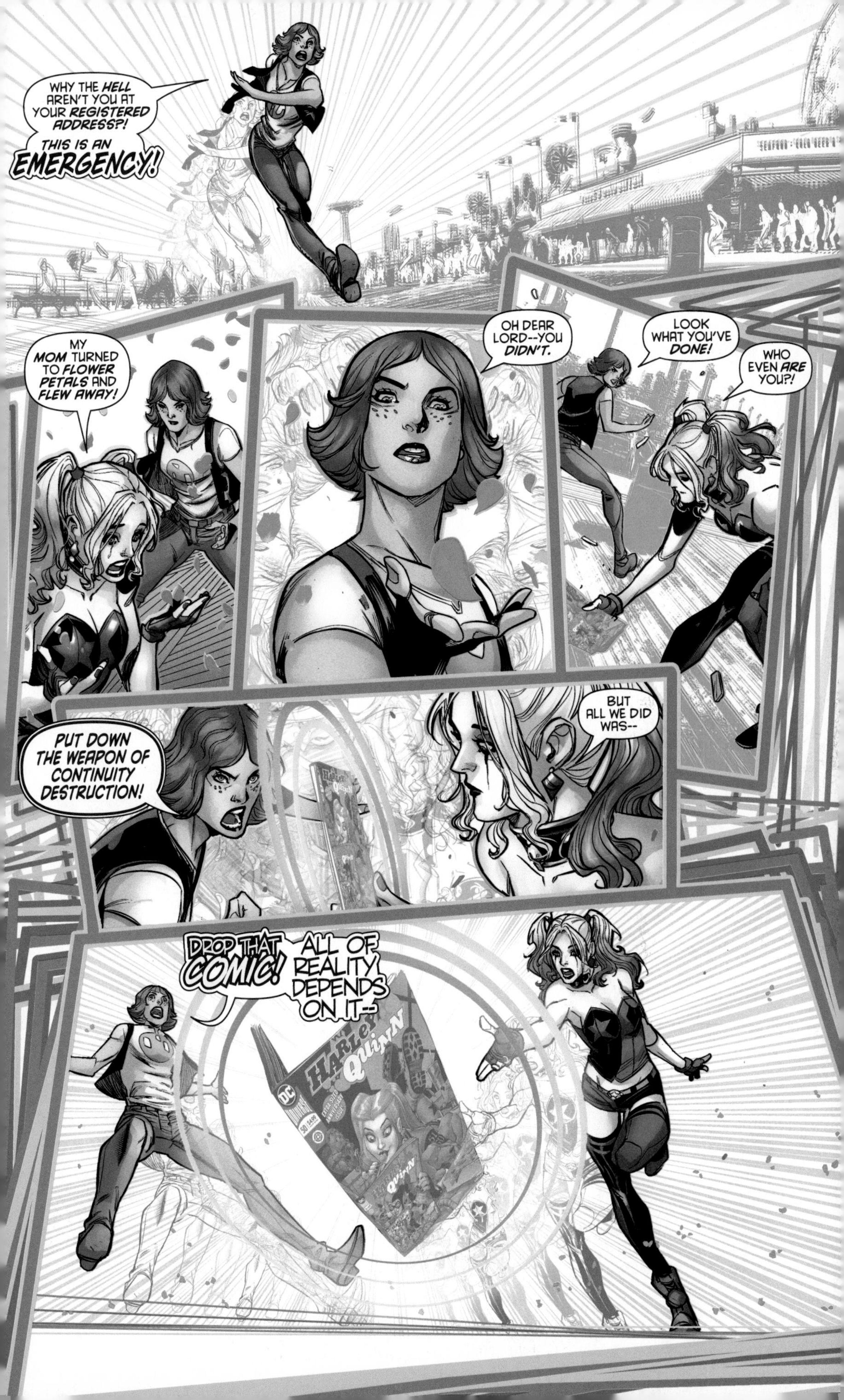
WHY THE HELL AREN'T YOU AT YOUR REGISTERED ADDRESS?!
THIS IS AN EMERGENCY!
MY MOM TURNED TO FLOWER PETALS AND FLEW AWAY!
OH DEAR LORD--YOU DIDN'T.
LOOK WHAT YOU'VE DONE!
WHO EVEN ARE YOU?!
PUT DOWN THE WEAPON OF CONTINUITY DESTRUCTION!
BUT ALL WE DID WAS--
DROP THAT COMIC!
ALL OF REALITY DEPENDS ON IT--

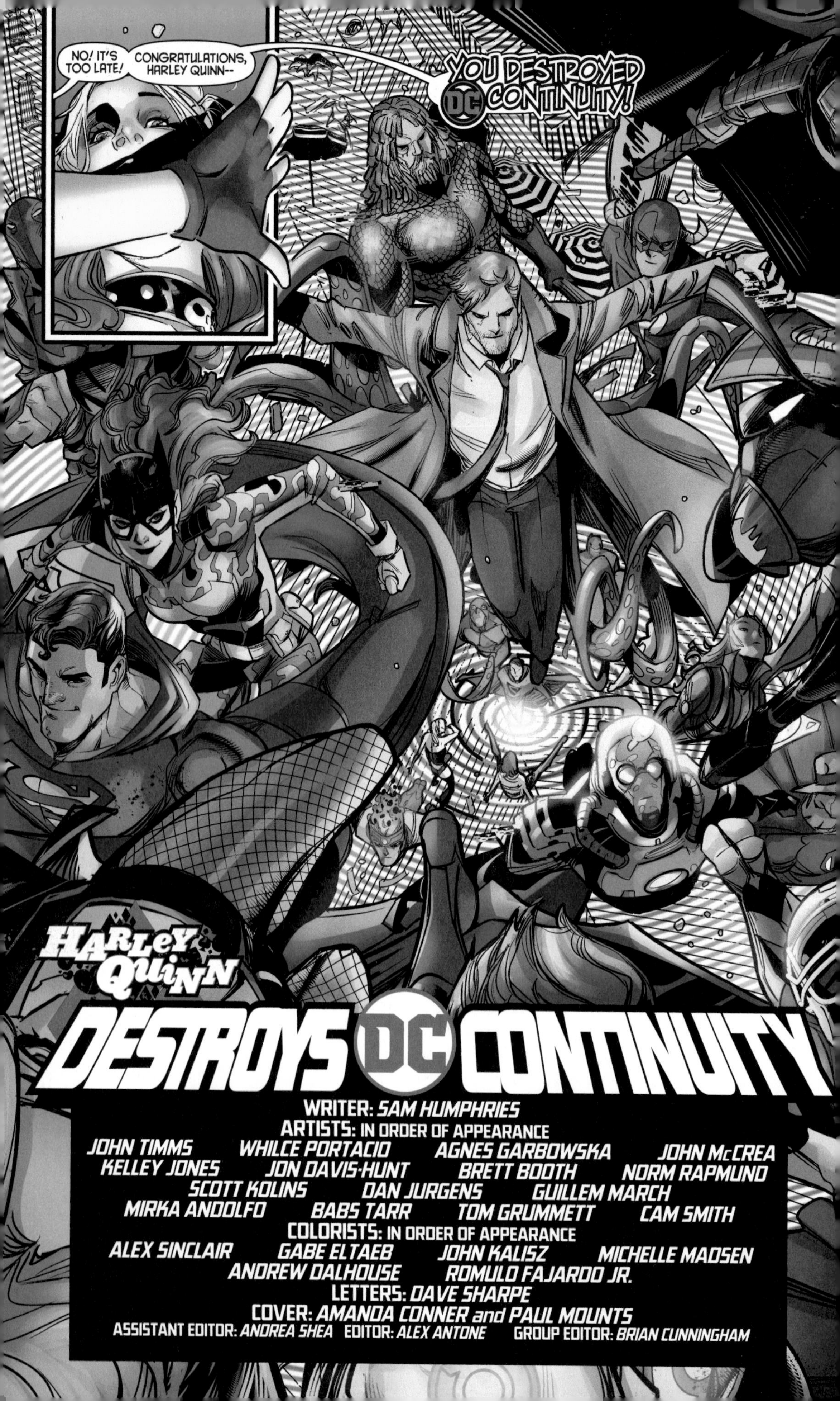
NO! IT'S TOO LATE!
CONGRATULATIONS, HARLEY QUINN--
YOU DESTROYED DC CONTINUITY!

HARLEY QUINN DESTROYS DC CONTINUITY

WRITER: *SAM HUMPHRIES*

ARTISTS: IN ORDER OF APPEARANCE

JOHN TIMMS WHILCE PORTACIO AGNES GARBOWSKA JOHN McCREA KELLEY JONES JON DAVIS-HUNT BRETT BOOTH NORM RAPMUND SCOTT KOLINS DAN JURGENS GUILLEM MARCH MIRKA ANDOLFO BABS TARR TOM GRUMMETT CAM SMITH

COLORISTS: IN ORDER OF APPEARANCE

ALEX SINCLAIR GABE ELTAEB JOHN KALISZ MICHELLE MADSEN ANDREW DALHOUSE ROMULO FAJARDO JR.

LETTERS: *DAVE SHARPE*

COVER: *AMANDA CONNER and PAUL MOUNTS*

ASSISTANT EDITOR: *ANDREA SHEA* **EDITOR:** *ALEX ANTONE* **GROUP EDITOR:** *BRIAN CUNNINGHAM*

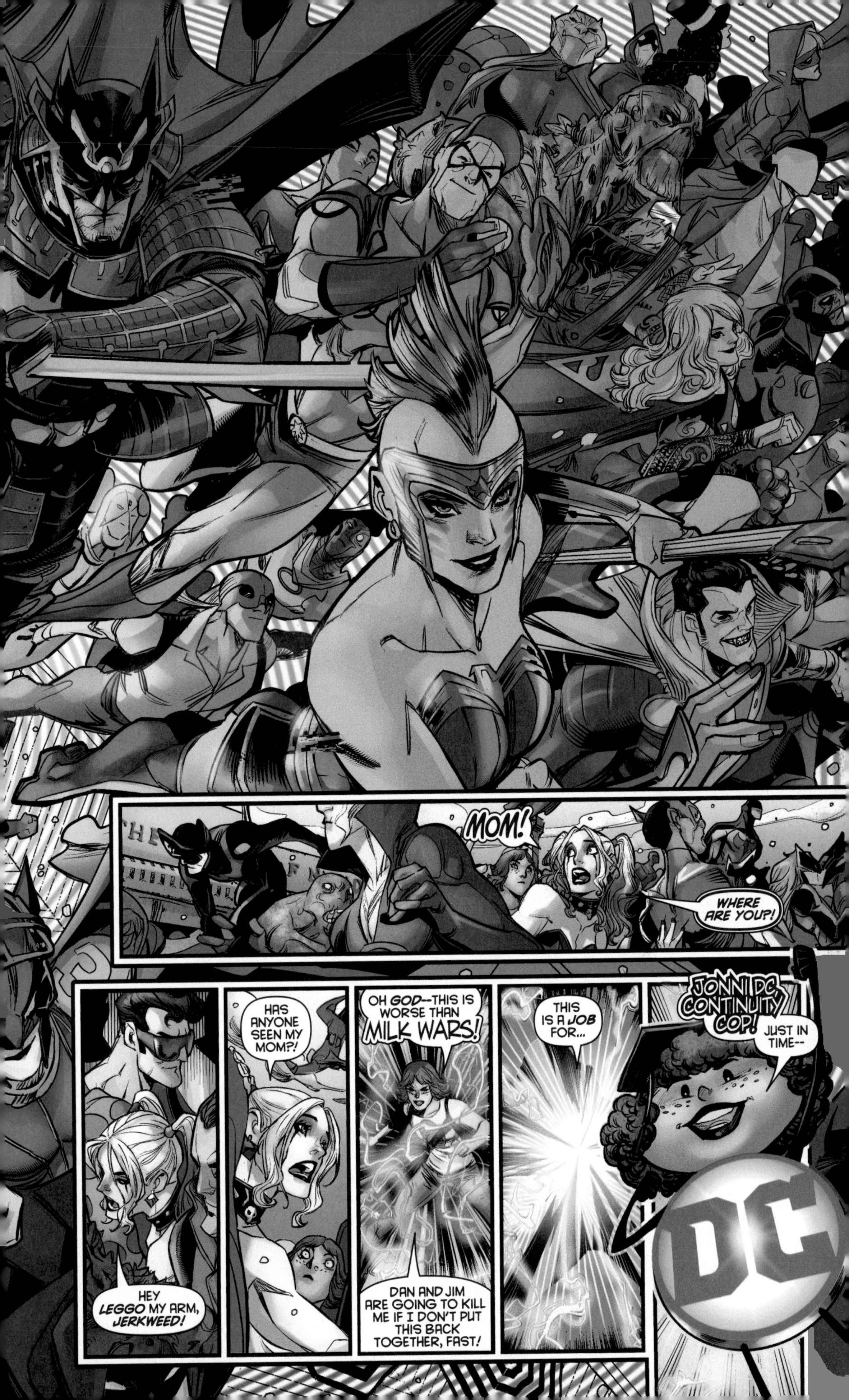
MOM!
WHERE ARE YOU?!
HEY LEGGO MY ARM, JERKWEED!
HAS ANYONE SEEN MY MOM?!
OH GOD--THIS IS WORSE THAN MILK WARS!
DAN AND JIM ARE GOING TO KILL ME IF I DON'T PUT THIS BACK TOGETHER, FAST!
THIS IS A JOB FOR...
JONNI DC CONTINUITY COP!
JUST IN TIME--

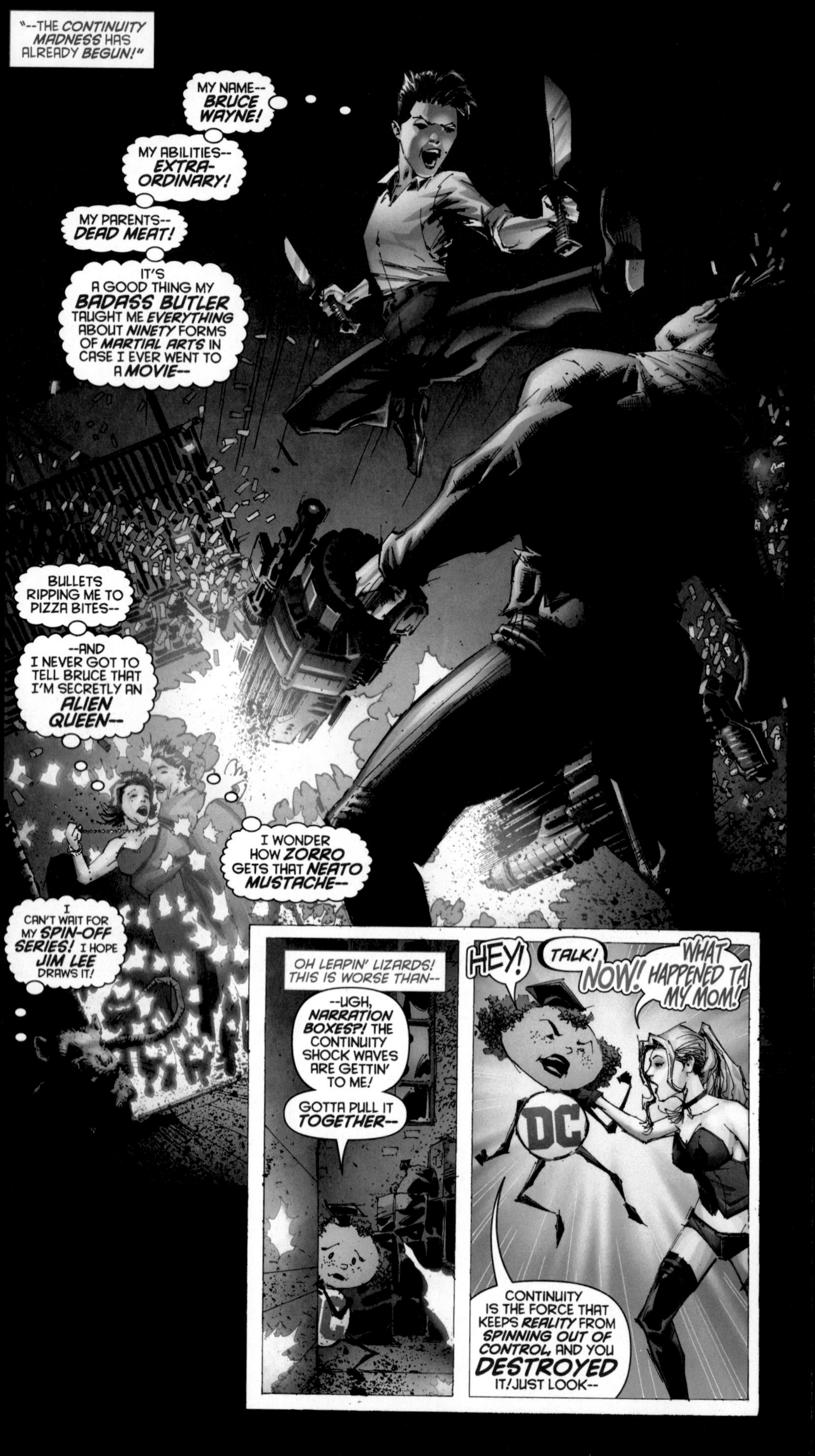
"--THE CONTINUITY MADNESS HAS ALREADY BEGUN!"
MY NAME-- BRUCE WAYNE!
MY ABILITIES-- EXTRA-ORDINARY!
MY PARENTS-- DEAD MEAT!
IT'S A GOOD THING MY BADASS BUTLER TAUGHT ME EVERYTHING ABOUT NINETY FORMS OF MARTIAL ARTS IN CASE I EVER WENT TO A MOVIE--
BULLETS RIPPING ME TO PIZZA BITES--
--AND I NEVER GOT TO TELL BRUCE THAT I'M SECRETLY AN ALIEN QUEEN--
I WONDER HOW ZORRO GETS THAT NEATO MUSTACHE--
I CAN'T WAIT FOR MY SPIN-OFF SERIES! I HOPE JIM LEE DRAWS IT!
OH LEAPIN' LIZARDS! THIS IS WORSE THAN--
--UGH, NARRATION BOXES?! THE CONTINUITY SHOCK WAVES ARE GETTIN' TO ME!
GOTTA PULL IT TOGETHER--
HEY!
TALK!
NOW!
WHAT HAPPENED TA MY MOM!
CONTINUITY IS THE FORCE THAT KEEPS REALITY FROM SPINNING OUT OF CONTROL, AND YOU DESTROYED IT! JUST LOOK--

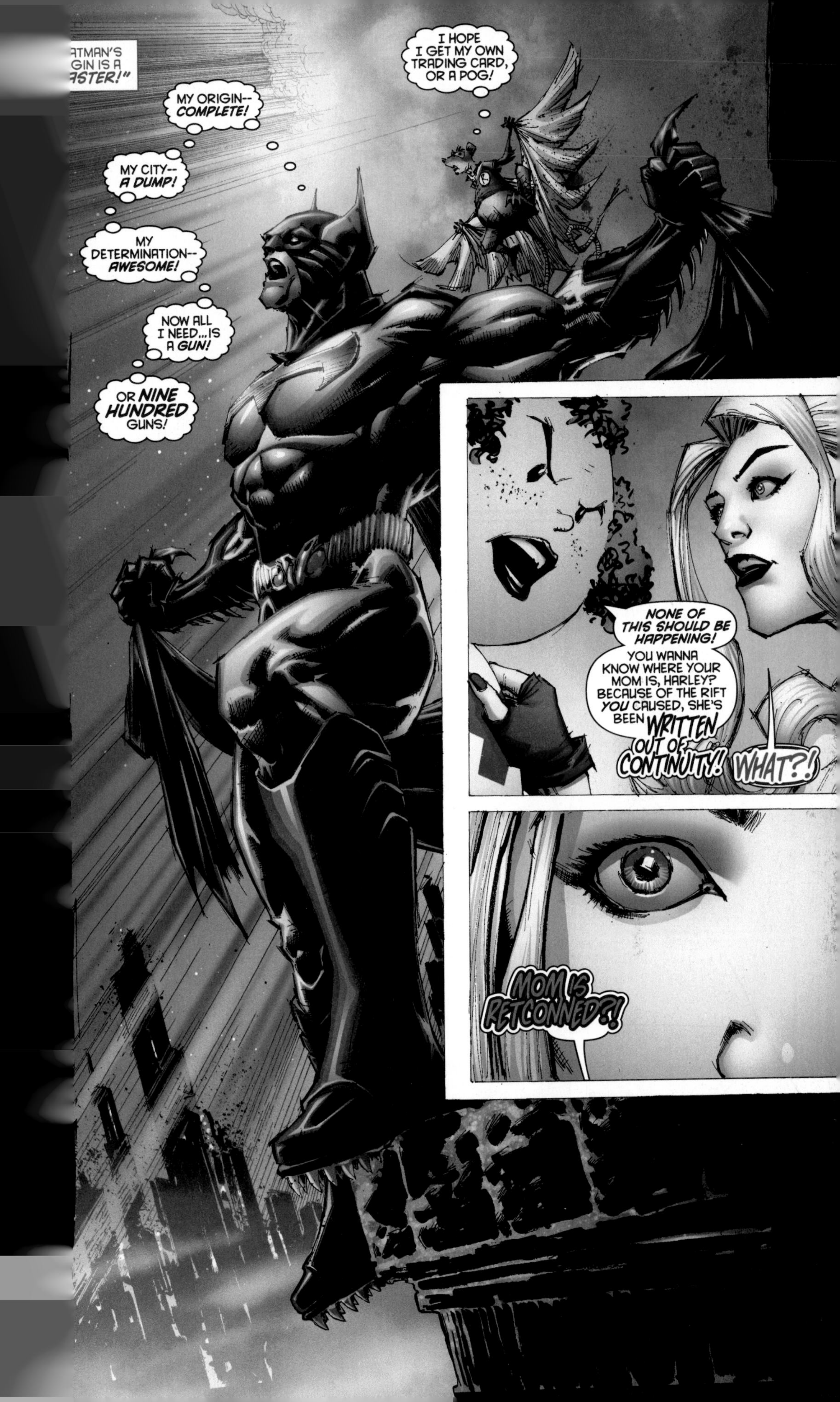

ATMAN'S GIN IS A ASTER!"
I HOPE I GET MY OWN TRADING CARD, OR A POG!
MY ORIGIN-- COMPLETE!
MY CITY-- A DUMP!
MY DETERMINATION-- AWESOME!
NOW ALL I NEED...IS A GUN!
OR NINE HUNDRED GUNS!
NONE OF THIS SHOULD BE HAPPENING!
YOU WANNA KNOW WHERE YOUR MOM IS, HARLEY? BECAUSE OF THE RIFT YOU CAUSED, SHE'S BEEN WRITTEN OUT OF CONTINUITY!
WHAT?!
MOM IS RETCONNED?!

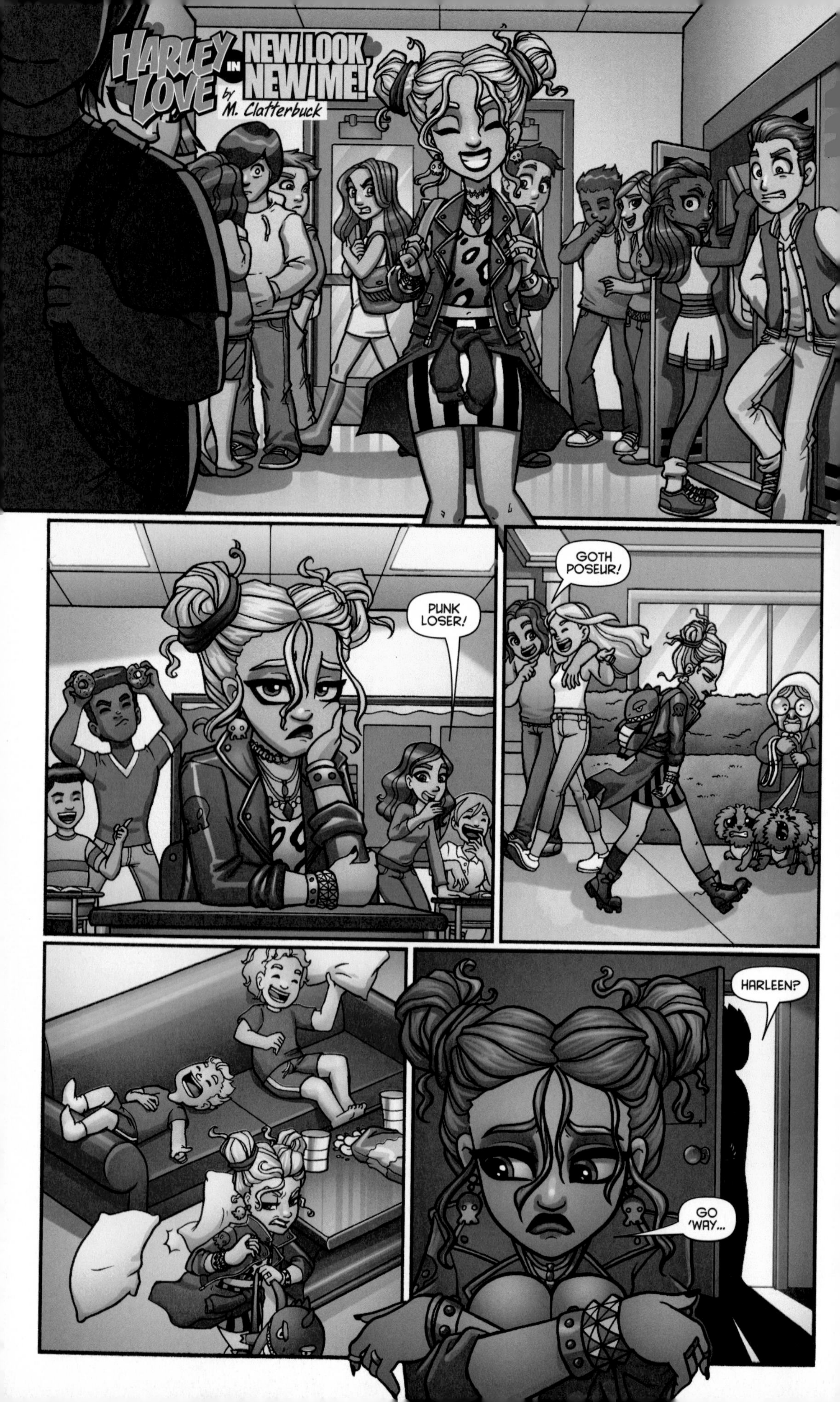
HARLEY LOVE
IN
NEW LOOK, NEW ME!
by
M. Clatterbuck
PUNK LOSER!
GOTH POSEUR!
HARLEEN?
GO 'WAY...

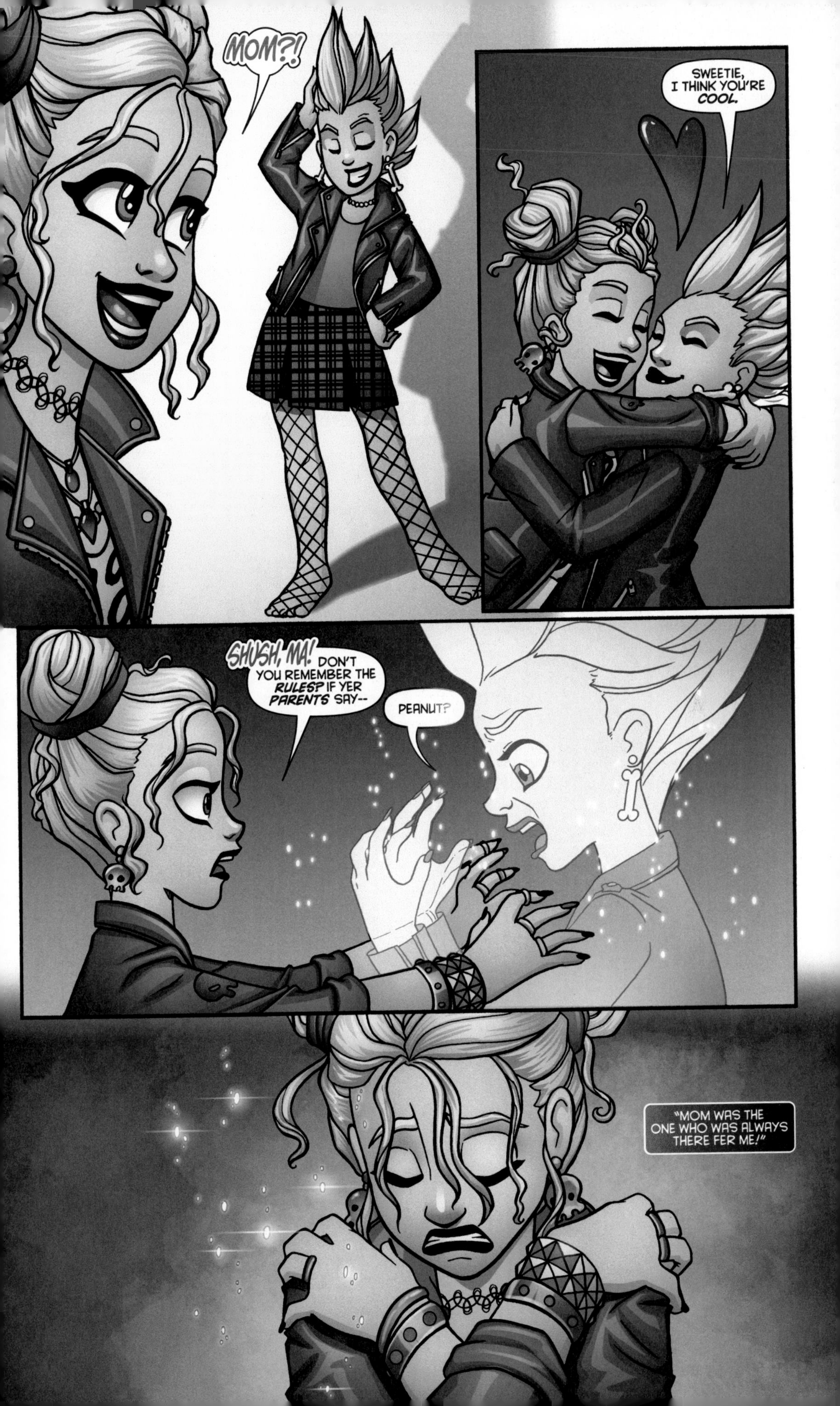
MOM?!
SWEETIE, I THINK YOU'RE COOL.
SHUSH, MA! DON'T YOU REMEMBER THE RULES? IF YER PARENTS SAY--
PEANUT?
"MOM WAS THE ONE WHO WAS ALWAYS THERE FER ME!"

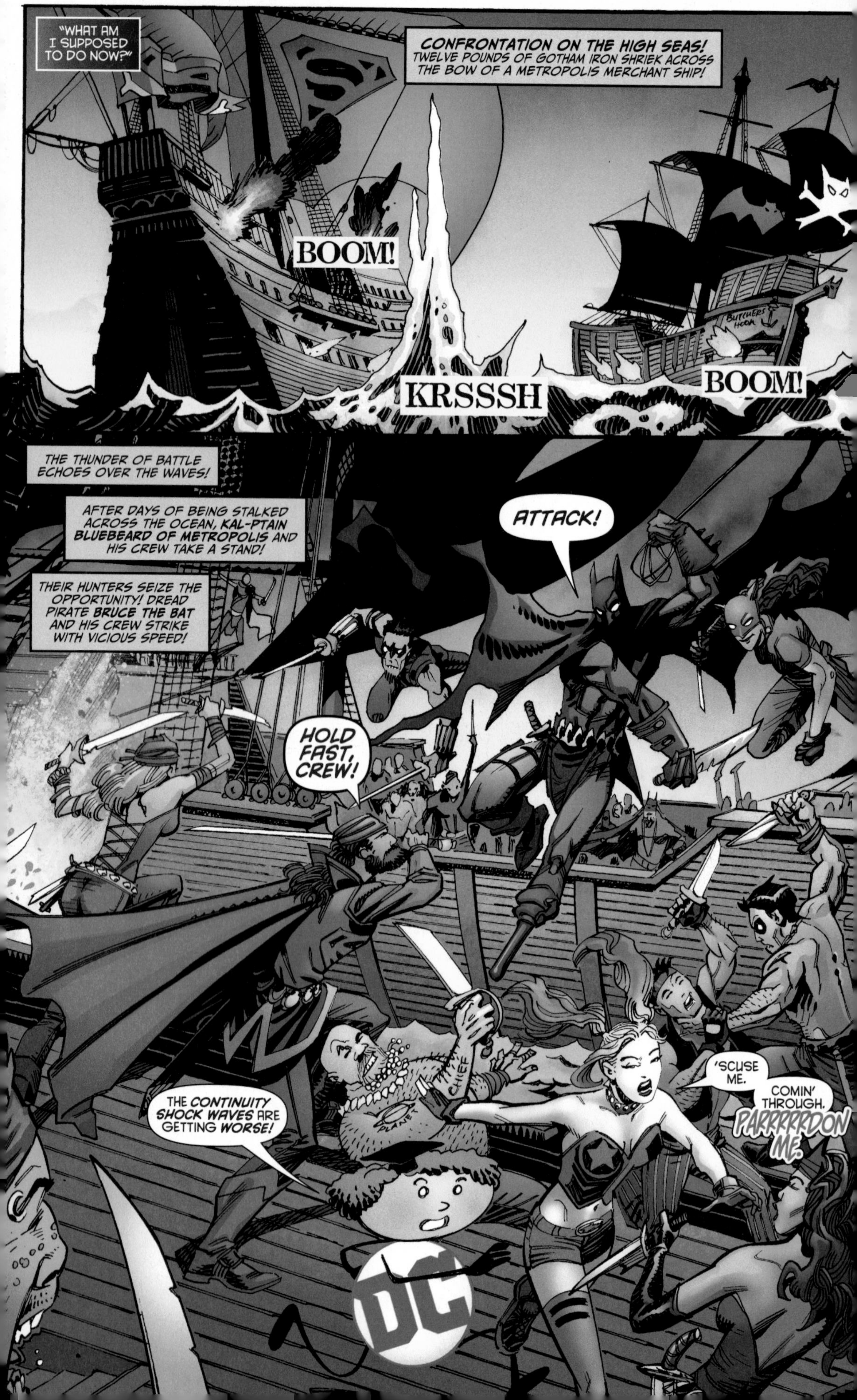

"WHAT AM I SUPPOSED TO DO NOW?"
CONFRONTATION ON THE HIGH SEAS! TWELVE POUNDS OF GOTHAM IRON SHRIEK ACROSS THE BOW OF A METROPOLIS MERCHANT SHIP!
BOOM!
KRSSSH
BOOM!
THE THUNDER OF BATTLE ECHOES OVER THE WAVES!
AFTER DAYS OF BEING STALKED ACROSS THE OCEAN, KAL-PTAIN BLUEBEARD OF METROPOLIS AND HIS CREW TAKE A STAND!
THEIR HUNTERS SEIZE THE OPPORTUNITY! DREAD PIRATE BRUCE THE BAT AND HIS CREW STRIKE WITH VICIOUS SPEED!
ATTACK!
HOLD FAST, CREW!
'SCUSE ME.
COMIN' THROUGH.
PARRRRRDON ME.
THE CONTINUITY SHOCK WAVES ARE GETTING WORSE!

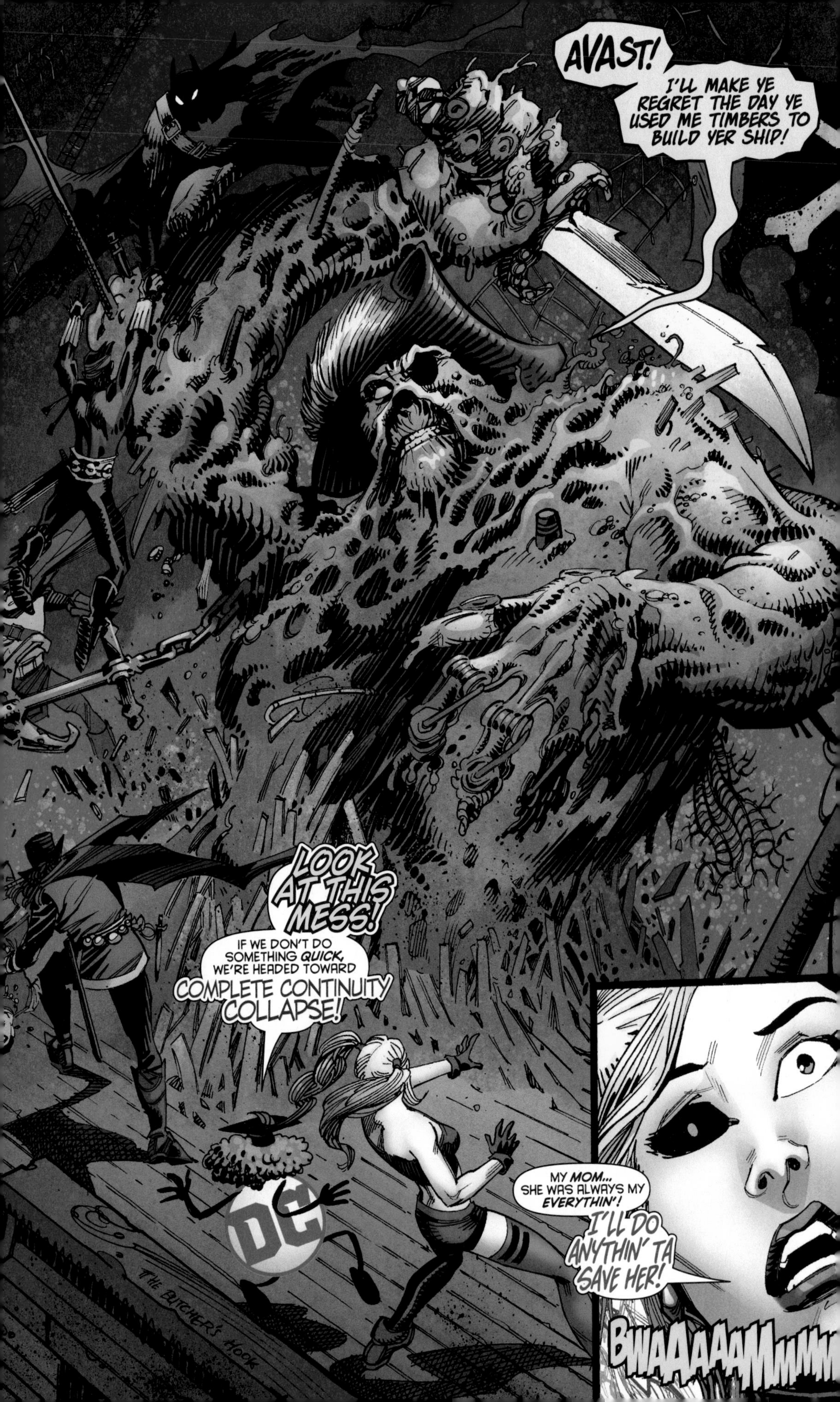
AVAST!
I'LL MAKE YE REGRET THE DAY YE USED ME TIMBERS TO BUILD YER SHIP!
LOOK AT THIS MESS!
IF WE DON'T DO SOMETHING QUICK, WE'RE HEADED TOWARD COMPLETE CONTINUITY COLLAPSE!
MY MOM... SHE WAS ALWAYS MY EVERYTHIN'!
I'LL DO ANYTHIN' TA SAVE HER!
BWAAAAAMMMMM
THE BUTCHER'S HOOK

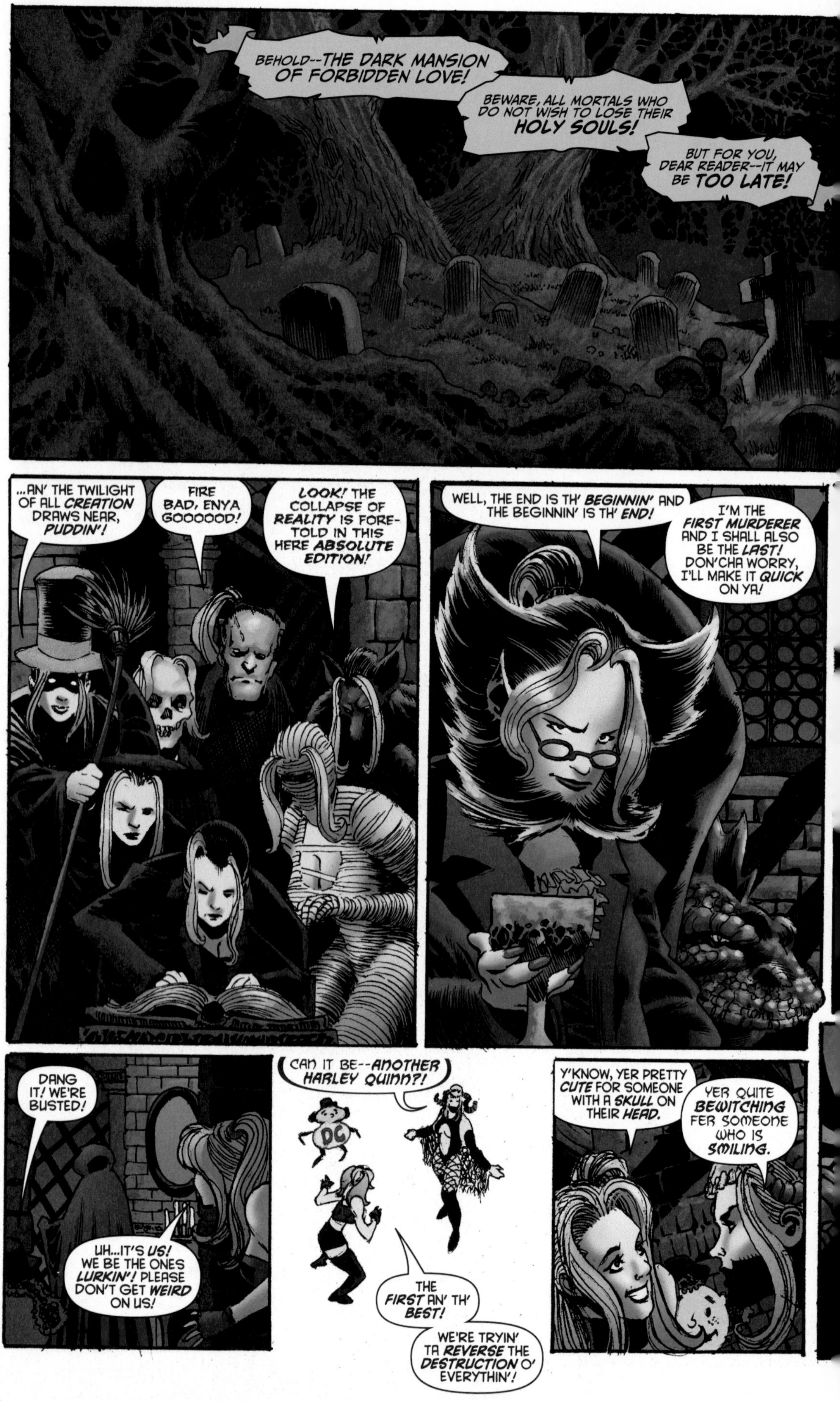
BEHOLD--THE DARK MANSION OF FORBIDDEN LOVE!
BEWARE, ALL MORTALS WHO DO NOT WISH TO LOSE THEIR HOLY SOULS!
BUT FOR YOU, DEAR READER--IT MAY BE TOO LATE!
...AN' THE TWILIGHT OF ALL CREATION DRAWS NEAR, PUDDIN'!
FIRE BAD, ENYA GOOOOOD!
LOOK! THE COLLAPSE OF REALITY IS FORETOLD IN THIS HERE ABSOLUTE EDITION!
WELL, THE END IS TH' BEGINNIN' AND THE BEGINNIN' IS TH' END!
I'M THE FIRST MURDERER AND I SHALL ALSO BE THE LAST! DON'CHA WORRY, I'LL MAKE IT QUICK ON YA!
DANG IT! WE'RE BUSTED!
UH...IT'S US! WE BE THE ONES LURKIN'! PLEASE DON'T GET WEIRD ON US!
CAN IT BE--ANOTHER HARLEY QUINN?!
DC
THE FIRST AN' TH' BEST!
WE'RE TRYIN' TA REVERSE THE DESTRUCTION O' EVERYTHIN'!
Y'KNOW, YER PRETTY CUTE FOR SOMEONE WITH A SKULL ON THEIR HEAD.
YER QUITE BEWITCHING FER SOMEONE WHO IS SMILING.

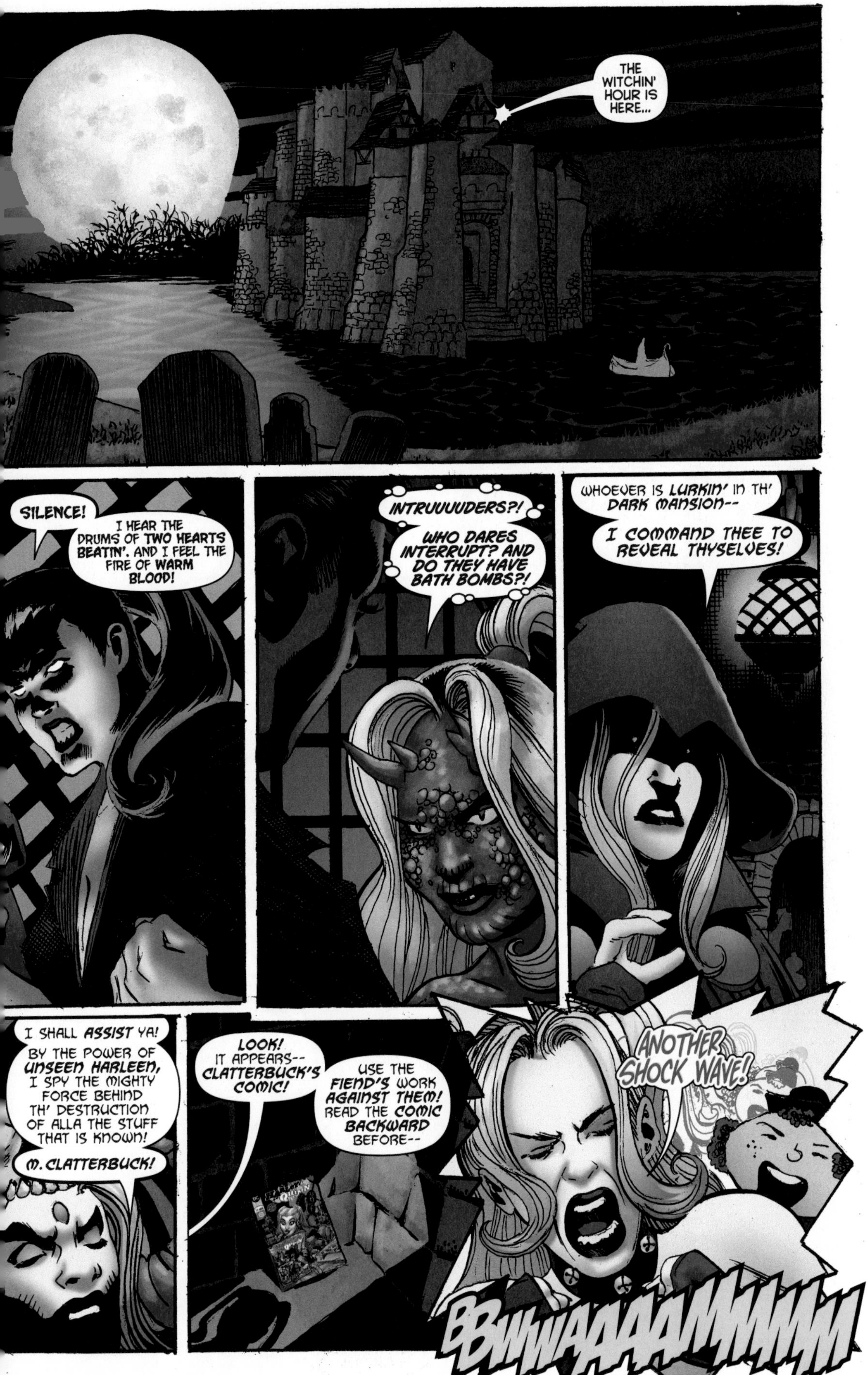
THE WITCHIN' HOUR IS HERE...
SILENCE!
I HEAR THE DRUMS OF TWO HEARTS BEATIN'. AND I FEEL THE FIRE OF WARM BLOOD!
INTRUUUUDERS?!
WHO DARES INTERRUPT? AND DO THEY HAVE BATH BOMBS?!
WHOEVER IS LURKIN' IN TH' DARK MANSION--
I COMMAND THEE TO REVEAL THYSELVES!
I SHALL ASSIST YA!
BY THE POWER OF UNSEEN HARLEEN, I SPY THE MIGHTY FORCE BEHIND TH' DESTRUCTION OF ALLA THE STUFF THAT IS KNOWN!
M. CLATTERBUCK!
LOOK!
IT APPEARS--
CLATTERBUCK'S COMIC!
USE THE FIEND'S WORK AGAINST THEM! READ THE COMIC BACKWARD BEFORE--
ANOTHER SHOCK WAVE!
BBWWAAAAMMMMM

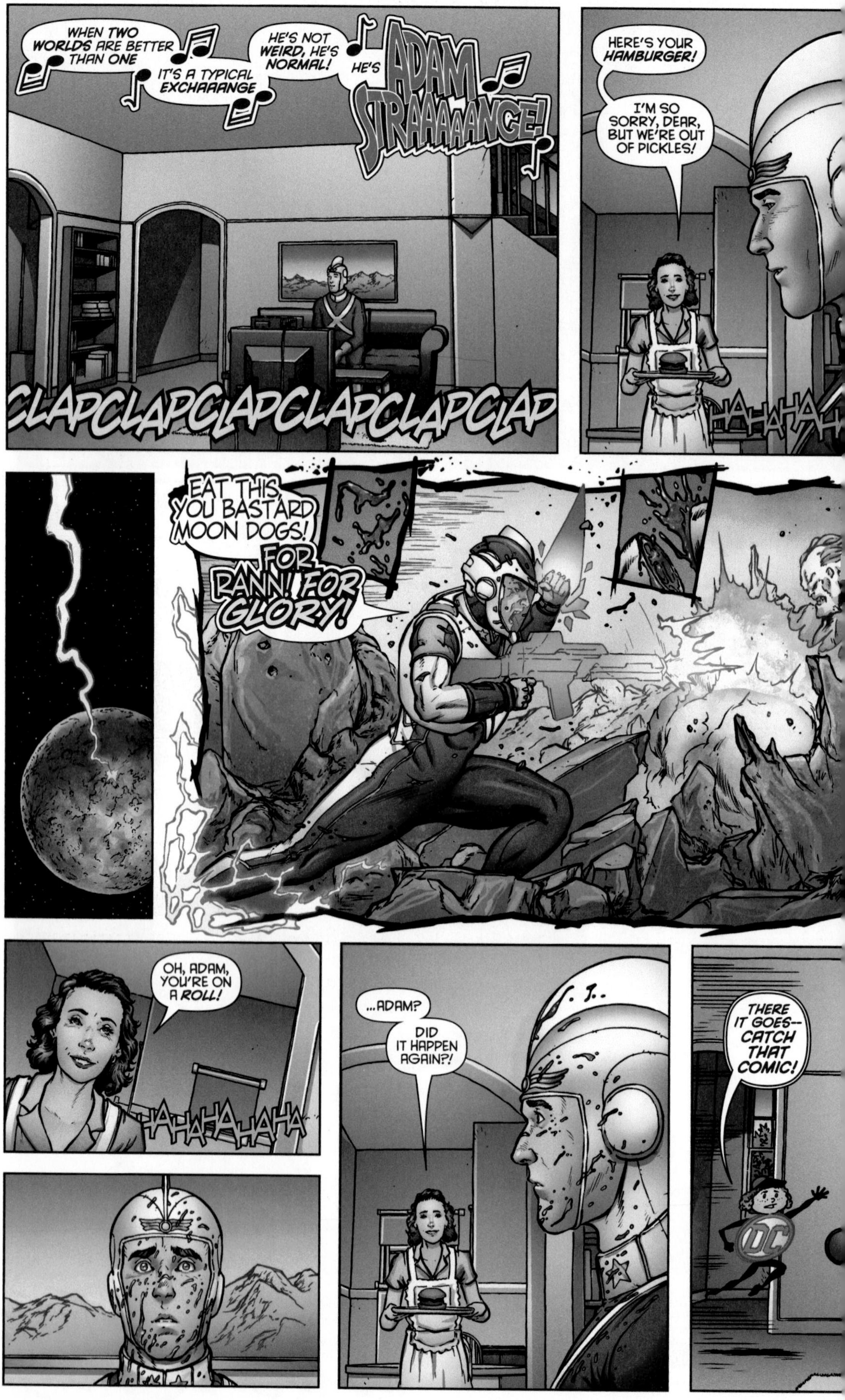
WHEN TWO WORLDS ARE BETTER THAN ONE
IT'S A TYPICAL EXCHAAAANGE
HE'S NOT WEIRD, HE'S NORMAL!
HE'S ADAM STRAAAAAANGE!
CLAPCLAPCLAPCLAPCLAPCLAP
HERE'S YOUR HAMBURGER!
I'M SO SORRY, DEAR, BUT WE'RE OUT OF PICKLES!
HAHAHAHA
EAT THIS, YOU BASTARD MOON DOGS!
FOR RANN! FOR GLORY!
OH, ADAM, YOU'RE ON A ROLL!
HAHAHAHAHAHA
...ADAM?
DID IT HAPPEN AGAIN?!
THERE IT GOES-- CATCH THAT COMIC!

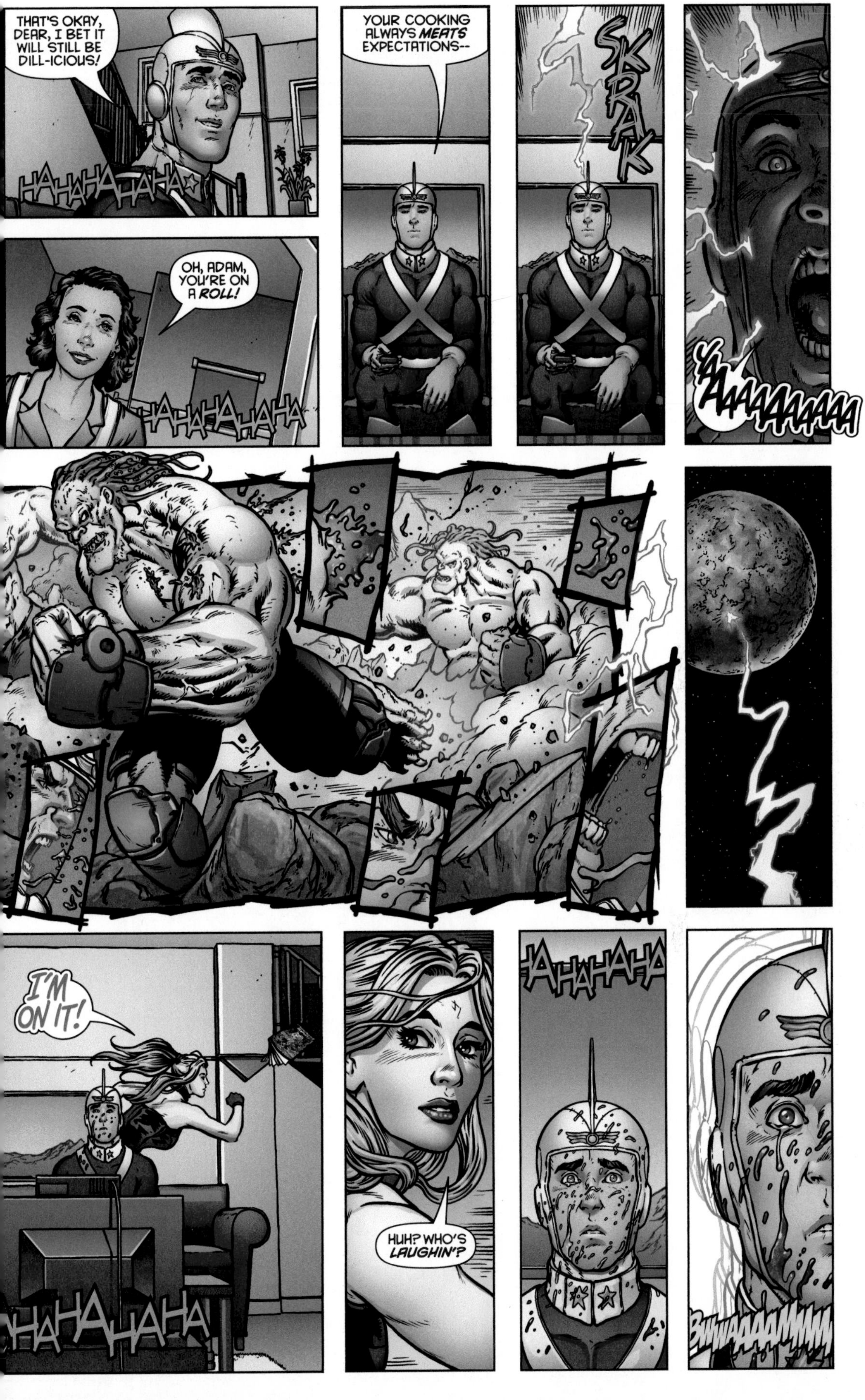
THAT'S OKAY, DEAR, I BET IT WILL STILL BE DILL-ICIOUS!
HAHAHAHAHAHA
OH, ADAM, YOU'RE ON A ROLL!
HAHAHAHAHAHA
YOUR COOKING ALWAYS MEATS EXPECTATIONS--
SKRAK
YAAAAAAAAAA
I'M ON IT!
HAHAHAHAHA
HUH? WHO'S LAUGHIN'?
HAHAHAHA
BWWAAAAMMM

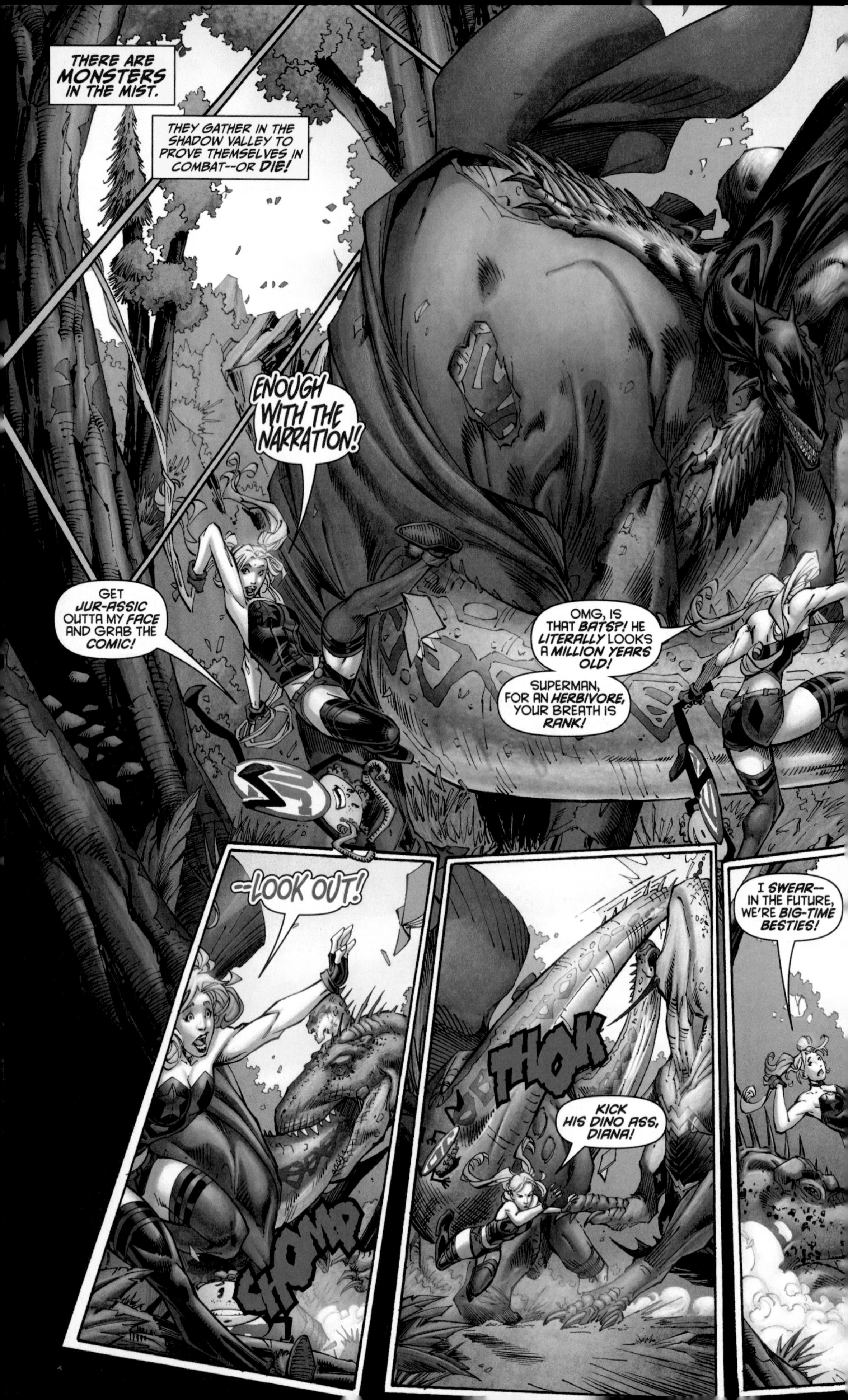
THERE ARE MONSTERS IN THE MIST.
THEY GATHER IN THE SHADOW VALLEY TO PROVE THEMSELVES IN COMBAT--OR DIE!
ENOUGH WITH THE NARRATION!
GET JUR-ASSIC OUTTA MY FACE AND GRAB THE COMIC!
OMG, IS THAT BATS?! HE LITERALLY LOOKS A MILLION YEARS OLD!
SUPERMAN, FOR AN HERBIVORE, YOUR BREATH IS RANK!
--LOOK OUT!
CHOMP
THOK
KICK HIS DINO ASS, DIANA!
I SWEAR-- IN THE FUTURE, WE'RE BIG-TIME BESTIES!

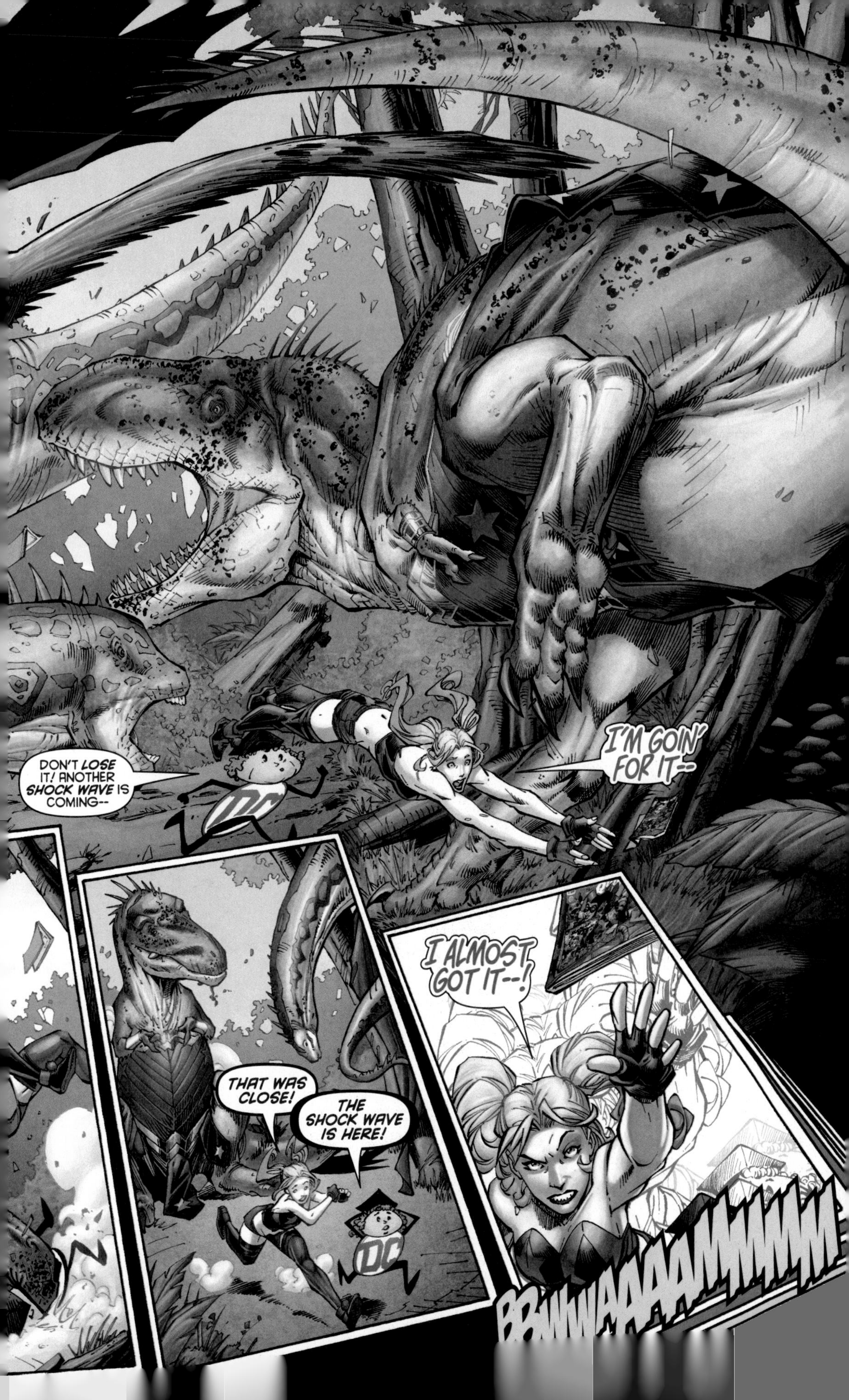
DON'T LOSE IT! ANOTHER SHOCK WAVE IS COMING--
I'M GOIN' FOR IT--
THAT WAS CLOSE!
THE SHOCK WAVE IS HERE!
I ALMOST GOT IT--!
BBWWAAAAMMMMM

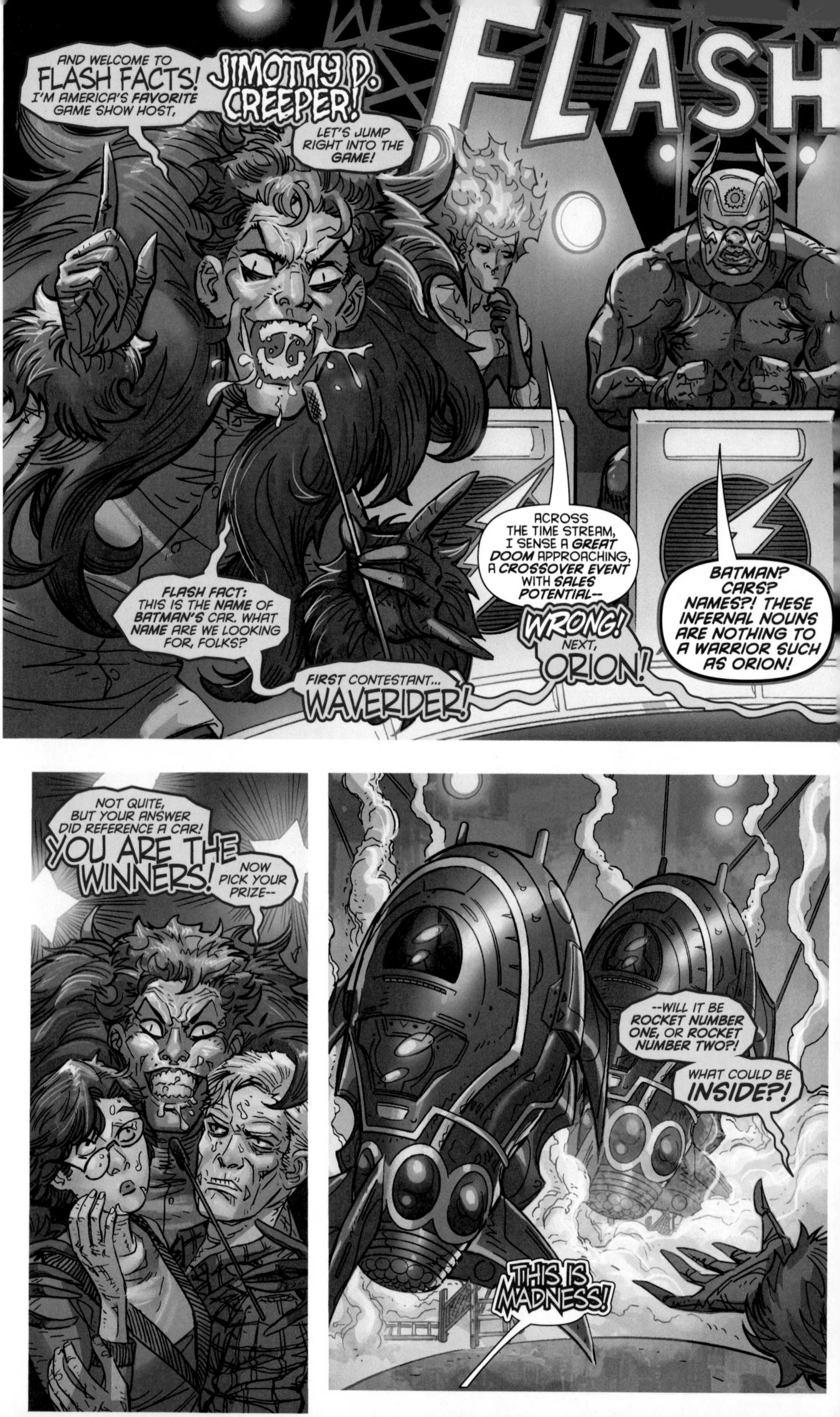
FLASH
AND WELCOME TO FLASH FACTS! I'M AMERICA'S FAVORITE GAME SHOW HOST, JIMOTHY D. CREEPER!
LET'S JUMP RIGHT INTO THE GAME!
FLASH FACT: THIS IS THE NAME OF BATMAN'S CAR. WHAT NAME ARE WE LOOKING FOR, FOLKS?
FIRST CONTESTANT... WAVERIDER!
ACROSS THE TIME STREAM, I SENSE A GREAT DOOM APPROACHING, A CROSSOVER EVENT WITH SALES POTENTIAL--
WRONG! NEXT, ORION!
BATMAN? CARS? NAMES?! THESE INFERNAL NOUNS ARE NOTHING TO A WARRIOR SUCH AS ORION!
NOT QUITE, BUT YOUR ANSWER DID REFERENCE A CAR! YOU ARE THE WINNERS!
NOW PICK YOUR PRIZE--
--WILL IT BE ROCKET NUMBER ONE, OR ROCKET NUMBER TWO?!
WHAT COULD BE INSIDE?!
THIS IS MADNESS!

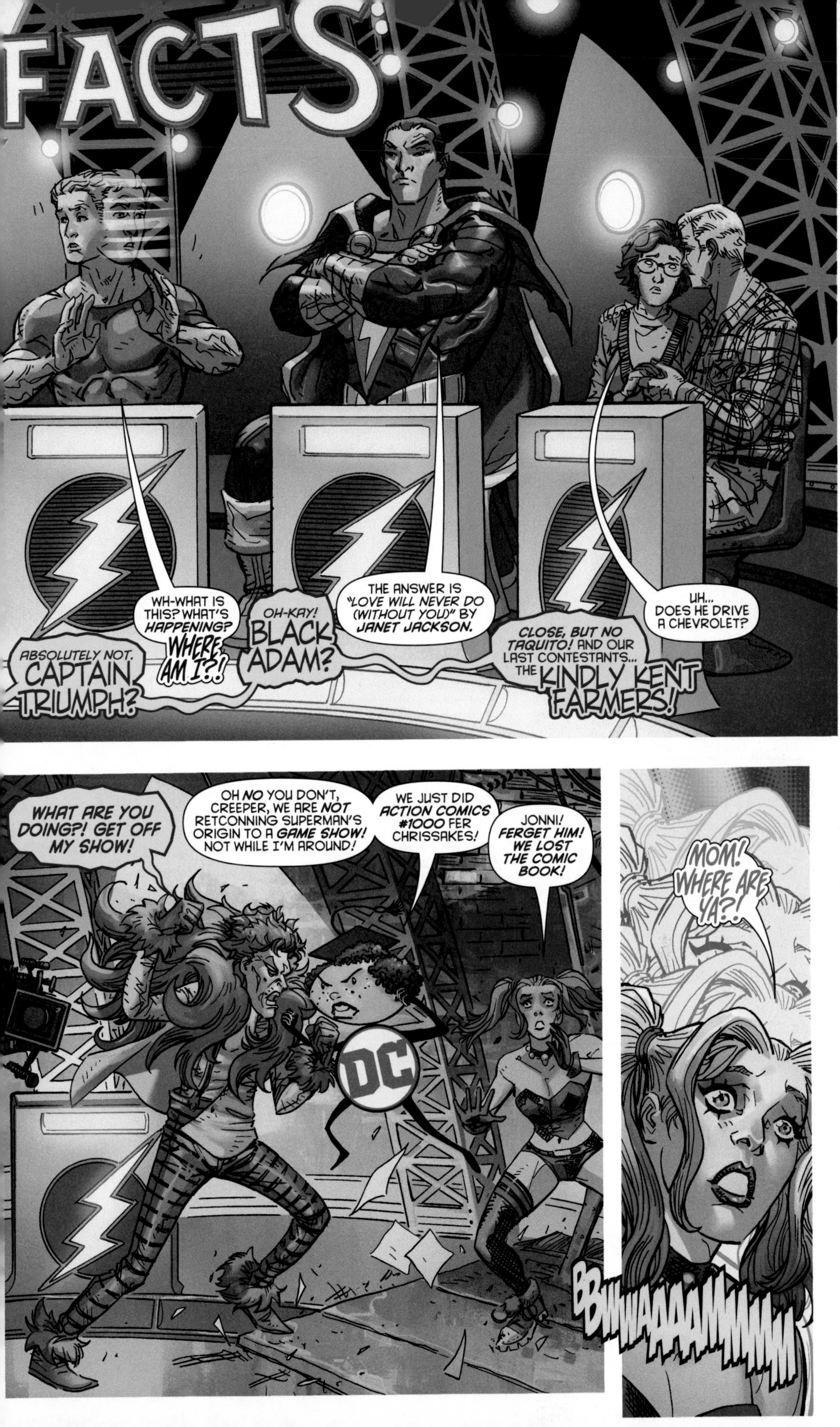
FACTS!
WH-WHAT IS THIS? WHAT'S HAPPENING? WHERE AM I?!
OH-KAY! BLACK ADAM?
THE ANSWER IS "LOVE WILL NEVER DO (WITHOUT YOU)" BY JANET JACKSON.
UH... DOES HE DRIVE A CHEVROLET?
ABSOLUTELY NOT. CAPTAIN TRIUMPH?
CLOSE, BUT NO TAQUITO! AND OUR LAST CONTESTANTS... THE KINDLY KENT FARMERS!
WHAT ARE YOU DOING?! GET OFF MY SHOW!
OH NO YOU DON'T, CREEPER, WE ARE NOT RETCONNING SUPERMAN'S ORIGIN TO A GAME SHOW! NOT WHILE I'M AROUND!
WE JUST DID ACTION COMICS #1000 FER CHRISSAKES!
JONNI! FERGET HIM! WE LOST THE COMIC BOOK!
MOM! WHERE ARE YA?!
BBWWAAAAMMMM

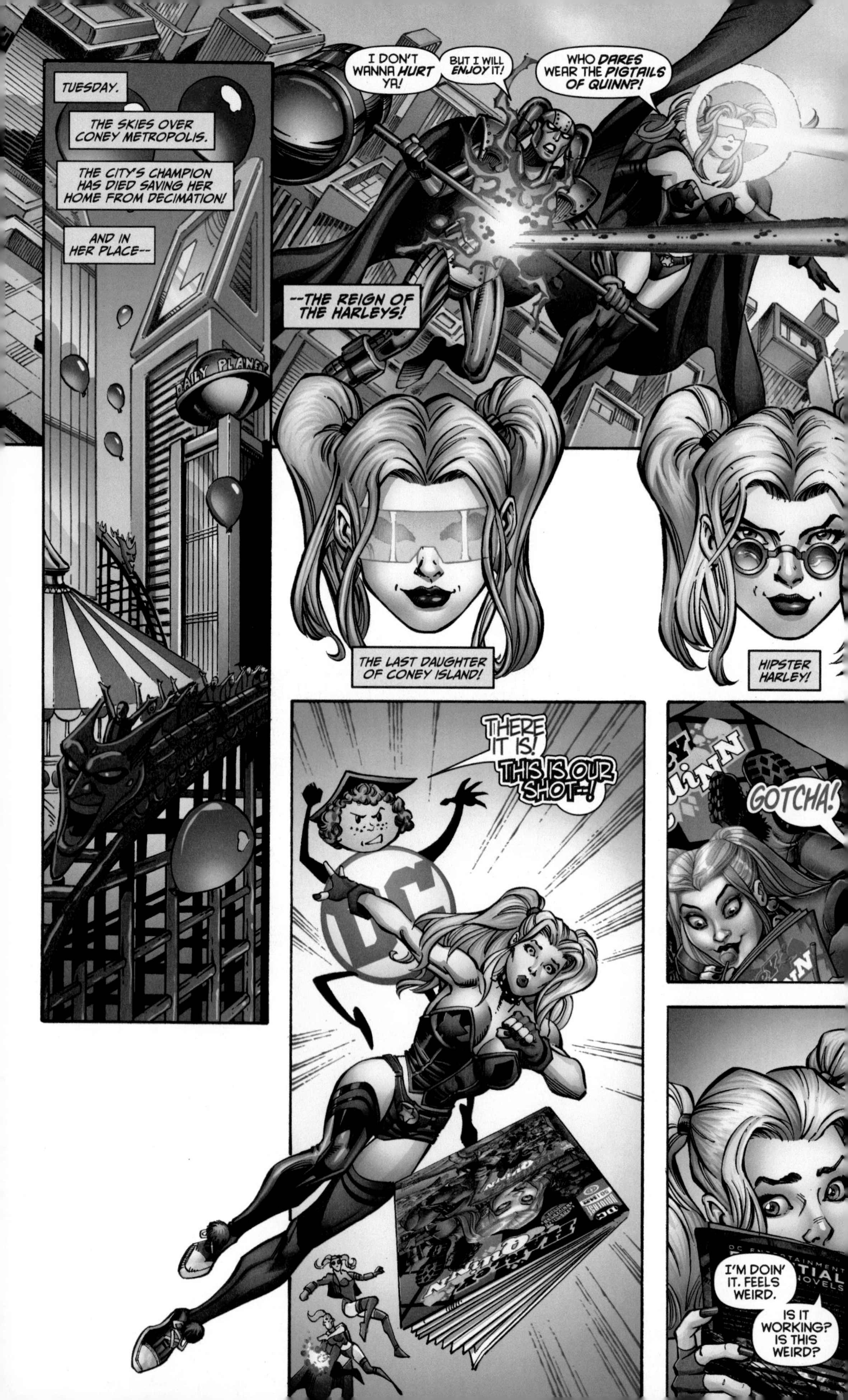
TUESDAY.
THE SKIES OVER CONEY METROPOLIS.
THE CITY'S CHAMPION HAS DIED SAVING HER HOME FROM DECIMATION!
AND IN HER PLACE--
--THE REIGN OF THE HARLEYS!
I DON'T WANNA HURT YA!
BUT I WILL ENJOY IT!
WHO DARES WEAR THE PIGTAILS OF QUINN?!
DAILY PLANET
THE LAST DAUGHTER OF CONEY ISLAND!
HIPSTER HARLEY!
THERE IT IS! THIS IS OUR SHOT--!
GOTCHA!
I'M DOIN' IT. FEELS WEIRD.
IS IT WORKING? IS THIS WEIRD?

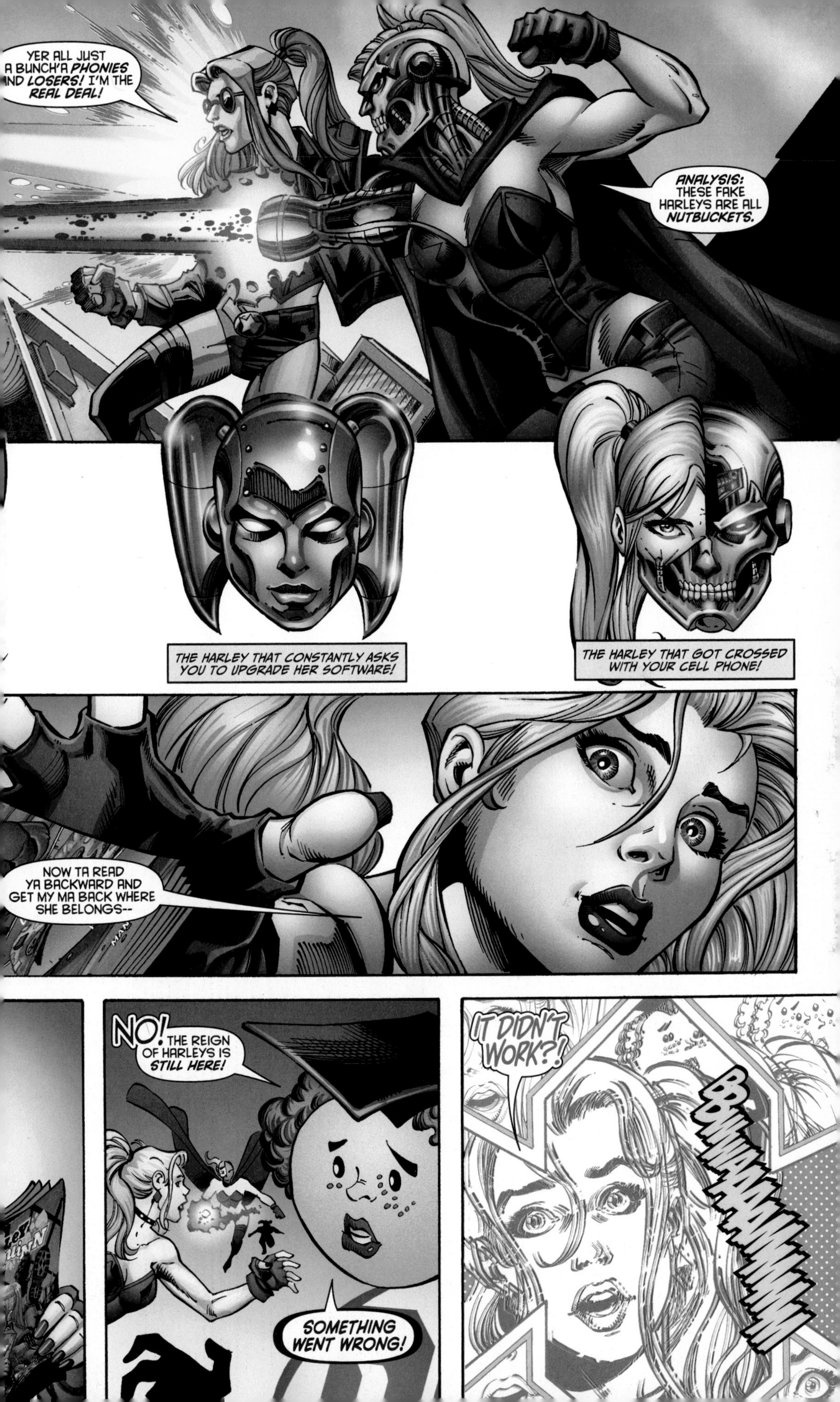
YER ALL JUST A BUNCH'A PHONIES AND LOSERS! I'M THE REAL DEAL!
ANALYSIS: THESE FAKE HARLEYS ARE ALL NUTBUCKETS.
THE HARLEY THAT CONSTANTLY ASKS YOU TO UPGRADE HER SOFTWARE!
THE HARLEY THAT GOT CROSSED WITH YOUR CELL PHONE!
NOW TA READ YA BACKWARD AND GET MY MA BACK WHERE SHE BELONGS--
NO! THE REIGN OF HARLEYS IS STILL HERE!
SOMETHING WENT WRONG!
IT DIDN'T WORK?!
BBWHAAAAMMM

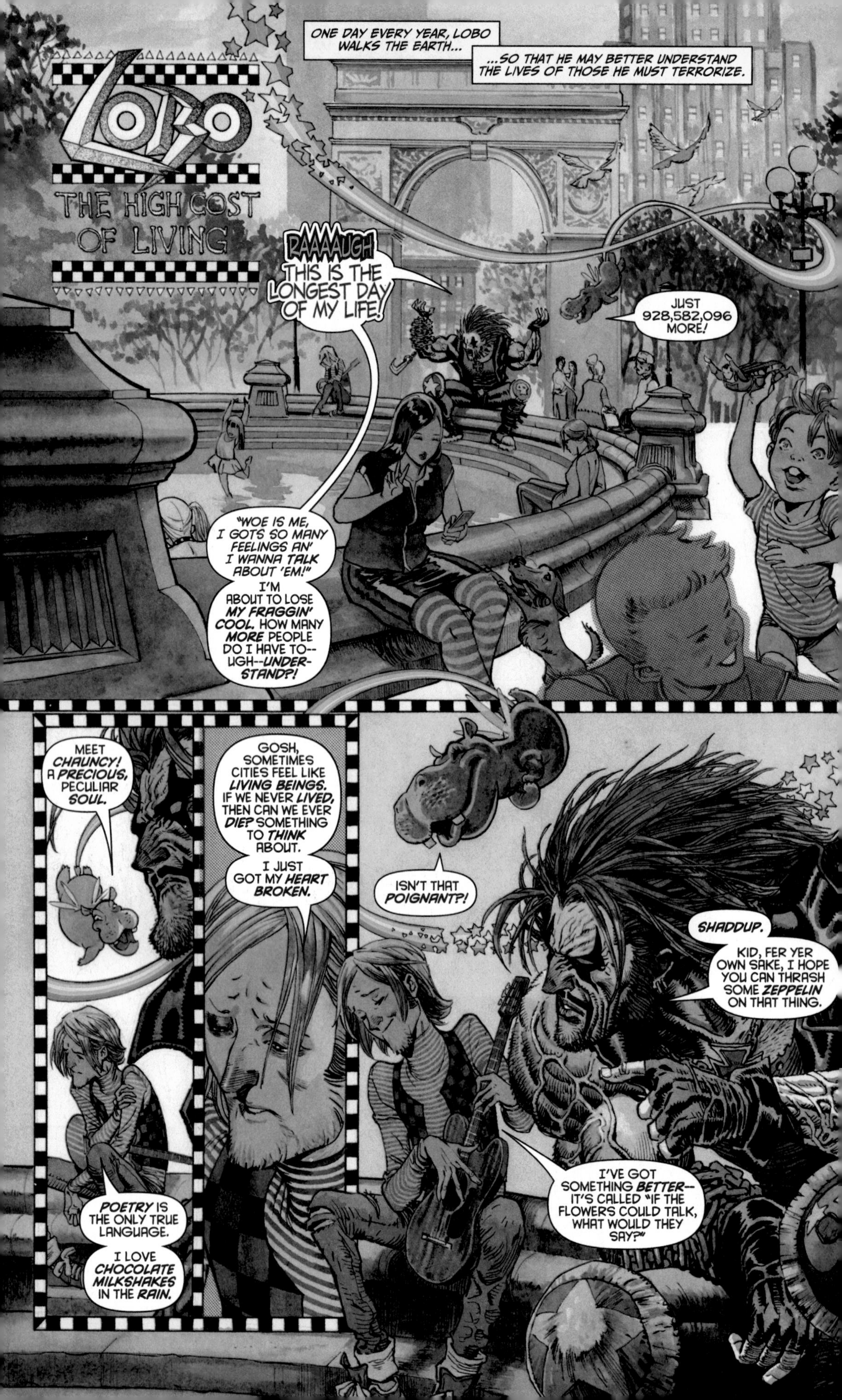

ONE DAY EVERY YEAR, LOBO WALKS THE EARTH...
...SO THAT HE MAY BETTER UNDERSTAND THE LIVES OF THOSE HE MUST TERRORIZE.
LOBO
THE HIGH COST OF LIVING
RAAAAUGH THIS IS THE LONGEST DAY OF MY LIFE!
JUST 928,582,096 MORE!
"WOE IS ME, I GOTS SO MANY FEELINGS AN' I WANNA TALK ABOUT 'EM!"
I'M ABOUT TO LOSE MY FRAGGIN' COOL. HOW MANY MORE PEOPLE DO I HAVE TO-- UGH--UNDERSTAND?!
MEET CHAUNCY! A PRECIOUS, PECULIAR SOUL.
POETRY IS THE ONLY TRUE LANGUAGE.
I LOVE CHOCOLATE MILKSHAKES IN THE RAIN.
GOSH, SOMETIMES CITIES FEEL LIKE LIVING BEINGS. IF WE NEVER LIVED, THEN CAN WE EVER DIE? SOMETHING TO THINK ABOUT.
I JUST GOT MY HEART BROKEN.
ISN'T THAT POIGNANT?!
SHADDUP.
KID, FER YER OWN SAKE, I HOPE YOU CAN THRASH SOME ZEPPELIN ON THAT THING.
I'VE GOT SOMETHING BETTER-- IT'S CALLED "IF THE FLOWERS COULD TALK, WHAT WOULD THEY SAY?"

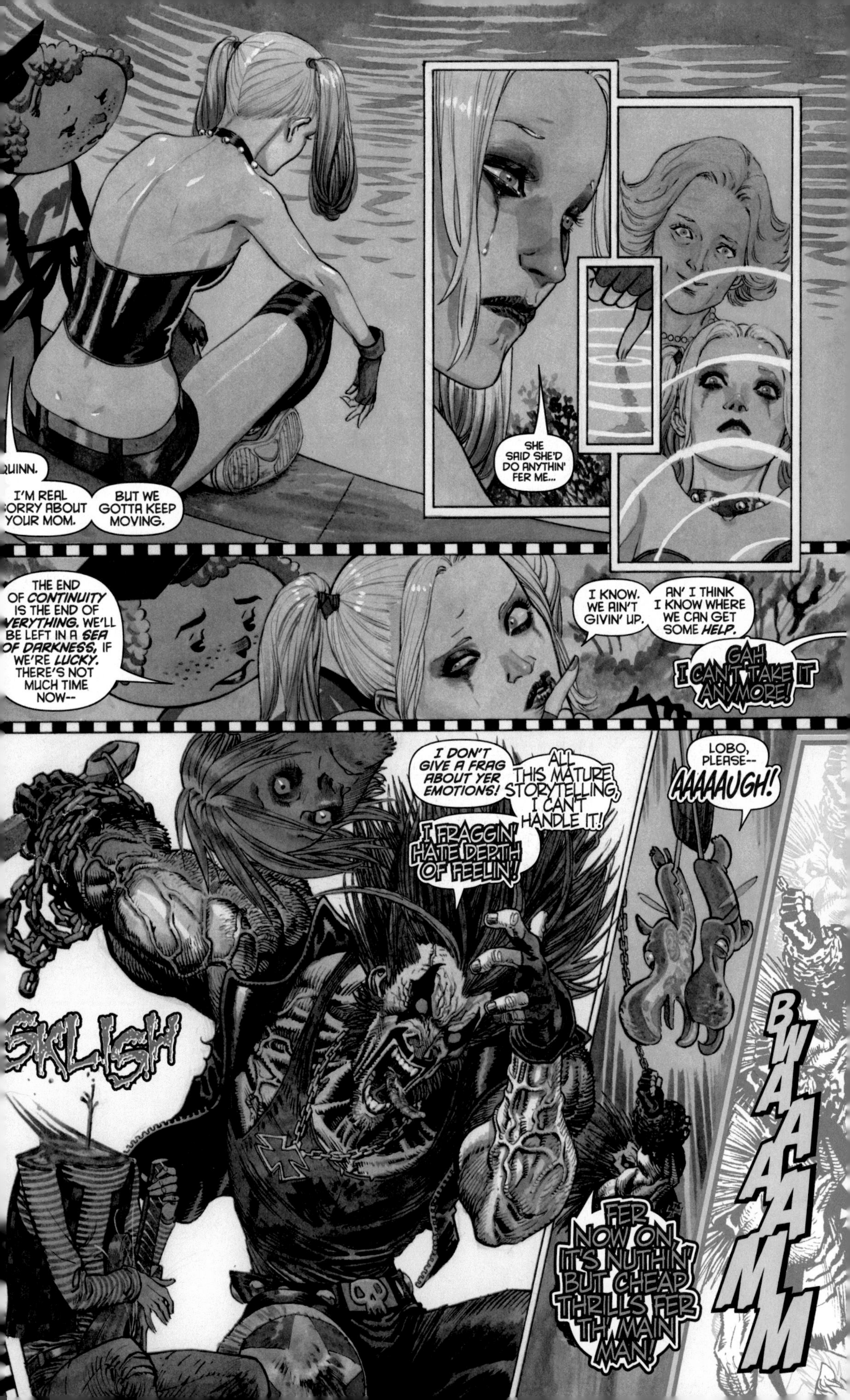
QUINN.
I'M REAL SORRY ABOUT YOUR MOM.
BUT WE GOTTA KEEP MOVING.
SHE SAID SHE'D DO ANYTHIN' FER ME...
THE END OF CONTINUITY IS THE END OF EVERYTHING. WE'LL BE LEFT IN A SEA OF DARKNESS, IF WE'RE LUCKY. THERE'S NOT MUCH TIME NOW--
I KNOW. WE AIN'T GIVIN' UP.
AN' I THINK I KNOW WHERE WE CAN GET SOME HELP.
GAH I CAN'T TAKE IT ANYMORE!
I DON'T GIVE A FRAG ABOUT YER EMOTIONS!
ALL THIS MATURE STORYTELLING, I CAN'T HANDLE IT!
I FRAGGIN' HATE DEPTH OF FEELIN'!
LOBO, PLEASE--
AAAAAUGH!
SKLISH
FER NOW ON IT'S NUTHIN' BUT CHEAP THRILLS FER TH' MAIN MAN!
BWAAAAMM

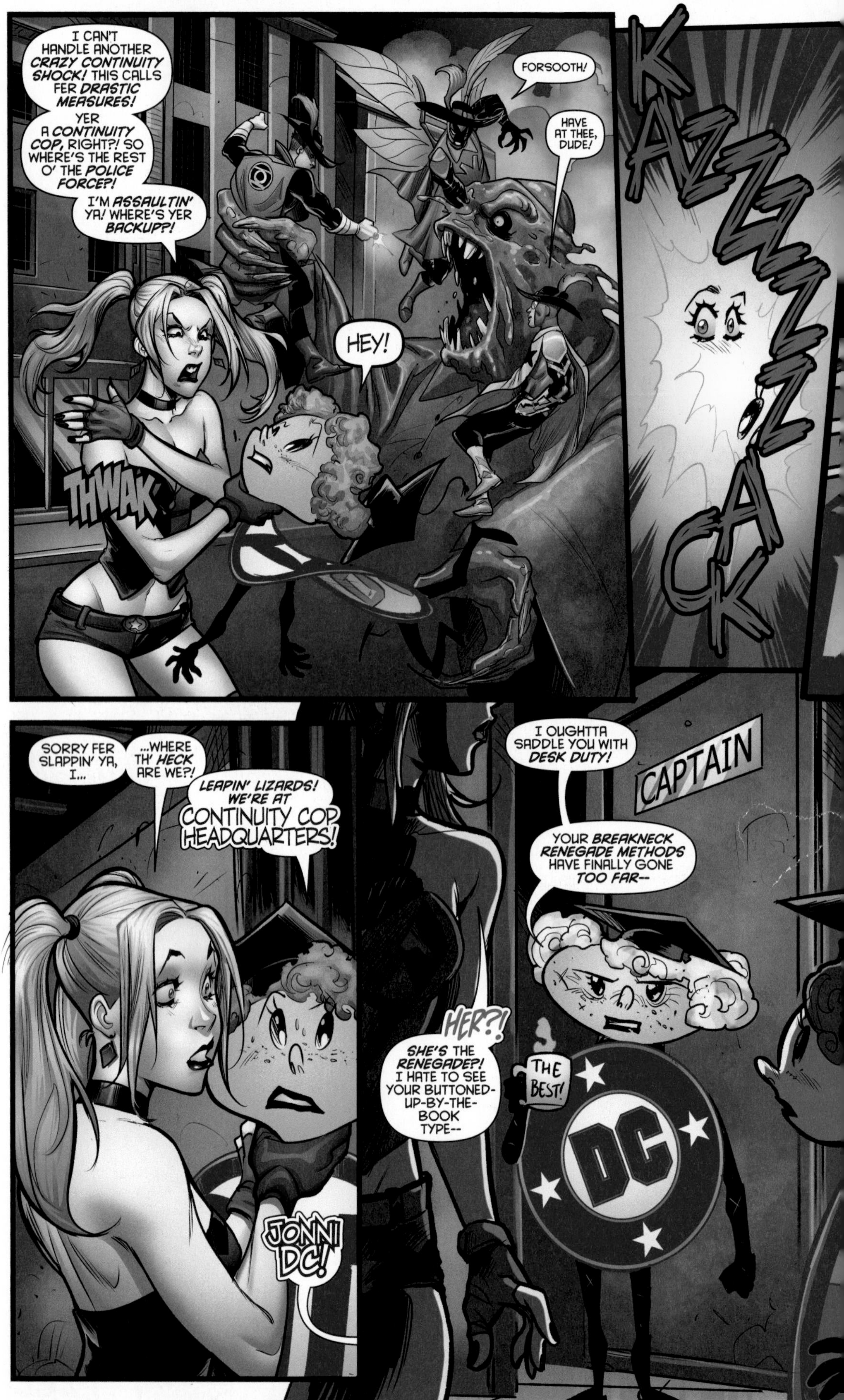

I CAN'T HANDLE ANOTHER CRAZY CONTINUITY SHOCK! THIS CALLS FER DRASTIC MEASURES!
YER A CONTINUITY COP, RIGHT?! SO WHERE'S THE REST O' THE POLICE FORCE?!
I'M ASSAULTIN' YA! WHERE'S YER BACKUP?!
FORSOOTH!
HAVE AT THEE, DUDE!
HEY!
THWAK
KAZZZZZZAACK
SORRY FER SLAPPIN' YA, I...
...WHERE TH' HECK ARE WE?!
LEAPIN' LIZARDS! WE'RE AT CONTINUITY COP HEADQUARTERS!
JONNI DC!
CAPTAIN
I OUGHTTA SADDLE YOU WITH DESK DUTY!
YOUR BREAKNECK RENEGADE METHODS HAVE FINALLY GONE TOO FAR--
HER?!
SHE'S THE RENEGADE?! I HATE TO SEE YOUR BUTTONED-UP-BY-THE-BOOK TYPE--
THE BEST!
DC

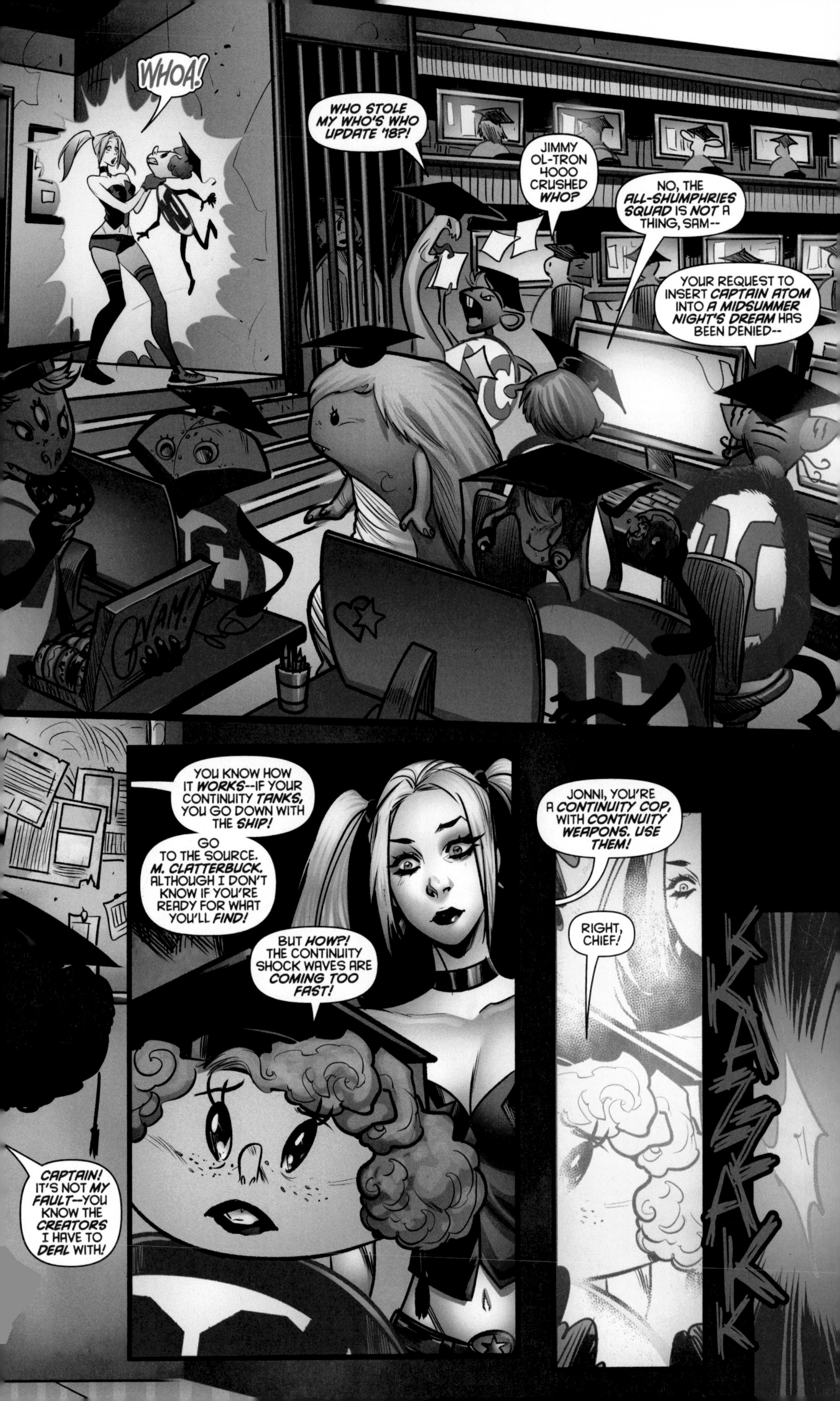

WHOA!
WHO STOLE MY WHO'S WHO UPDATE '18?!
JIMMY OL-TRON 4000 CRUSHED WHO?
NO, THE ALL-SHUMPHRIES SQUAD IS NOT A THING, SAM--
YOUR REQUEST TO INSERT CAPTAIN ATOM INTO A MIDSUMMER NIGHT'S DREAM HAS BEEN DENIED--
CAPTAIN! IT'S NOT MY FAULT--YOU KNOW THE CREATORS I HAVE TO DEAL WITH!
YOU KNOW HOW IT WORKS--IF YOUR CONTINUITY TANKS, YOU GO DOWN WITH THE SHIP!
GO TO THE SOURCE. M. CLATTERBUCK. ALTHOUGH I DON'T KNOW IF YOU'RE READY FOR WHAT YOU'LL FIND!
BUT HOW?! THE CONTINUITY SHOCK WAVES ARE COMING TOO FAST!
JONNI, YOU'RE A CONTINUITY COP, WITH CONTINUITY WEAPONS. USE THEM!
RIGHT, CHIEF!

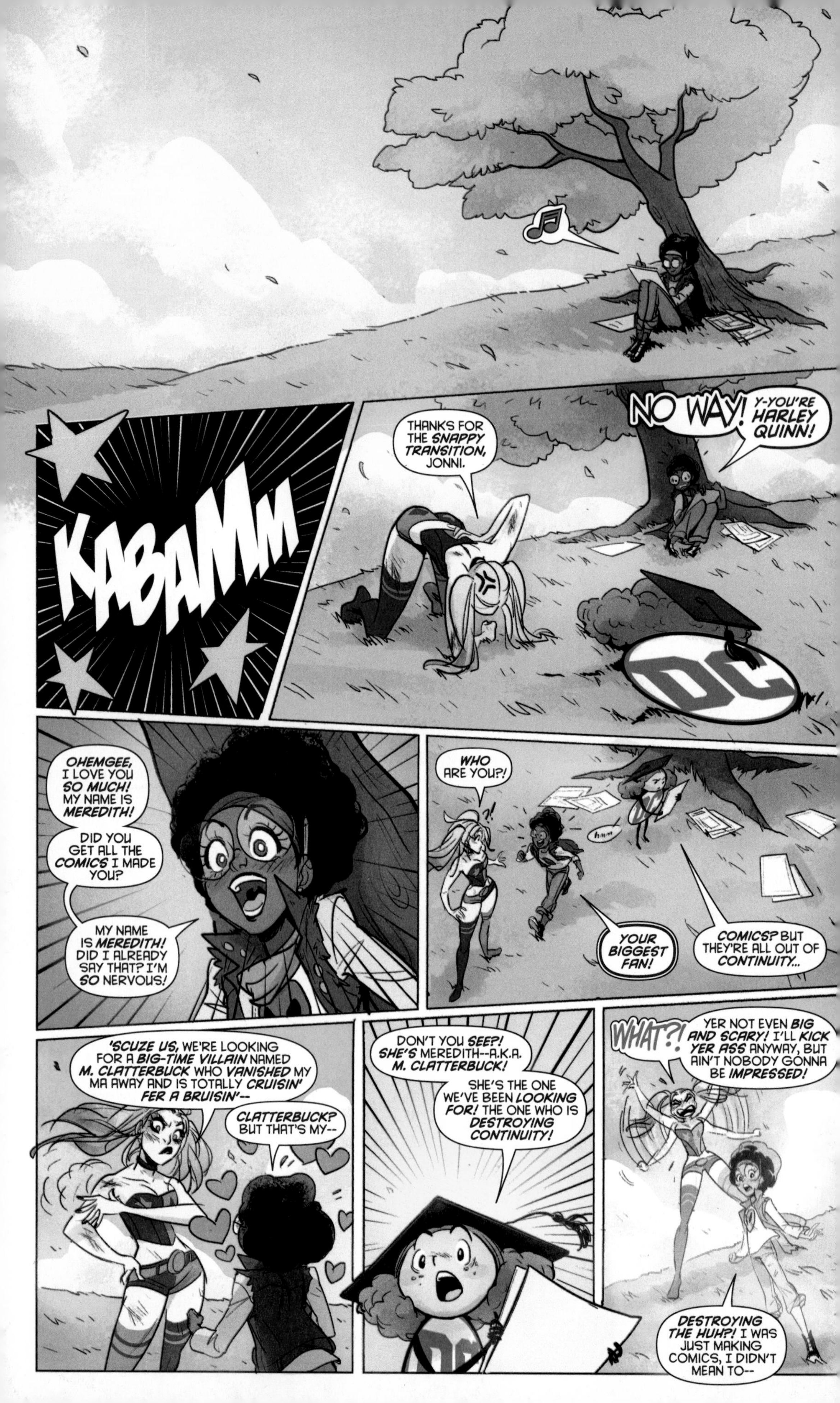

KABAMM
THANKS FOR THE SNAPPY TRANSITION, JONNI.
NO WAY!
Y-YOU'RE HARLEY QUINN!
OHEMGEE, I LOVE YOU SO MUCH! MY NAME IS MEREDITH!
DID YOU GET ALL THE COMICS I MADE YOU?
MY NAME IS MEREDITH! DID I ALREADY SAY THAT? I'M SO NERVOUS!
WHO ARE YOU?!
hmm
YOUR BIGGEST FAN!
COMICS? BUT THEY'RE ALL OUT OF CONTINUITY...
'SCUZE US, WE'RE LOOKING FOR A BIG-TIME VILLAIN NAMED M. CLATTERBUCK WHO VANISHED MY MA AWAY AND IS TOTALLY CRUISIN' FER A BRUISIN'--
CLATTERBUCK? BUT THAT'S MY--
DON'T YOU SEE?! SHE'S MEREDITH--A.K.A. M. CLATTERBUCK!
SHE'S THE ONE WE'VE BEEN LOOKING FOR! THE ONE WHO IS DESTROYING CONTINUITY!
WHAT?!
YER NOT EVEN BIG AND SCARY! I'LL KICK YER ASS ANYWAY, BUT AIN'T NOBODY GONNA BE IMPRESSED!
DESTROYING THE HUH?! I WAS JUST MAKING COMICS, I DIDN'T MEAN TO--

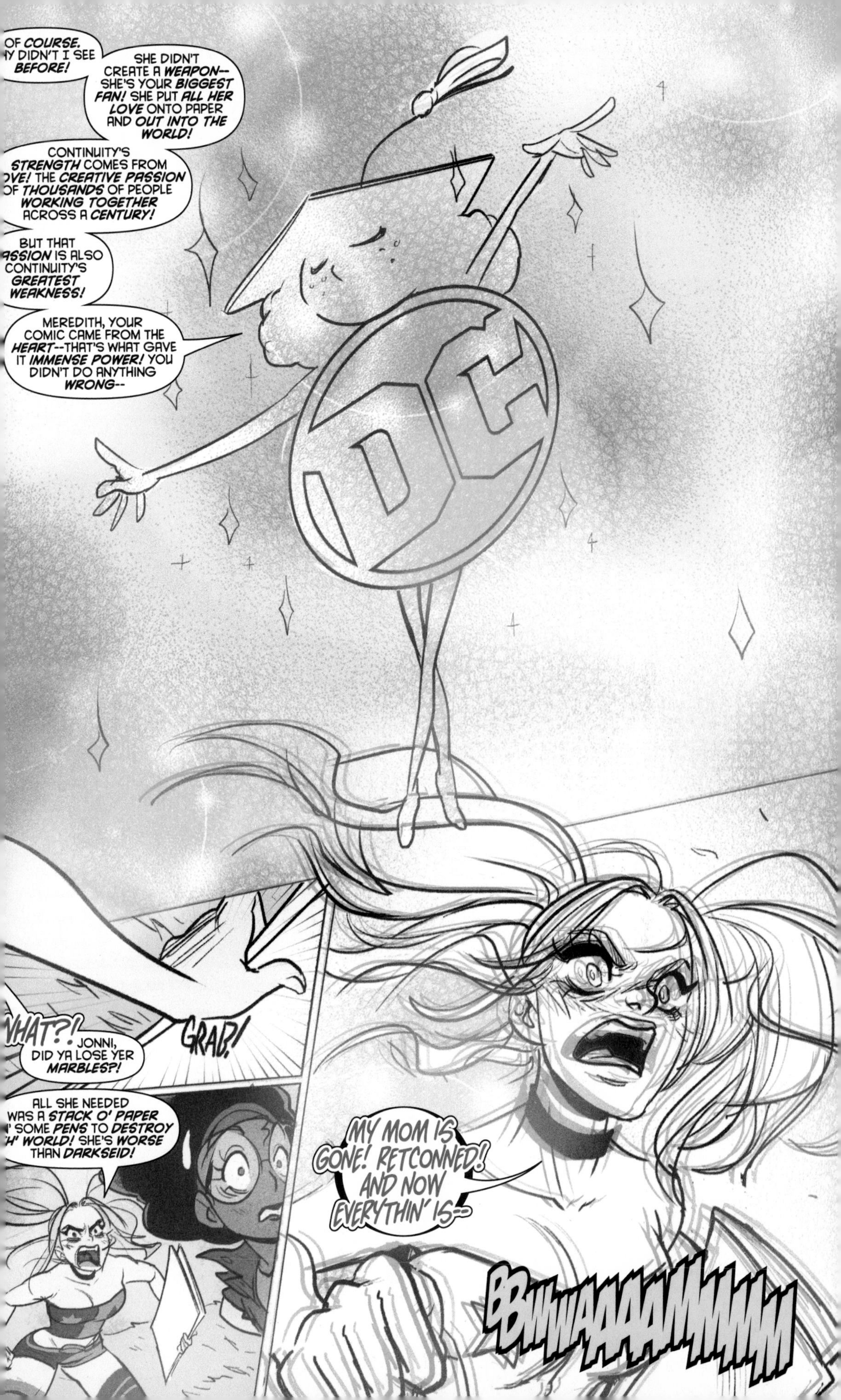

OF COURSE. ...Y DIDN'T I SEE BEFORE!
SHE DIDN'T CREATE A WEAPON-- SHE'S YOUR BIGGEST FAN! SHE PUT ALL HER LOVE ONTO PAPER AND OUT INTO THE WORLD!
CONTINUITY'S STRENGTH COMES FROM ...OVE! THE CREATIVE PASSION OF THOUSANDS OF PEOPLE WORKING TOGETHER ACROSS A CENTURY!
BUT THAT ...ASSION IS ALSO CONTINUITY'S GREATEST WEAKNESS!
MEREDITH, YOUR COMIC CAME FROM THE HEART--THAT'S WHAT GAVE IT IMMENSE POWER! YOU DIDN'T DO ANYTHING WRONG--
...HAT?!
GRAB!
JONNI, DID YA LOSE YER MARBLES?!
ALL SHE NEEDED WAS A STACK O' PAPER ...' SOME PENS TO DESTROY ...H' WORLD! SHE'S WORSE THAN DARKSEID!
MY MOM IS GONE! RETCONNED! AND NOW EVERYTHIN' IS--
BBWWAAAAMMMMM

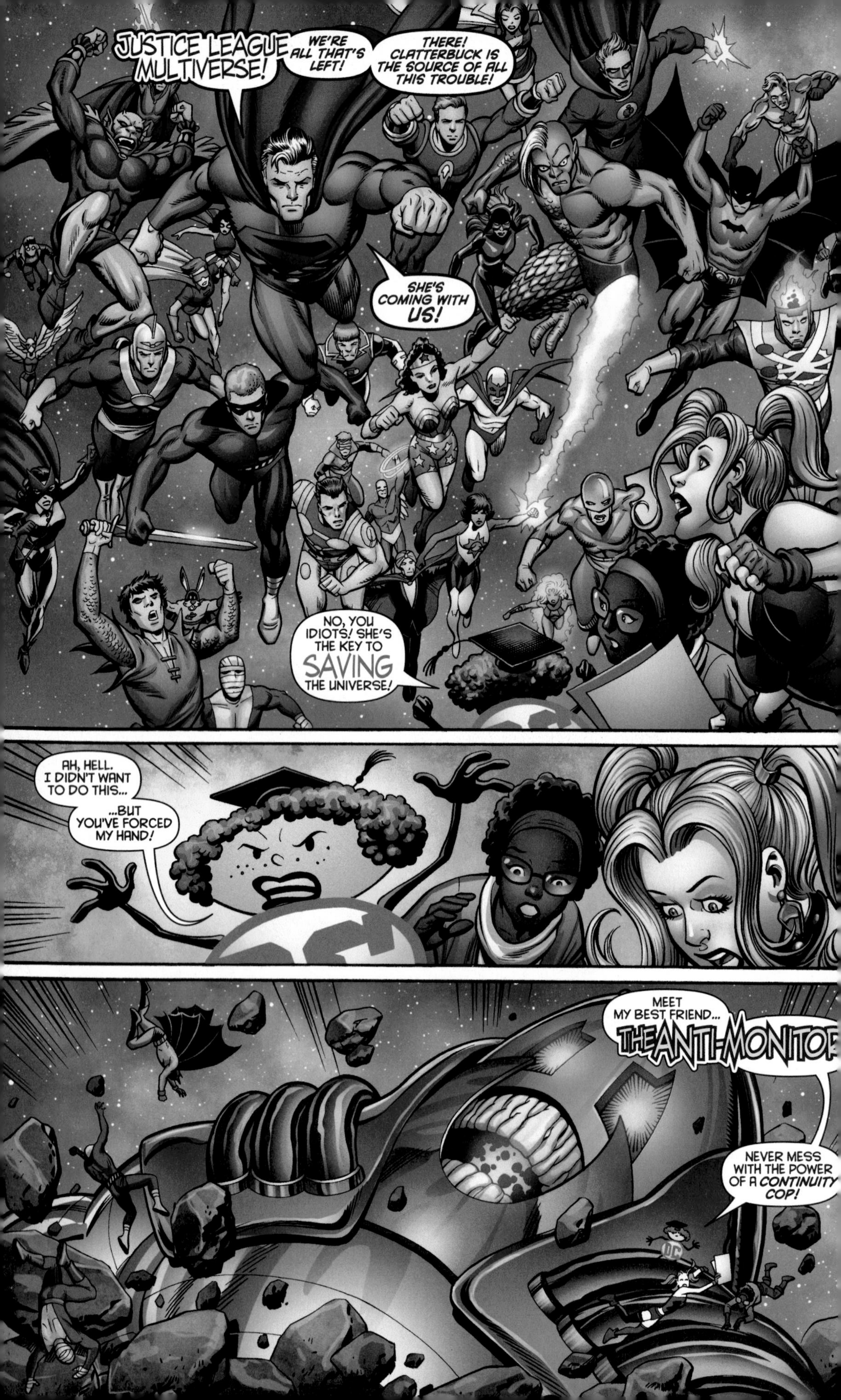
JUSTICE LEAGUE MULTIVERSE!
WE'RE ALL THAT'S LEFT!
THERE! CLATTERBUCK IS THE SOURCE OF ALL THIS TROUBLE!
SHE'S COMING WITH US!
NO, YOU IDIOTS! SHE'S THE KEY TO SAVING THE UNIVERSE!
AH, HELL. I DIDN'T WANT TO DO THIS...
...BUT YOU'VE FORCED MY HAND!
MEET MY BEST FRIEND... THE ANTI-MONITOR!
NEVER MESS WITH THE POWER OF A CONTINUITY COP!

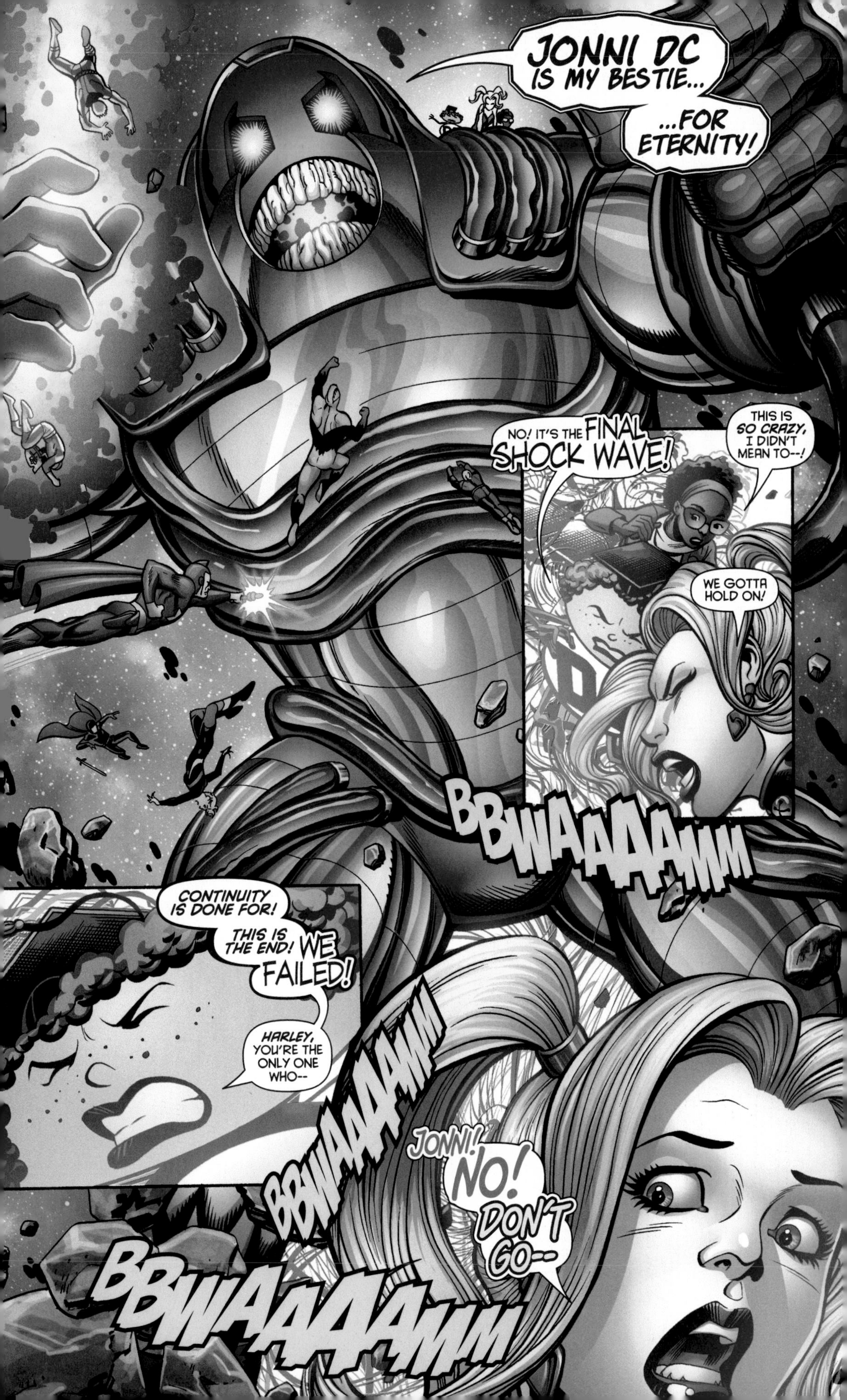

JONNI DC IS MY BESTIE...
...FOR ETERNITY!
NO! IT'S THE FINAL SHOCK WAVE!
THIS IS SO CRAZY, I DIDN'T MEAN TO--!
WE GOTTA HOLD ON!
BBWAAAAMM
CONTINUITY IS DONE FOR!
THIS IS THE END! WE FAILED!
HARLEY, YOU'RE THE ONLY ONE WHO--
BBWAAAAMM
JONNI! NO! DON'T GO--
BBWAAAAMM

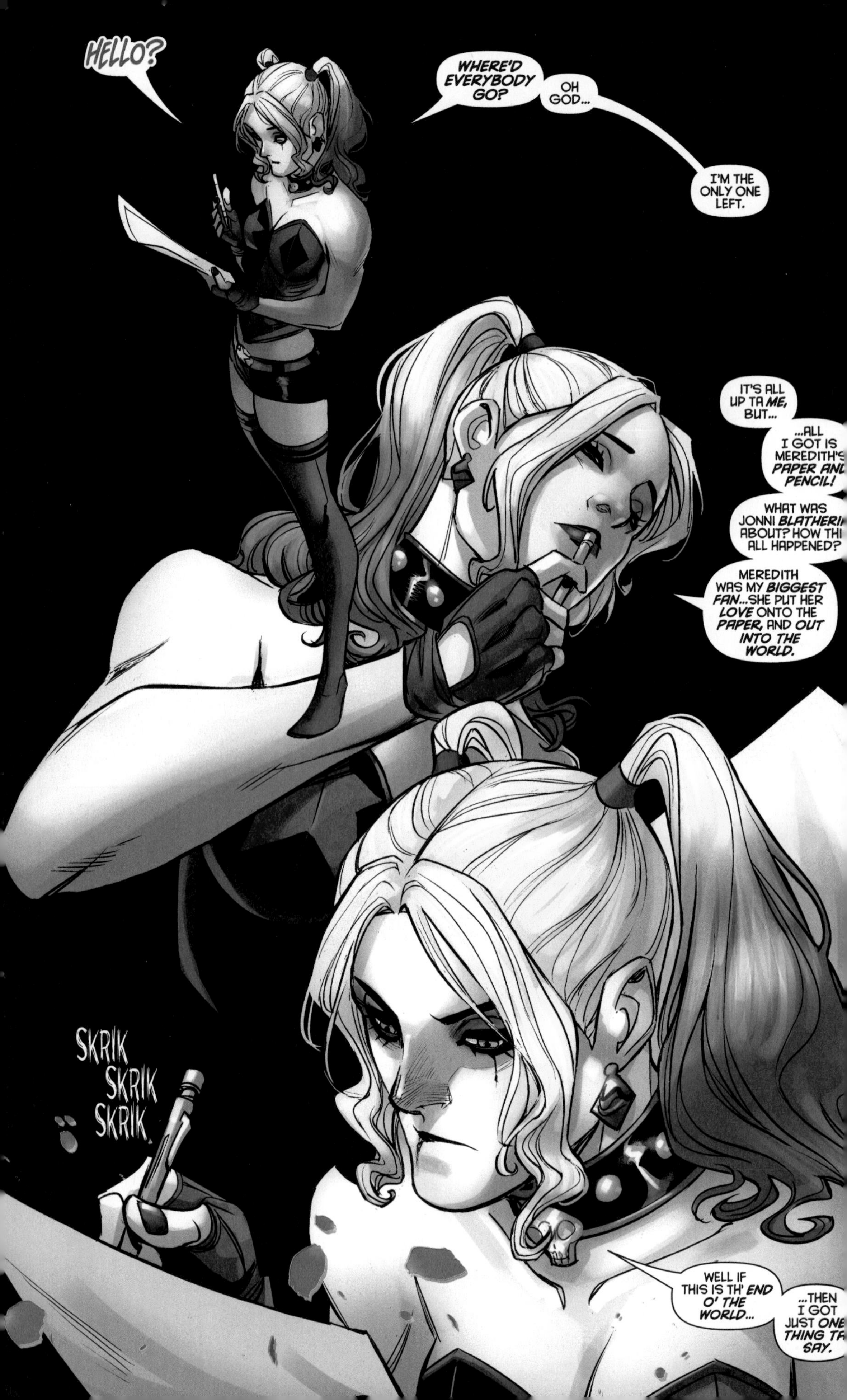
HELLO?
WHERE'D EVERYBODY GO?
OH GOD...
I'M THE ONLY ONE LEFT.
IT'S ALL UP TA ME, BUT...
...ALL I GOT IS MEREDITH'S PAPER AN PENCIL!
WHAT WAS JONNI BLATHERI ABOUT? HOW THI ALL HAPPENED?
MEREDITH WAS MY BIGGEST FAN...SHE PUT HER LOVE ONTO THE PAPER, AND OUT INTO THE WORLD.
SKRIK SKRIK SKRIK
WELL IF THIS IS TH' END O' THE WORLD...
...THEN I GOT JUST ON THING T SAY.

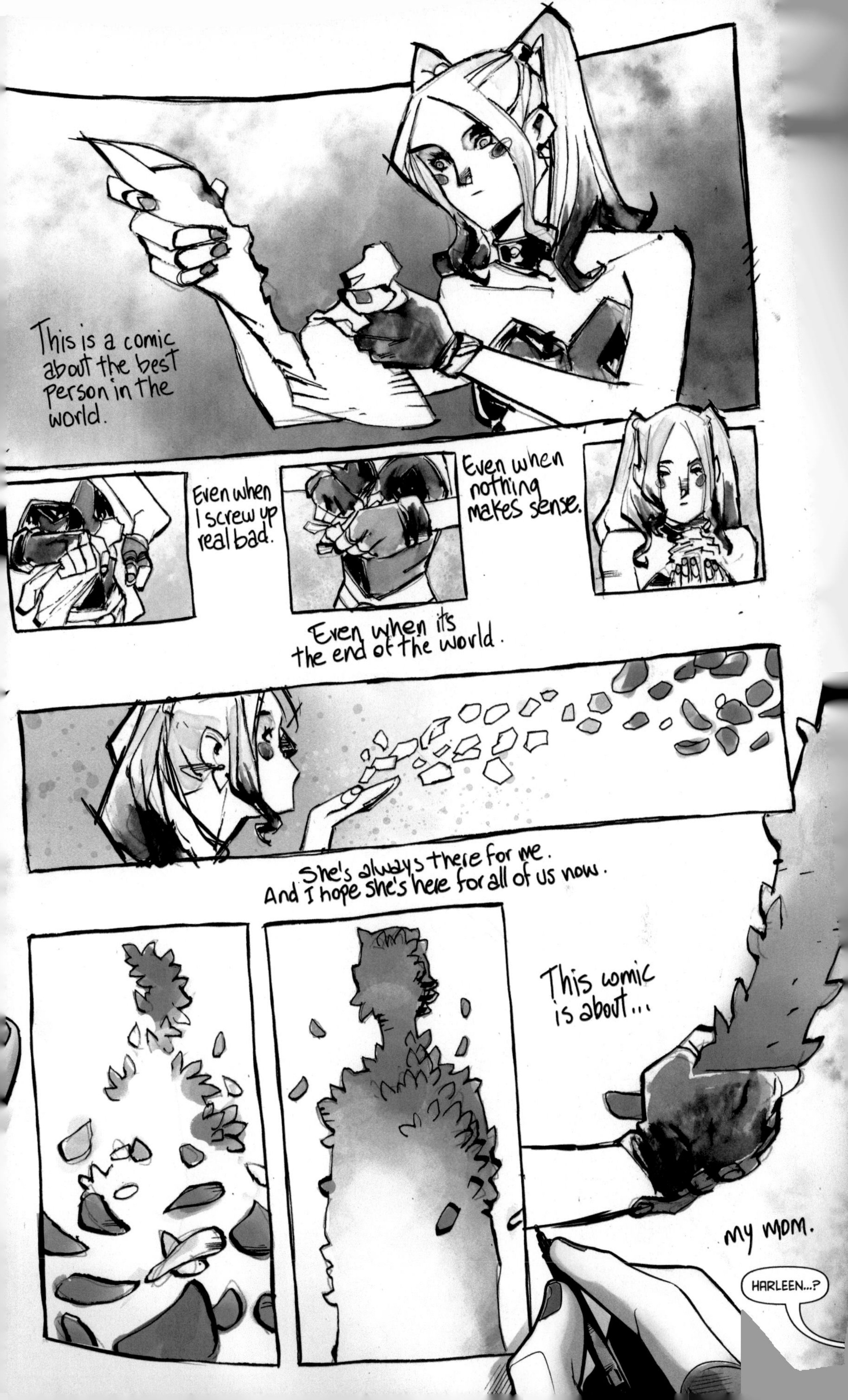

This is a comic about the best person in the world.
Even when I screw up real bad.
Even when nothing makes sense.
Even when it's the end of the world.
She's always there for me. And I hope she's here for all of us now.
This comic is about...
my mom.
HARLEEN...?

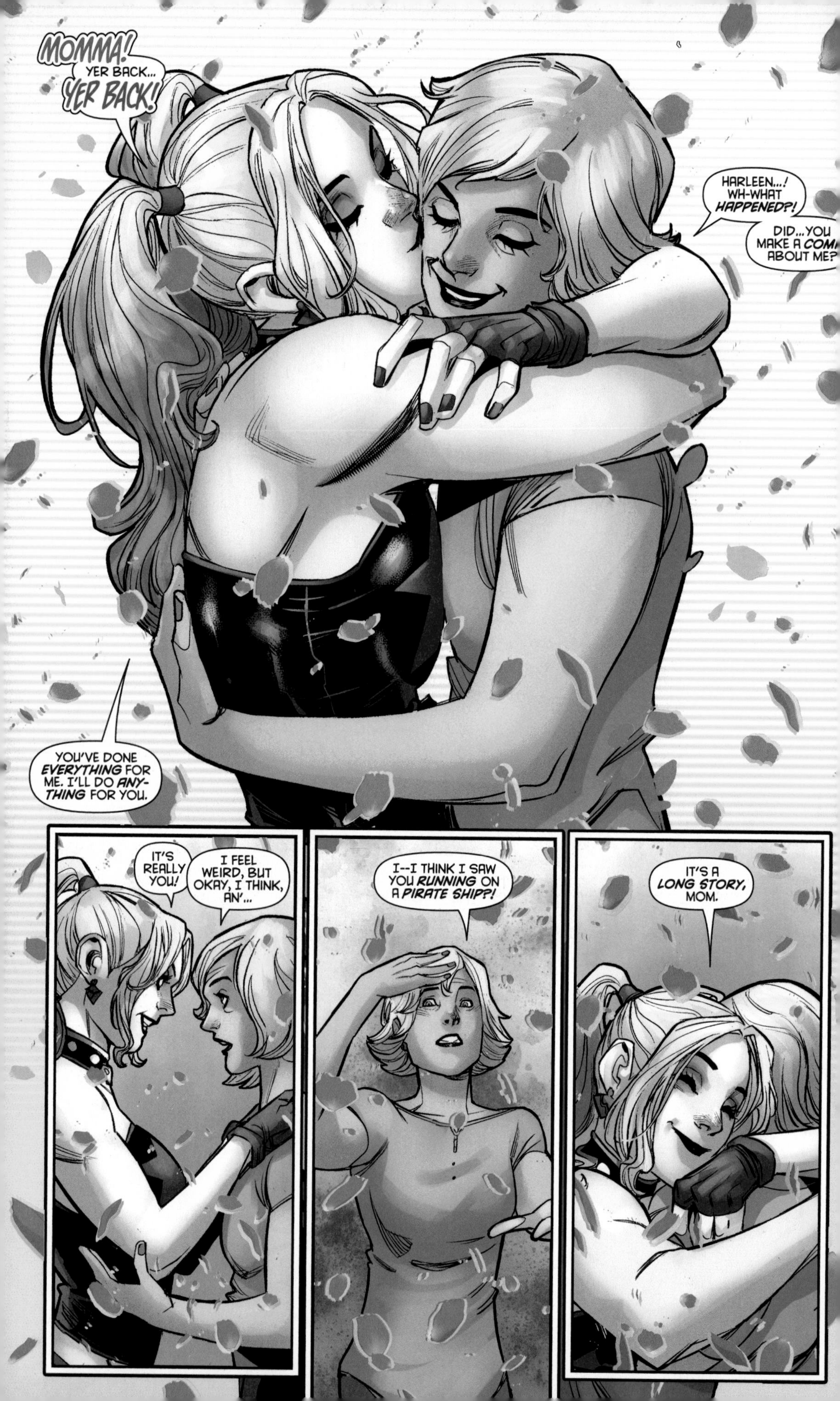

MOMMA! YER BACK... YER BACK!
HARLEEN...! WH-WHAT HAPPENED?!
DID...YOU MAKE A COM ABOUT ME?
YOU'VE DONE EVERYTHING FOR ME. I'LL DO ANY-THING FOR YOU.
IT'S REALLY YOU!
I FEEL WEIRD, BUT OKAY, I THINK, AN'...
I--I THINK I SAW YOU RUNNING ON A PIRATE SHIP?!
IT'S A LONG STORY, MOM.

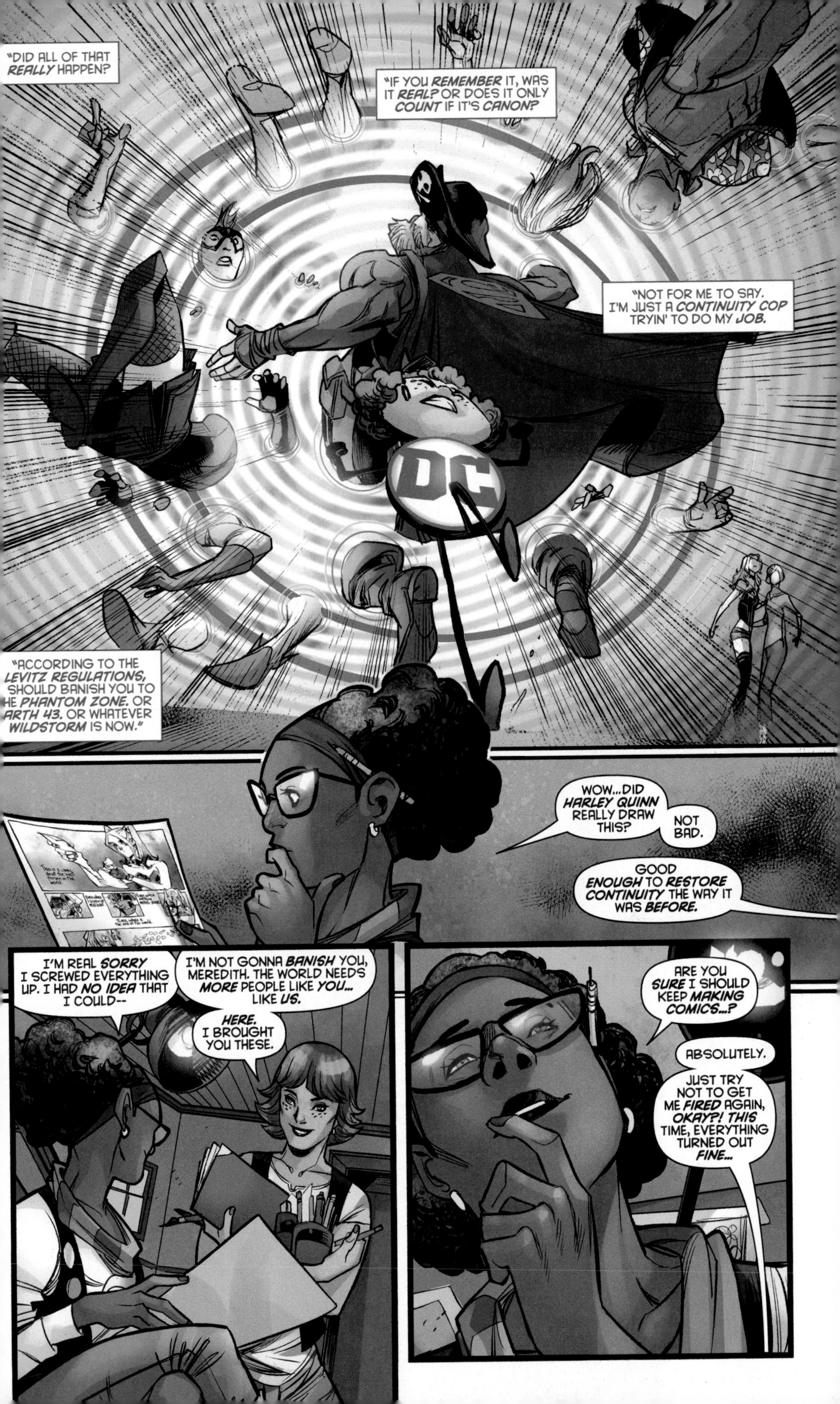

"DID ALL OF THAT *REALLY* HAPPEN?
"IF YOU *REMEMBER* IT, WAS IT *REAL?* OR DOES IT ONLY *COUNT* IF IT'S *CANON?*
"NOT FOR ME TO SAY. I'M JUST A *CONTINUITY COP* TRYIN' TO DO MY *JOB.*
"ACCORDING TO THE *LEVITZ REGULATIONS,* SHOULD BANISH YOU TO HE *PHANTOM ZONE.* OR ARTH 43. OR WHATEVER *WILDSTORM* IS NOW."
WOW...DID *HARLEY QUINN* REALLY DRAW THIS?
NOT BAD.
GOOD *ENOUGH* TO *RESTORE CONTINUITY* THE WAY IT WAS *BEFORE.*
I'M REAL *SORRY* I SCREWED EVERYTHING UP. I HAD *NO IDEA* THAT I COULD--
I'M NOT GONNA *BANISH* YOU, MEREDITH. THE WORLD NEEDS *MORE* PEOPLE LIKE *YOU*... LIKE *US.*
HERE. I BROUGHT YOU THESE.
ARE YOU *SURE* I SHOULD KEEP *MAKING COMICS...?*
ABSOLUTELY.
JUST TRY NOT TO GET ME *FIRED* AGAIN, *OKAY?! THIS* TIME, EVERYTHING TURNED OUT *FINE...*

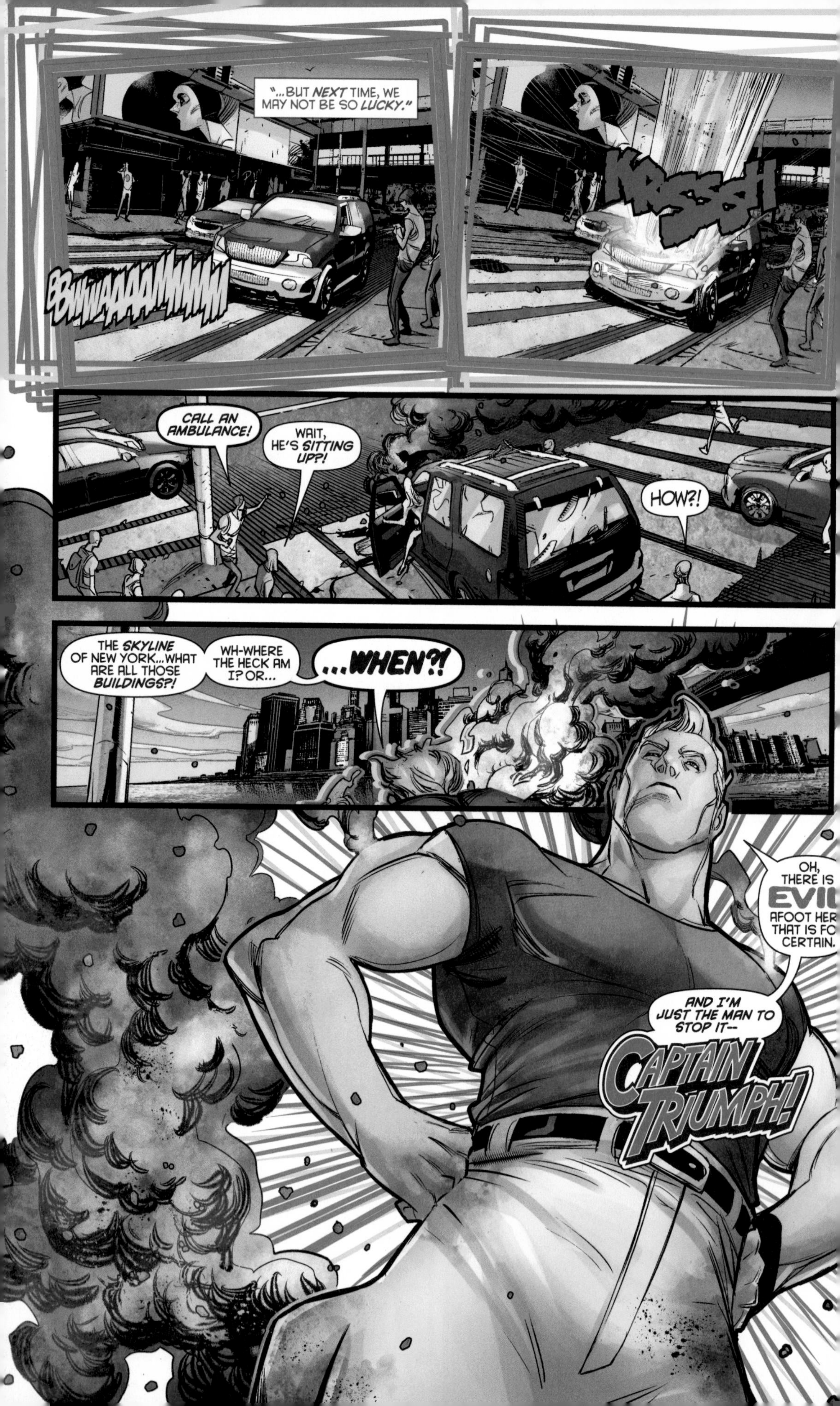
"...BUT NEXT TIME, WE MAY NOT BE SO LUCKY."
BBWWAAAAMMMM
KRSSSH
CALL AN AMBULANCE!
WAIT, HE'S SITTING UP?!
HOW?!
THE SKYLINE OF NEW YORK...WHAT ARE ALL THOSE BUILDINGS?!
WH-WHERE THE HECK AM I? OR...
...WHEN?!
AND I'M JUST THE MAN TO STOP IT--
CAPTAIN TRIUMPH!

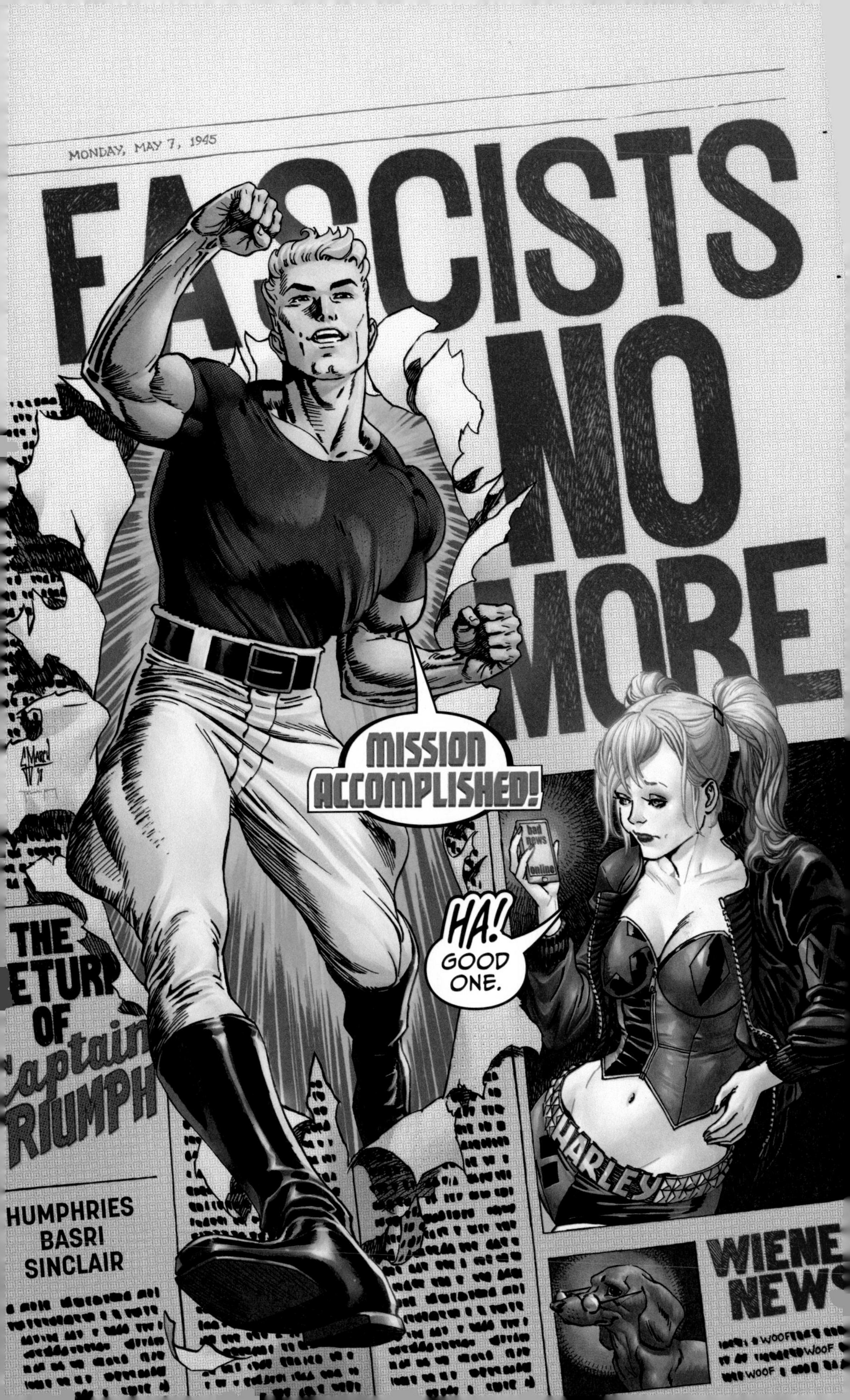

MONDAY, MAY 7, 1945
FASCISTS NO MORE
MISSION ACCOMPLISHED!
bad news online
HA! GOOD ONE.
THE
OF
HUMPHRIES
BASRI
SINCLAIR
HARLEY
WOOF
WOOF
WOOF

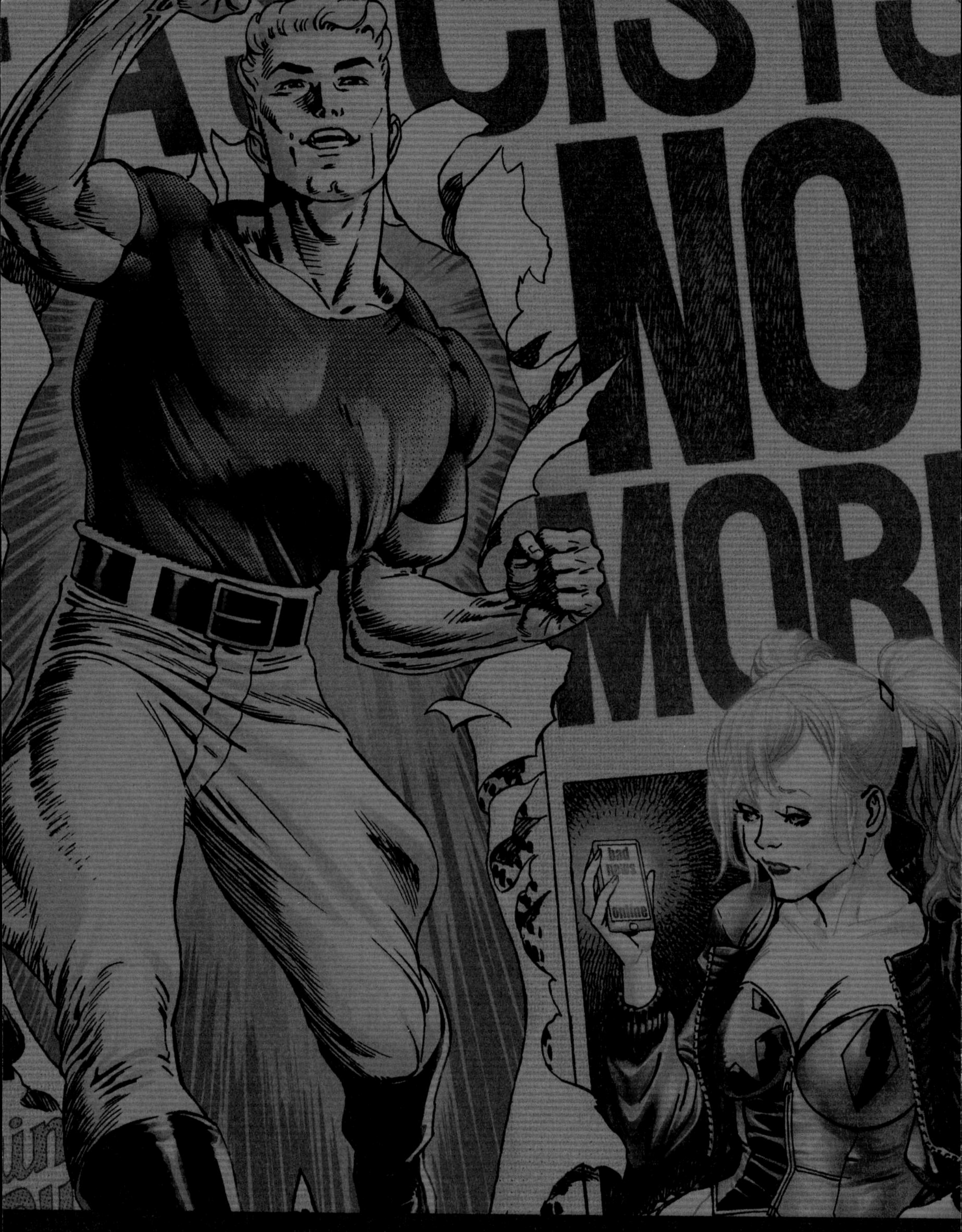
NO

HARLEY QUINN
#51

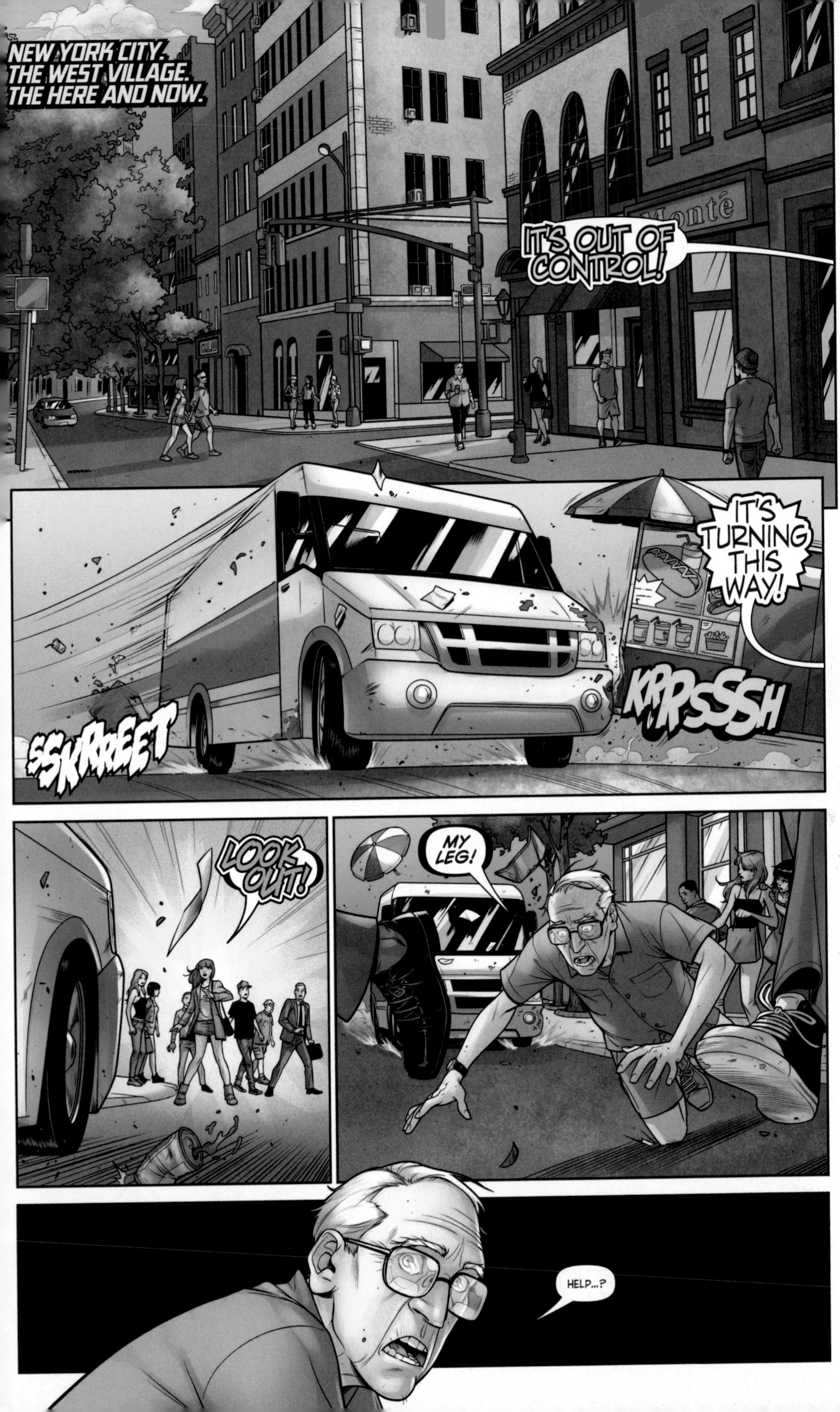
NEW YORK CITY.
THE WEST VILLAGE.
THE HERE AND NOW.
Monté
IT'S OUT OF CONTROL!
IT'S TURNING THIS WAY!
SSKRREET
KRRSSSH
LOOK OUT!
MY LEG!
HELP...?

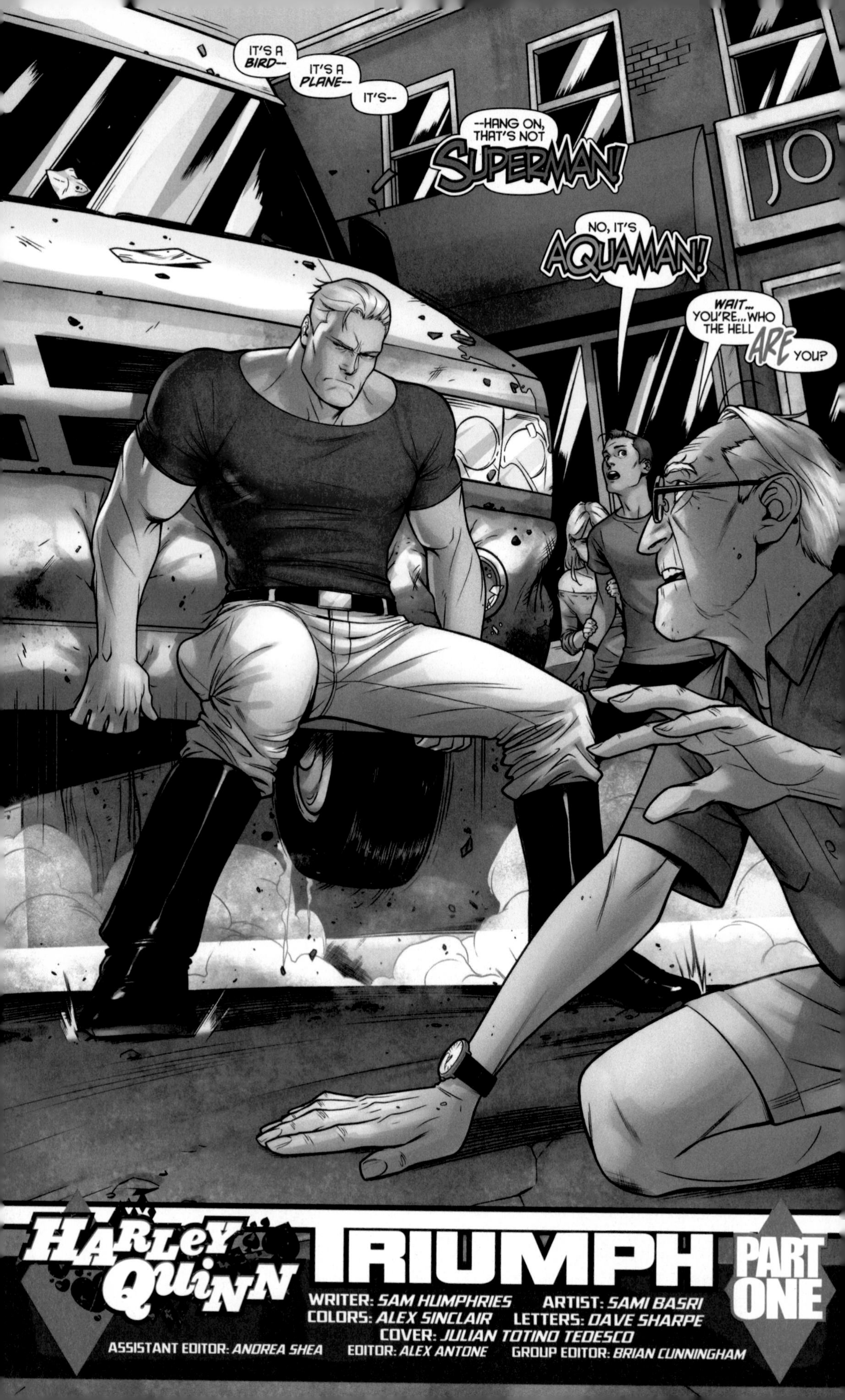
IT'S A BIRD--
IT'S A PLANE--
IT'S--
--HANG ON, THAT'S NOT SUPERMAN!
NO, IT'S AQUAMAN!
WAIT... YOU'RE...WHO THE HELL ARE YOU?
HARLEY QUINN
TRIUMPH
PART ONE
WRITER: SAM HUMPHRIES ARTIST: SAMI BASRI
COLORS: ALEX SINCLAIR LETTERS: DAVE SHARPE
COVER: JULIAN TOTINO TEDESCO
ASSISTANT EDITOR: ANDREA SHEA EDITOR: ALEX ANTONE GROUP EDITOR: BRIAN CUNNINGHAM

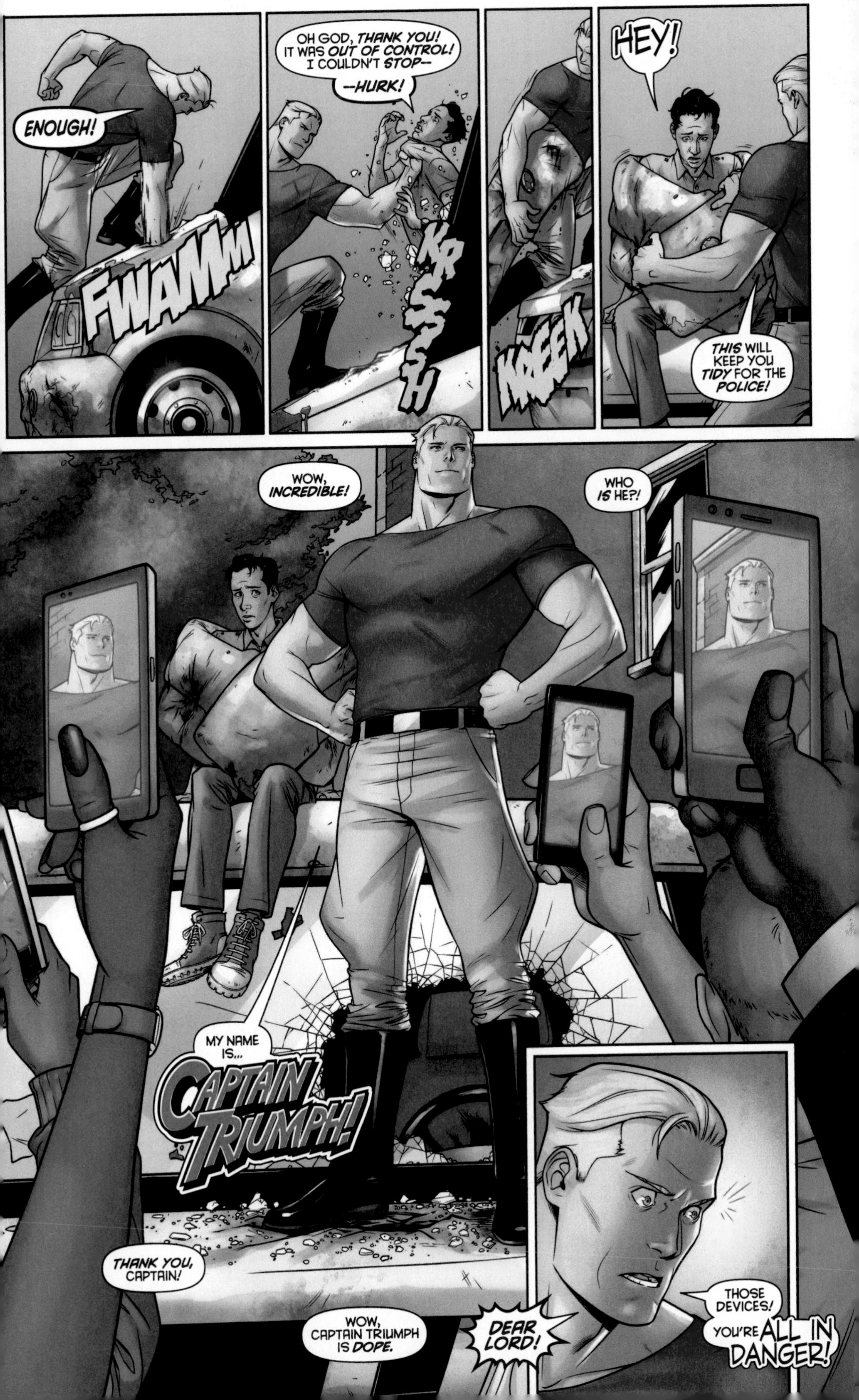

ENOUGH!
FWAMM
OH GOD, THANK YOU! IT WAS OUT OF CONTROL! I COULDN'T STOP--
--HURK!
KRSSSH
KREEK
HEY!
THIS WILL KEEP YOU TIDY FOR THE POLICE!
WOW, INCREDIBLE!
WHO IS HE?!
MY NAME IS...
CAPTAIN TRIUMPH!
THANK YOU, CAPTAIN!
WOW, CAPTAIN TRIUMPH IS DOPE.
DEAR LORD!
THOSE DEVICES!
YOU'RE ALL IN DANGER!

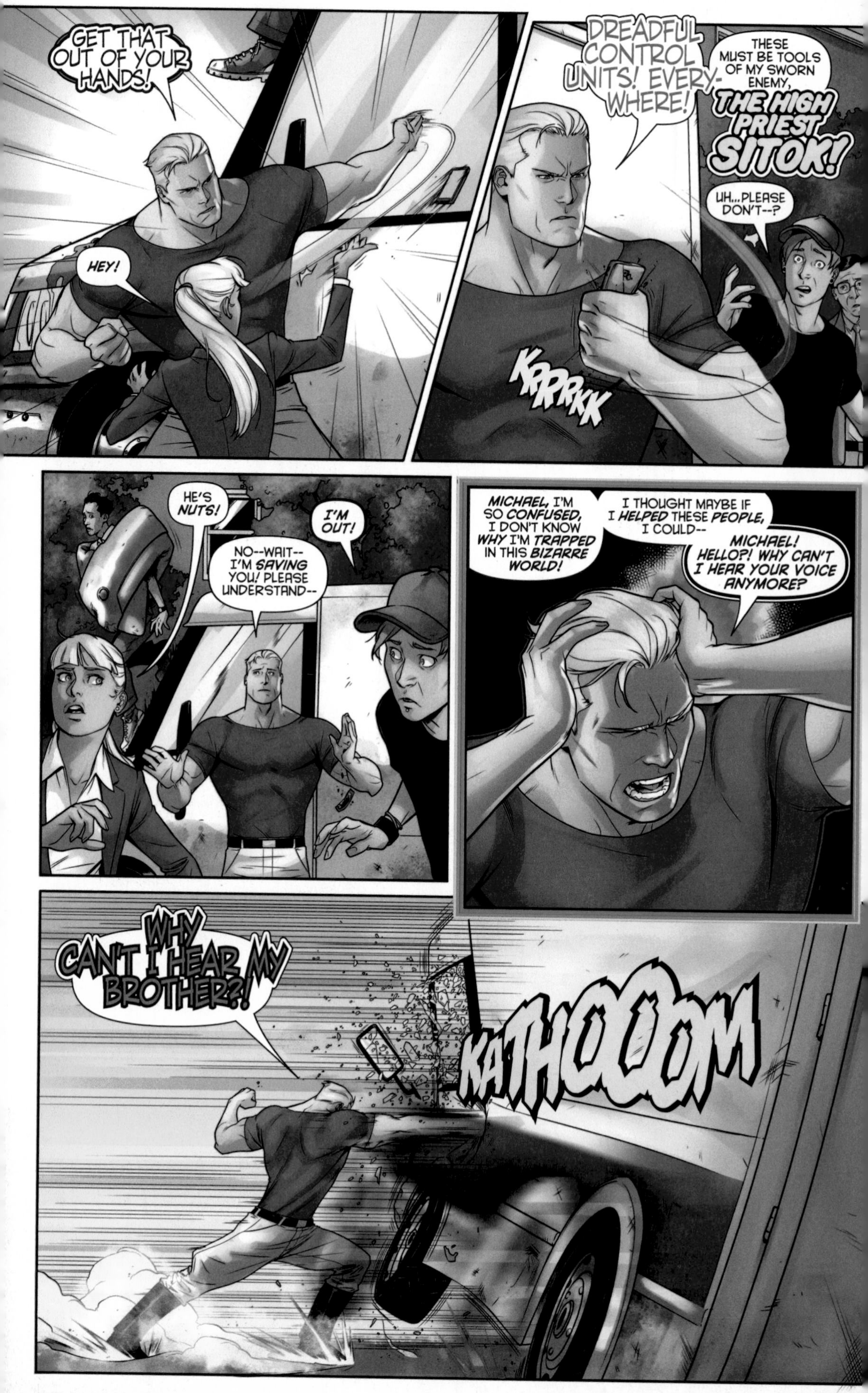
GET THAT OUT OF YOUR HANDS!
HEY!
DREADFUL CONTROL UNITS! EVERY-WHERE!
THESE MUST BE TOOLS OF MY SWORN ENEMY, THE HIGH PRIEST SITOK!
UH...PLEASE DON'T--?
KRRRKK
HE'S NUTS!
I'M OUT!
NO--WAIT-- I'M SAVING YOU! PLEASE UNDERSTAND--
MICHAEL, I'M SO CONFUSED, I DON'T KNOW WHY I'M TRAPPED IN THIS BIZARRE WORLD!
I THOUGHT MAYBE IF I HELPED THESE PEOPLE, I COULD--
MICHAEL! HELLO?! WHY CAN'T I HEAR YOUR VOICE ANYMORE?
WHY CAN'T I HEAR MY BROTHER?!
KATHOOOM

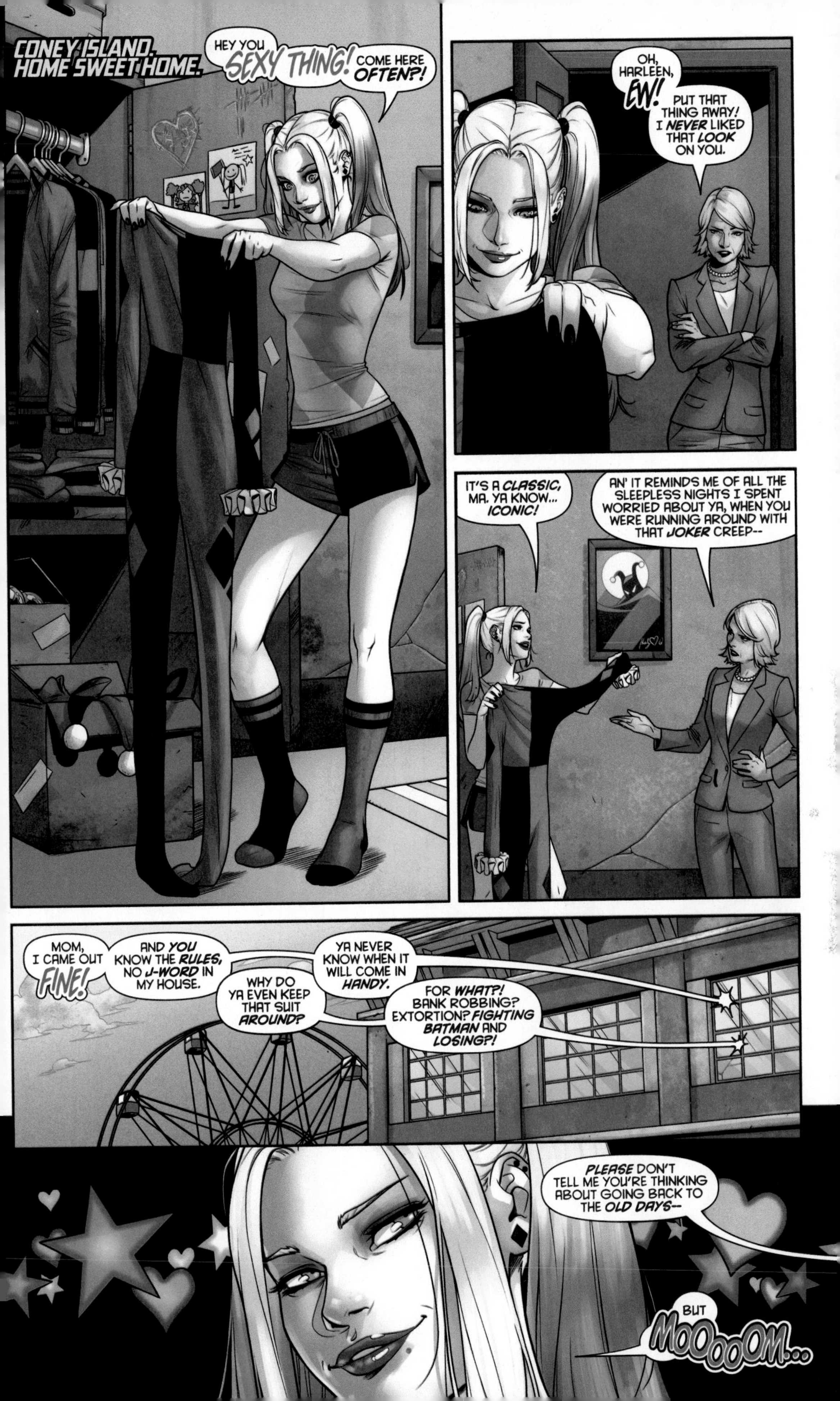
CONEY ISLAND. HOME SWEET HOME.
HEY YOU SEXY THING! COME HERE OFTEN?!
OH, HARLEEN, EW! PUT THAT THING AWAY! I NEVER LIKED THAT LOOK ON YOU.
IT'S A CLASSIC, MA. YA KNOW... ICONIC!
AN' IT REMINDS ME OF ALL THE SLEEPLESS NIGHTS I SPENT WORRIED ABOUT YA, WHEN YOU WERE RUNNING AROUND WITH THAT JOKER CREEP--
MOM, I CAME OUT FINE!
AND YOU KNOW THE RULES, NO J-WORD IN MY HOUSE.
WHY DO YA EVEN KEEP THAT SUIT AROUND?
YA NEVER KNOW WHEN IT WILL COME IN HANDY.
FOR WHAT?! BANK ROBBING? EXTORTION? FIGHTING BATMAN AND LOSING?!
PLEASE DON'T TELL ME YOU'RE THINKING ABOUT GOING BACK TO THE OLD DAYS--
BUT MOOOOOM...

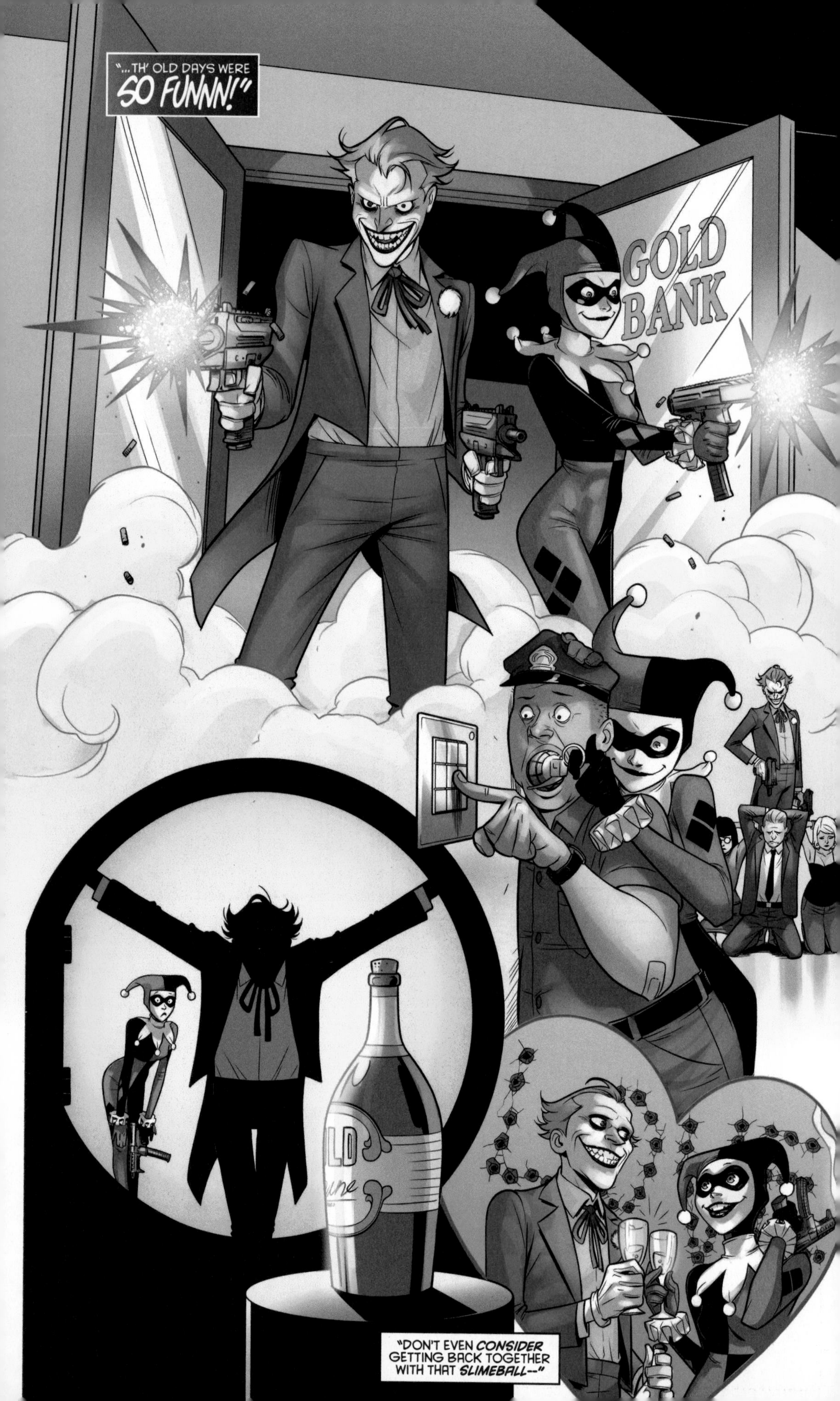
"...TH' OLD DAYS WERE SO FUNNN!"
GOLD BANK
"DON'T EVEN CONSIDER GETTING BACK TOGETHER WITH THAT SLIMEBALL--"

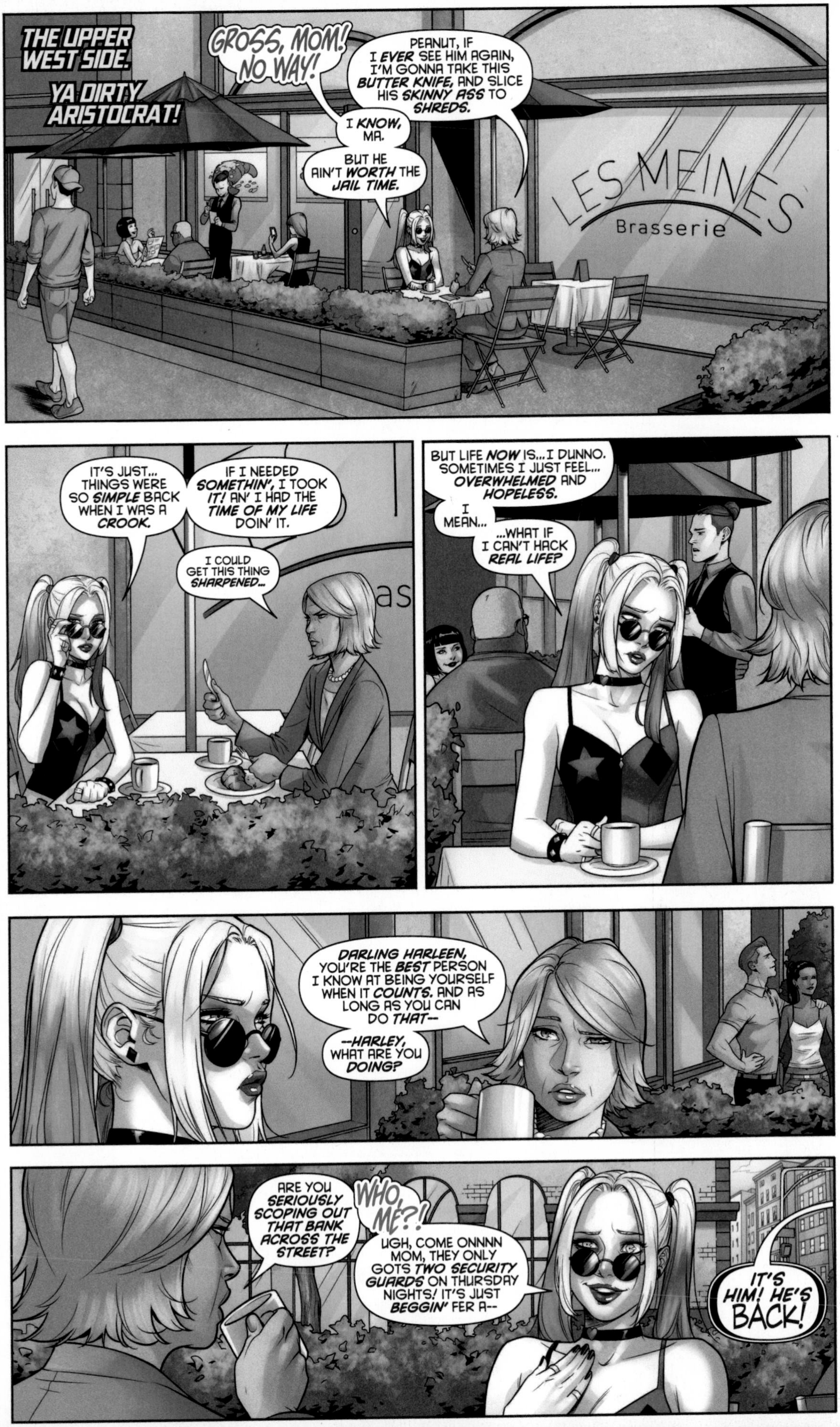
THE UPPER WEST SIDE.
YA DIRTY ARISTOCRAT!
GROSS, MOM! NO WAY!
PEANUT, IF I EVER SEE HIM AGAIN, I'M GONNA TAKE THIS BUTTER KNIFE, AND SLICE HIS SKINNY ASS TO SHREDS.
I KNOW, MA.
BUT HE AIN'T WORTH THE JAIL TIME.
LES MEINES
Brasserie
IT'S JUST... THINGS WERE SO SIMPLE BACK WHEN I WAS A CROOK.
IF I NEEDED SOMETHIN', I TOOK IT! AN' I HAD THE TIME OF MY LIFE DOIN' IT.
I COULD GET THIS THING SHARPENED...
BUT LIFE NOW IS... I DUNNO. SOMETIMES I JUST FEEL... OVERWHELMED AND HOPELESS.
I MEAN...
...WHAT IF I CAN'T HACK REAL LIFE?
DARLING HARLEEN, YOU'RE THE BEST PERSON I KNOW AT BEING YOURSELF WHEN IT COUNTS. AND AS LONG AS YOU CAN DO THAT--
--HARLEY, WHAT ARE YOU DOING?
ARE YOU SERIOUSLY SCOPING OUT THAT BANK ACROSS THE STREET?
WHO, ME?!
UGH, COME ONNNN MOM, THEY ONLY GOTS TWO SECURITY GUARDS ON THURSDAY NIGHTS! IT'S JUST BEGGIN' FER A--
IT'S HIM! HE'S BACK!

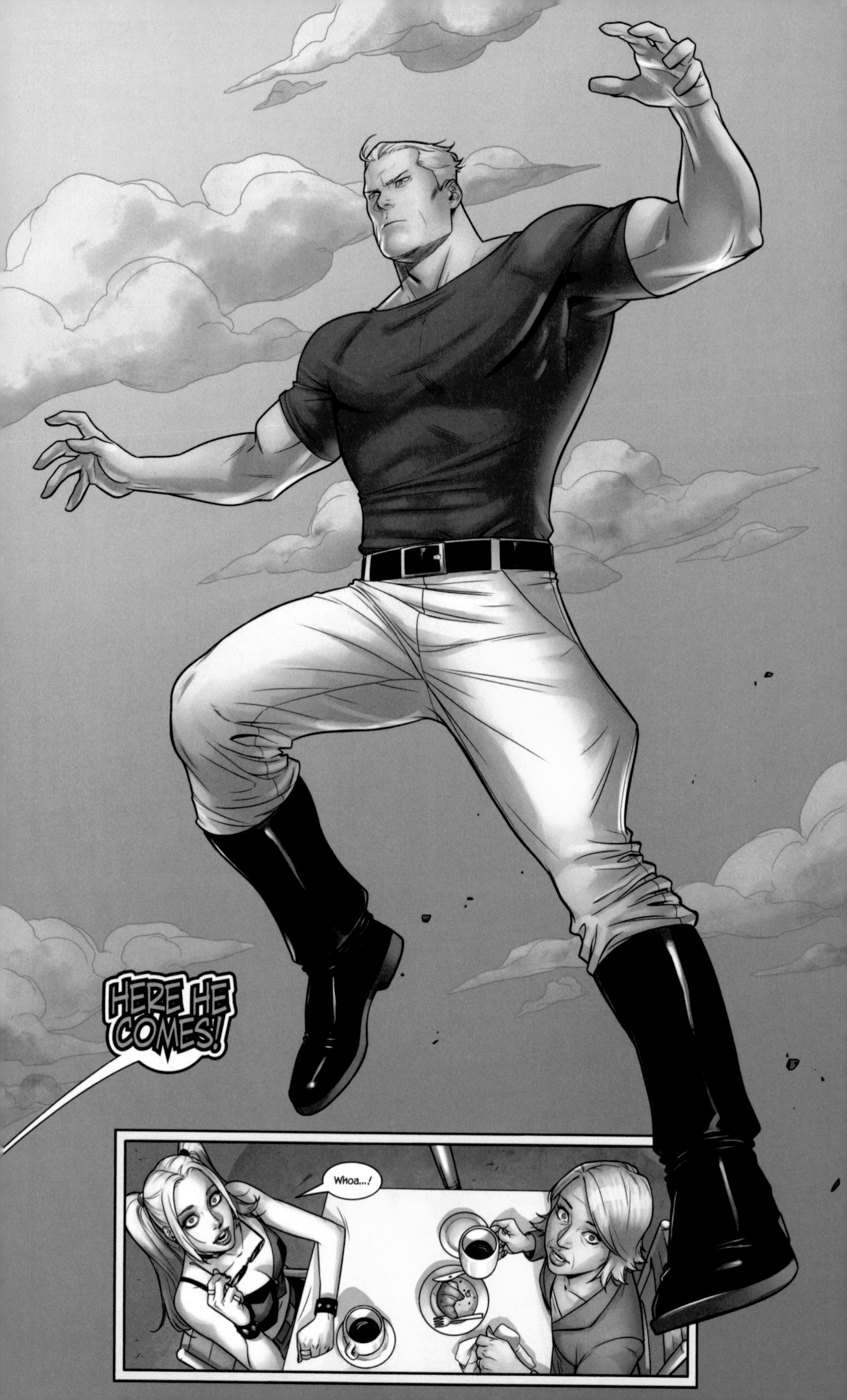
HERE HE COMES!
Whoa...!

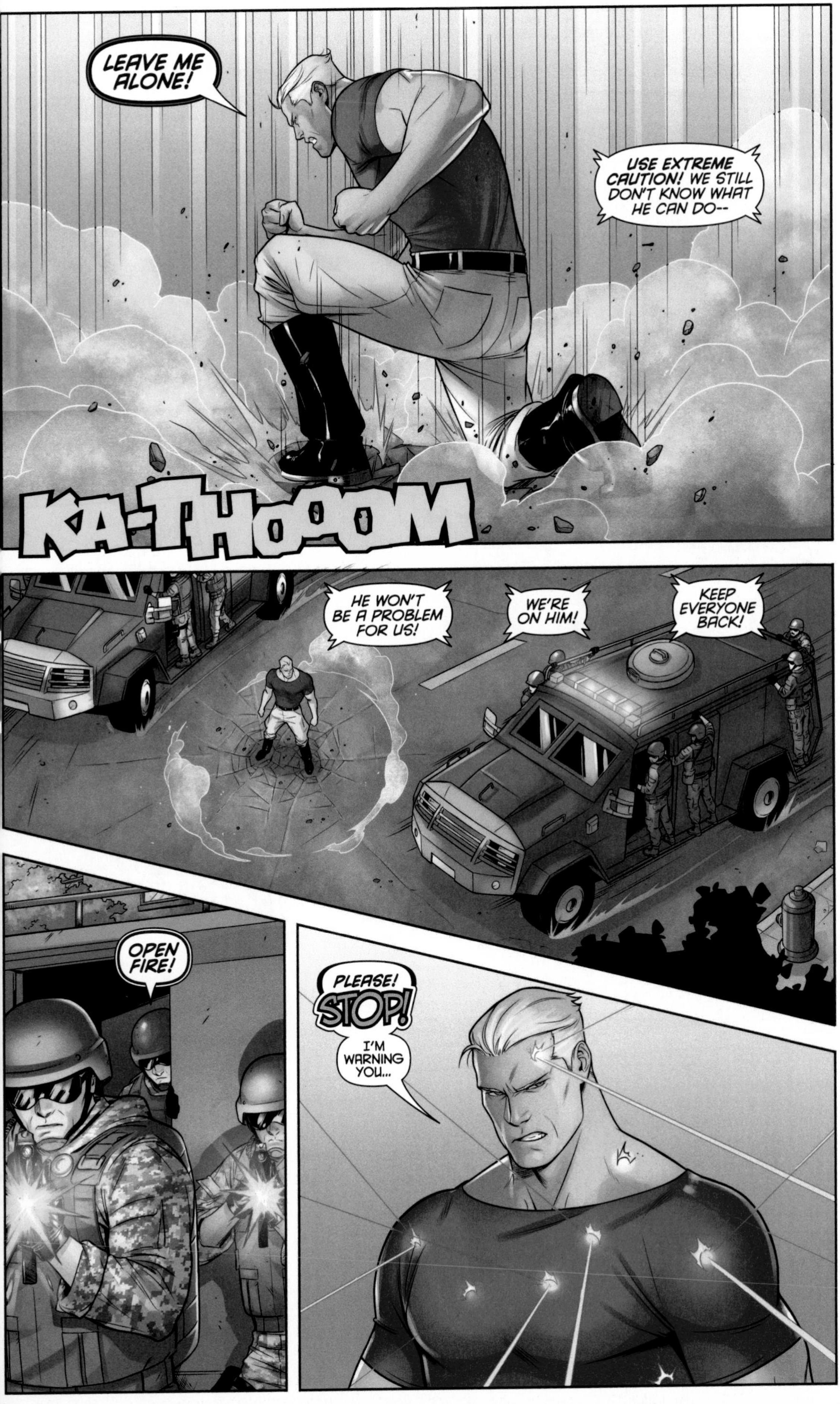
LEAVE ME ALONE!
USE EXTREME CAUTION! WE STILL DON'T KNOW WHAT HE CAN DO--
KA-THOOOM
HE WON'T BE A PROBLEM FOR US!
WE'RE ON HIM!
KEEP EVERYONE BACK!
OPEN FIRE!
PLEASE! STOP!
I'M WARNING YOU...

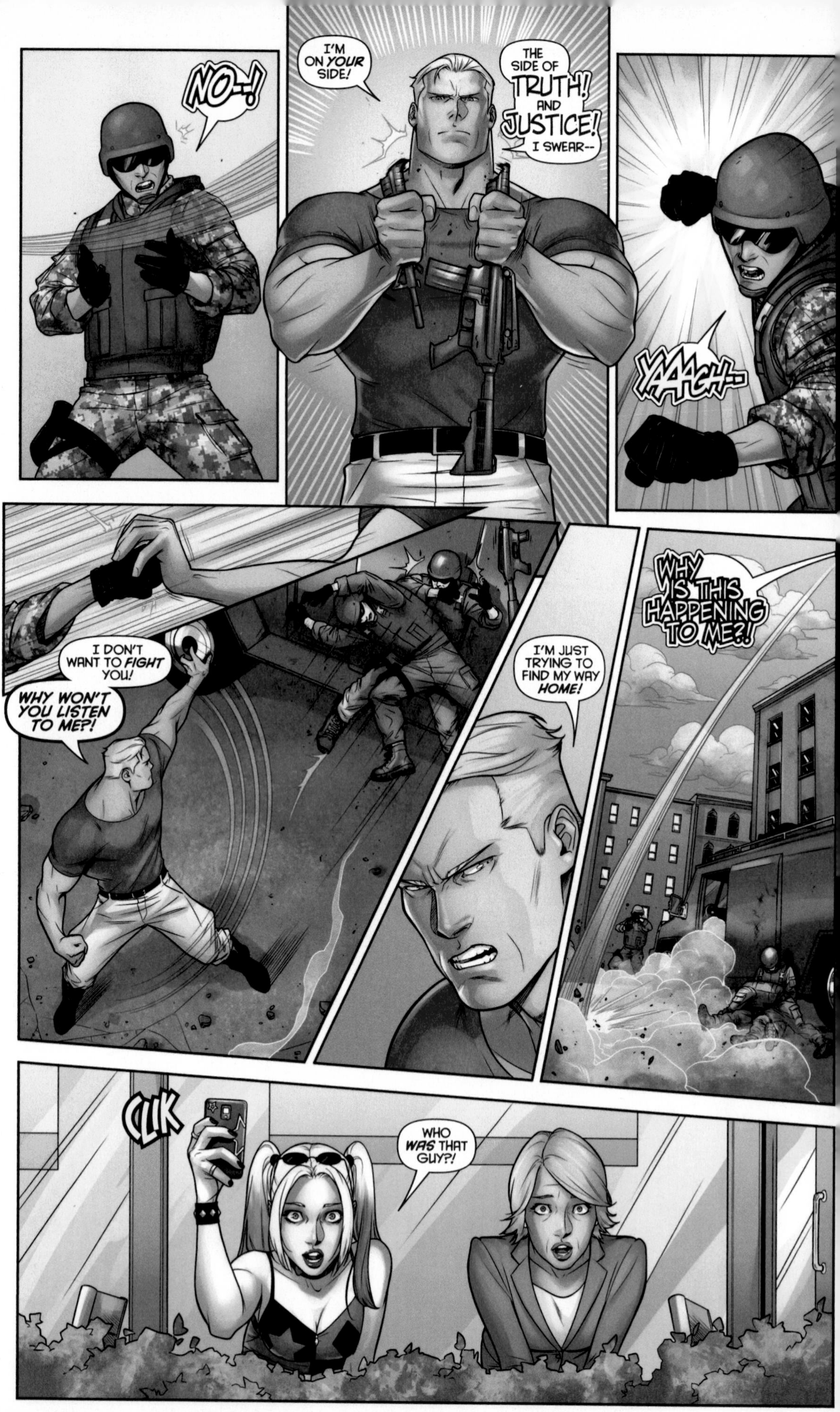

NO--!
I'M ON YOUR SIDE!
THE SIDE OF TRUTH! AND JUSTICE! I SWEAR--
YAAAGH--
I DON'T WANT TO FIGHT YOU!
WHY WON'T YOU LISTEN TO ME?!
I'M JUST TRYING TO FIND MY WAY HOME!
WHY IS THIS HAPPENING TO ME?!
CLIK
WHO WAS THAT GUY?!

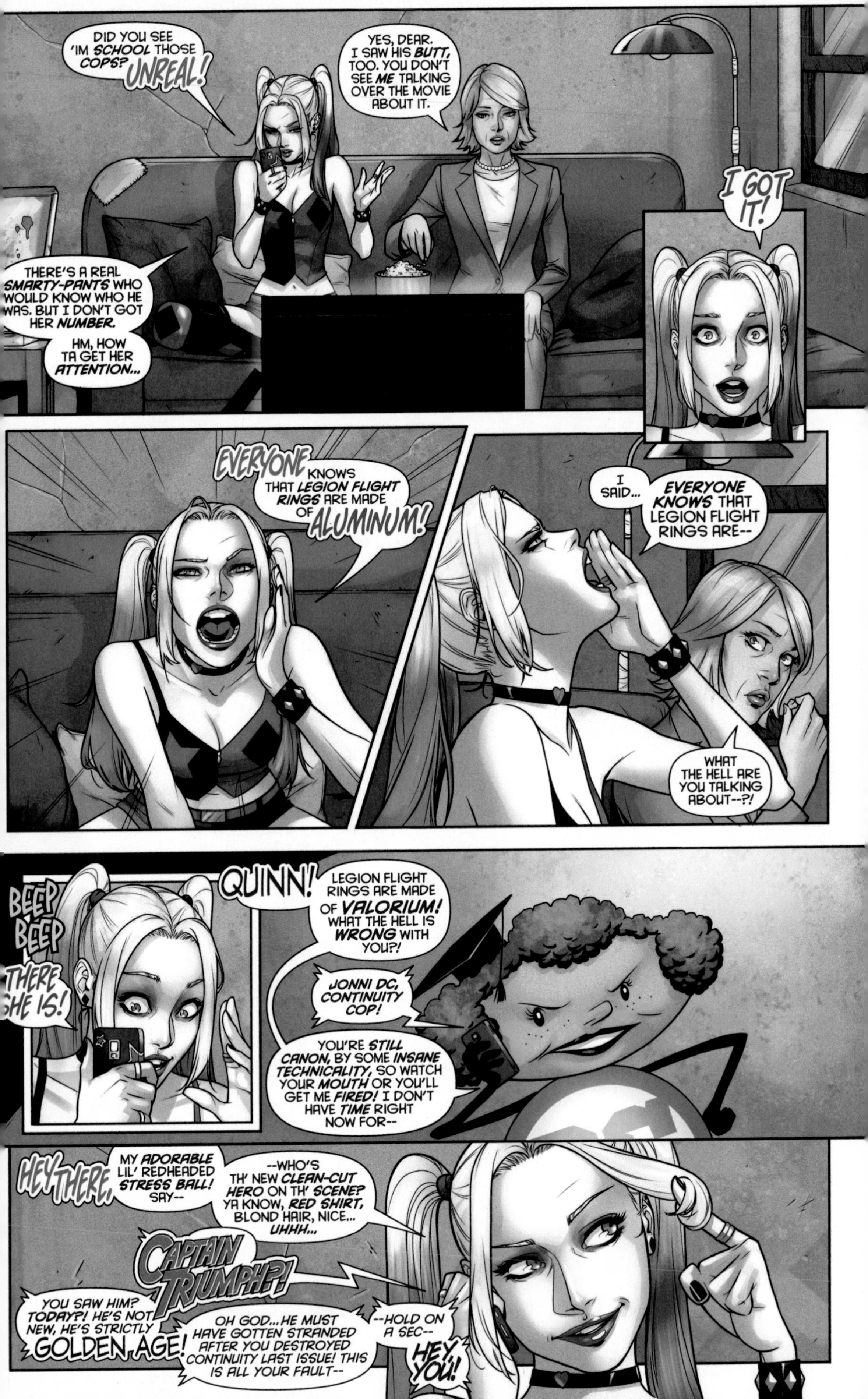
DID YOU SEE 'IM SCHOOL THOSE COPS? UNREAL!
YES, DEAR. I SAW HIS BUTT, TOO. YOU DON'T SEE ME TALKING OVER THE MOVIE ABOUT IT.
THERE'S A REAL SMARTY-PANTS WHO WOULD KNOW WHO HE WAS. BUT I DON'T GOT HER NUMBER.
HM, HOW TA GET HER ATTENTION...
I GOT IT!
EVERYONE KNOWS THAT LEGION FLIGHT RINGS ARE MADE OF ALUMINUM!
I SAID... EVERYONE KNOWS THAT LEGION FLIGHT RINGS ARE--
WHAT THE HELL ARE YOU TALKING ABOUT--?!
BEEP BEEP
THERE SHE IS!
QUINN!
LEGION FLIGHT RINGS ARE MADE OF VALORIUM! WHAT THE HELL IS WRONG WITH YOU?!
JONNI DC, CONTINUITY COP!
YOU'RE STILL CANON, BY SOME INSANE TECHNICALITY, SO WATCH YOUR MOUTH OR YOU'LL GET ME FIRED! I DON'T HAVE TIME RIGHT NOW FOR--
HEY THERE,
MY ADORABLE LIL' REDHEADED STRESS BALL! SAY--
--WHO'S TH' NEW CLEAN-CUT HERO ON TH' SCENE? YA KNOW, RED SHIRT, BLOND HAIR, NICE... UHHH...
CAPTAIN TRIUMPH?!
YOU SAW HIM? TODAY?! HE'S NOT NEW, HE'S STRICTLY GOLDEN AGE!
OH GOD... HE MUST HAVE GOTTEN STRANDED AFTER YOU DESTROYED CONTINUITY LAST ISSUE! THIS IS ALL YOUR FAULT--
--HOLD ON A SEC--
HEY YOU!

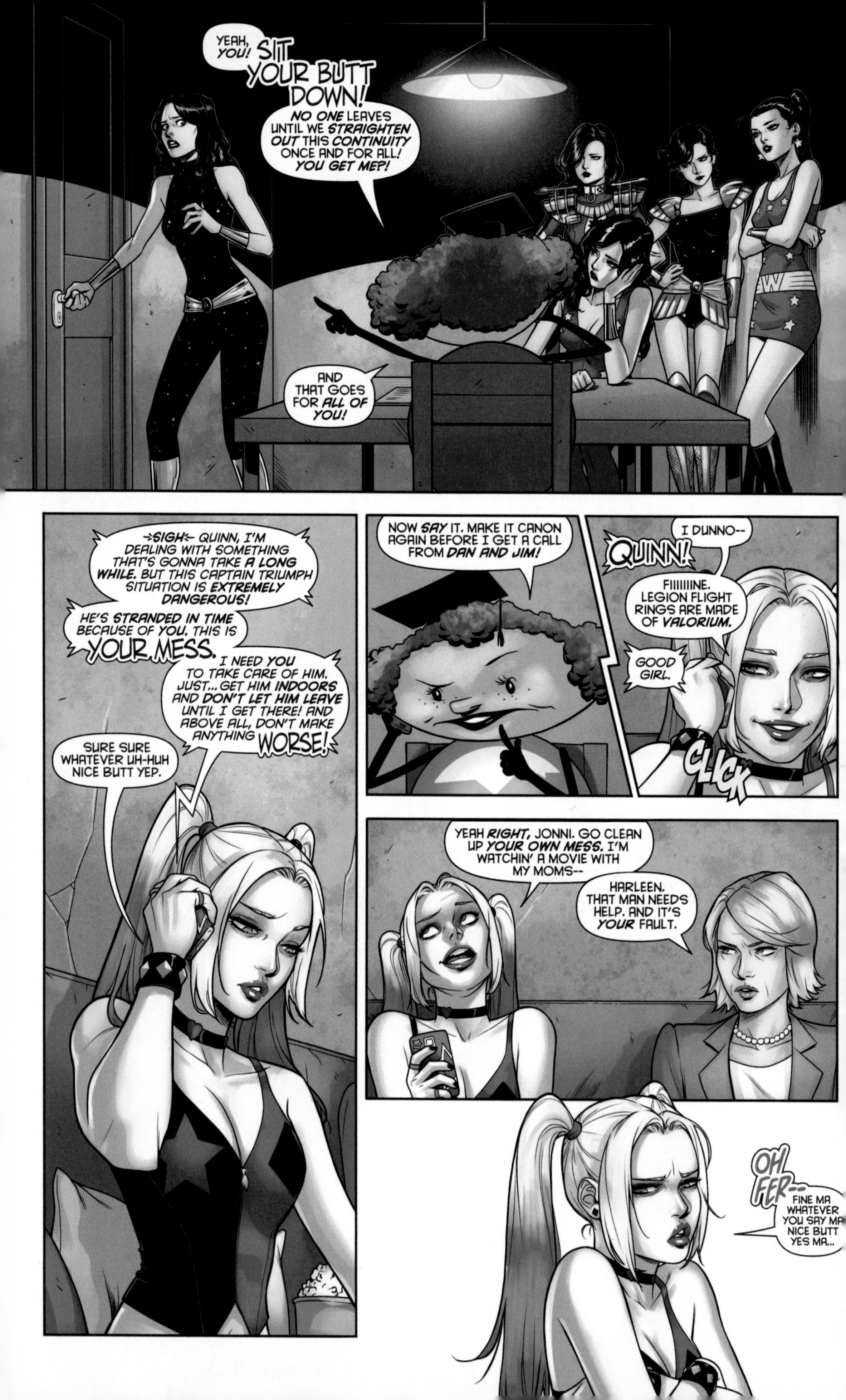

YEAH, YOU! SIT YOUR BUTT DOWN!
NO ONE LEAVES UNTIL WE STRAIGHTEN OUT THIS CONTINUITY ONCE AND FOR ALL! YOU GET ME?!
AND THAT GOES FOR ALL OF YOU!
>SIGH< QUINN, I'M DEALING WITH SOMETHING THAT'S GONNA TAKE A LONG WHILE. BUT THIS CAPTAIN TRIUMPH SITUATION IS EXTREMELY DANGEROUS!
HE'S STRANDED IN TIME BECAUSE OF YOU. THIS IS YOUR MESS.
I NEED YOU TO TAKE CARE OF HIM. JUST... GET HIM INDOORS AND DON'T LET HIM LEAVE UNTIL I GET THERE! AND ABOVE ALL, DON'T MAKE ANYTHING WORSE!
SURE SURE WHATEVER UH-HUH NICE BUTT YEP.
NOW SAY IT. MAKE IT CANON AGAIN BEFORE I GET A CALL FROM DAN AND JIM!
I DUNNO--
QUINN!
FIIIIIIINE. LEGION FLIGHT RINGS ARE MADE OF VALORIUM.
GOOD GIRL.
CLICK
YEAH RIGHT, JONNI. GO CLEAN UP YOUR OWN MESS. I'M WATCHIN' A MOVIE WITH MY MOMS--
HARLEEN. THAT MAN NEEDS HELP. AND IT'S YOUR FAULT.
OH FER--
FINE MA WHATEVER YOU SAY MA NICE BUTT YES MA...

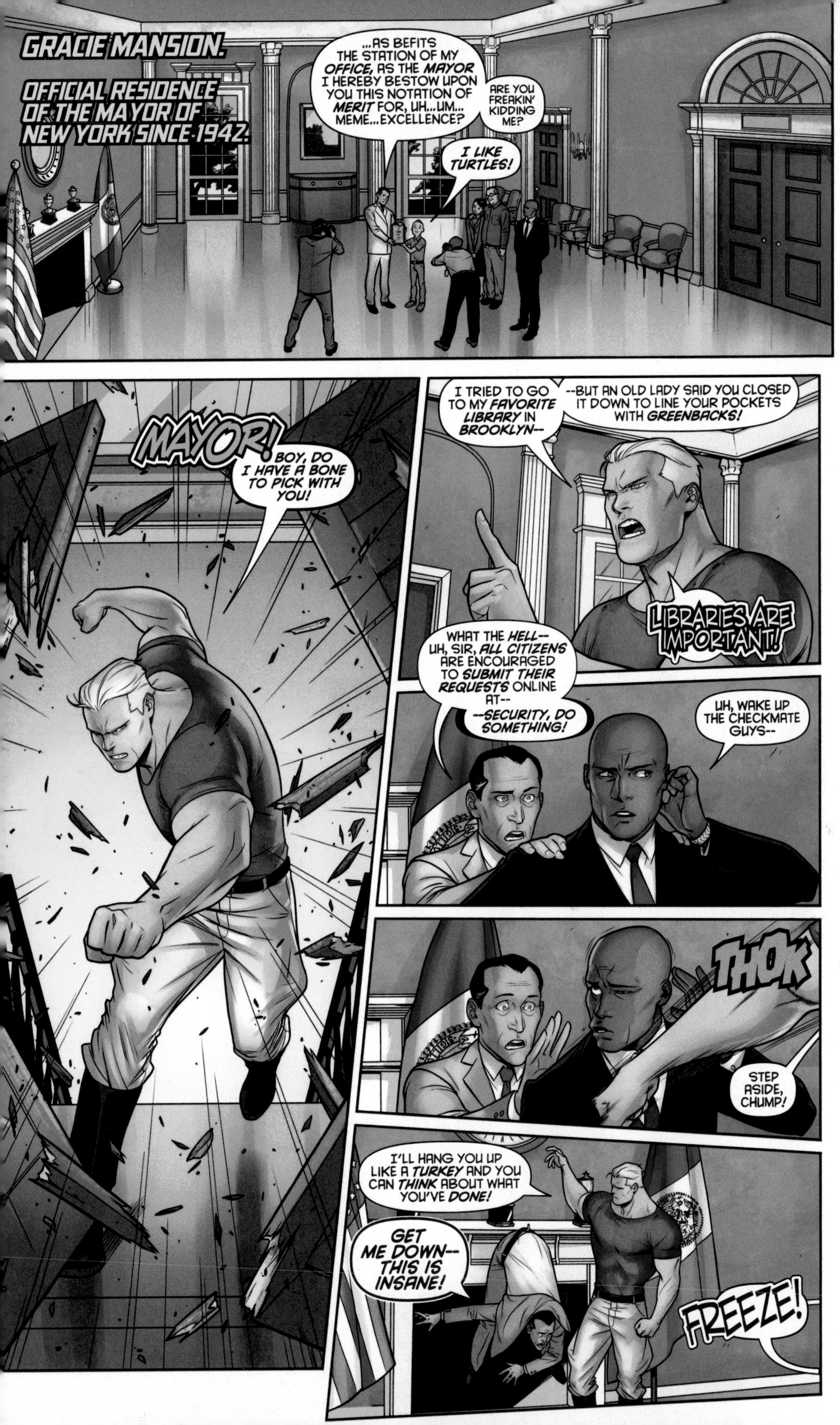
GRACIE MANSION.
OFFICIAL RESIDENCE OF THE MAYOR OF NEW YORK SINCE 1942.
...AS BEFITS THE STATION OF MY OFFICE, AS THE MAYOR I HEREBY BESTOW UPON YOU THIS NOTATION OF MERIT FOR, UH...UM... MEME...EXCELLENCE?
ARE YOU FREAKIN' KIDDING ME?
I LIKE TURTLES!
MAYOR!
BOY, DO I HAVE A BONE TO PICK WITH YOU!
I TRIED TO GO TO MY FAVORITE LIBRARY IN BROOKLYN--
--BUT AN OLD LADY SAID YOU CLOSED IT DOWN TO LINE YOUR POCKETS WITH GREENBACKS!
LIBRARIES ARE IMPORTANT!
WHAT THE HELL-- UH, SIR, ALL CITIZENS ARE ENCOURAGED TO SUBMIT THEIR REQUESTS ONLINE AT--
--SECURITY, DO SOMETHING!
UH, WAKE UP THE CHECKMATE GUYS--
THOK
STEP ASIDE, CHUMP!
I'LL HANG YOU UP LIKE A TURKEY AND YOU CAN THINK ABOUT WHAT YOU'VE DONE!
GET ME DOWN-- THIS IS INSANE!
FREEZE!

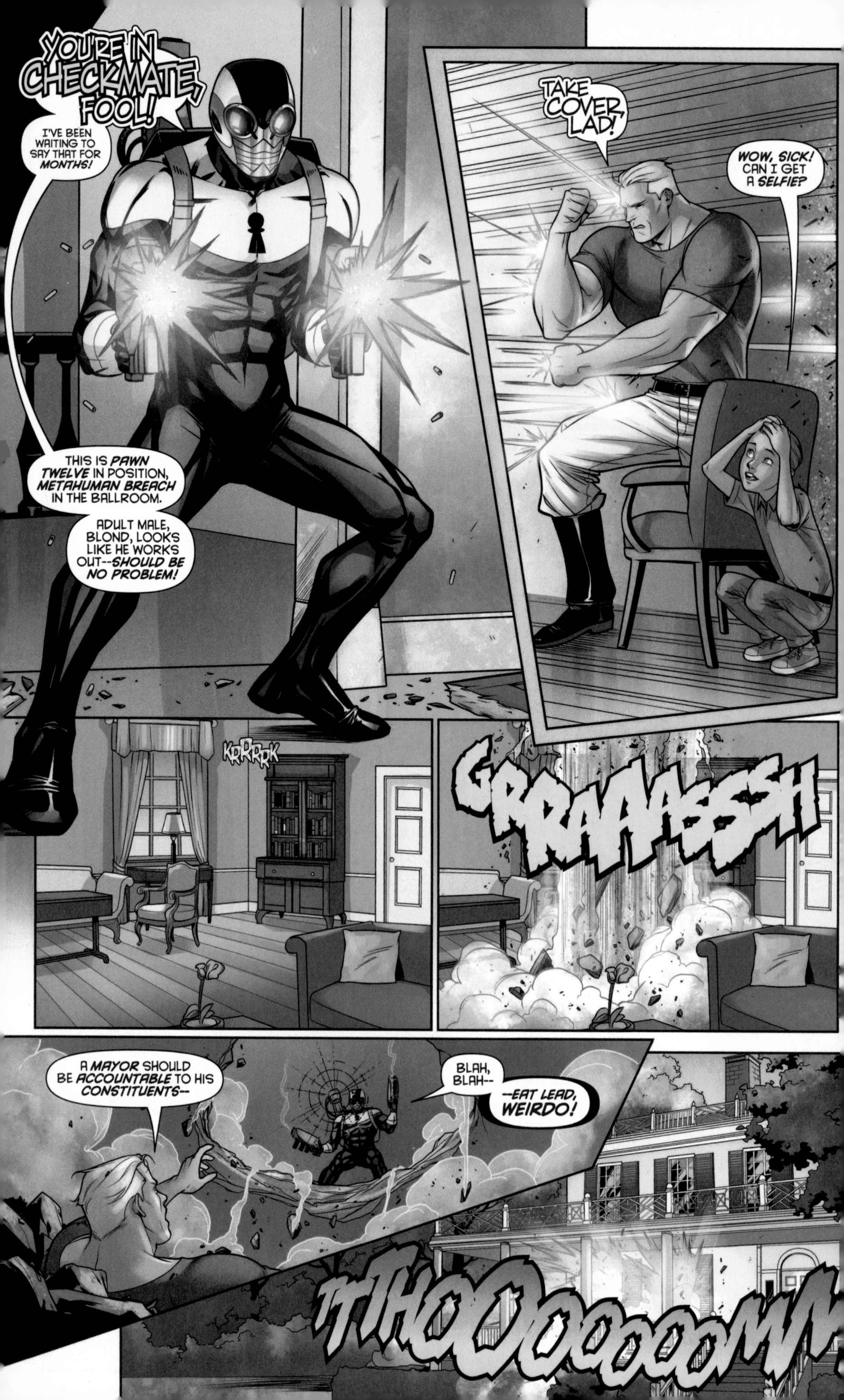
YOU'RE IN CHECKMATE, FOOL!
I'VE BEEN WAITING TO SAY THAT FOR MONTHS!
THIS IS PAWN TWELVE IN POSITION, METAHUMAN BREACH IN THE BALLROOM.
ADULT MALE, BLOND, LOOKS LIKE HE WORKS OUT--SHOULD BE NO PROBLEM!
TAKE COVER, LAD!
WOW, SICK! CAN I GET A SELFIE?
KRRRRK
GRAAASSH
A MAYOR SHOULD BE ACCOUNTABLE TO HIS CONSTITUENTS--
BLAH, BLAH--
--EAT LEAD, WEIRDO!
THOOOOOOOM

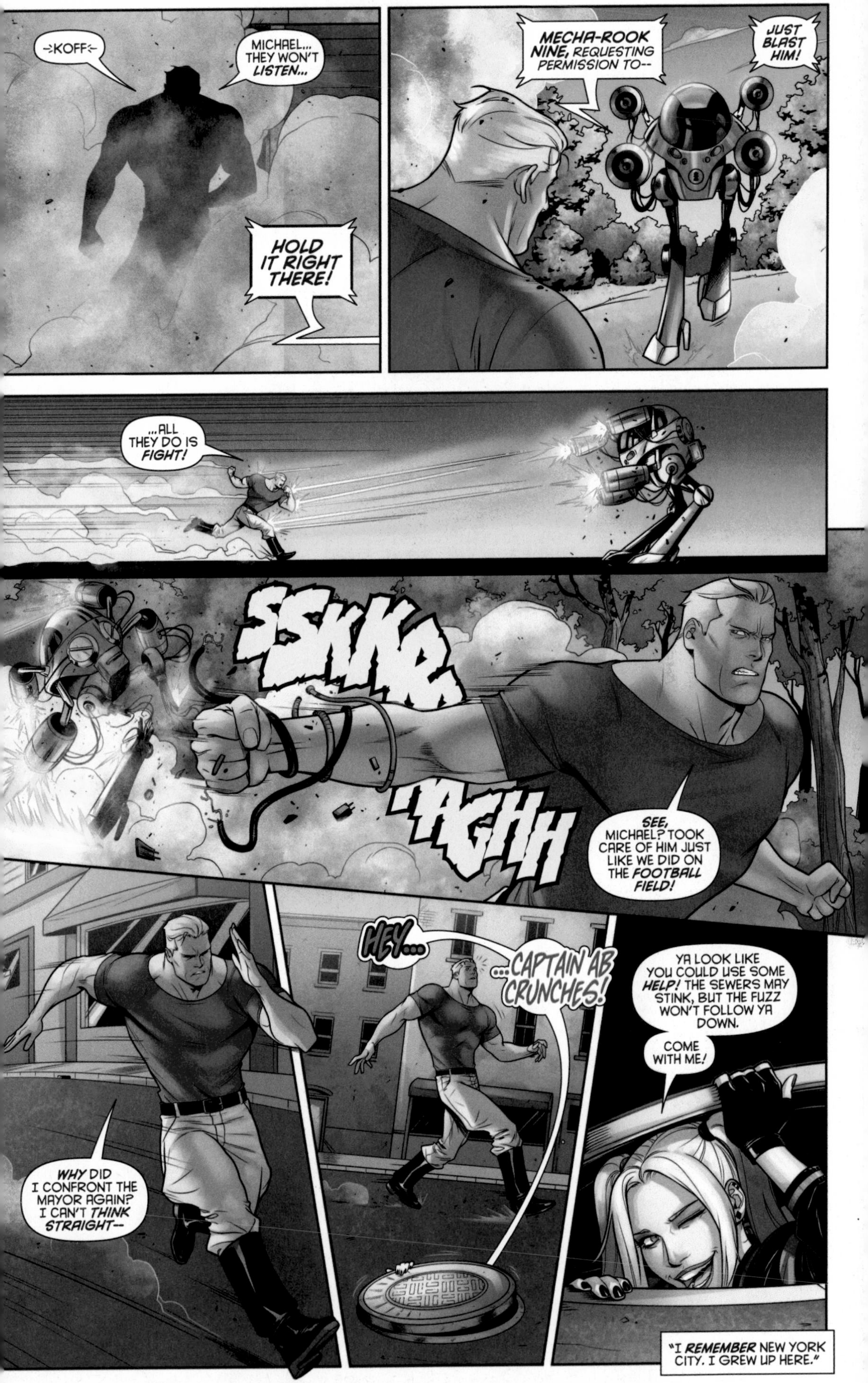
-KOFF-
MICHAEL... THEY WON'T LISTEN...
HOLD IT RIGHT THERE!
MECHA-ROOK NINE, REQUESTING PERMISSION TO--
JUST BLAST HIM!
...ALL THEY DO IS FIGHT!
SSKKR
TAGHH
SEE, MICHAEL? TOOK CARE OF HIM JUST LIKE WE DID ON THE FOOTBALL FIELD!
WHY DID I CONFRONT THE MAYOR AGAIN? I CAN'T THINK STRAIGHT--
HEY...
...CAPTAIN AB CRUNCHES!
YA LOOK LIKE YOU COULD USE SOME HELP! THE SEWERS MAY STINK, BUT THE FUZZ WON'T FOLLOW YA DOWN.
COME WITH ME!
"I REMEMBER NEW YORK CITY. I GREW UP HERE."

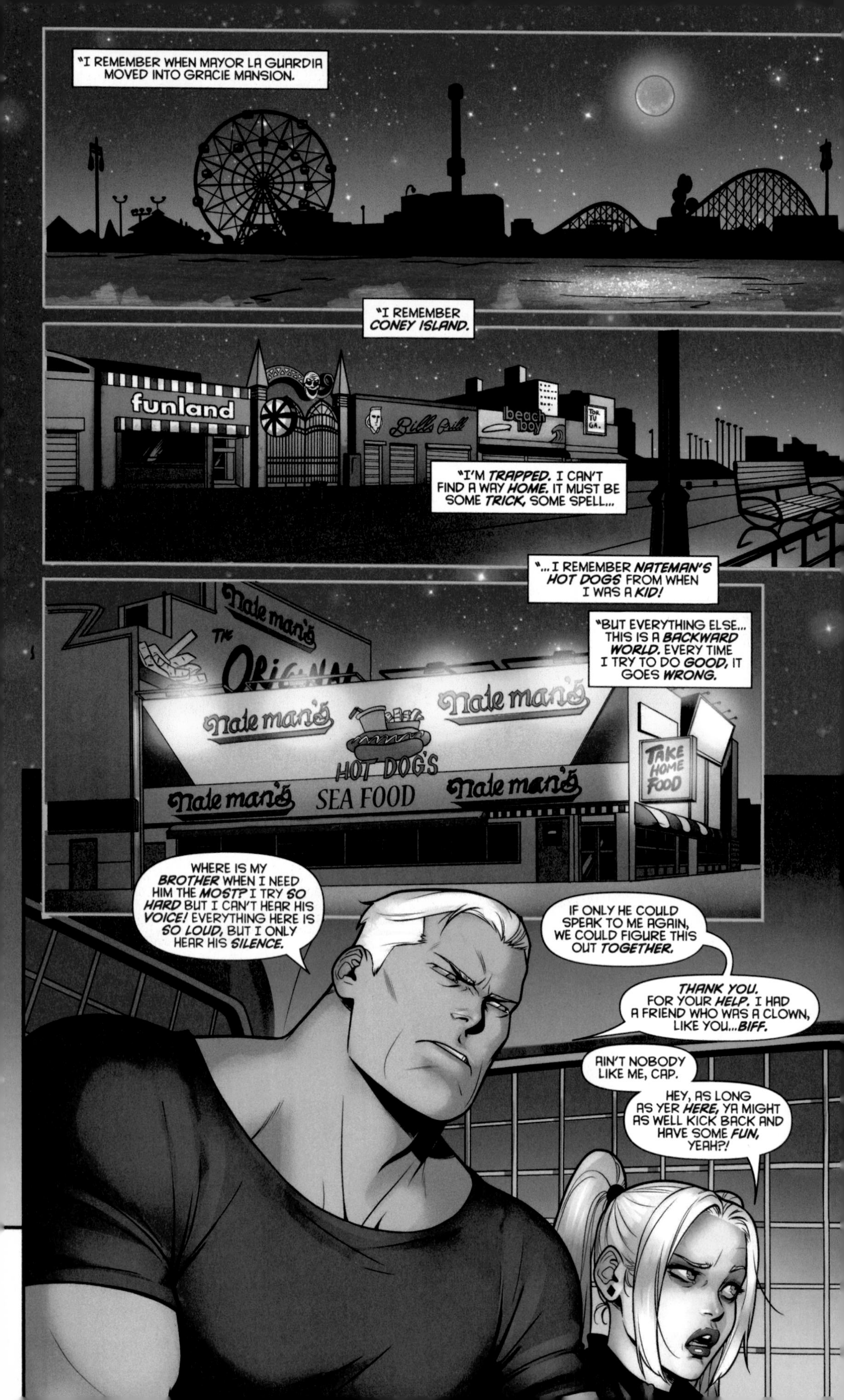

"I REMEMBER WHEN MAYOR LA GUARDIA MOVED INTO GRACIE MANSION.
"I REMEMBER CONEY ISLAND.
funland
Bill's Grill
beach boy
TOR TU GA.
"I'M TRAPPED. I CAN'T FIND A WAY HOME. IT MUST BE SOME TRICK, SOME SPELL...
"...I REMEMBER NATEMAN'S HOT DOGS FROM WHEN I WAS A KID!
"BUT EVERYTHING ELSE... THIS IS A BACKWARD WORLD. EVERY TIME I TRY TO DO GOOD, IT GOES WRONG.
Nateman's
THE
Nateman's
Nateman's
HOT DOG'S
Nateman's
SEA FOOD
Nateman's
TAKE HOME FOOD
WHERE IS MY BROTHER WHEN I NEED HIM THE MOST? I TRY SO HARD BUT I CAN'T HEAR HIS VOICE! EVERYTHING HERE IS SO LOUD, BUT I ONLY HEAR HIS SILENCE.
IF ONLY HE COULD SPEAK TO ME AGAIN, WE COULD FIGURE THIS OUT TOGETHER.
THANK YOU. FOR YOUR HELP. I HAD A FRIEND WHO WAS A CLOWN, LIKE YOU...BIFF.
AIN'T NOBODY LIKE ME, CAP.
HEY, AS LONG AS YER HERE, YA MIGHT AS WELL KICK BACK AND HAVE SOME FUN, YEAH?!

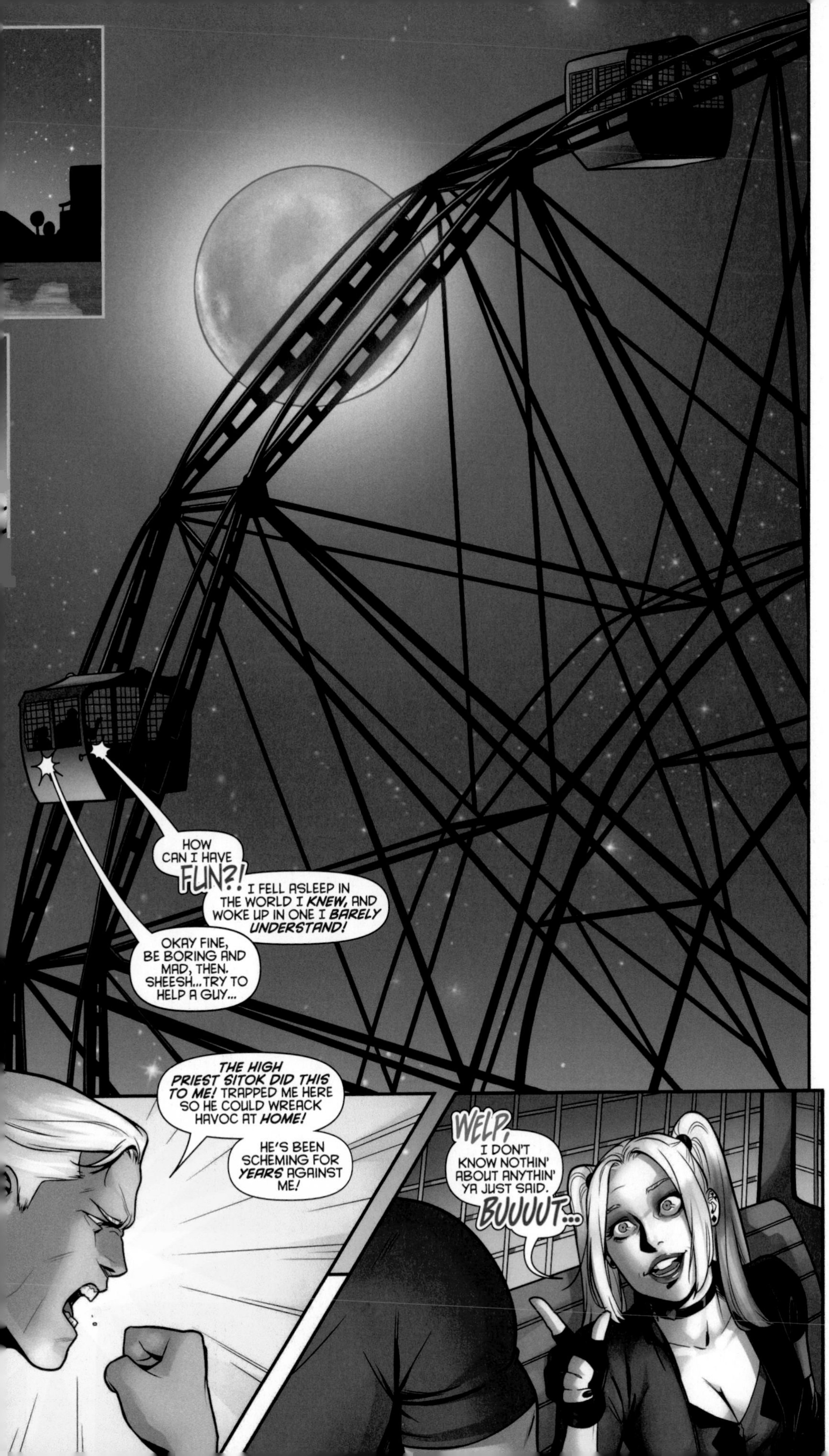
HOW CAN I HAVE FUN?! I FELL ASLEEP IN THE WORLD I KNEW, AND WOKE UP IN ONE I BARELY UNDERSTAND!
OKAY FINE, BE BORING AND MAD, THEN. SHEESH...TRY TO HELP A GUY...
THE HIGH PRIEST SITOK DID THIS TO ME! TRAPPED ME HERE SO HE COULD WREACK HAVOC AT HOME!
HE'S BEEN SCHEMING FOR YEARS AGAINST ME!
WELP, I DON'T KNOW NOTHIN' ABOUT ANYTHIN' YA JUST SAID. BUUUUT...

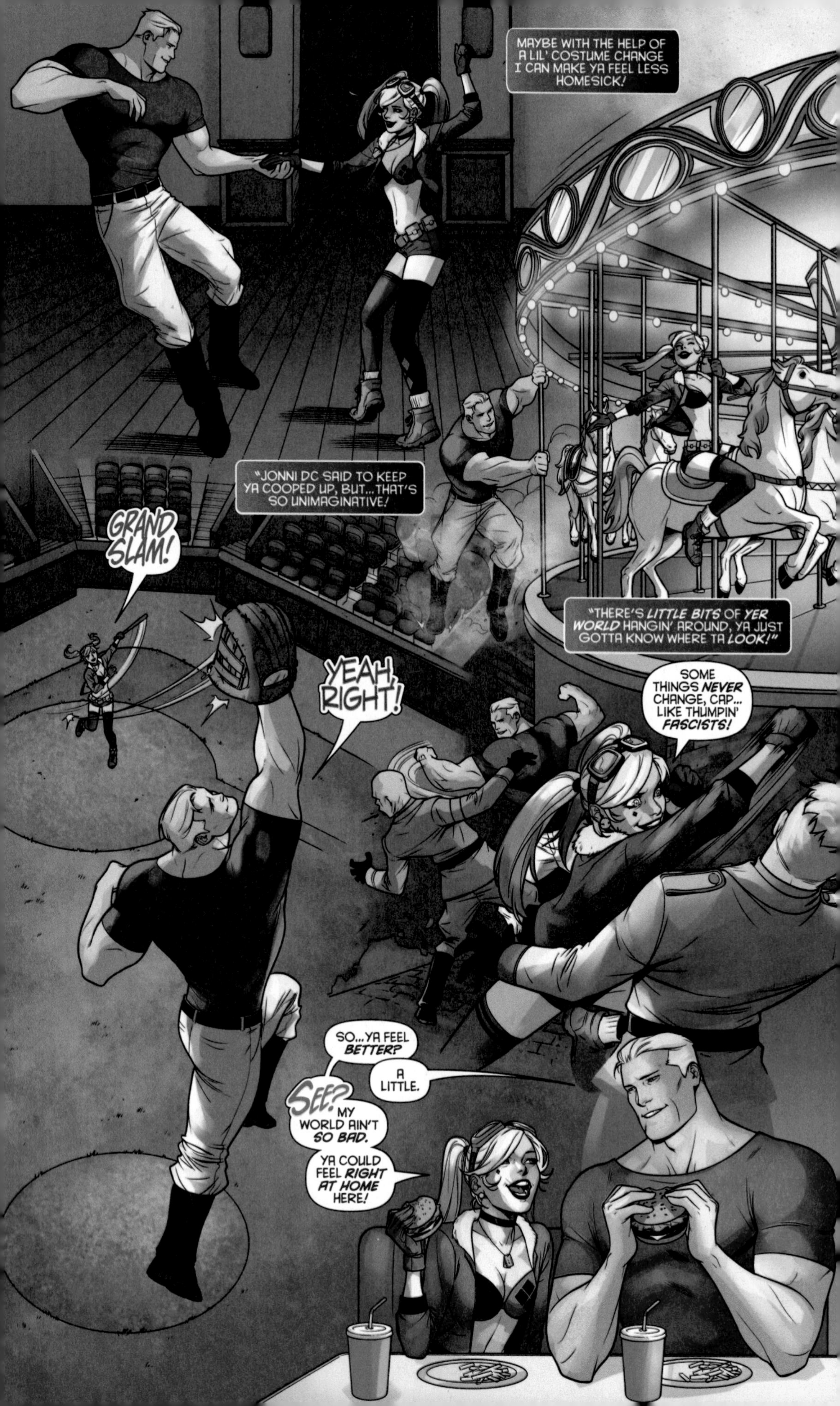

MAYBE WITH THE HELP OF A LIL' COSTUME CHANGE I CAN MAKE YA FEEL LESS HOMESICK!
"JONNI DC SAID TO KEEP YA COOPED UP, BUT... THAT'S SO UNIMAGINATIVE!
"THERE'S LITTLE BITS OF YER WORLD HANGIN' AROUND, YA JUST GOTTA KNOW WHERE TA LOOK!"
GRAND SLAM!
YEAH, RIGHT!
SOME THINGS NEVER CHANGE, CAP... LIKE THUMPIN' FASCISTS!
SO...YA FEEL BETTER?
A LITTLE.
SEE? MY WORLD AIN'T SO BAD.
YA COULD FEEL RIGHT AT HOME HERE!

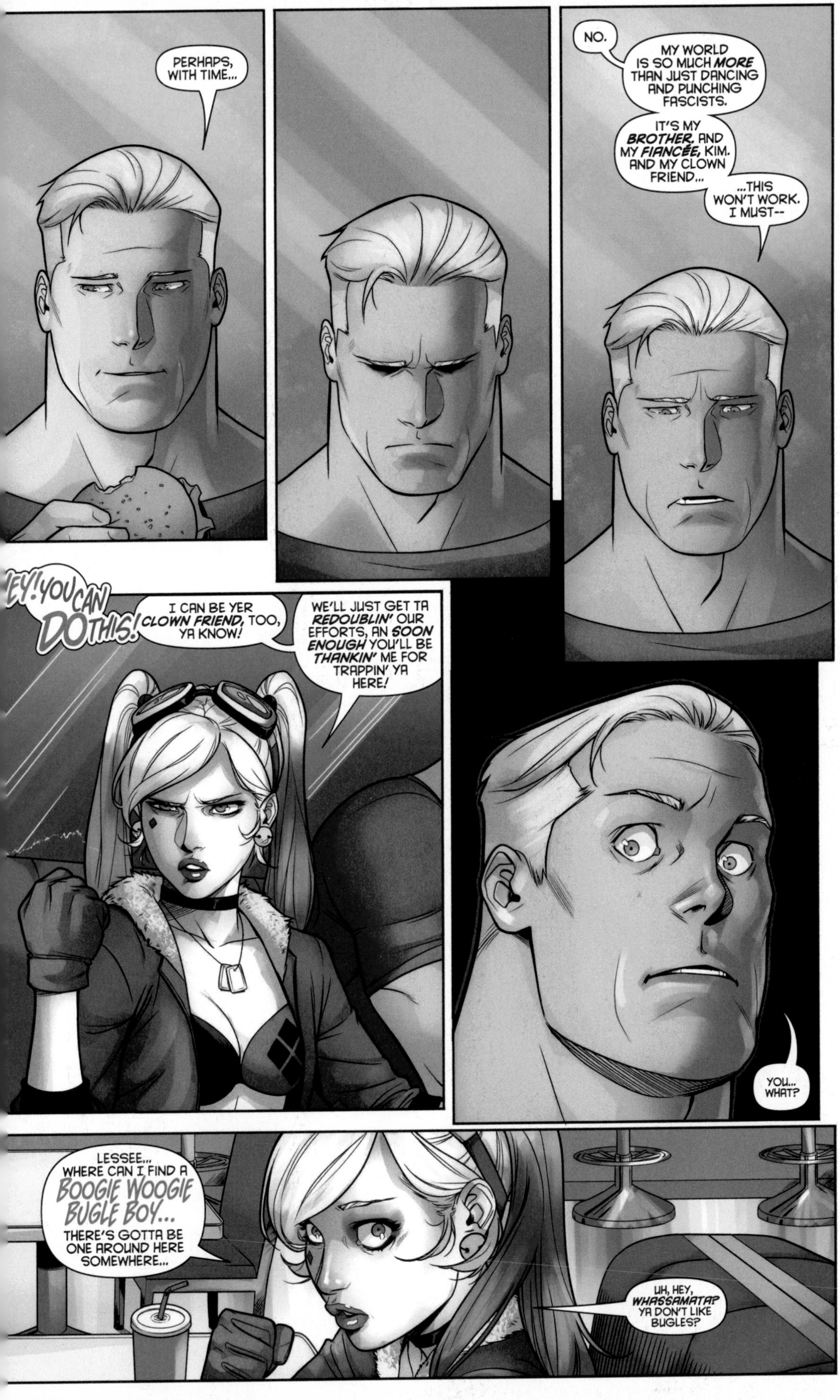
PERHAPS, WITH TIME...
NO.
MY WORLD IS SO MUCH MORE THAN JUST DANCING AND PUNCHING FASCISTS.
IT'S MY BROTHER, AND MY FIANCÉE, KIM. AND MY CLOWN FRIEND...
...THIS WON'T WORK. I MUST--
EY! YOU CAN DO THIS!
I CAN BE YER CLOWN FRIEND, TOO, YA KNOW!
WE'LL JUST GET TA REDOUBLIN' OUR EFFORTS, AN SOON ENOUGH YOU'LL BE THANKIN' ME FOR TRAPPIN' YA HERE!
YOU... WHAT?
LESSEE... WHERE CAN I FIND A BOOGIE WOOGIE BUGLE BOY... THERE'S GOTTA BE ONE AROUND HERE SOMEWHERE...
UH, HEY, WHASSAMATA? YA DON'T LIKE BUGLES?

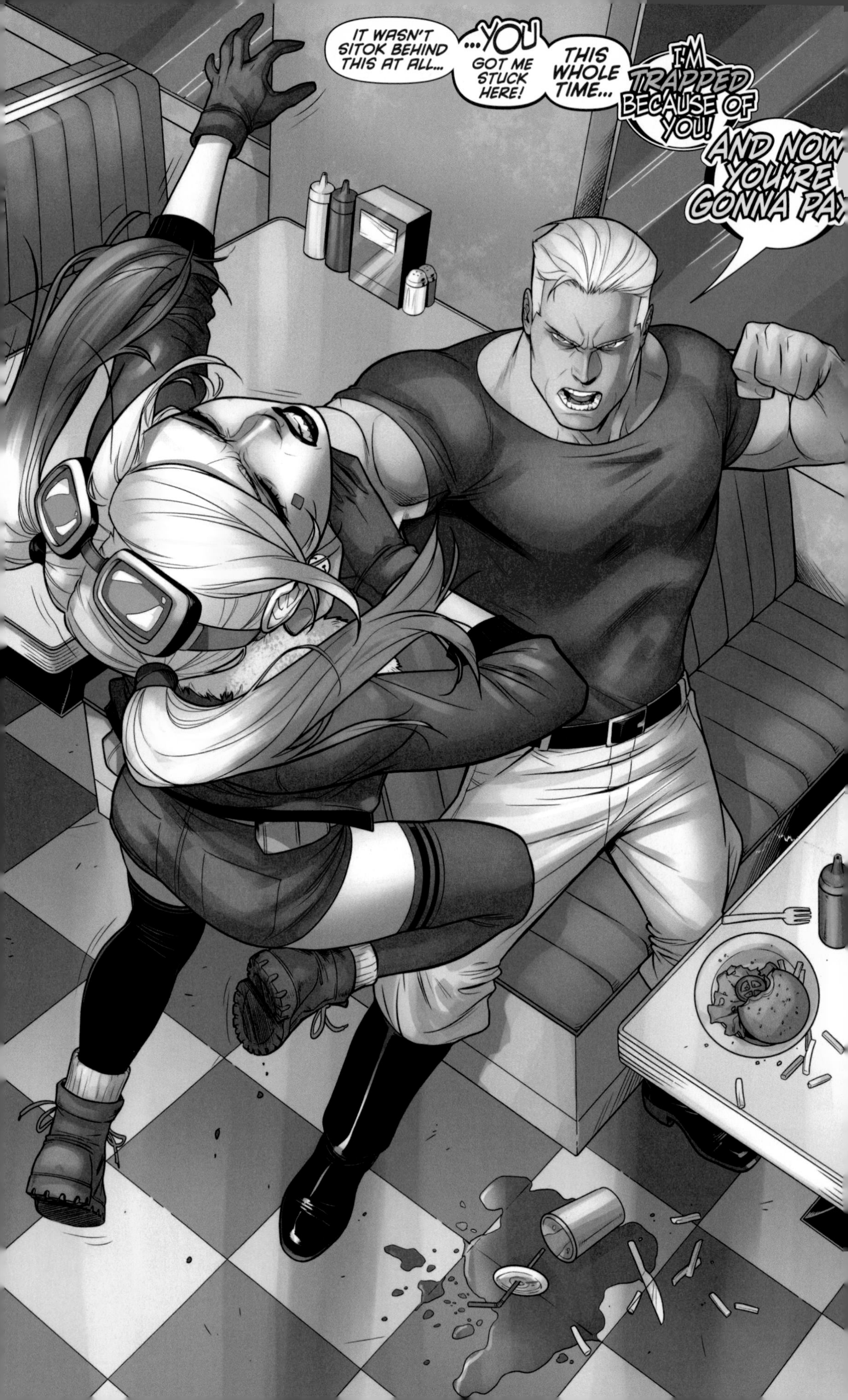
IT WASN'T SITOK BEHIND THIS AT ALL...
...YOU GOT ME STUCK HERE!
THIS WHOLE TIME...
I'M TRAPPED BECAUSE OF YOU!
AND NOW YOU'RE GONNA PAY

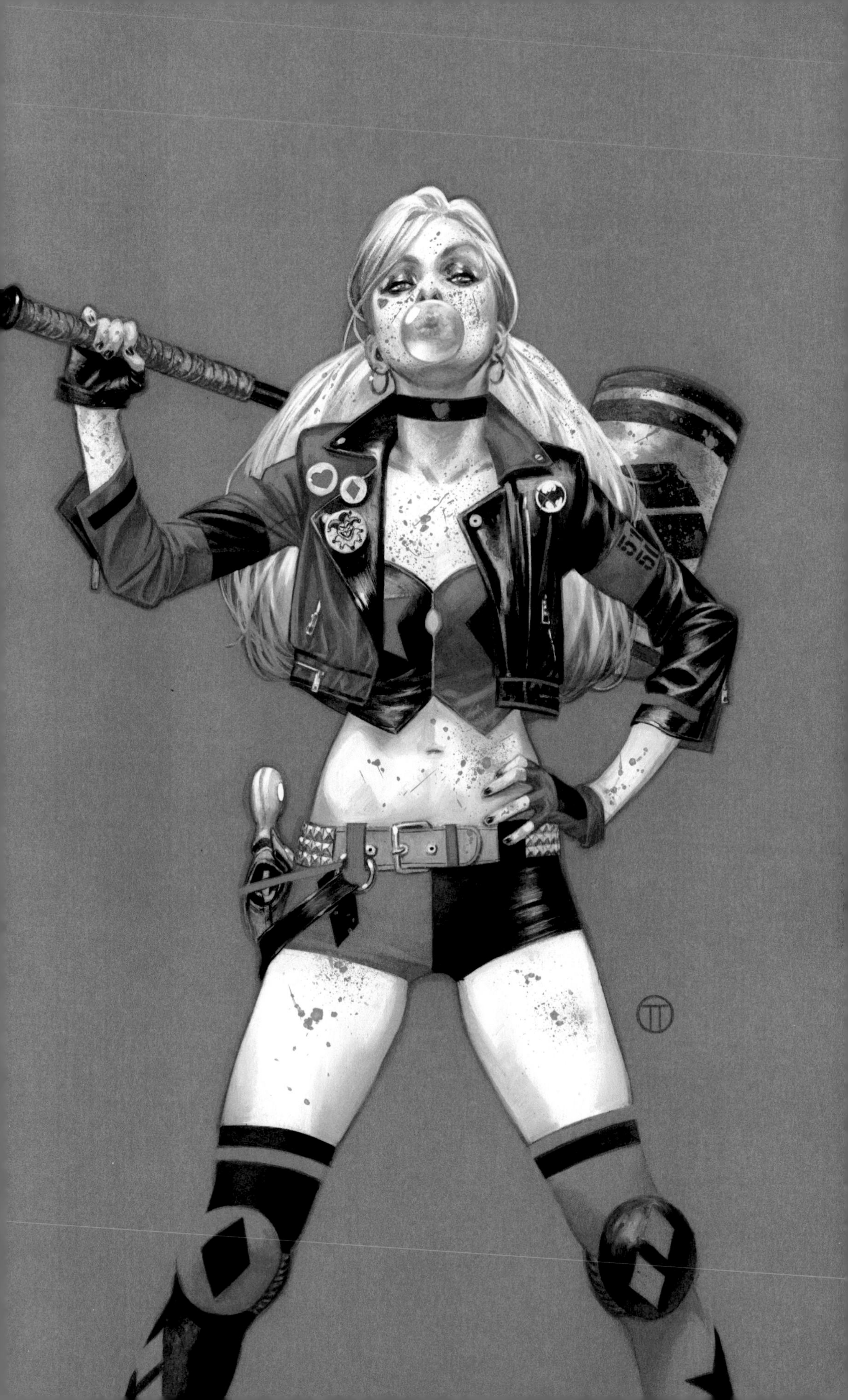

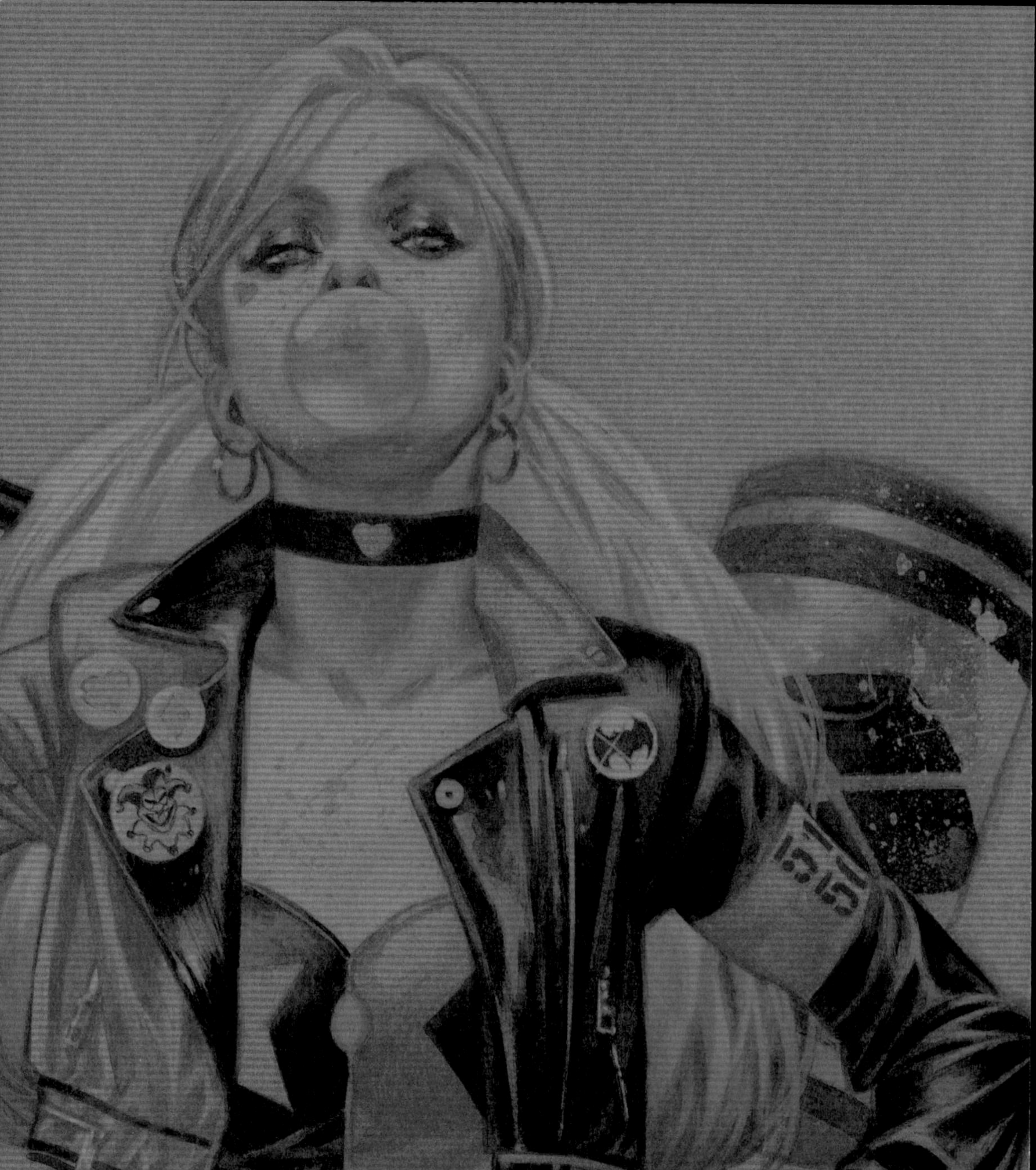

HARLEY QUINN
#52

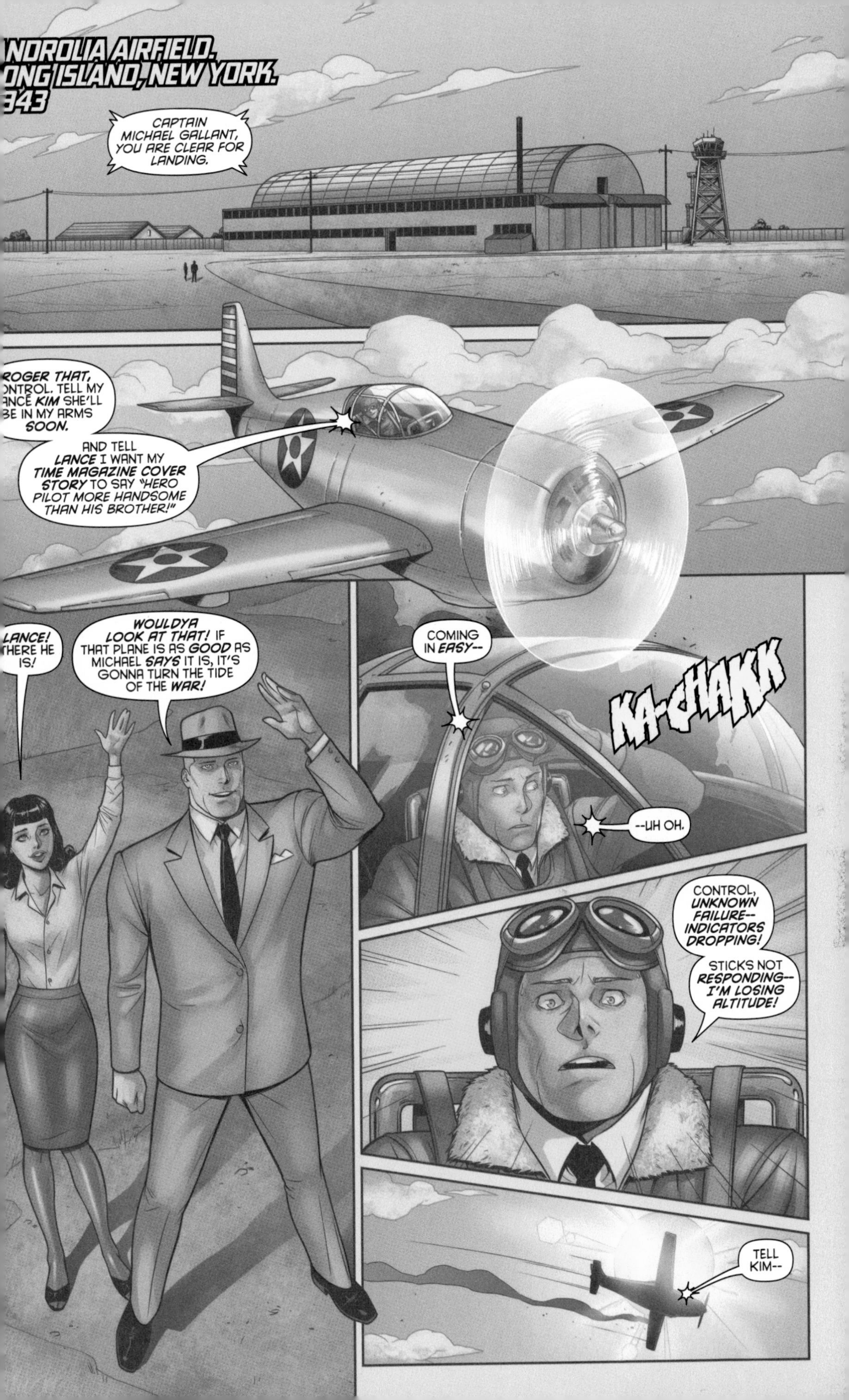
NDROLIA AIRFIELD.
ONG ISLAND, NEW YORK.
343
CAPTAIN MICHAEL GALLANT, YOU ARE CLEAR FOR LANDING.
ROGER THAT, ONTROL. TELL MY ANCÉ KIM SHE'LL BE IN MY ARMS SOON.
AND TELL LANCE I WANT MY TIME MAGAZINE COVER STORY TO SAY "HERO PILOT MORE HANDSOME THAN HIS BROTHER!"
LANCE! THERE HE IS!
WOULDYA LOOK AT THAT! IF THAT PLANE IS AS GOOD AS MICHAEL SAYS IT IS, IT'S GONNA TURN THE TIDE OF THE WAR!
COMING IN EASY--
KA-CHAKK
--UH OH.
CONTROL, UNKNOWN FAILURE-- INDICATORS DROPPING!
STICKS NOT RESPONDING-- I'M LOSING ALTITUDE!
TELL KIM--

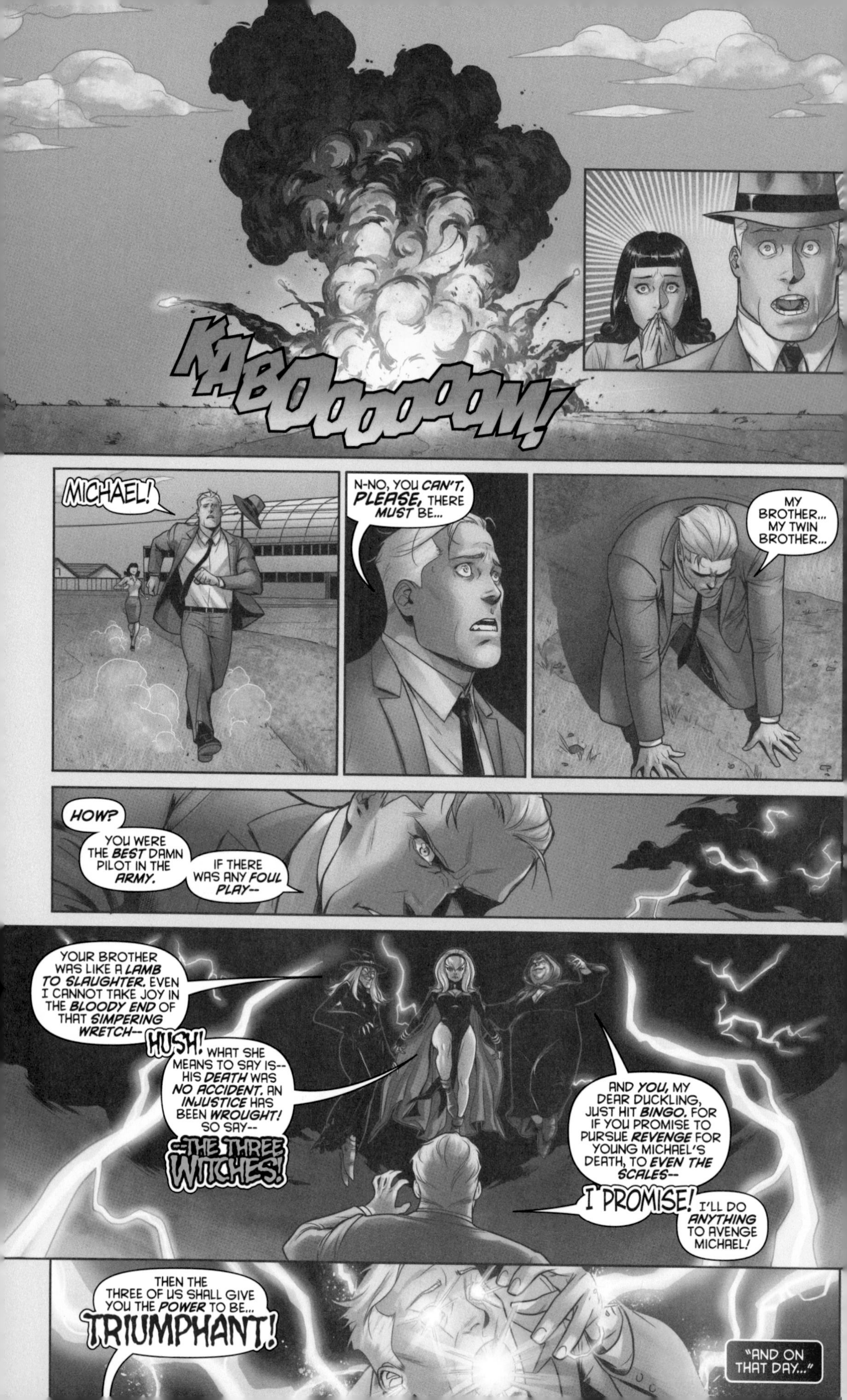

KA-BOOOOOOOM!
MICHAEL!
N-NO, YOU CAN'T, PLEASE, THERE MUST BE...
MY BROTHER... MY TWIN BROTHER...
HOW?
YOU WERE THE BEST DAMN PILOT IN THE ARMY.
IF THERE WAS ANY FOUL PLAY--
YOUR BROTHER WAS LIKE A LAMB TO SLAUGHTER. EVEN I CANNOT TAKE JOY IN THE BLOODY END OF THAT SIMPERING WRETCH--
HUSH! WHAT SHE MEANS TO SAY IS-- HIS DEATH WAS NO ACCIDENT. AN INJUSTICE HAS BEEN WROUGHT! SO SAY--
--THE THREE WITCHES!
AND YOU, MY DEAR DUCKLING, JUST HIT BINGO. FOR IF YOU PROMISE TO PURSUE REVENGE FOR YOUNG MICHAEL'S DEATH, TO EVEN THE SCALES--
I PROMISE! I'LL DO ANYTHING TO AVENGE MICHAEL!
THEN THE THREE OF US SHALL GIVE YOU THE POWER TO BE... TRIUMPHANT!
"AND ON THAT DAY..."

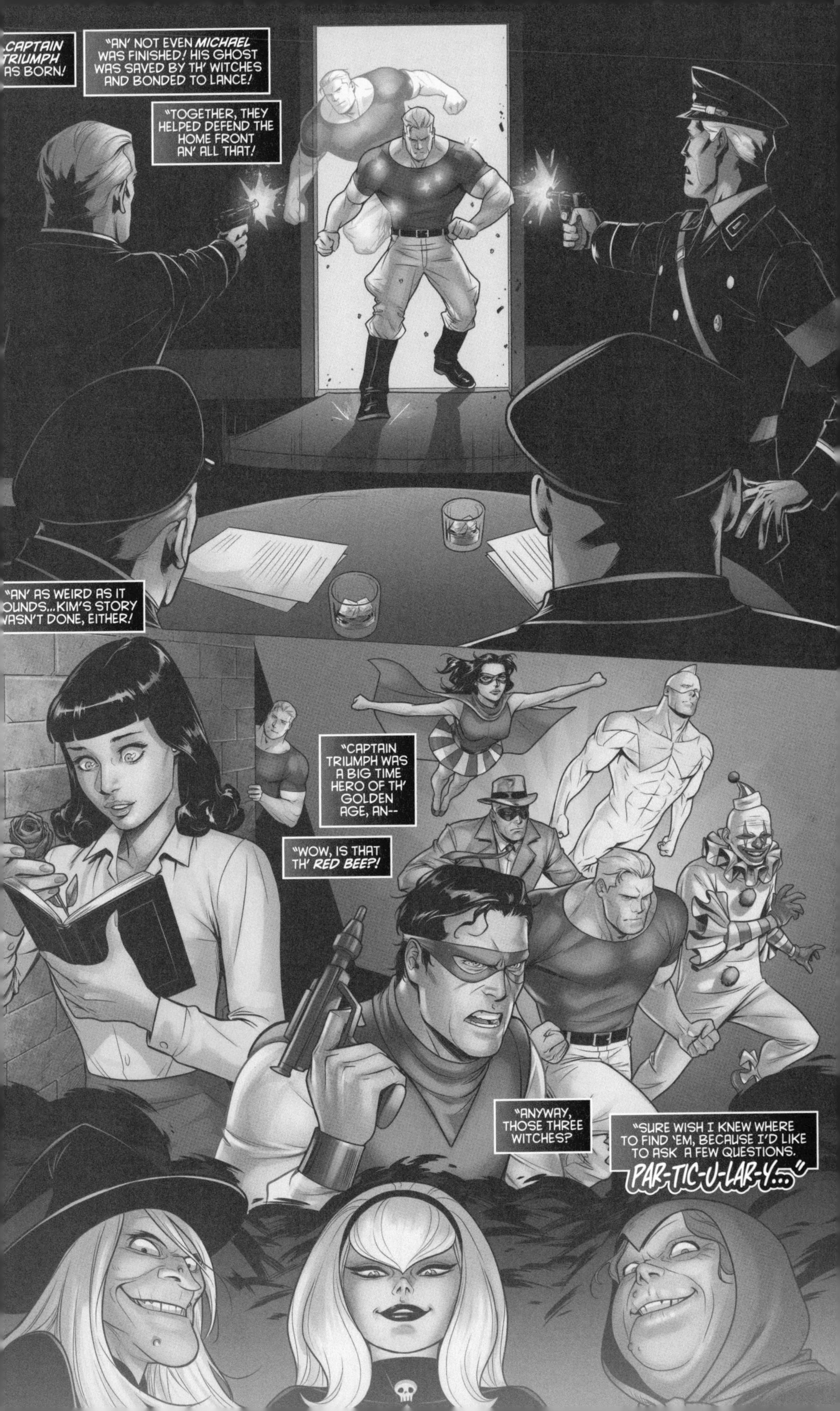
CAPTAIN TRIUMPH AS BORN!
"AN' NOT EVEN MICHAEL WAS FINISHED! HIS GHOST WAS SAVED BY TH' WITCHES AND BONDED TO LANCE!
"TOGETHER, THEY HELPED DEFEND THE HOME FRONT AN' ALL THAT!
"AN' AS WEIRD AS IT OUNDS...KIM'S STORY WASN'T DONE, EITHER!
"CAPTAIN TRIUMPH WAS A BIG TIME HERO OF TH' GOLDEN AGE, AN--
"WOW, IS THAT TH' RED BEE?!
"ANYWAY, THOSE THREE WITCHES?
"SURE WISH I KNEW WHERE TO FIND 'EM, BECAUSE I'D LIKE TO ASK A FEW QUESTIONS.
PAR-TIC-U-LAR-Y..."

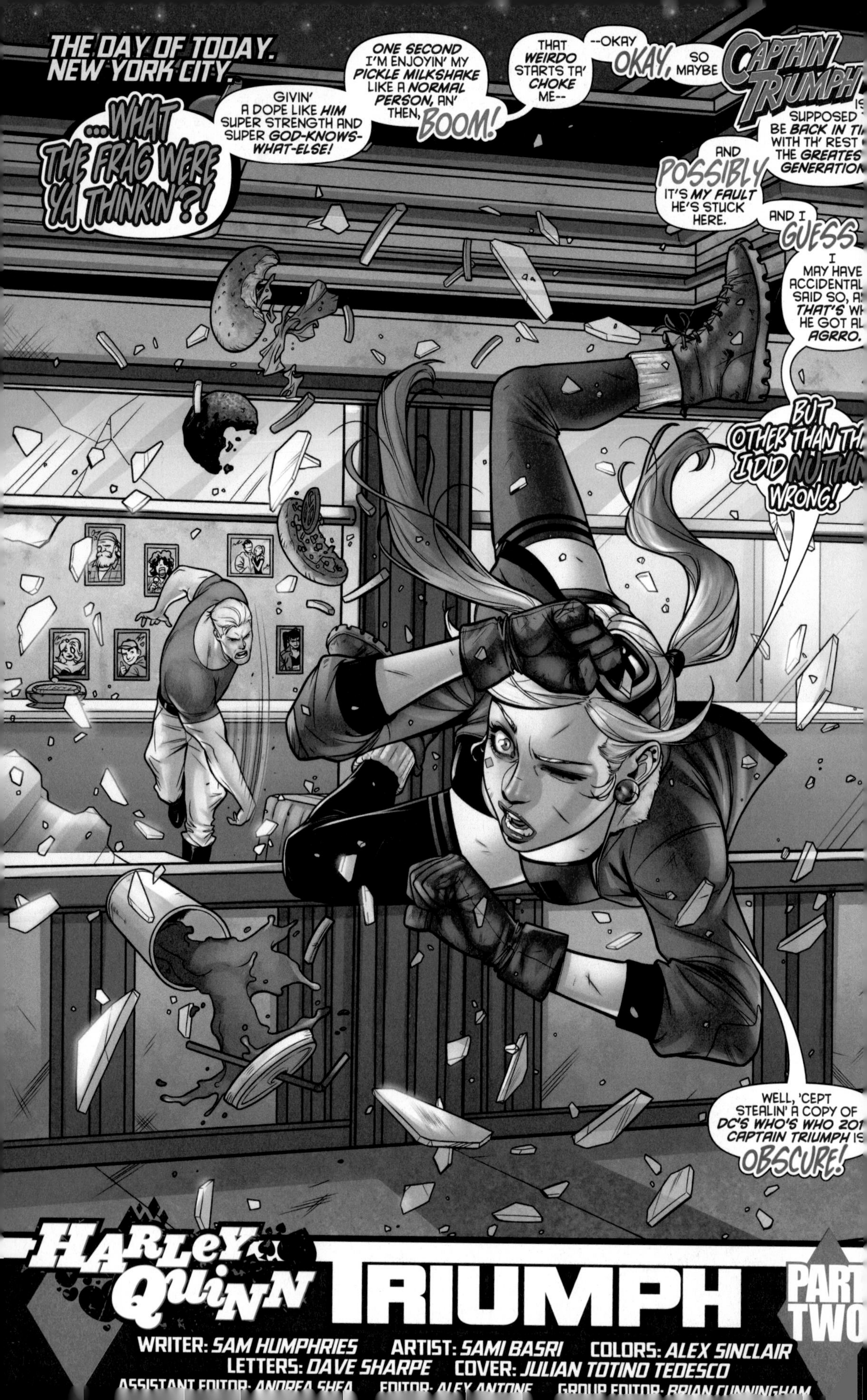
THE DAY OF TODAY. NEW YORK CITY.
...WHAT THE FRAG WERE YA THINKIN'?!
GIVIN' A DOPE LIKE HIM SUPER STRENGTH AND SUPER GOD-KNOWS-WHAT-ELSE!
ONE SECOND I'M ENJOYIN' MY PICKLE MILKSHAKE LIKE A NORMAL PERSON, AN' THEN, BOOM!
THAT WEIRDO STARTS TA' CHOKE ME--
--OKAY OKAY, SO MAYBE CAPTAIN TRIUMPH
SUPPOSED BE BACK IN TI WITH TH' REST THE GREATES GENERATION
AND POSSIBLY IT'S MY FAULT HE'S STUCK HERE.
AND I GUESS I MAY HAVE ACCIDENTAL SAID SO, AN THAT'S WH HE GOT AL AGRRO.
BUT OTHER THAN TH I DID NUTHIN WRONG!
WELL, 'CEPT STEALIN' A COPY OF DC'S WHO'S WHO 201 CAPTAIN TRIUMPH IS OBSCURE!
HARLEY QUINN
TRIUMPH
PART TWO
WRITER: SAM HUMPHRIES ARTIST: SAMI BASRI COLORS: ALEX SINCLAIR
LETTERS: DAVE SHARPE COVER: JULIAN TOTINO TEDESCO

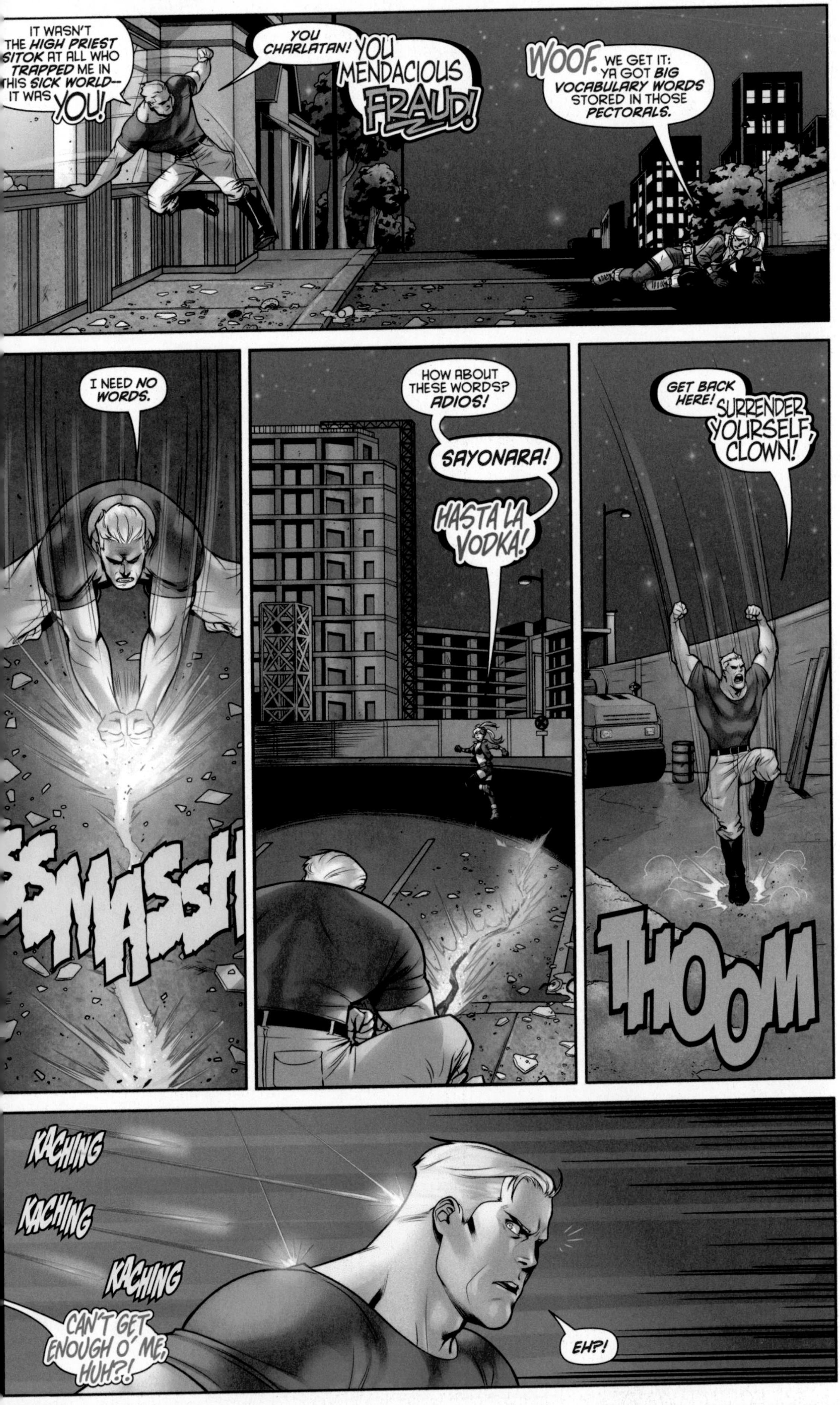
IT WASN'T THE HIGH PRIEST SITOK AT ALL WHO TRAPPED ME IN THIS SICK WORLD-- IT WAS YOU!
YOU CHARLATAN! YOU MENDACIOUS FRAUD!
WOOF. WE GET IT: YA GOT BIG VOCABULARY WORDS STORED IN THOSE PECTORALS.
I NEED NO WORDS.
SMASH
HOW ABOUT THESE WORDS? ADIOS!
SAYONARA!
HASTA LA VODKA!
GET BACK HERE!
SURRENDER YOURSELF, CLOWN!
THOOM
KACHING
KACHING
KACHING
CAN'T GET ENOUGH O' ME, HUH?!
EH?!

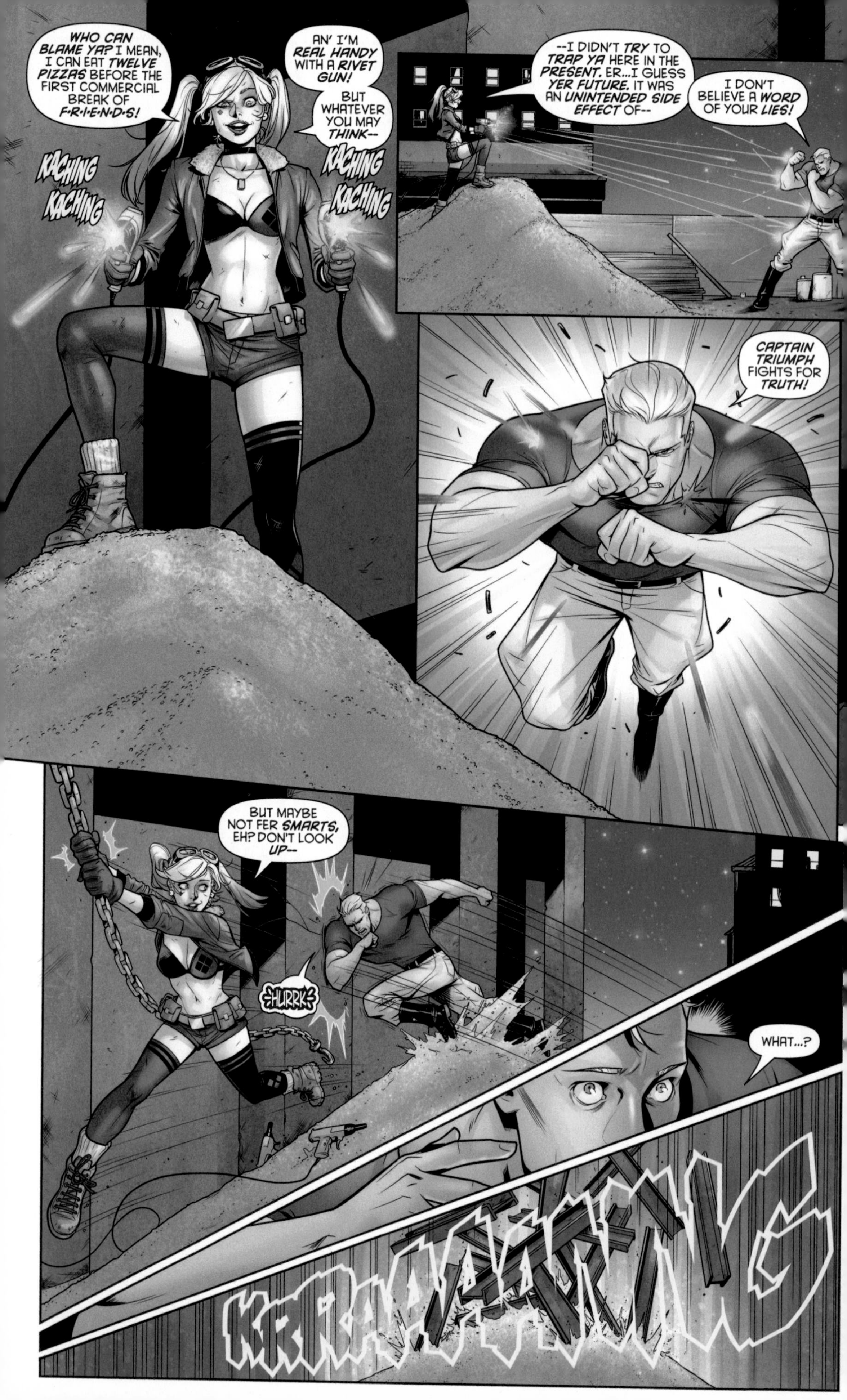
WHO CAN BLAME YA? I MEAN, I CAN EAT TWELVE PIZZAS BEFORE THE FIRST COMMERCIAL BREAK OF F·R·I·E·N·D·S!
AN' I'M REAL HANDY WITH A RIVET GUN!
BUT WHATEVER YOU MAY THINK--
KACHING
KACHING
KACHING
KACHING
--I DIDN'T TRY TO TRAP YA HERE IN THE PRESENT. ER...I GUESS YER FUTURE. IT WAS AN UNINTENDED SIDE EFFECT OF--
I DON'T BELIEVE A WORD OF YOUR LIES!
CAPTAIN TRIUMPH FIGHTS FOR TRUTH!
BUT MAYBE NOT FER SMARTS, EH? DON'T LOOK UP--
HURRK
WHAT...?
KRRAAAANNNG

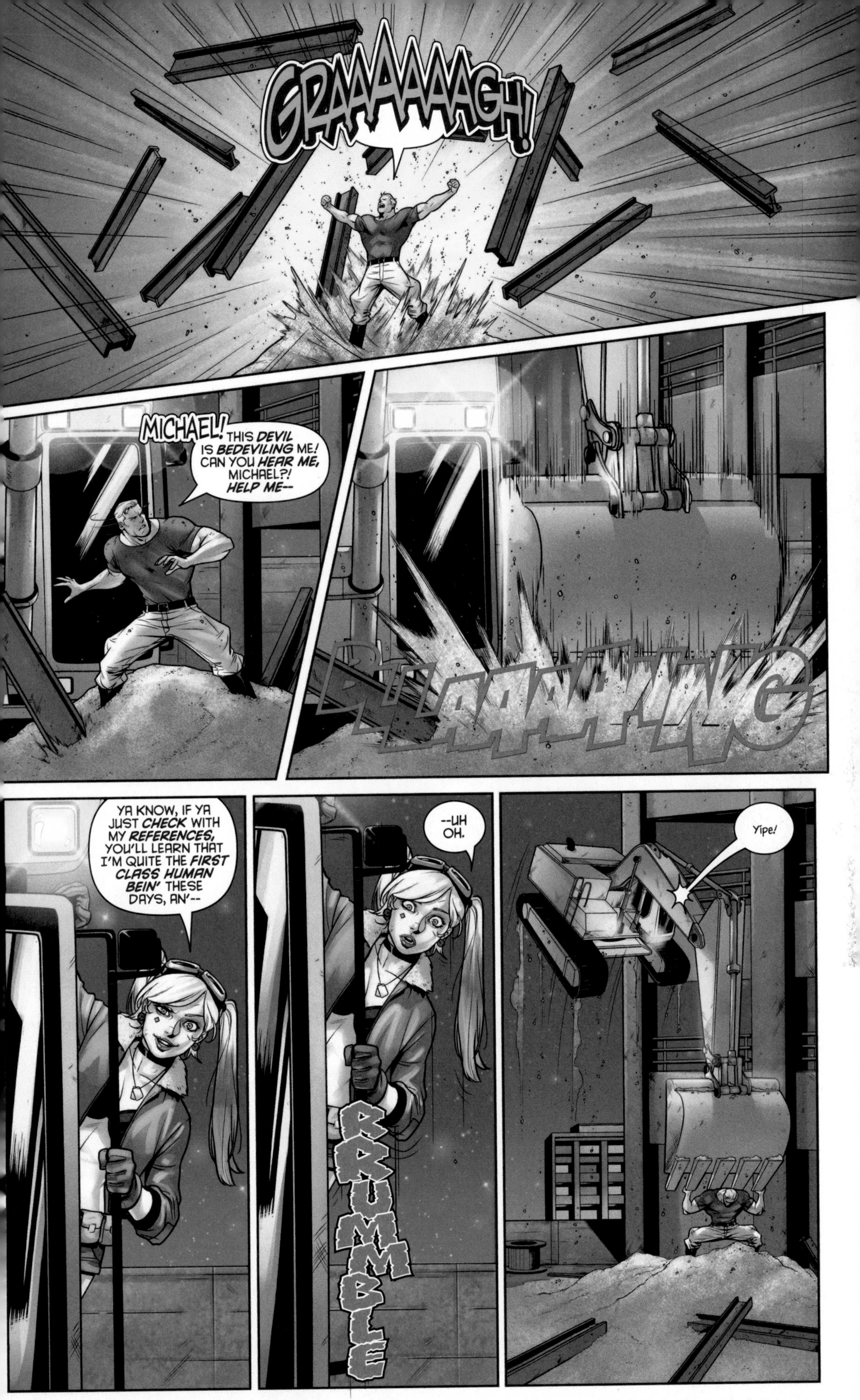
GRAAAAAAGH!
MICHAEL! THIS DEVIL IS BEDEVILING ME! CAN YOU HEAR ME, MICHAEL?! HELP ME--
YA KNOW, IF YA JUST CHECK WITH MY REFERENCES, YOU'LL LEARN THAT I'M QUITE THE FIRST CLASS HUMAN BEIN' THESE DAYS, AN'--
--UH OH.
RRUMMBLE
Yipe!

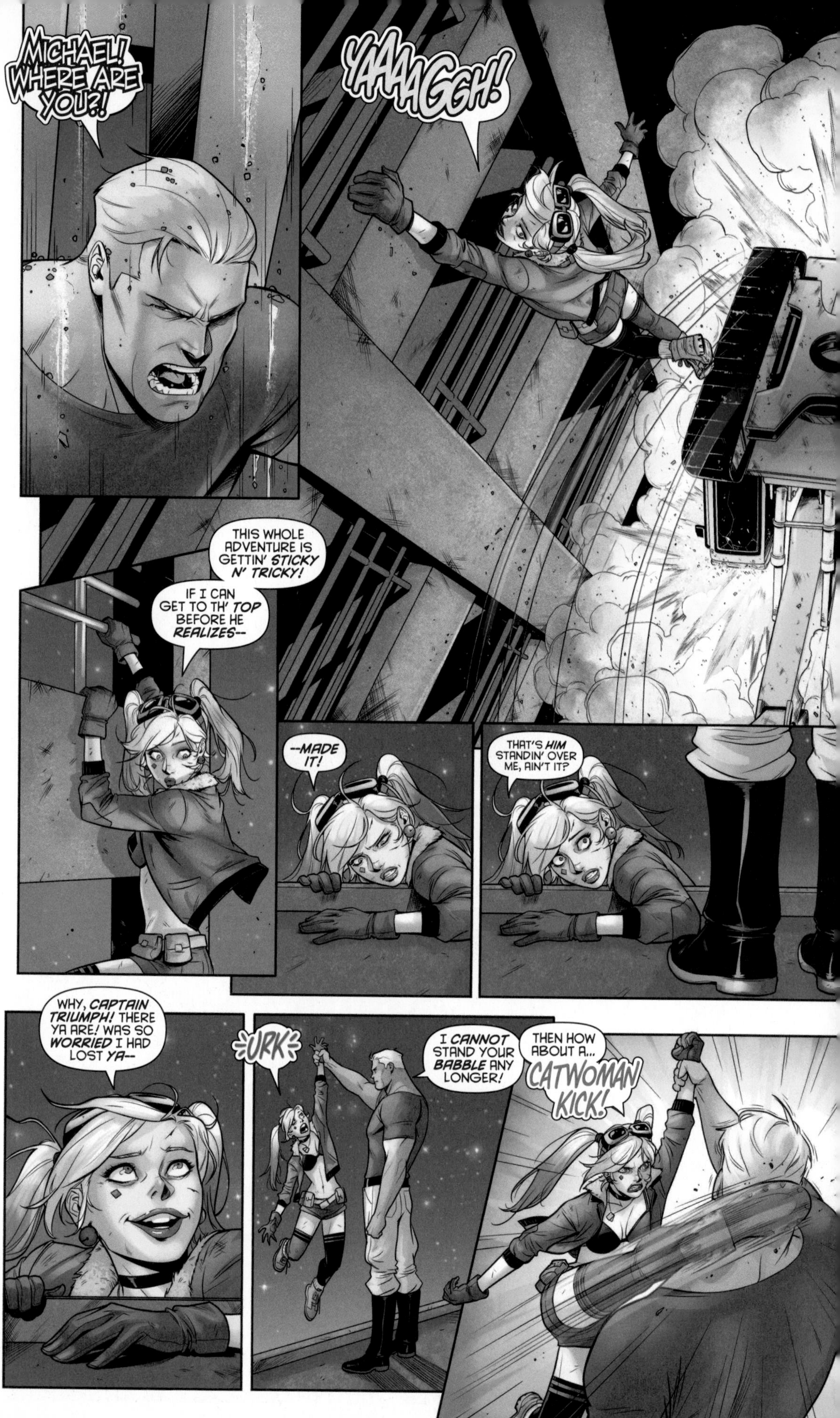
MICHAEL! WHERE ARE YOU?!
YAAAAGGH!
THIS WHOLE ADVENTURE IS GETTIN' STICKY N' TRICKY!
IF I CAN GET TO TH' TOP BEFORE HE REALIZES--
--MADE IT!
THAT'S HIM STANDIN' OVER ME, AIN'T IT?
WHY, CAPTAIN TRIUMPH! THERE YA ARE! WAS SO WORRIED I HAD LOST YA--
URK
I CANNOT STAND YOUR BABBLE ANY LONGER!
THEN HOW ABOUT A... CATWOMAN KICK!

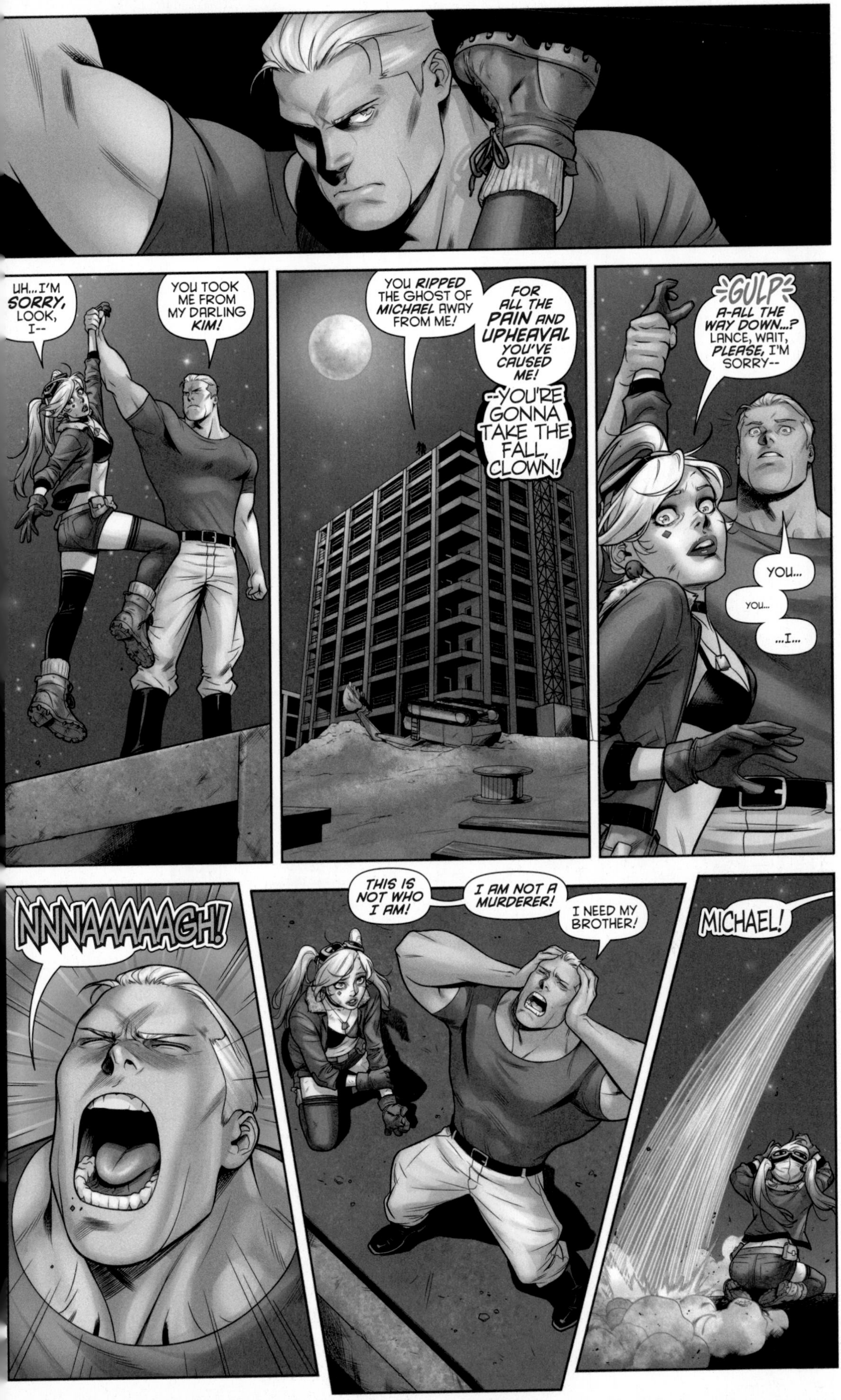

UH... I'M SORRY, LOOK, I--
YOU TOOK ME FROM MY DARLING KIM!
YOU RIPPED THE GHOST OF MICHAEL AWAY FROM ME!
FOR ALL THE PAIN AND UPHEAVAL YOU'VE CAUSED ME!
--YOU'RE GONNA TAKE THE FALL, CLOWN!
GULP
A-ALL THE WAY DOWN...? LANCE, WAIT, PLEASE, I'M SORRY--
YOU...
YOU...
...I...
NNNAAAAAAGH!
THIS IS NOT WHO I AM!
I AM NOT A MURDERER!
I NEED MY BROTHER!
MICHAEL!

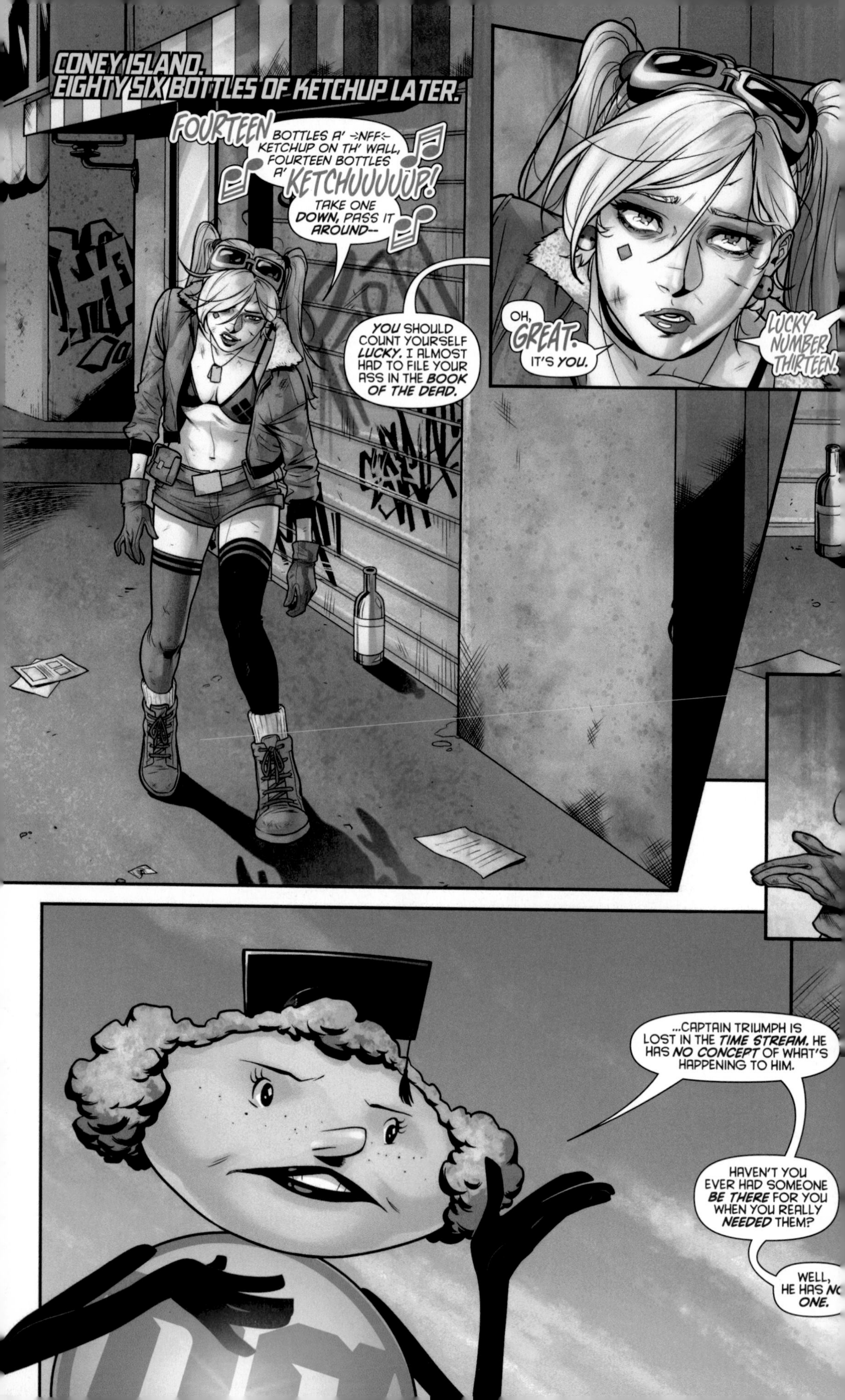
CONEY ISLAND.
EIGHTY SIX BOTTLES OF KETCHUP LATER.
FOURTEEN BOTTLES A' ⇒NFF⇐ KETCHUP ON TH' WALL, FOURTEEN BOTTLES A' KETCHUUUUUP!
TAKE ONE DOWN, PASS IT AROUND--
YOU SHOULD COUNT YOURSELF LUCKY. I ALMOST HAD TO FILE YOUR ASS IN THE BOOK OF THE DEAD.
OH, GREAT. IT'S YOU.
LUCKY NUMBER THIRTEEN.
...CAPTAIN TRIUMPH IS LOST IN THE TIME STREAM. HE HAS NO CONCEPT OF WHAT'S HAPPENING TO HIM.
HAVEN'T YOU EVER HAD SOMEONE BE THERE FOR YOU WHEN YOU REALLY NEEDED THEM?
WELL, HE HAS NO ONE.

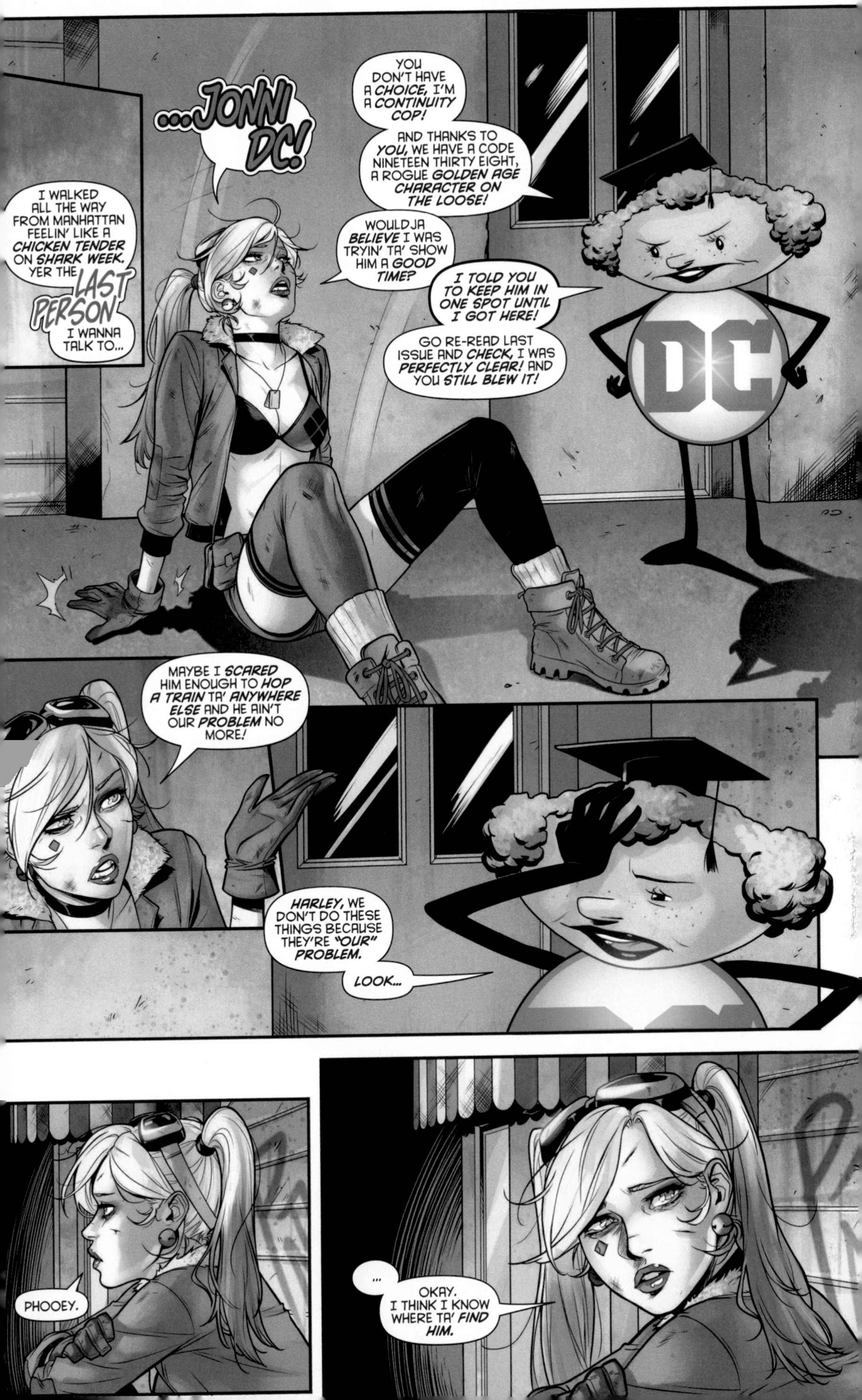
...JONNI DC!
I WALKED ALL THE WAY FROM MANHATTAN FEELIN' LIKE A CHICKEN TENDER ON SHARK WEEK. YER THE LAST PERSON I WANNA TALK TO...
YOU DON'T HAVE A CHOICE, I'M A CONTINUITY COP!
AND THANKS TO YOU, WE HAVE A CODE NINETEEN THIRTY EIGHT, A ROGUE GOLDEN AGE CHARACTER ON THE LOOSE!
WOULDJA BELIEVE I WAS TRYIN' TA' SHOW HIM A GOOD TIME?
I TOLD YOU TO KEEP HIM IN ONE SPOT UNTIL I GOT HERE!
GO RE-READ LAST ISSUE AND CHECK, I WAS PERFECTLY CLEAR! AND YOU STILL BLEW IT!
MAYBE I SCARED HIM ENOUGH TO HOP A TRAIN TA' ANYWHERE ELSE AND HE AIN'T OUR PROBLEM NO MORE!
HARLEY, WE DON'T DO THESE THINGS BECAUSE THEY'RE "OUR" PROBLEM.
LOOK...
PHOOEY.
...
OKAY. I THINK I KNOW WHERE TA' FIND HIM.

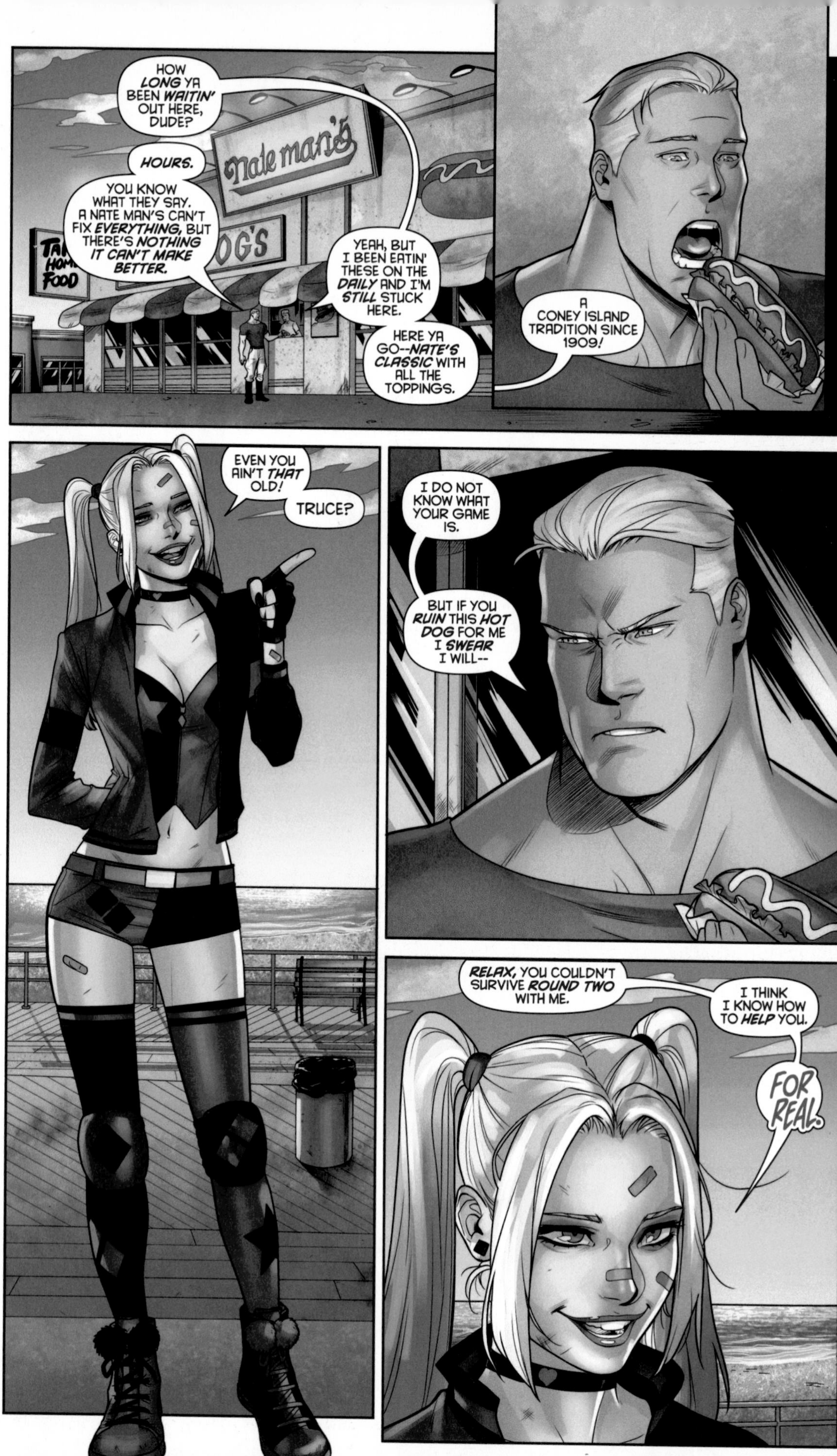
HOW LONG YA BEEN WAITIN' OUT HERE, DUDE?
nate man's
OG'S
HOURS.
YOU KNOW WHAT THEY SAY. A NATE MAN'S CAN'T FIX EVERYTHING, BUT THERE'S NOTHING IT CAN'T MAKE BETTER.
YEAH, BUT I BEEN EATIN' THESE ON THE DAILY AND I'M STILL STUCK HERE.
HERE YA GO--NATE'S CLASSIC WITH ALL THE TOPPINGS.
A CONEY ISLAND TRADITION SINCE 1909!
EVEN YOU AIN'T THAT OLD!
TRUCE?
I DO NOT KNOW WHAT YOUR GAME IS.
BUT IF YOU RUIN THIS HOT DOG FOR ME I SWEAR I WILL--
RELAX, YOU COULDN'T SURVIVE ROUND TWO WITH ME.
I THINK I KNOW HOW TO HELP YOU.
FOR REAL.

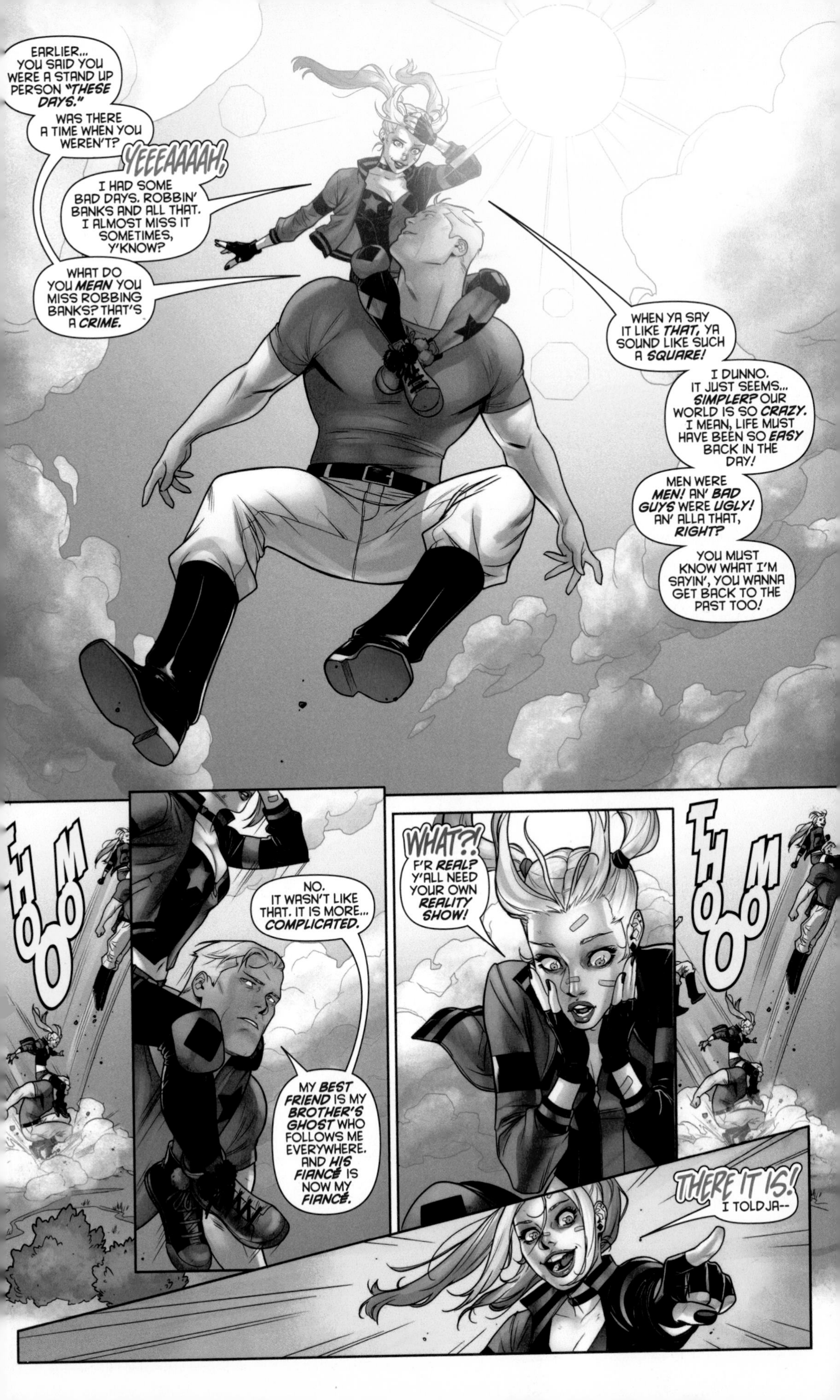
EARLIER... YOU SAID YOU WERE A STAND UP PERSON "THESE DAYS."
WAS THERE A TIME WHEN YOU WEREN'T?
YEEEAAAAH,
I HAD SOME BAD DAYS. ROBBIN' BANKS AND ALL THAT. I ALMOST MISS IT SOMETIMES, Y'KNOW?
WHAT DO YOU MEAN YOU MISS ROBBING BANKS? THAT'S A CRIME.
WHEN YA SAY IT LIKE THAT, YA SOUND LIKE SUCH A SQUARE!
I DUNNO. IT JUST SEEMS... SIMPLER? OUR WORLD IS SO CRAZY. I MEAN, LIFE MUST HAVE BEEN SO EASY BACK IN THE DAY!
MEN WERE MEN! AN' BAD GUYS WERE UGLY! AN' ALLA THAT, RIGHT?
YOU MUST KNOW WHAT I'M SAYIN', YOU WANNA GET BACK TO THE PAST TOO!
THWOOOM
NO. IT WASN'T LIKE THAT. IT IS MORE... COMPLICATED.
MY BEST FRIEND IS MY BROTHER'S GHOST WHO FOLLOWS ME EVERYWHERE. AND HIS FIANCÉ IS NOW MY FIANCÉ.
WHAT?!
F'R REAL? Y'ALL NEED YOUR OWN REALITY SHOW!
THWOOOM
THERE IT IS!
I TOLDJA--

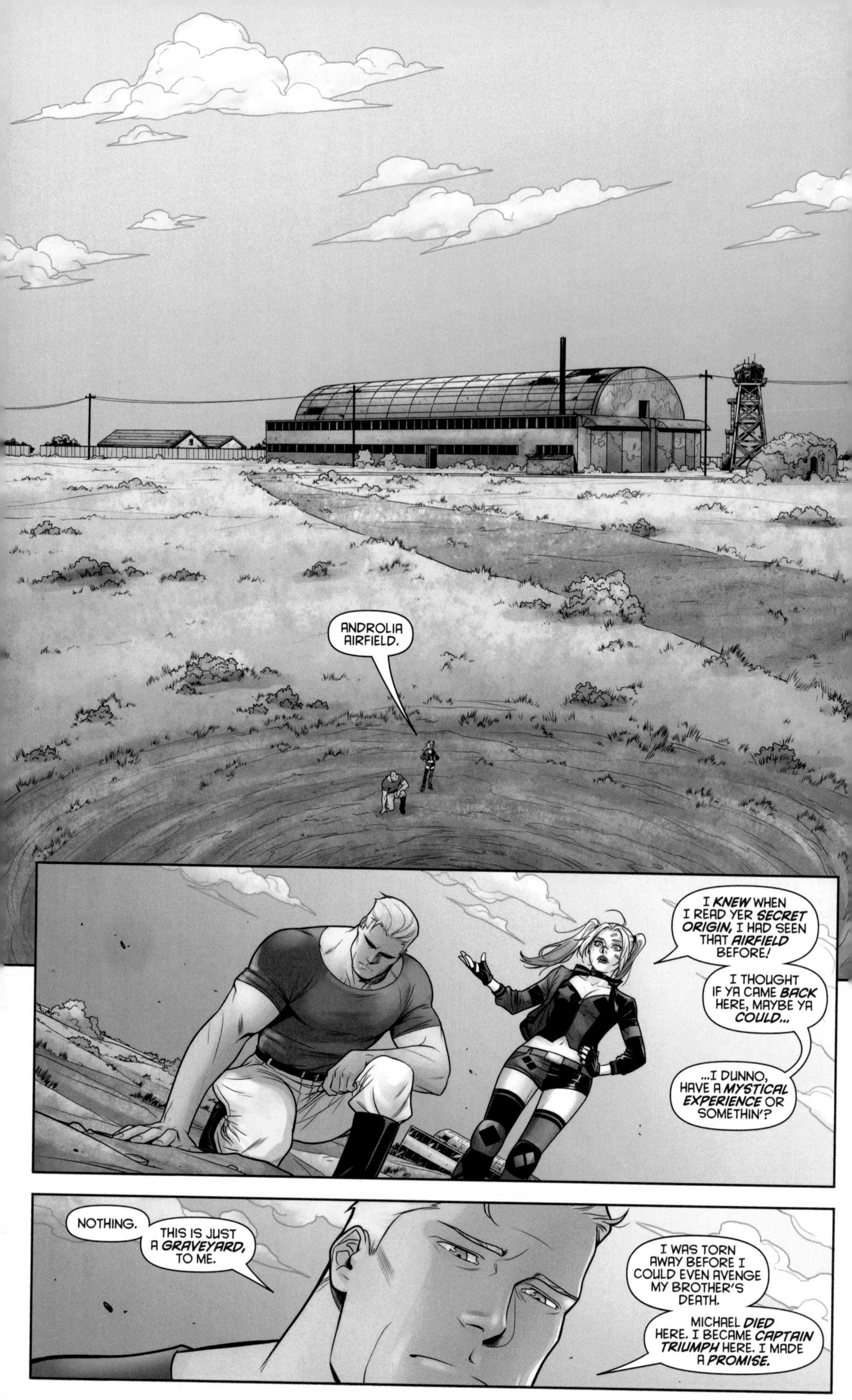
ANDROLIA AIRFIELD.
I KNEW WHEN I READ YER SECRET ORIGIN, I HAD SEEN THAT AIRFIELD BEFORE!
I THOUGHT IF YA CAME BACK HERE, MAYBE YA COULD...
...I DUNNO, HAVE A MYSTICAL EXPERIENCE OR SOMETHIN'?
NOTHING.
THIS IS JUST A GRAVEYARD, TO ME.
I WAS TORN AWAY BEFORE I COULD EVEN AVENGE MY BROTHER'S DEATH.
MICHAEL DIED HERE. I BECAME CAPTAIN TRIUMPH HERE. I MADE A PROMISE.

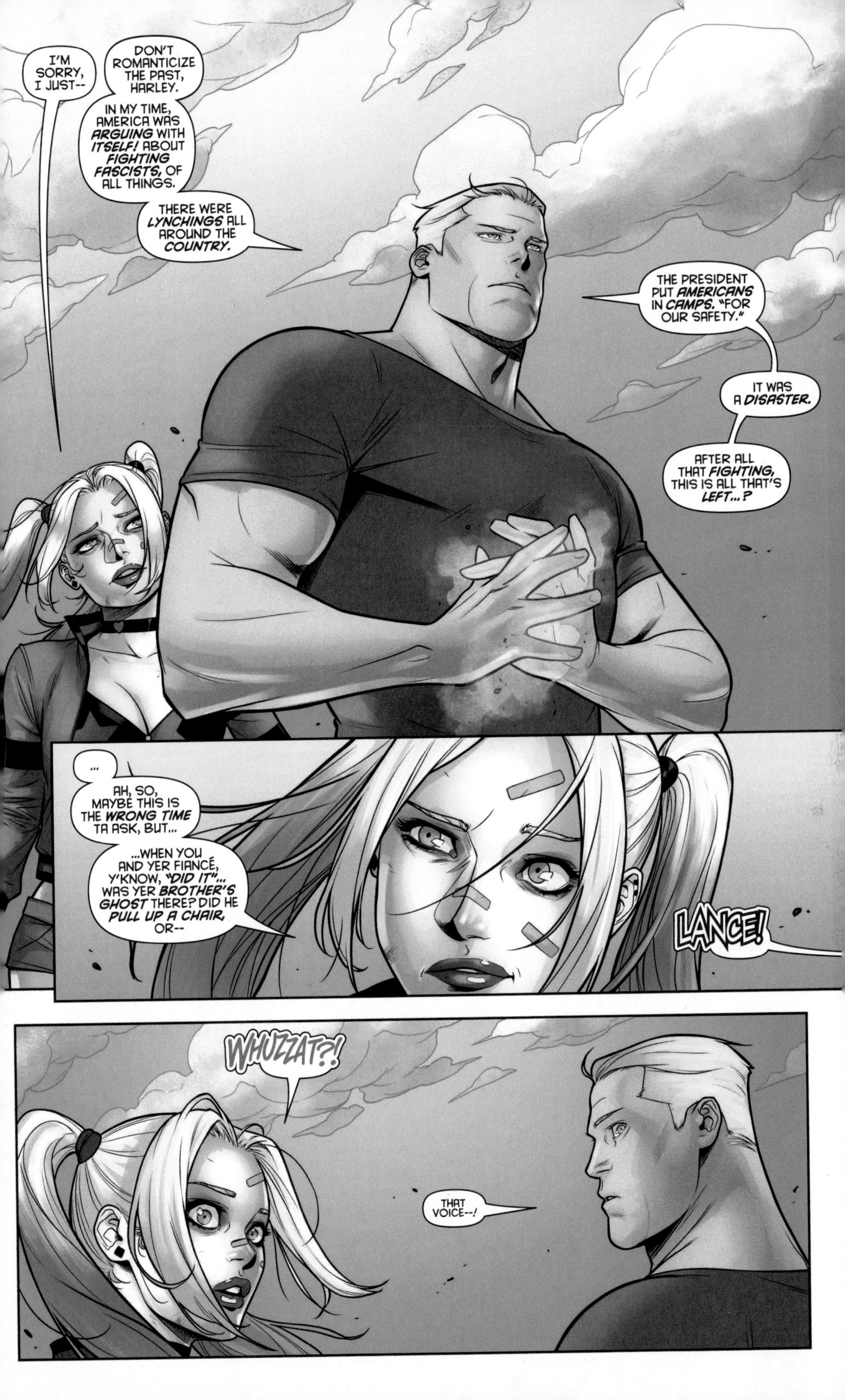

I'M SORRY, I JUST--
DON'T ROMANTICIZE THE PAST, HARLEY.
IN MY TIME, AMERICA WAS ARGUING WITH ITSELF! ABOUT FIGHTING FASCISTS, OF ALL THINGS.
THERE WERE LYNCHINGS ALL AROUND THE COUNTRY.
THE PRESIDENT PUT AMERICANS IN CAMPS. "FOR OUR SAFETY."
IT WAS A DISASTER.
AFTER ALL THAT FIGHTING, THIS IS ALL THAT'S LEFT...?
...
AH, SO, MAYBE THIS IS THE WRONG TIME TA ASK, BUT...
...WHEN YOU AND YER FIANCÉ, Y'KNOW, "DID IT"... WAS YER BROTHER'S GHOST THERE? DID HE PULL UP A CHAIR, OR--
LANCE!
WHUZZAT?!
THAT VOICE--!

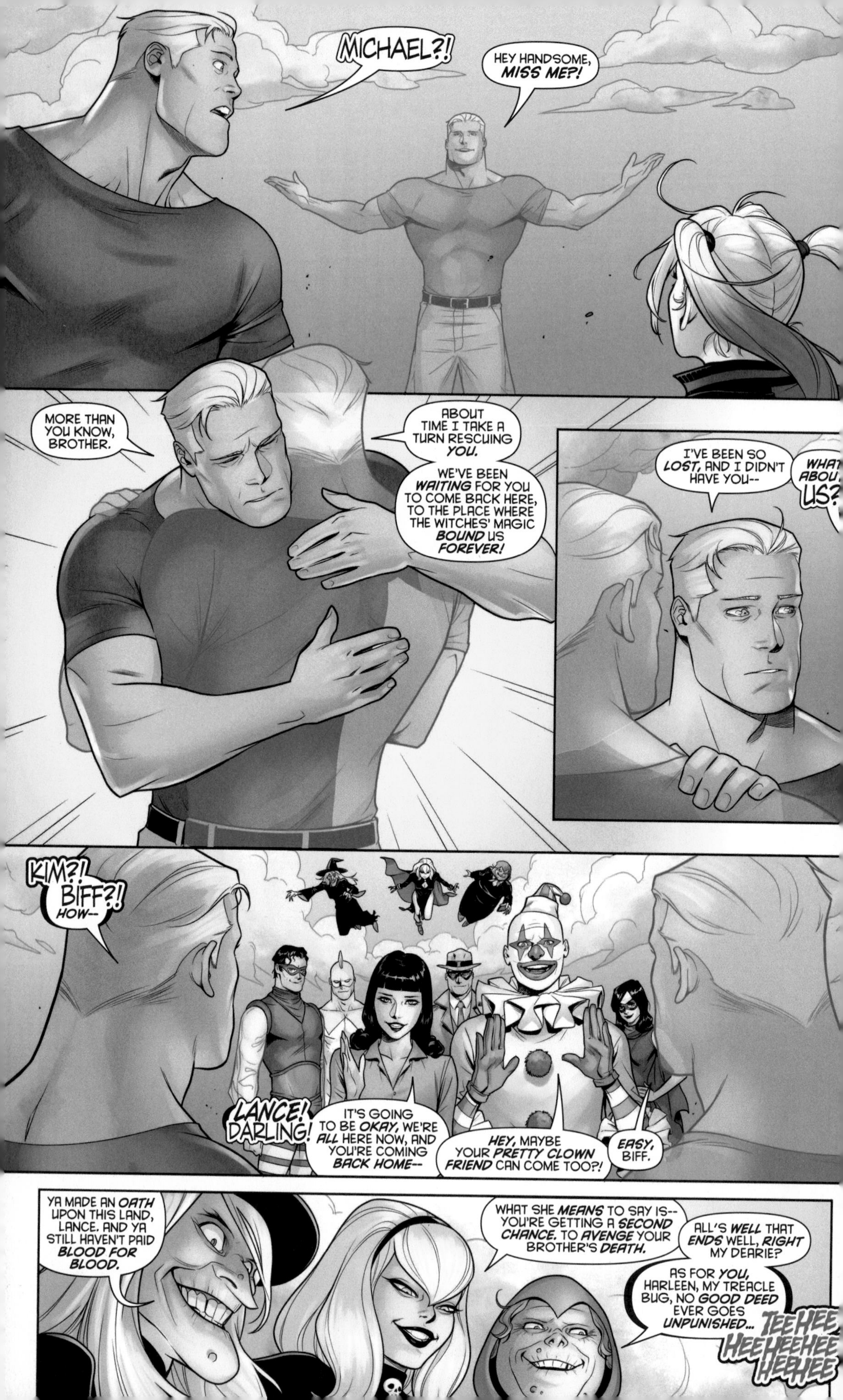
MICHAEL?!
HEY HANDSOME, MISS ME?!
MORE THAN YOU KNOW, BROTHER.
ABOUT TIME I TAKE A TURN RESCUING YOU.
WE'VE BEEN WAITING FOR YOU TO COME BACK HERE, TO THE PLACE WHERE THE WITCHES' MAGIC BOUND US FOREVER!
I'VE BEEN SO LOST, AND I DIDN'T HAVE YOU--
KIM?! BIFF?! HOW--
LANCE! DARLING!
IT'S GOING TO BE OKAY, WE'RE ALL HERE NOW, AND YOU'RE COMING BACK HOME--
HEY, MAYBE YOUR PRETTY CLOWN FRIEND CAN COME TOO?!
EASY, BIFF.
YA MADE AN OATH UPON THIS LAND, LANCE. AND YA STILL HAVEN'T PAID BLOOD FOR BLOOD.
WHAT SHE MEANS TO SAY IS-- YOU'RE GETTING A SECOND CHANCE. TO AVENGE YOUR BROTHER'S DEATH.
ALL'S WELL THAT ENDS WELL, RIGHT MY DEARIE?
AS FOR YOU, HARLEEN, MY TREACLE BUG, NO GOOD DEED EVER GOES UNPUNISHED...
TEEHEE HEEHEEHEE HEEHEE

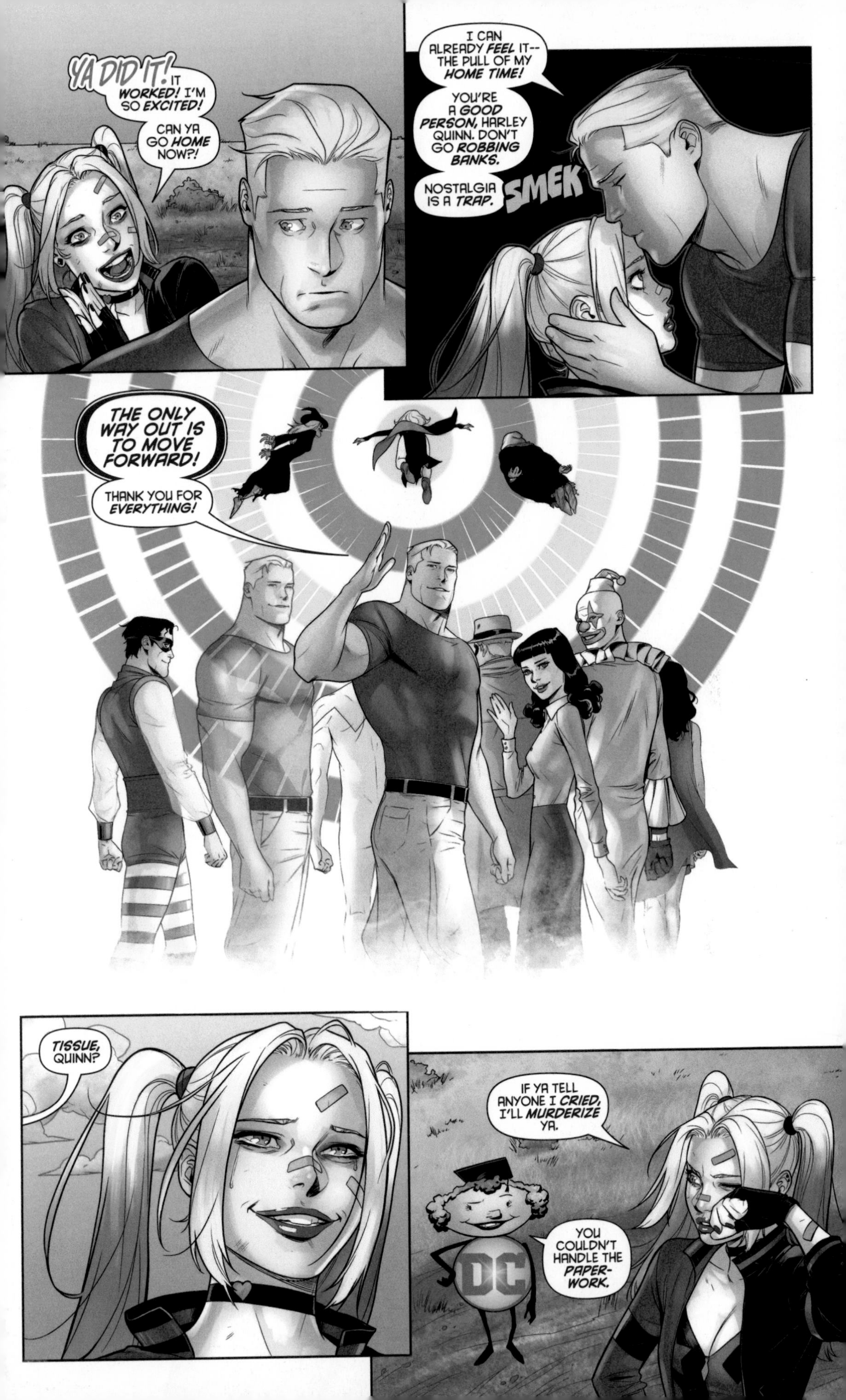
YA DID IT! IT WORKED! I'M SO EXCITED!
CAN YA GO HOME NOW?!
I CAN ALREADY FEEL IT-- THE PULL OF MY HOME TIME!
YOU'RE A GOOD PERSON, HARLEY QUINN. DON'T GO ROBBING BANKS.
NOSTALGIA IS A TRAP.
SMEK
THE ONLY WAY OUT IS TO MOVE FORWARD!
THANK YOU FOR EVERYTHING!
TISSUE, QUINN?
IF YA TELL ANYONE I CRIED, I'LL MURDERIZE YA.
YOU COULDN'T HANDLE THE PAPER-WORK.

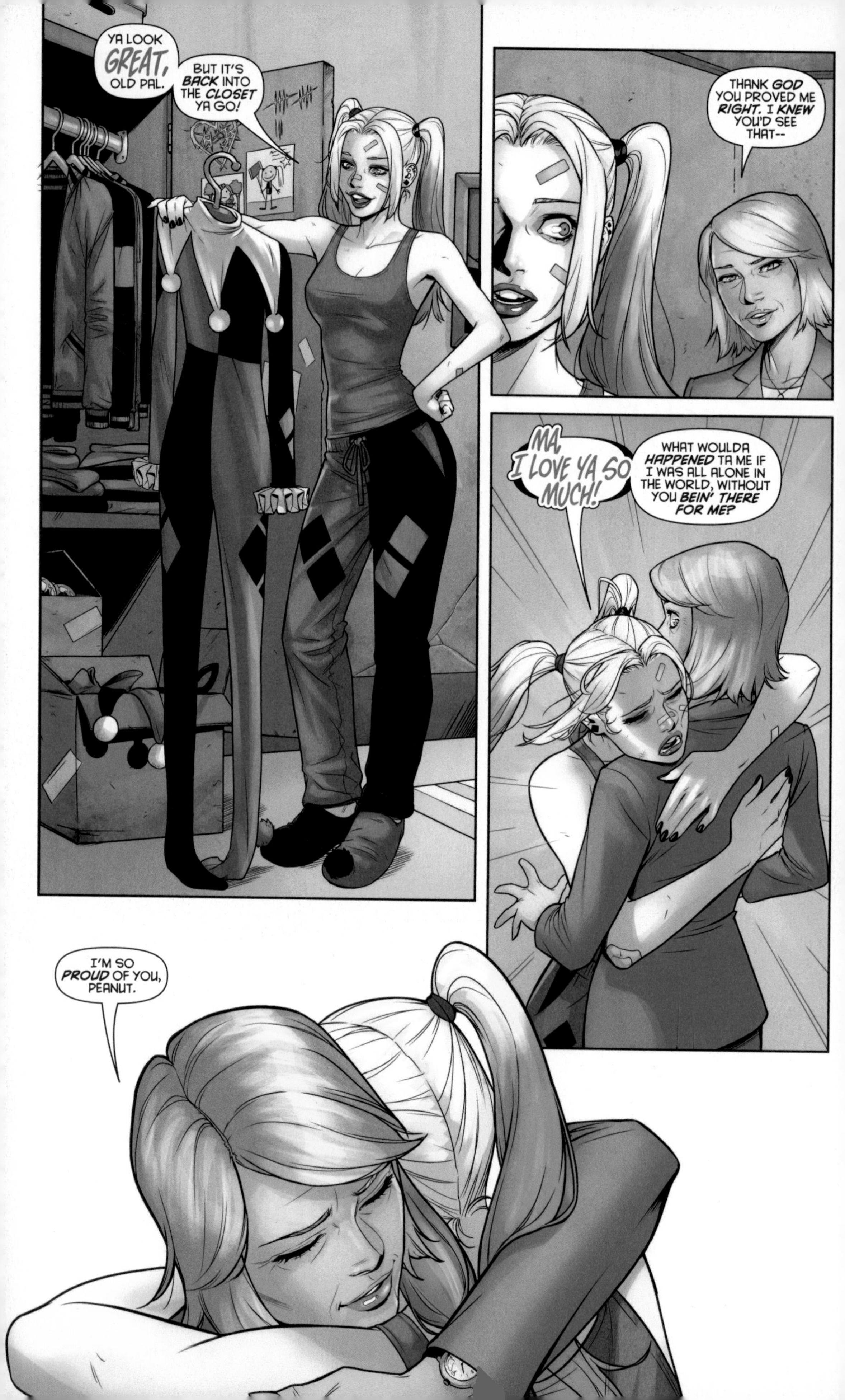
YA LOOK GREAT, OLD PAL.
BUT IT'S BACK INTO THE CLOSET YA GO!
THANK GOD YOU PROVED ME RIGHT. I KNEW YOU'D SEE THAT--
MA, I LOVE YA SO MUCH!
WHAT WOULDA HAPPENED TA ME IF I WAS ALL ALONE IN THE WORLD, WITHOUT YOU BEIN' THERE FOR ME?
I'M SO PROUD OF YOU, PEANUT.

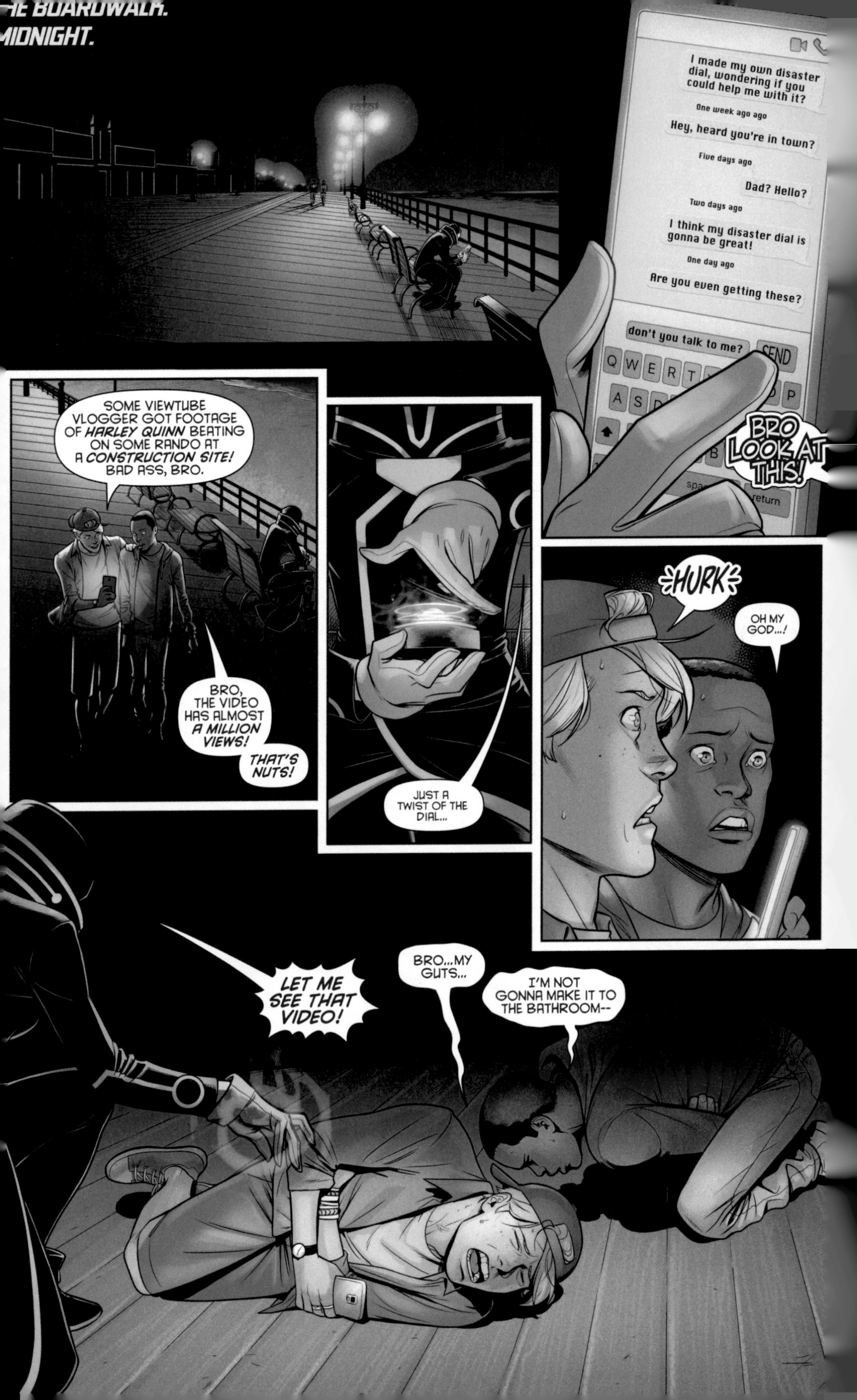

BOARDWALK.
MIDNIGHT.
I made my own disaster dial, wondering if you could help me with it?
One week ago ago
Hey, heard you're in town?
Five days ago
Dad? Hello?
Two days ago
I think my disaster dial is gonna be great!
One day ago
Are you even getting these?
don't you talk to me?
SEND
SOME VIEWTUBE VLOGGER GOT FOOTAGE OF HARLEY QUINN BEATING ON SOME RANDO AT A CONSTRUCTION SITE! BAD ASS, BRO.
BRO, THE VIDEO HAS ALMOST A MILLION VIEWS!
THAT'S NUTS!
JUST A TWIST OF THE DIAL...
BRO LOOK AT THIS!
HURK
OH MY GOD...!
LET ME SEE THAT VIDEO!
BRO...MY GUTS...
I'M NOT GONNA MAKE IT TO THE BATHROOM--

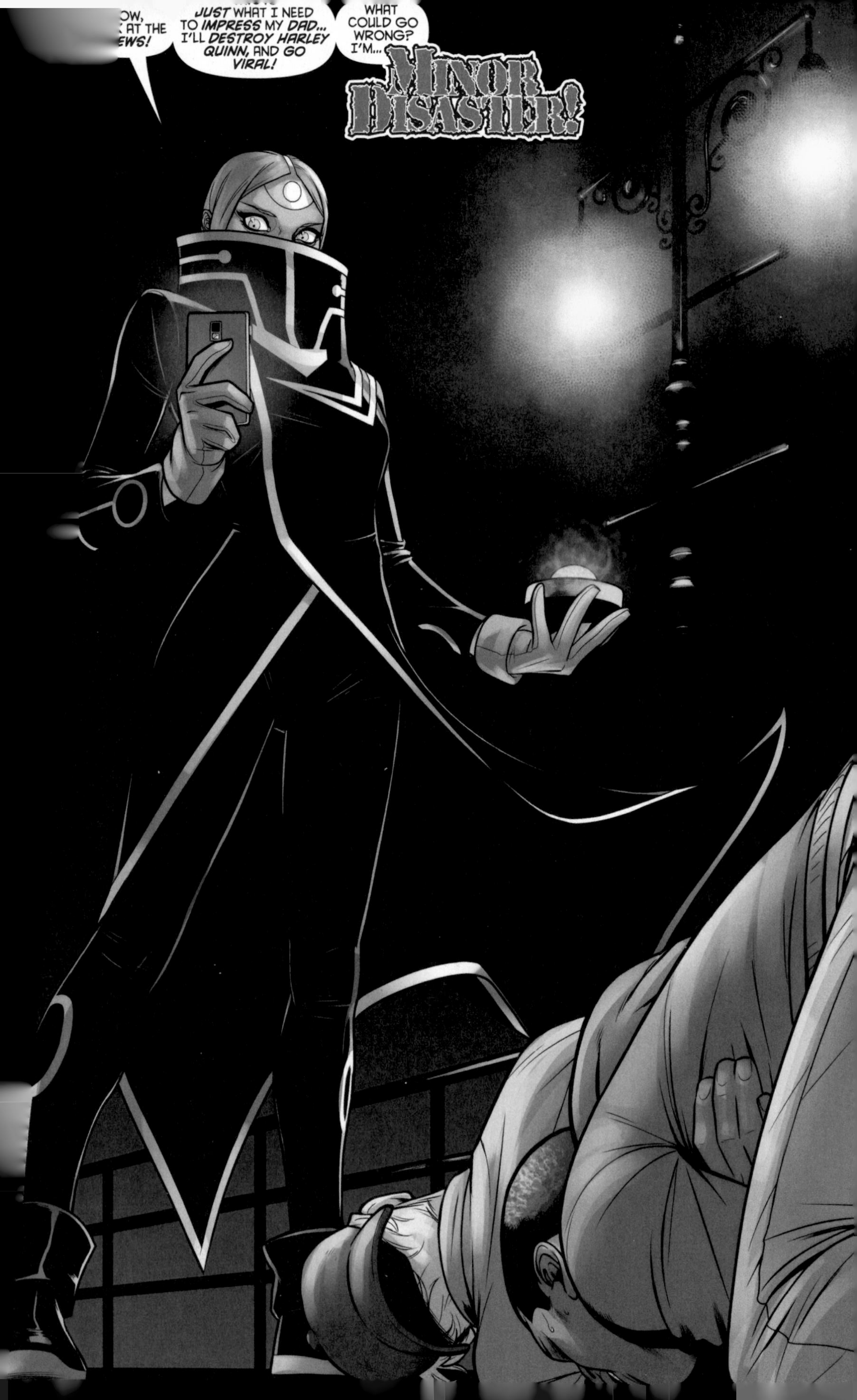

JUST WHAT I NEED TO IMPRESS MY DAD... I'LL DESTROY HARLEY QUINN, AND GO VIRAL!
WHAT COULD GO WRONG? I'M...
MINOR DISASTER!

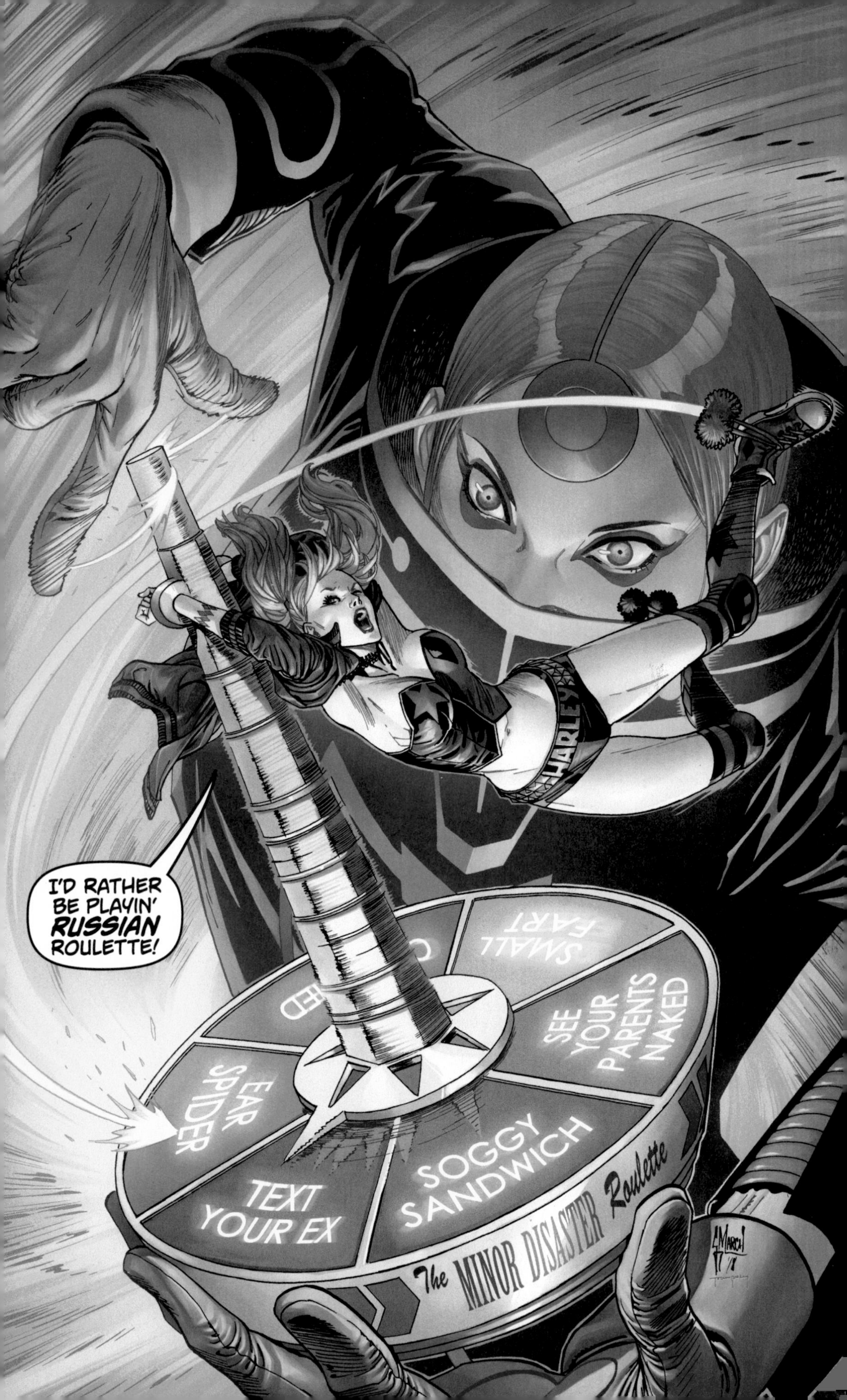
I'D RATHER BE PLAYIN' RUSSIAN ROULETTE!
SMALL FART
SEE YOUR PARENTS NAKED
EAR SPIDER
SOGGY SANDWICH
TEXT YOUR EX
The MINOR DISASTER Roulette
HARLEY

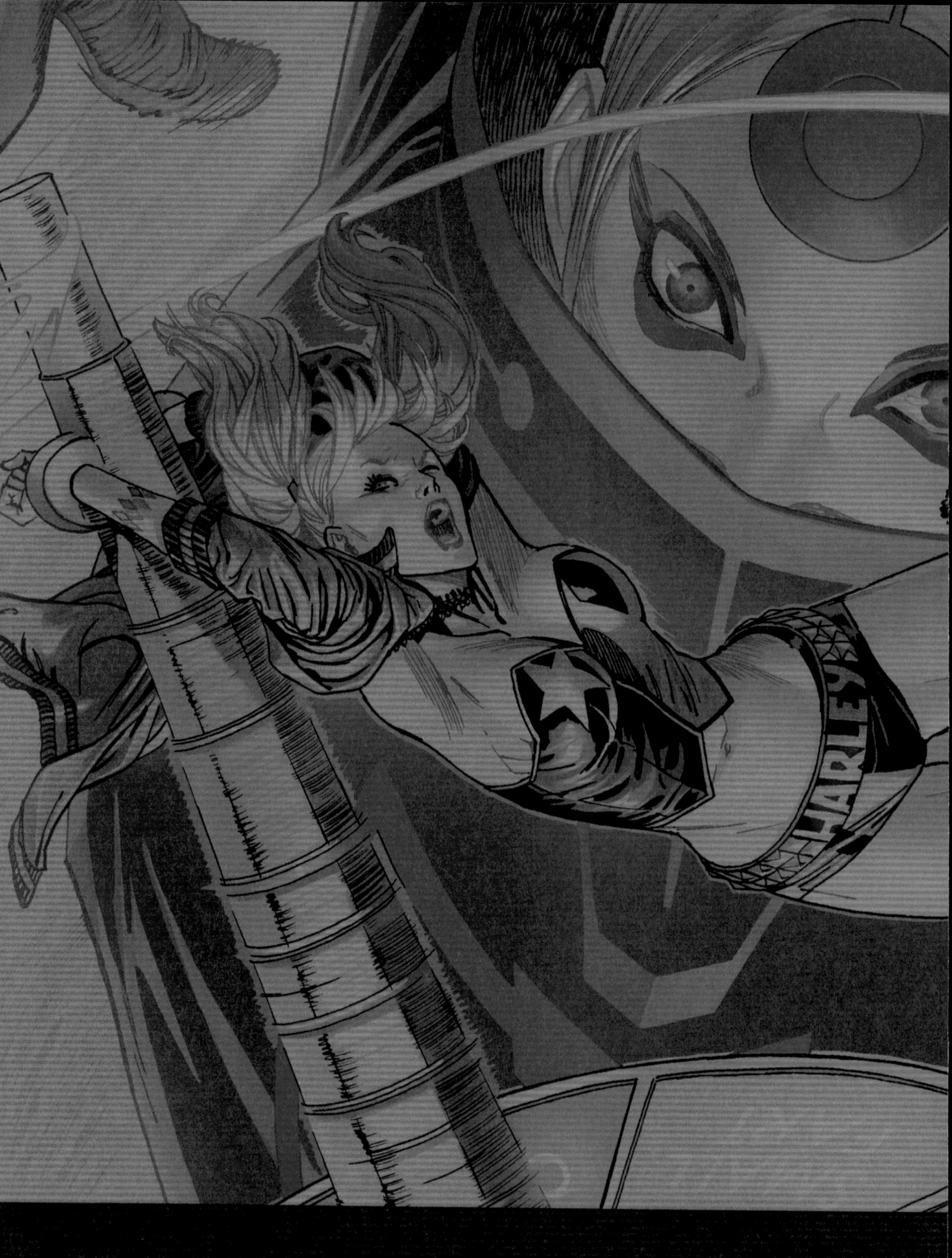

HARLEY QUINN
#53

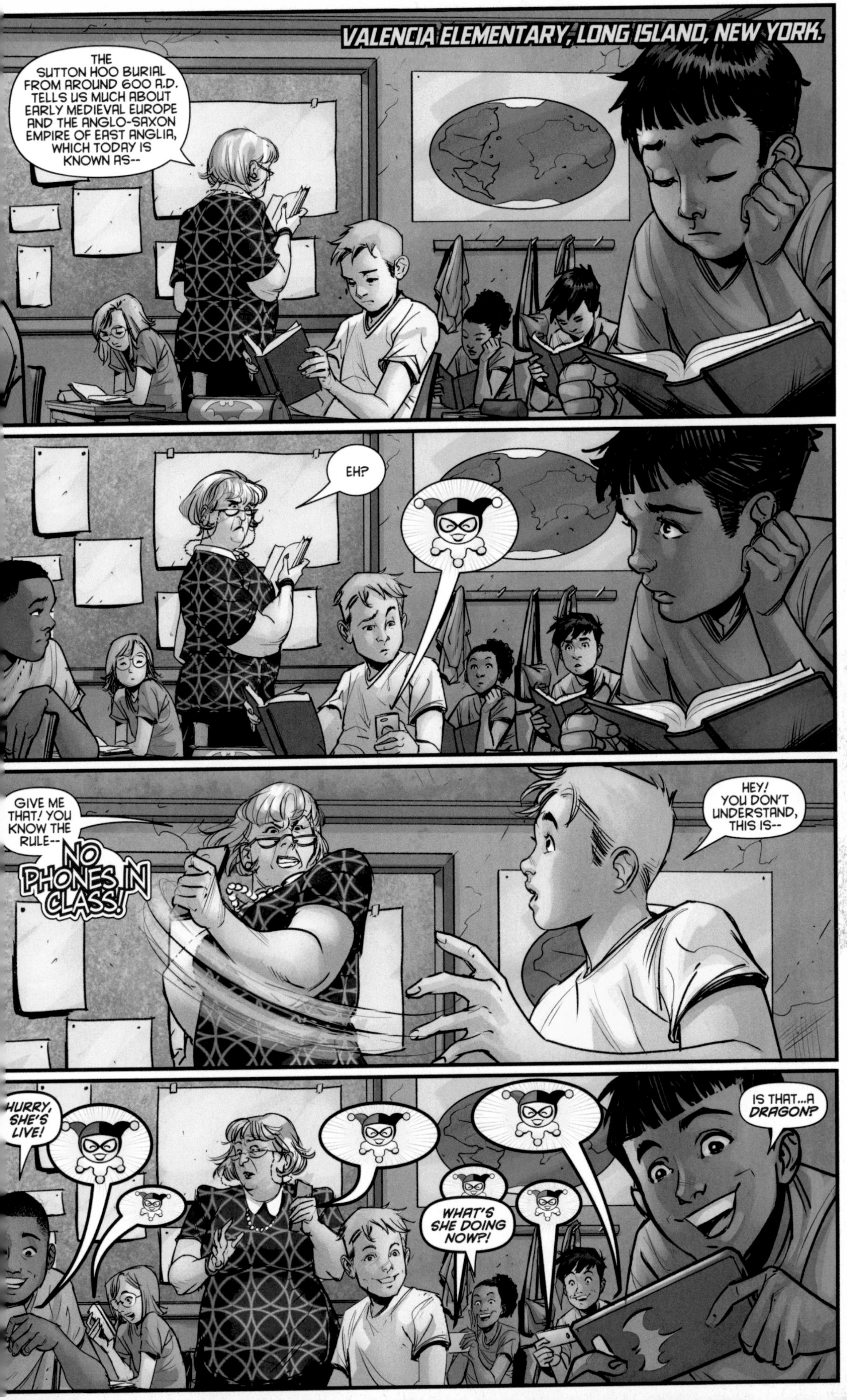
VALENCIA ELEMENTARY, LONG ISLAND, NEW YORK.
THE SUTTON HOO BURIAL FROM AROUND 600 A.D. TELLS US MUCH ABOUT EARLY MEDIEVAL EUROPE AND THE ANGLO-SAXON EMPIRE OF EAST ANGLIA, WHICH TODAY IS KNOWN AS--
EH?
GIVE ME THAT! YOU KNOW THE RULE--
NO PHONES IN CLASS!
HEY! YOU DON'T UNDERSTAND, THIS IS--
HURRY, SHE'S LIVE!
WHAT'S SHE DOING NOW?!
IS THAT...A DRAGON?

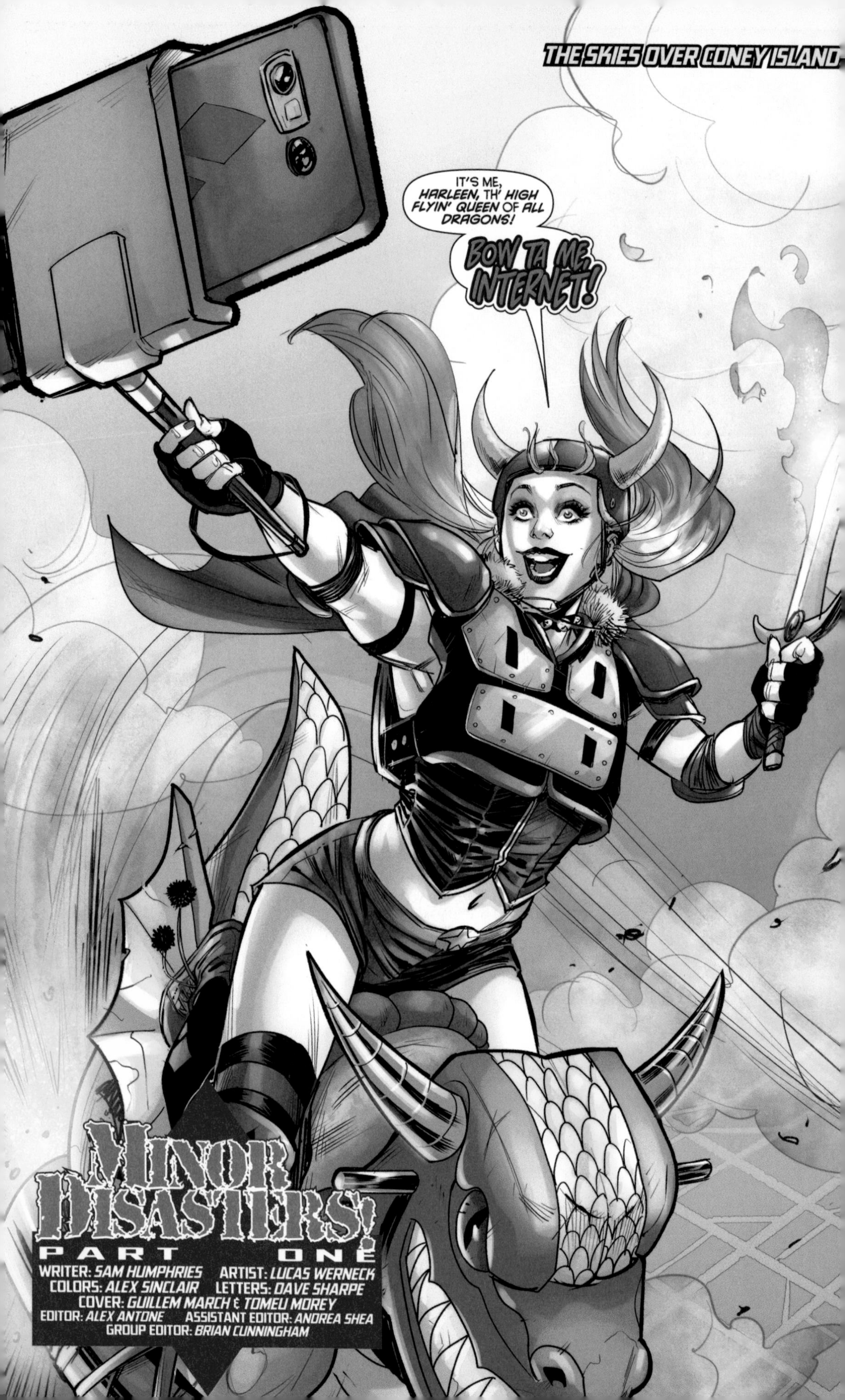
THE SKIES OVER CONEY ISLAND
IT'S ME, HARLEEN, TH' HIGH FLYIN' QUEEN OF ALL DRAGONS!
BOW TA ME, INTERNET!
MINOR DISASTERS!
PART ONE
WRITER: SAM HUMPHRIES ARTIST: LUCAS WERNECK
COLORS: ALEX SINCLAIR LETTERS: DAVE SHARPE
COVER: GUILLEM MARCH & TOMEU MOREY
EDITOR: ALEX ANTONE ASSISTANT EDITOR: ANDREA SHEA
GROUP EDITOR: BRIAN CUNNINGHAM

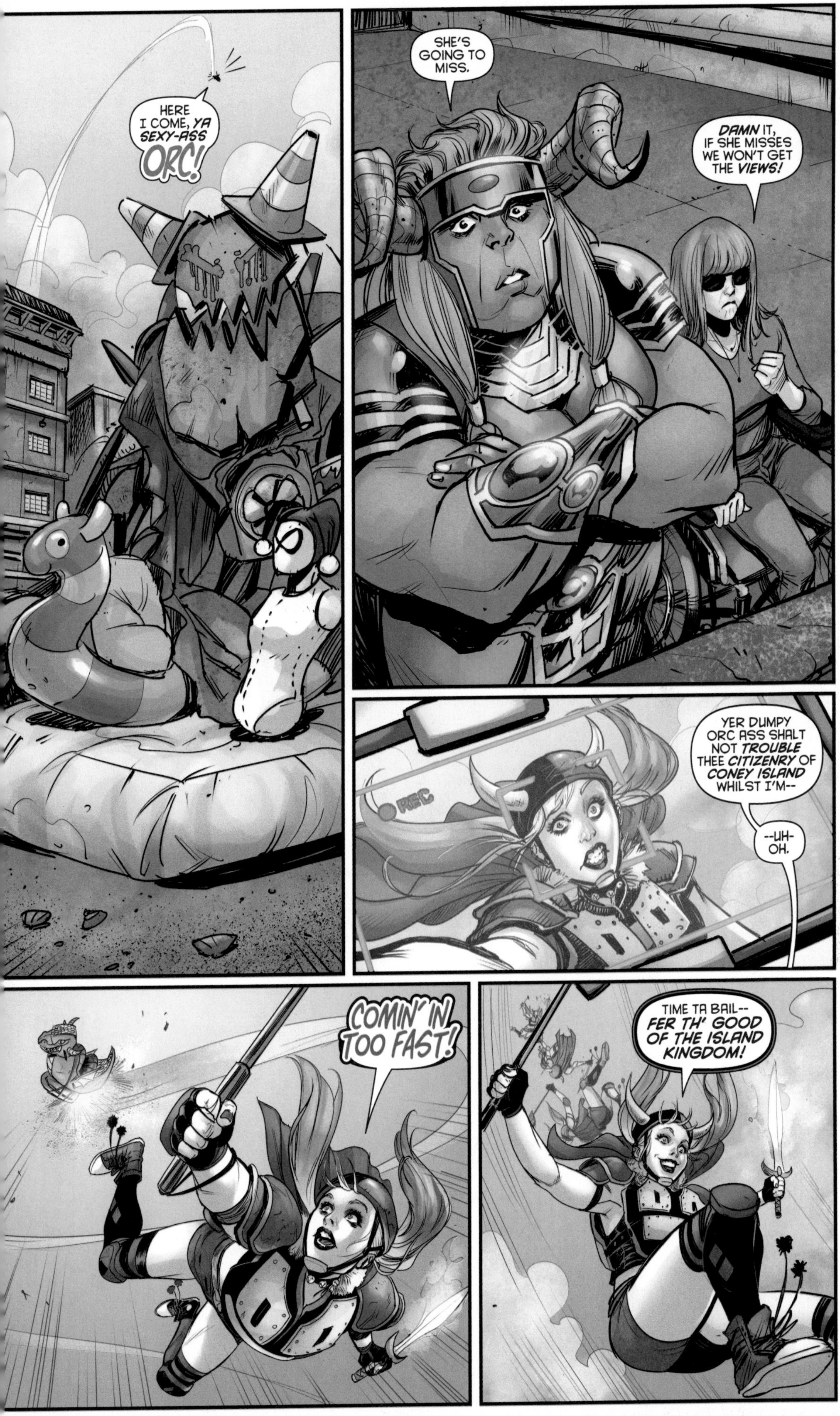
HERE I COME, YA SEXY-ASS ORC!
SHE'S GOING TO MISS.
DAMN IT, IF SHE MISSES WE WON'T GET THE VIEWS!
REC
YER DUMPY ORC ASS SHALT NOT TROUBLE THEE CITIZENRY OF CONEY ISLAND WHILST I'M--
--UH-OH.
COMIN' IN TOO FAST!
TIME TA BAIL-- FER TH' GOOD OF THE ISLAND KINGDOM!

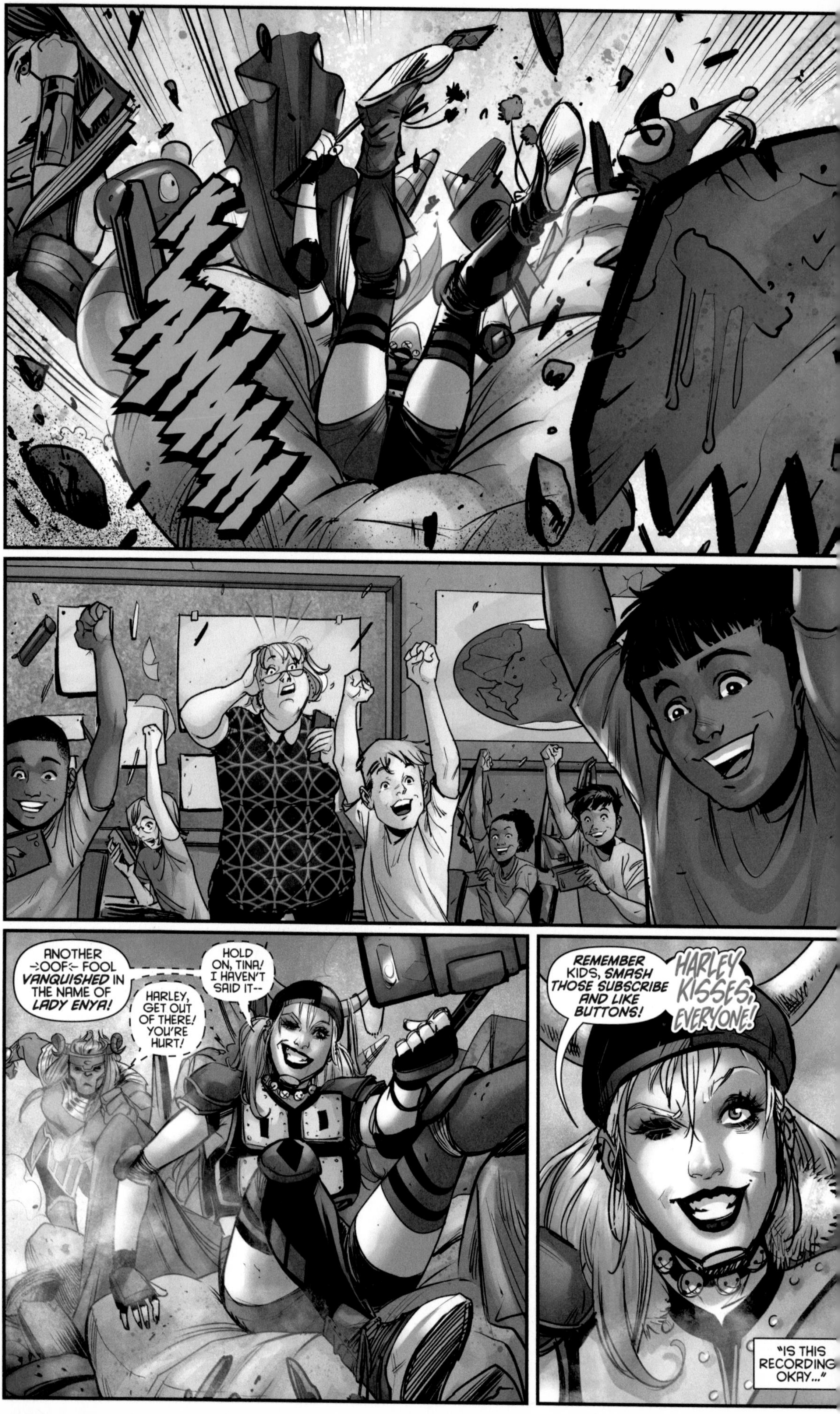
ANOTHER ⇒OOF⇐ FOOL VANQUISHED IN THE NAME OF LADY ENYA!
HARLEY, GET OUT OF THERE! YOU'RE HURT!
HOLD ON, TINA! I HAVEN'T SAID IT--
REMEMBER KIDS, SMASH THOSE SUBSCRIBE AND LIKE BUTTONS!
HARLEY KISSES, EVERYONE!
"IS THIS RECORDING OKAY..."

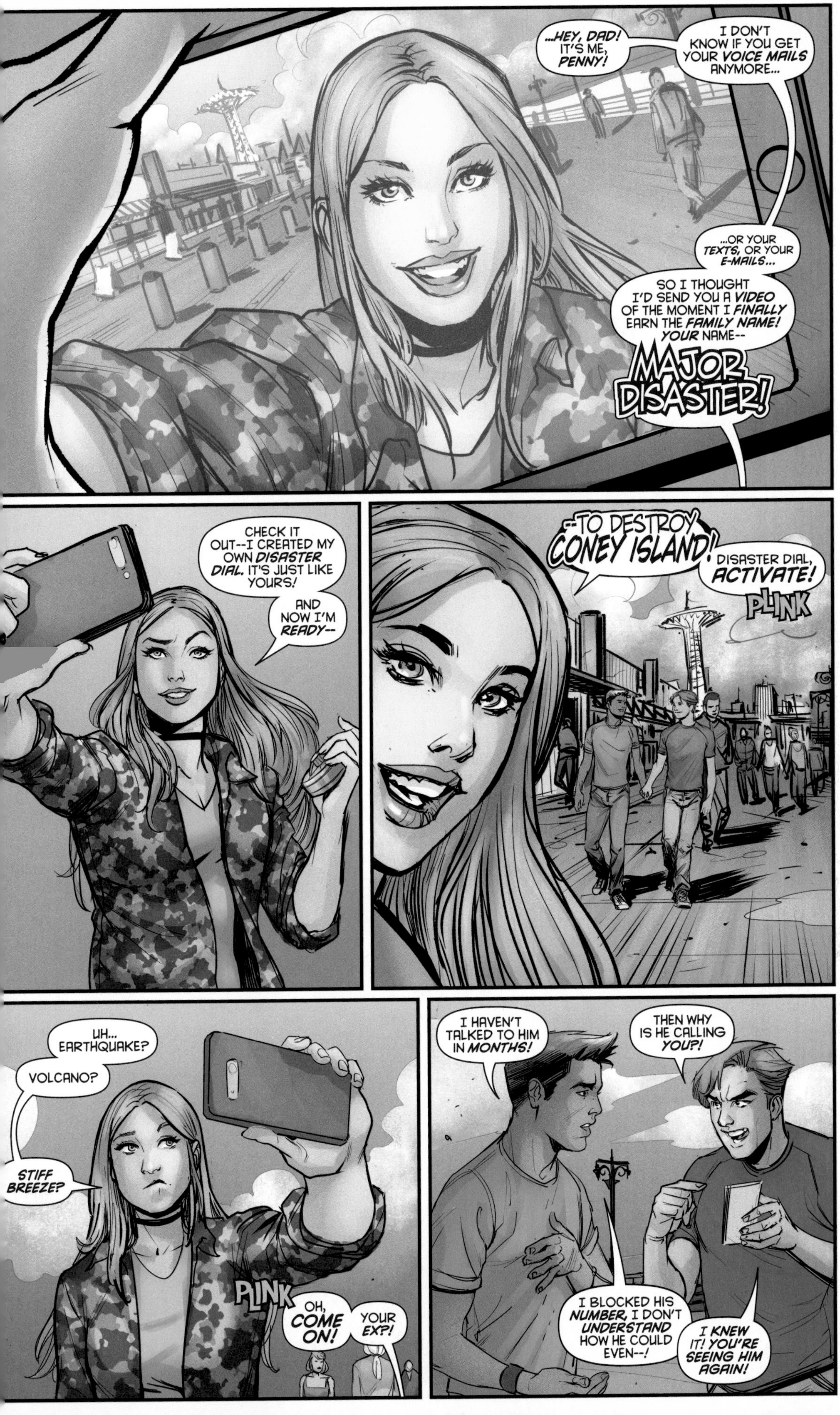
...HEY, DAD! IT'S ME, PENNY!
I DON'T KNOW IF YOU GET YOUR VOICE MAILS ANYMORE...
...OR YOUR TEXTS, OR YOUR E-MAILS...
SO I THOUGHT I'D SEND YOU A VIDEO OF THE MOMENT I FINALLY EARN THE FAMILY NAME! YOUR NAME--
MAJOR DISASTER!
CHECK IT OUT--I CREATED MY OWN DISASTER DIAL. IT'S JUST LIKE YOURS!
AND NOW I'M READY--
--TO DESTROY CONEY ISLAND!
DISASTER DIAL, ACTIVATE!
PLINK
UH... EARTHQUAKE?
VOLCANO?
STIFF BREEZE?
PLINK
OH, COME ON!
YOUR EX?!
I HAVEN'T TALKED TO HIM IN MONTHS!
THEN WHY IS HE CALLING YOU?!
I BLOCKED HIS NUMBER, I DON'T UNDERSTAND HOW HE COULD EVEN--!
I KNEW IT! YOU'RE SEEING HIM AGAIN!

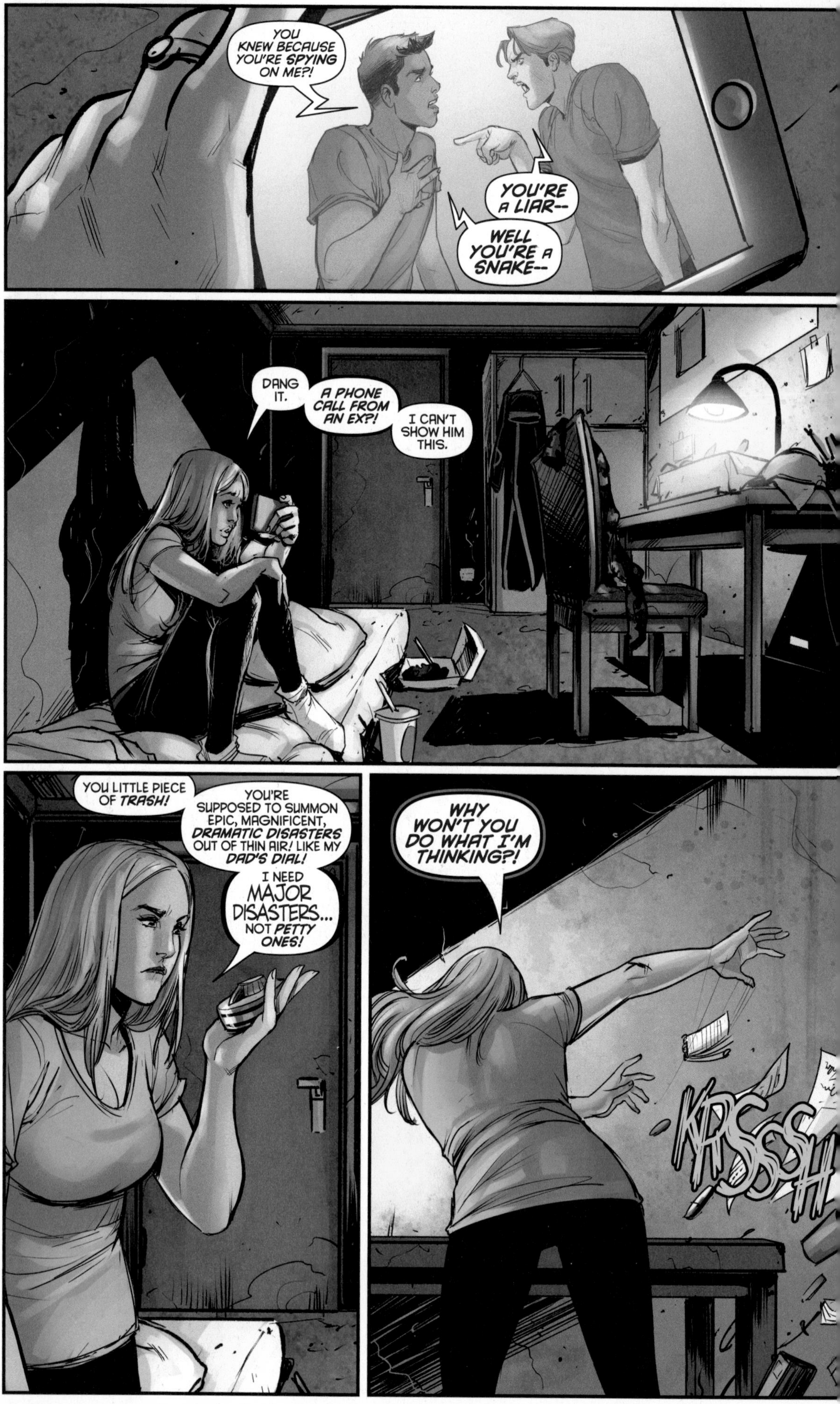
YOU KNEW BECAUSE YOU'RE SPYING ON ME?!
YOU'RE A LIAR--
WELL YOU'RE A SNAKE--
DANG IT.
A PHONE CALL FROM AN EX?!
I CAN'T SHOW HIM THIS.
YOU LITTLE PIECE OF TRASH!
YOU'RE SUPPOSED TO SUMMON EPIC, MAGNIFICENT, DRAMATIC DISASTERS OUT OF THIN AIR! LIKE MY DAD'S DIAL!
I NEED MAJOR DISASTERS... NOT PETTY ONES!
WHY WON'T YOU DO WHAT I'M THINKING?!
KRSSSH

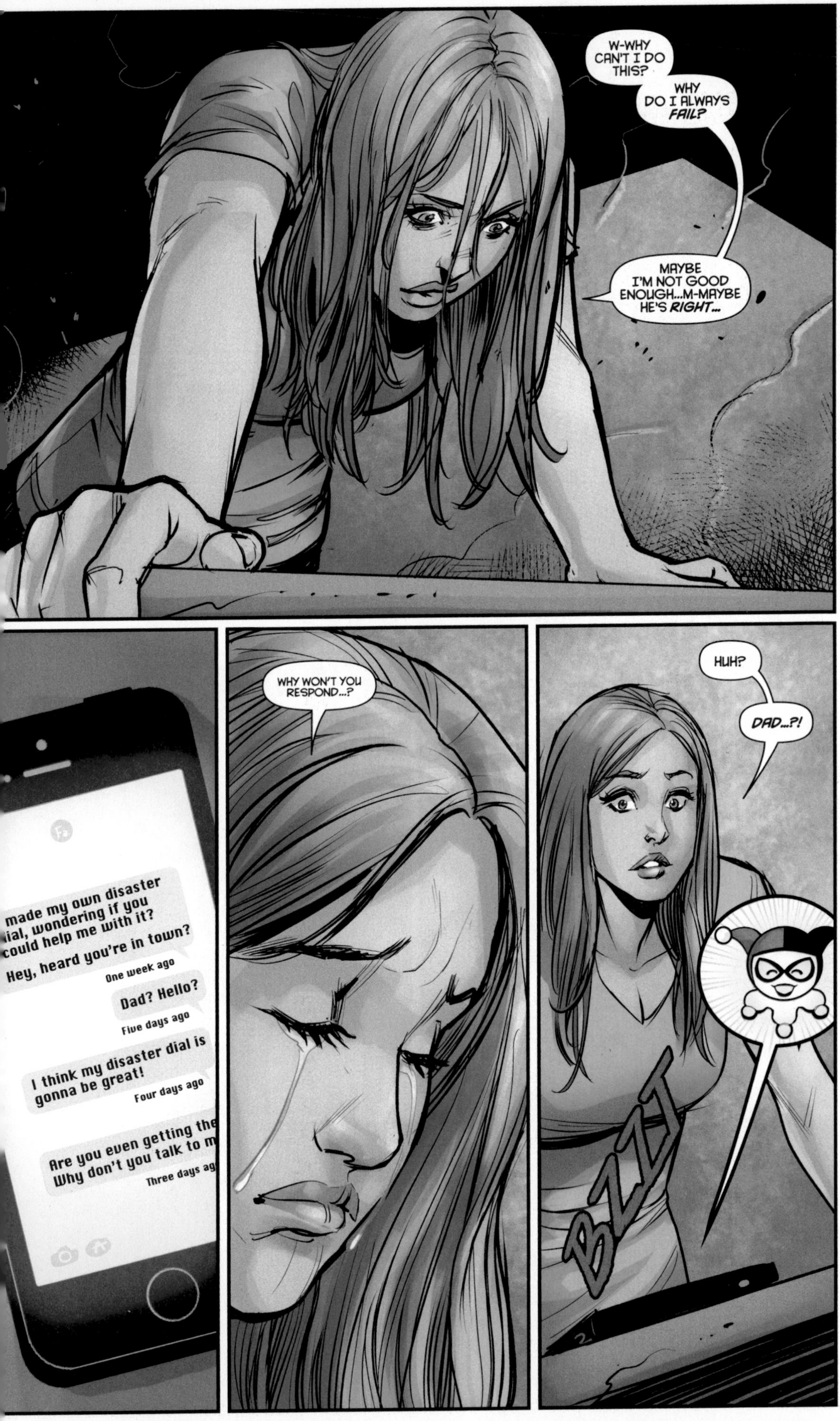
W-WHY CAN'T I DO THIS?
WHY DO I ALWAYS *FAIL?*
MAYBE I'M NOT GOOD ENOUGH...M-MAYBE HE'S *RIGHT...*
made my own disaster
ial, wondering if you
could help me with it?
Hey, heard you're in town?
One week ago
Dad? Hello?
Five days ago
I think my disaster dial is gonna be great!
Four days ago
Are you even getting the
Why don't you talk to m
Three days ag
WHY WON'T YOU RESPOND...?
HUH?
DAD...?!
BZZT

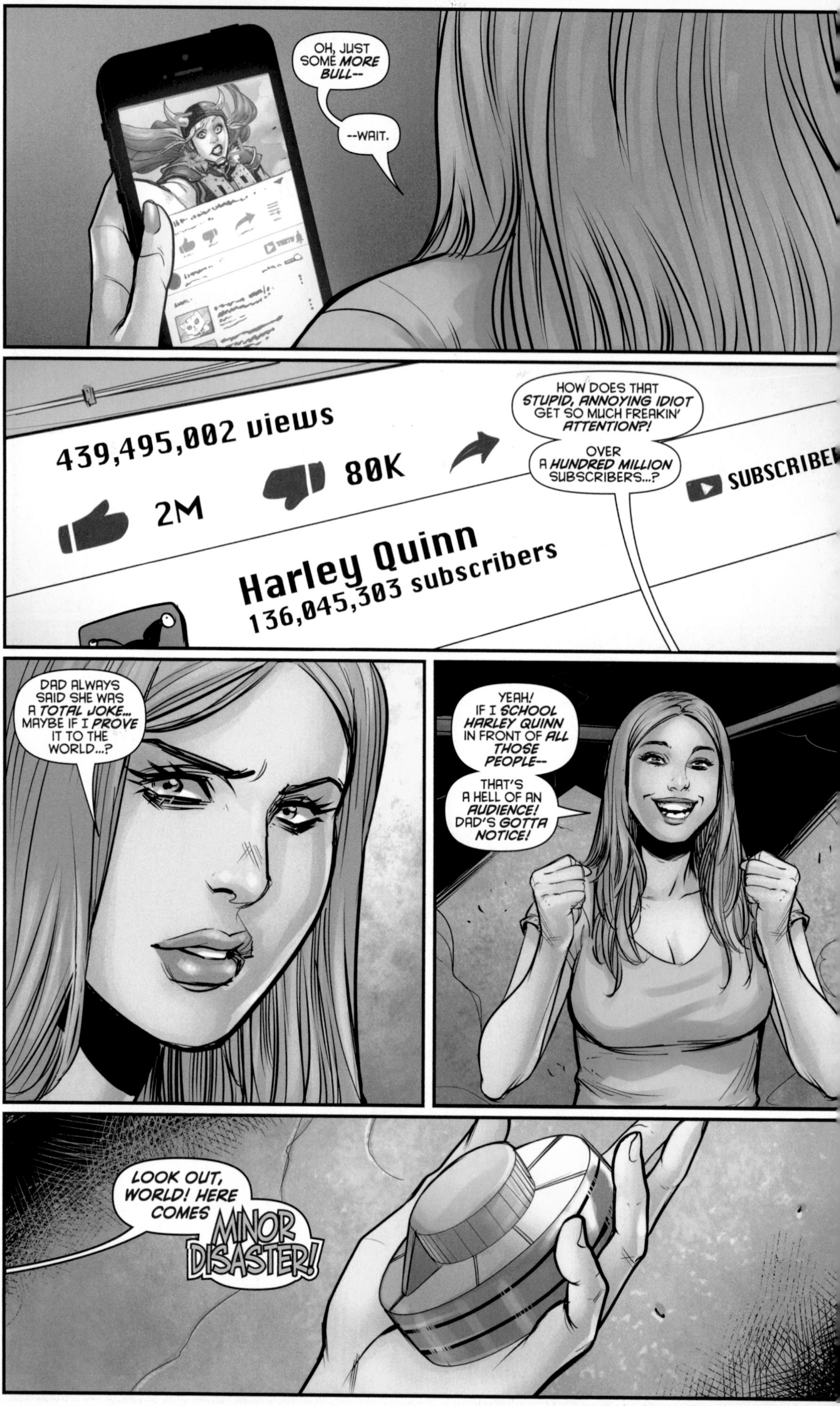
OH, JUST SOME MORE BULL--
--WAIT.
439,495,002 views
2M
80K
SUBSCRIBE
Harley Quinn
136,045,303 subscribers
HOW DOES THAT STUPID, ANNOYING IDIOT GET SO MUCH FREAKIN' ATTENTION?!
OVER A HUNDRED MILLION SUBSCRIBERS...?
DAD ALWAYS SAID SHE WAS A TOTAL JOKE... MAYBE IF I PROVE IT TO THE WORLD...?
YEAH! IF I SCHOOL HARLEY QUINN IN FRONT OF ALL THOSE PEOPLE--
THAT'S A HELL OF AN AUDIENCE! DAD'S GOTTA NOTICE!
LOOK OUT, WORLD! HERE COMES MINOR DISASTER!

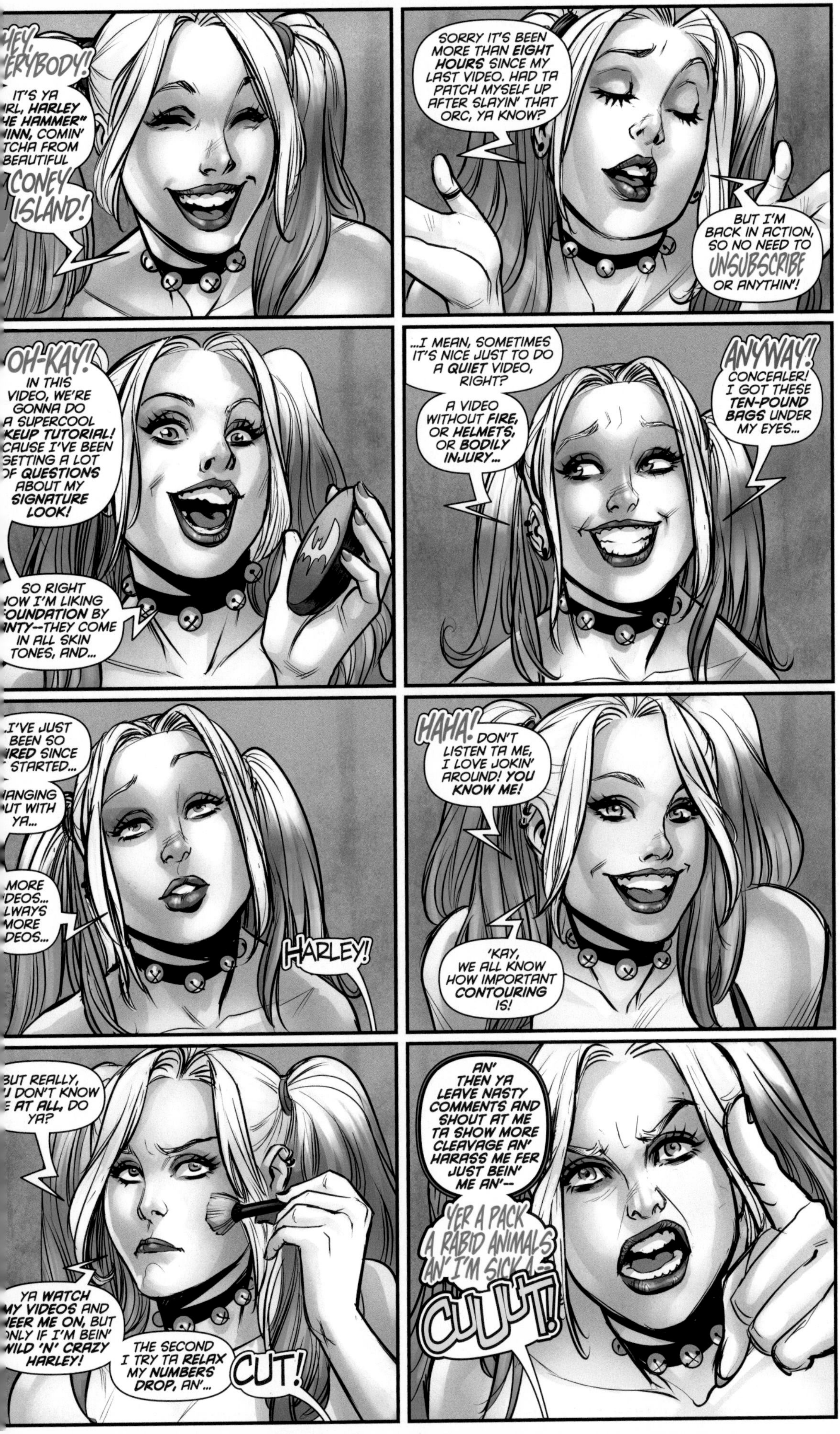
HEY, ERYBODY!
IT'S YA IRL, HARLEY HE HAMMER" INN, COMIN' TCHA FROM BEAUTIFUL CONEY ISLAND!
SORRY IT'S BEEN MORE THAN EIGHT HOURS SINCE MY LAST VIDEO. HAD TA PATCH MYSELF UP AFTER SLAYIN' THAT ORC, YA KNOW?
BUT I'M BACK IN ACTION, SO NO NEED TO UNSUBSCRIBE OR ANYTHIN'!
OH-KAY! IN THIS VIDEO, WE'RE GONNA DO A SUPERCOOL KEUP TUTORIAL! CAUSE I'VE BEEN GETTING A LOT OF QUESTIONS ABOUT MY SIGNATURE LOOK!
SO RIGHT NOW I'M LIKING FOUNDATION BY NTY--THEY COME IN ALL SKIN TONES, AND...
...I MEAN, SOMETIMES IT'S NICE JUST TO DO A QUIET VIDEO, RIGHT?
A VIDEO WITHOUT FIRE, OR HELMETS, OR BODILY INJURY...
ANYWAY! CONCEALER! I GOT THESE TEN-POUND BAGS UNDER MY EYES...
I'VE JUST BEEN SO IRED SINCE STARTED...
HANGING UT WITH YA...
MORE IDEOS... ALWAYS MORE IDEOS...
HARLEY!
HAHA! DON'T LISTEN TA ME, I LOVE JOKIN' AROUND! YOU KNOW ME!
'KAY, WE ALL KNOW HOW IMPORTANT CONTOURING IS!
BUT REALLY, U DON'T KNOW E AT ALL, DO YA?
YA WATCH MY VIDEOS AND HEER ME ON, BUT NLY IF I'M BEIN' WILD 'N' CRAZY HARLEY!
THE SECOND I TRY TA RELAX MY NUMBERS DROP, AN'...
CUT!
AN' THEN YA LEAVE NASTY COMMENTS AND SHOUT AT ME TA SHOW MORE CLEAVAGE AN' HARASS ME FER JUST BEIN' ME AN'--
YER A PACK A RABID ANIMALS AN' I'M SICK A...
CUUUT!

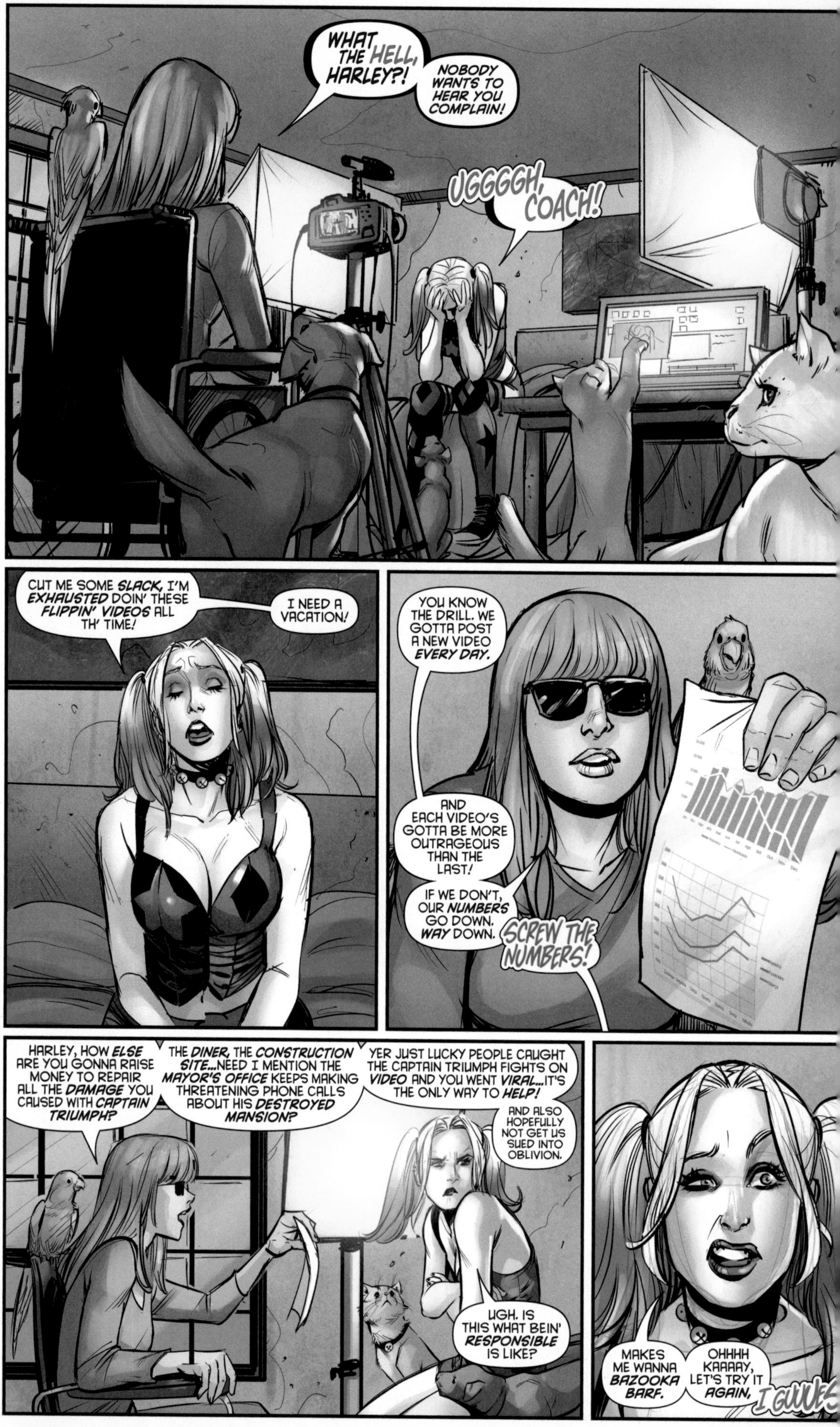
WHAT THE HELL, HARLEY?!
NOBODY WANTS TO HEAR YOU COMPLAIN!
UGGGGH, COACH!
CUT ME SOME SLACK, I'M EXHAUSTED DOIN' THESE FLIPPIN' VIDEOS ALL TH' TIME!
I NEED A VACATION!
YOU KNOW THE DRILL. WE GOTTA POST A NEW VIDEO EVERY DAY.
AND EACH VIDEO'S GOTTA BE MORE OUTRAGEOUS THAN THE LAST!
IF WE DON'T, OUR NUMBERS GO DOWN. WAY DOWN.
SCREW THE NUMBERS!
HARLEY, HOW ELSE ARE YOU GONNA RAISE MONEY TO REPAIR ALL THE DAMAGE YOU CAUSED WITH CAPTAIN TRIUMPH?
THE DINER, THE CONSTRUCTION SITE...NEED I MENTION THE MAYOR'S OFFICE KEEPS MAKING THREATENING PHONE CALLS ABOUT HIS DESTROYED MANSION?
YER JUST LUCKY PEOPLE CAUGHT THE CAPTAIN TRIUMPH FIGHTS ON VIDEO AND YOU WENT VIRAL...IT'S THE ONLY WAY TO HELP!
AND ALSO HOPEFULLY NOT GET US SUED INTO OBLIVION.
UGH. IS THIS WHAT BEIN' RESPONSIBLE IS LIKE?
MAKES ME WANNA BAZOOKA BARF.
OHHHH KAAAAY, LET'S TRY IT AGAIN.

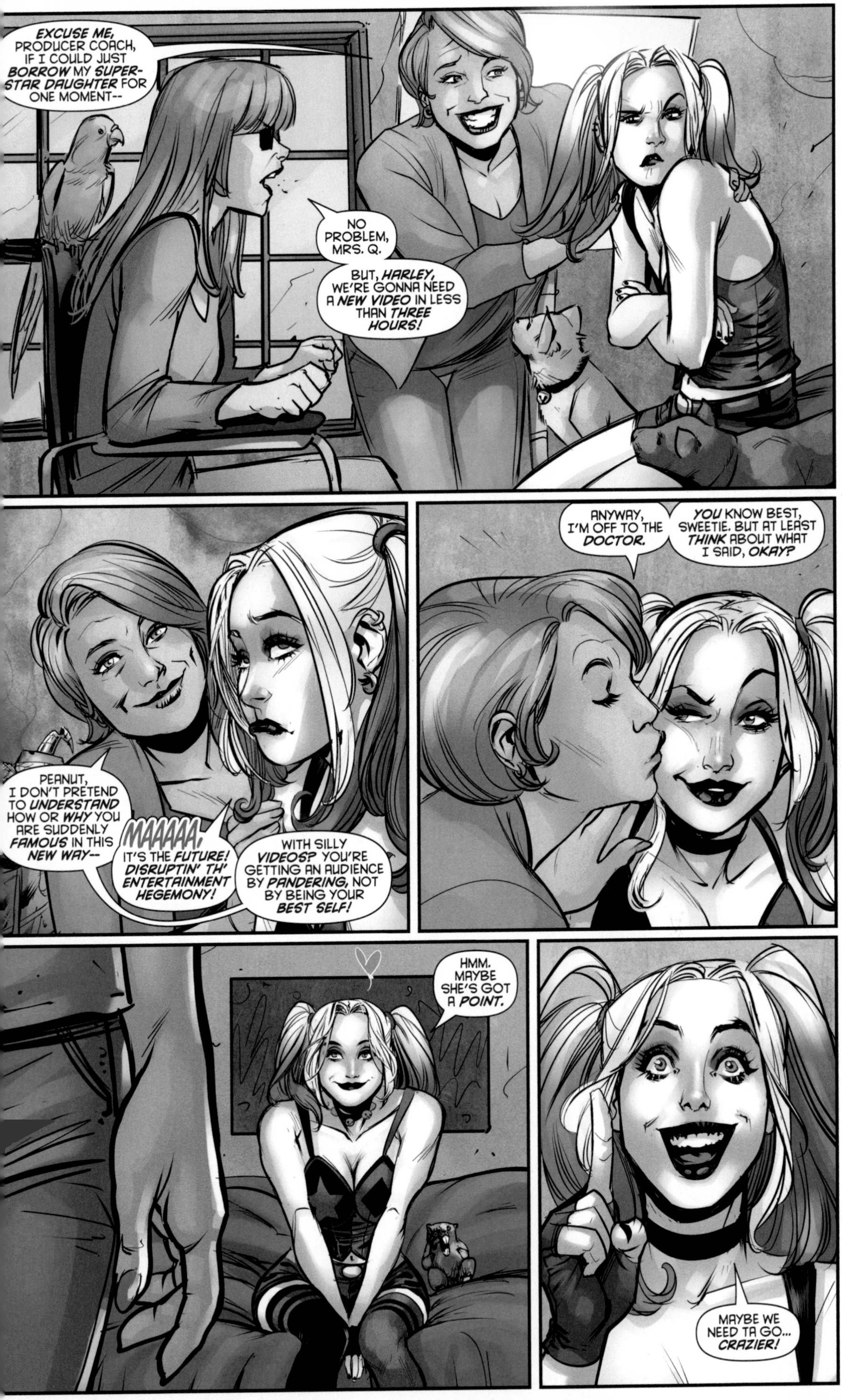

EXCUSE ME, PRODUCER COACH, IF I COULD JUST BORROW MY SUPER-STAR DAUGHTER FOR ONE MOMENT--
NO PROBLEM, MRS. Q.
BUT, HARLEY, WE'RE GONNA NEED A NEW VIDEO IN LESS THAN THREE HOURS!
PEANUT, I DON'T PRETEND TO UNDERSTAND HOW OR WHY YOU ARE SUDDENLY FAMOUS IN THIS NEW WAY--
MAAAAA, IT'S THE FUTURE! DISRUPTIN' TH' ENTERTAINMENT HEGEMONY!
WITH SILLY VIDEOS? YOU'RE GETTING AN AUDIENCE BY PANDERING, NOT BY BEING YOUR BEST SELF!
YOU KNOW BEST, SWEETIE. BUT AT LEAST THINK ABOUT WHAT I SAID, OKAY?
ANYWAY, I'M OFF TO THE DOCTOR.
HMM. MAYBE SHE'S GOT A POINT.
MAYBE WE NEED TA GO... CRAZIER!

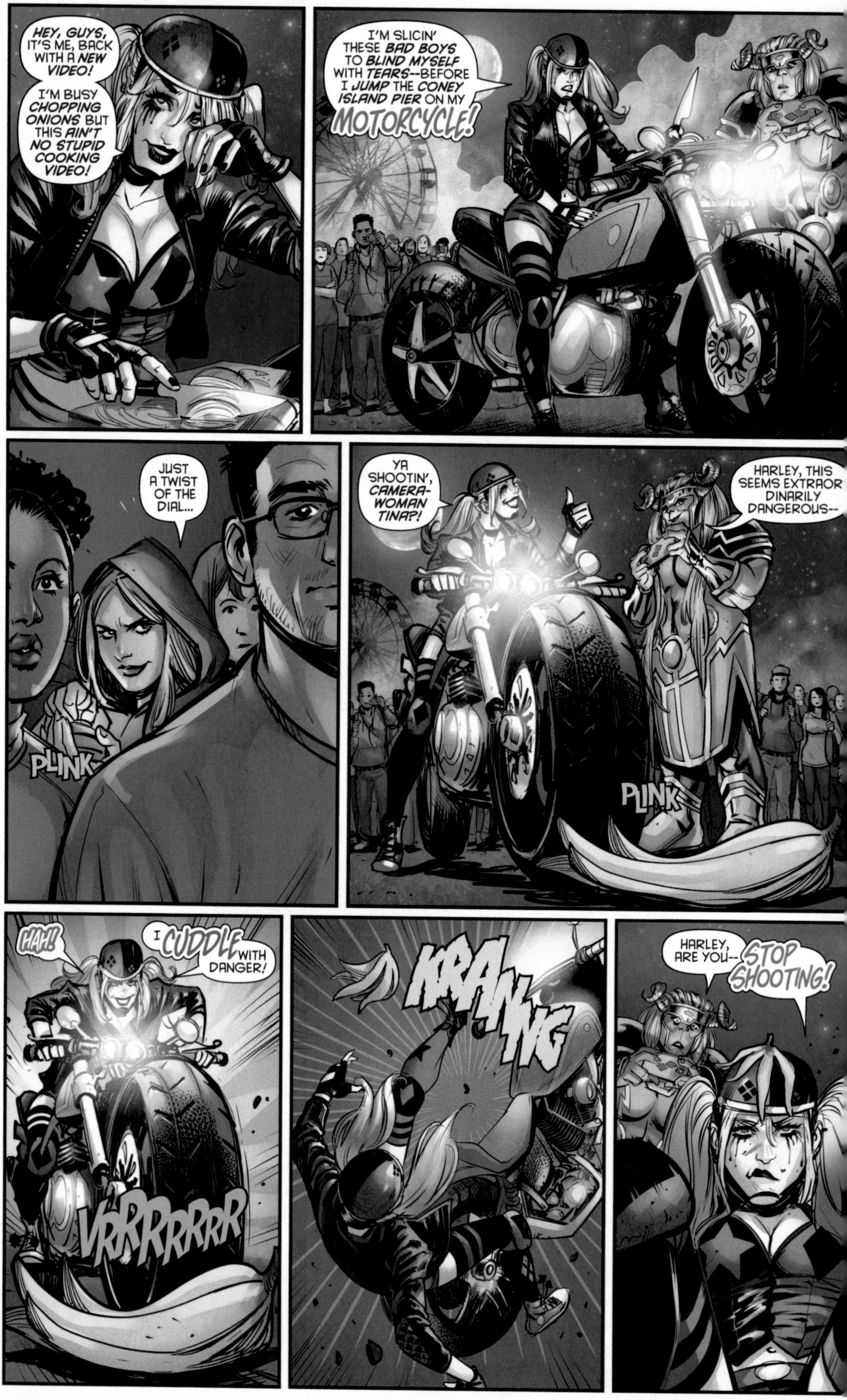
HEY, GUYS, IT'S ME, BACK WITH A NEW VIDEO!
I'M BUSY CHOPPING ONIONS BUT THIS AIN'T NO STUPID COOKING VIDEO!
I'M SLICIN' THESE BAD BOYS TO BLIND MYSELF WITH TEARS--BEFORE I JUMP THE CONEY ISLAND PIER ON MY MOTORCYCLE!
JUST A TWIST OF THE DIAL...
PLINK
YA SHOOTIN', CAMERA-WOMAN TINA?!
HARLEY, THIS SEEMS EXTRAOR DINARILY DANGEROUS--
PLINK
HAH!
I CUDDLE WITH DANGER!
VRRRRRRR
KRANNG
HARLEY, ARE YOU--
STOP SHOOTING!

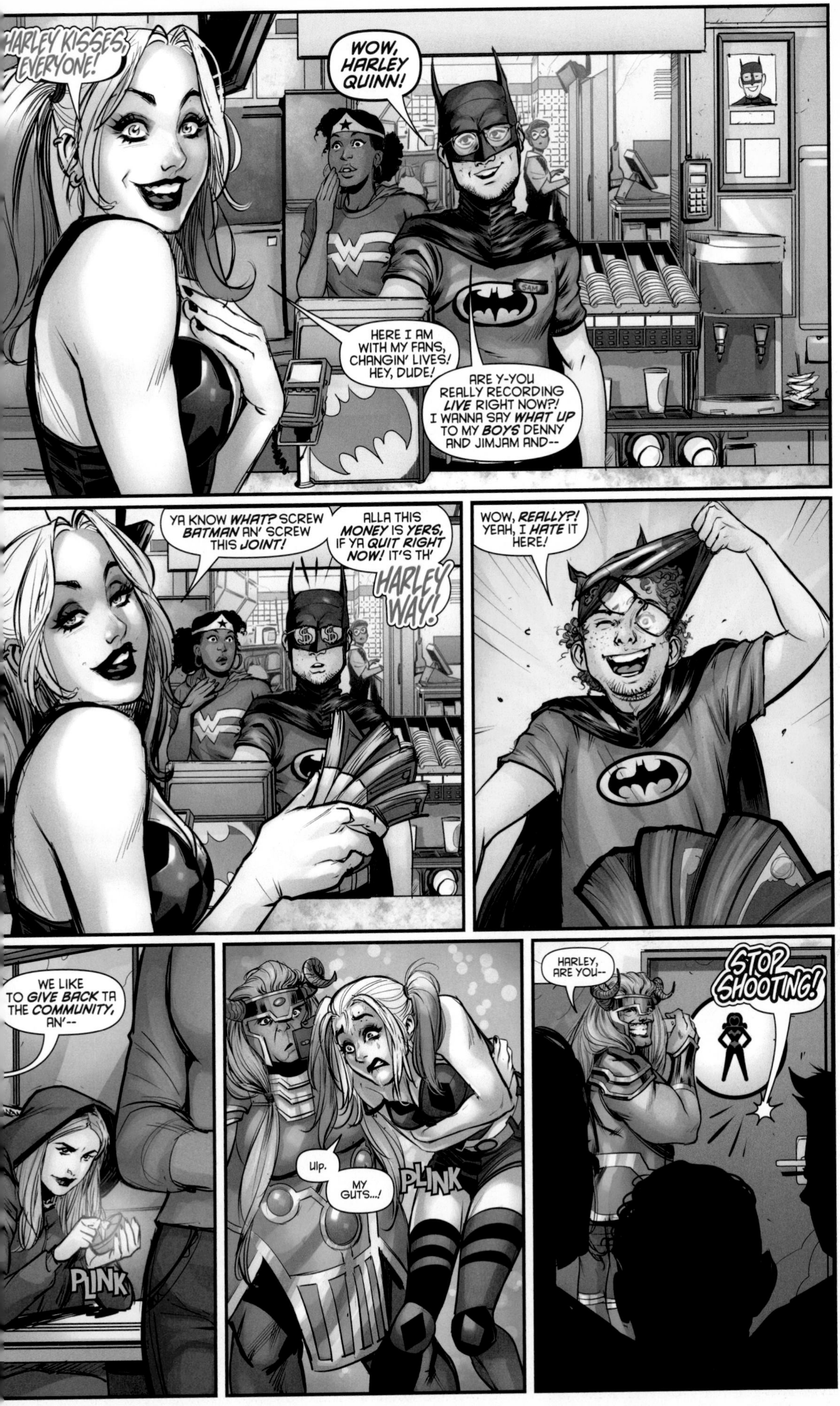

HARLEY KISSES, EVERYONE!
WOW, HARLEY QUINN!
HERE I AM WITH MY FANS, CHANGIN' LIVES! HEY, DUDE!
ARE Y-YOU REALLY RECORDING LIVE RIGHT NOW?! I WANNA SAY WHAT UP TO MY BOYS DENNY AND JIMJAM AND--
YA KNOW WHAT? SCREW BATMAN AN' SCREW THIS JOINT!
ALLA THIS MONEY IS YERS, IF YA QUIT RIGHT NOW! IT'S TH' HARLEY WAY!
WOW, REALLY?! YEAH, I HATE IT HERE!
WE LIKE TO GIVE BACK TA THE COMMUNITY, AN'--
PLINK
Ulp.
MY GUTS...!
PLINK
HARLEY, ARE YOU--
STOP SHOOTING!

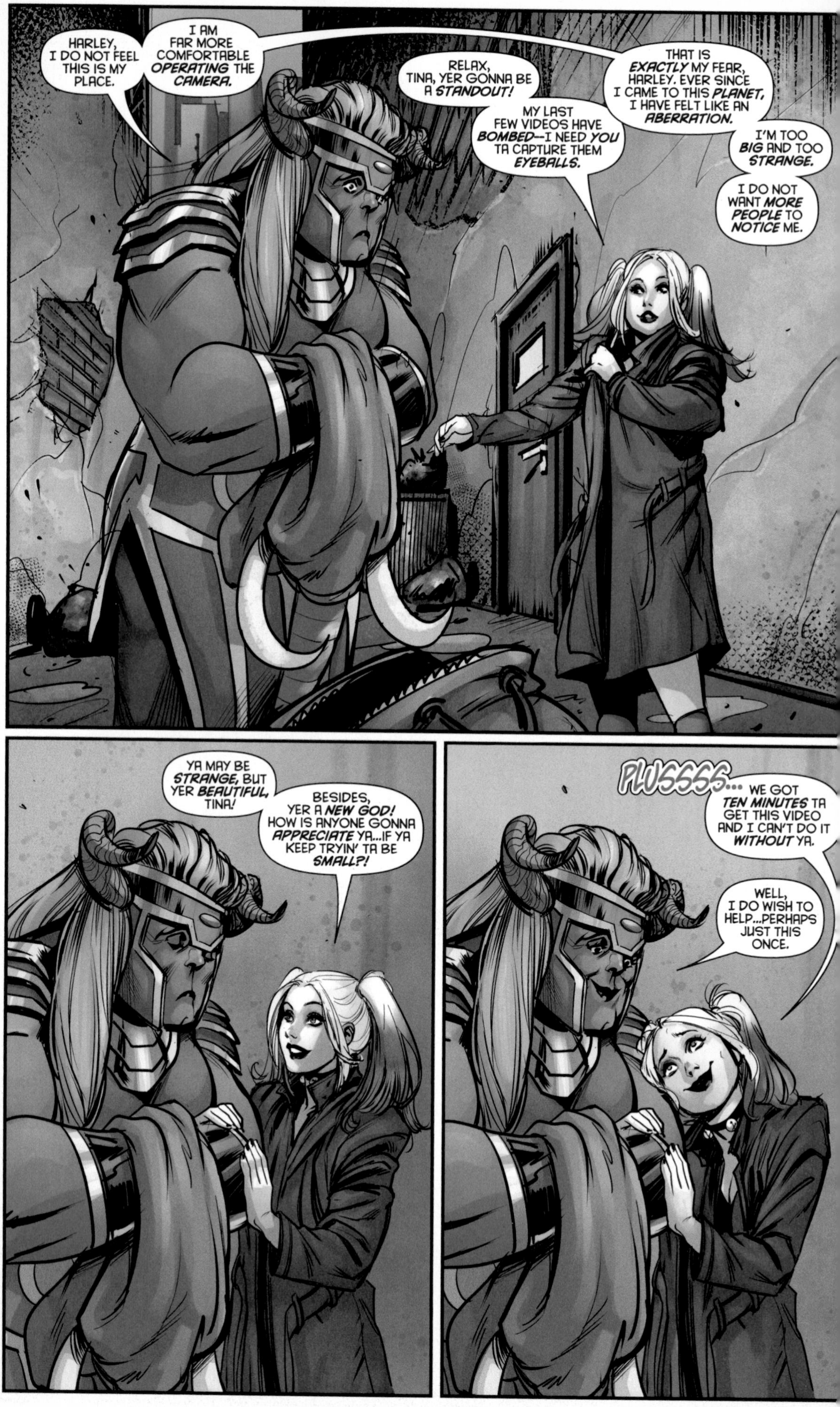
HARLEY, I DO NOT FEEL THIS IS MY PLACE.
I AM FAR MORE COMFORTABLE *OPERATING* THE *CAMERA.*
RELAX, TINA, YER GONNA BE A *STANDOUT!*
MY LAST FEW VIDEOS HAVE *BOMBED*--I NEED *YOU* TA CAPTURE THEM *EYEBALLS.*
THAT IS *EXACTLY* MY FEAR, HARLEY. EVER SINCE I CAME TO THIS *PLANET,* I HAVE FELT LIKE AN *ABERRATION.*
I'M TOO *BIG* AND TOO *STRANGE.*
I DO NOT WANT *MORE PEOPLE* TO *NOTICE* ME.
YA MAY BE *STRANGE,* BUT YER *BEAUTIFUL,* TINA!
BESIDES, YER A *NEW GOD!* HOW IS ANYONE GONNA *APPRECIATE* YA...IF YA KEEP TRYIN' TA BE *SMALL?!*
PLUSSSS...
WE GOT *TEN MINUTES* TA GET THIS VIDEO AND I CAN'T DO IT *WITHOUT* YA.
WELL, I DO WISH TO HELP...PERHAPS JUST THIS ONCE.

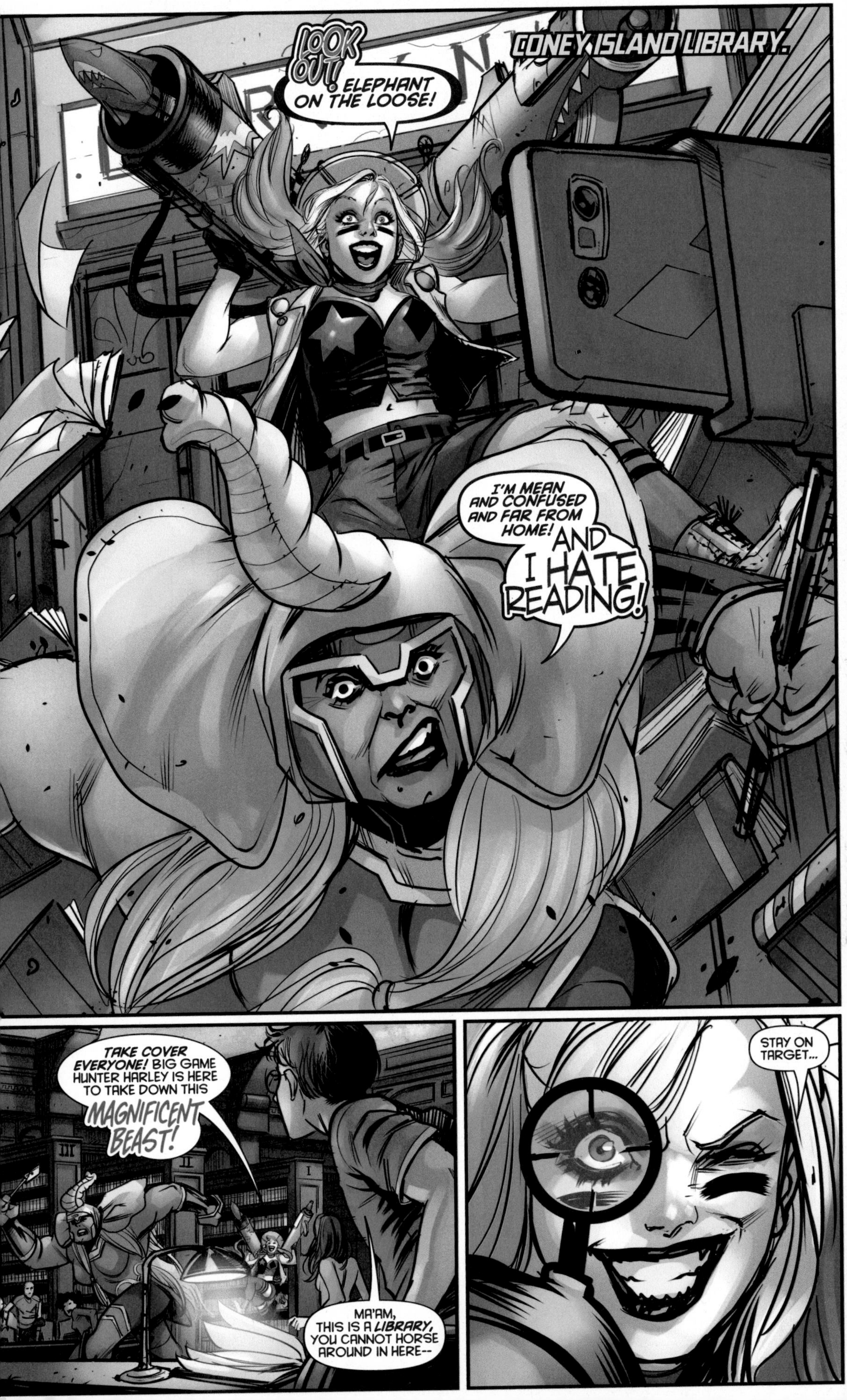
CONEY ISLAND LIBRARY.
LOOK OUT! ELEPHANT ON THE LOOSE!
I'M MEAN AND CONFUSED AND FAR FROM HOME! AND I HATE READING!
TAKE COVER EVERYONE! BIG GAME HUNTER HARLEY IS HERE TO TAKE DOWN THIS MAGNIFICENT BEAST!
MA'AM, THIS IS A LIBRARY, YOU CANNOT HORSE AROUND IN HERE--
STAY ON TARGET...

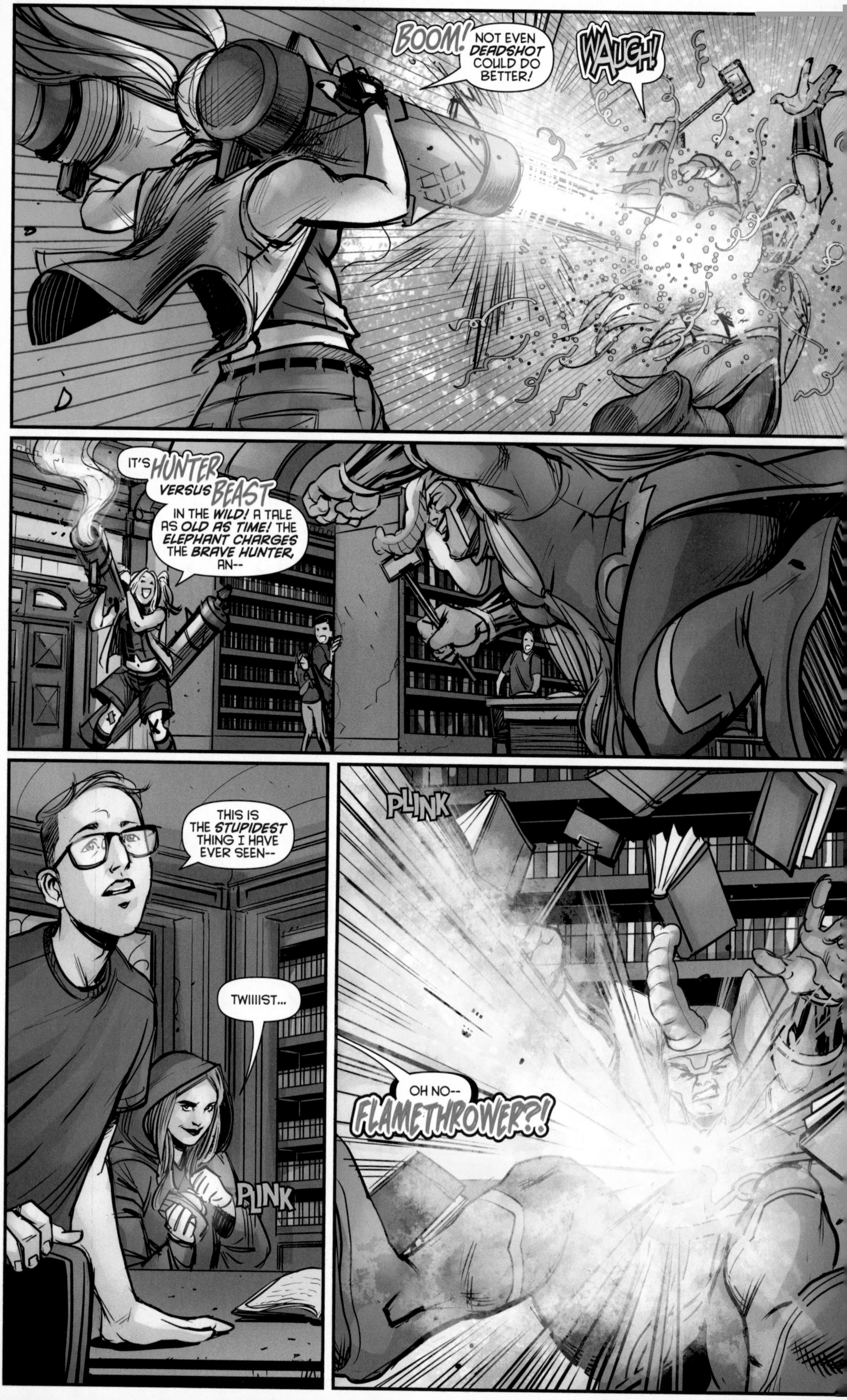
BOOM!
NOT EVEN DEADSHOT COULD DO BETTER!
WAUGH!
IT'S HUNTER VERSUS BEAST IN THE WILD! A TALE AS OLD AS TIME! THE ELEPHANT CHARGES THE BRAVE HUNTER, AN--
THIS IS THE STUPIDEST THING I HAVE EVER SEEN--
TWIIIIST...
PLINK
PLINK
OH NO--
FLAMETHROWER?!

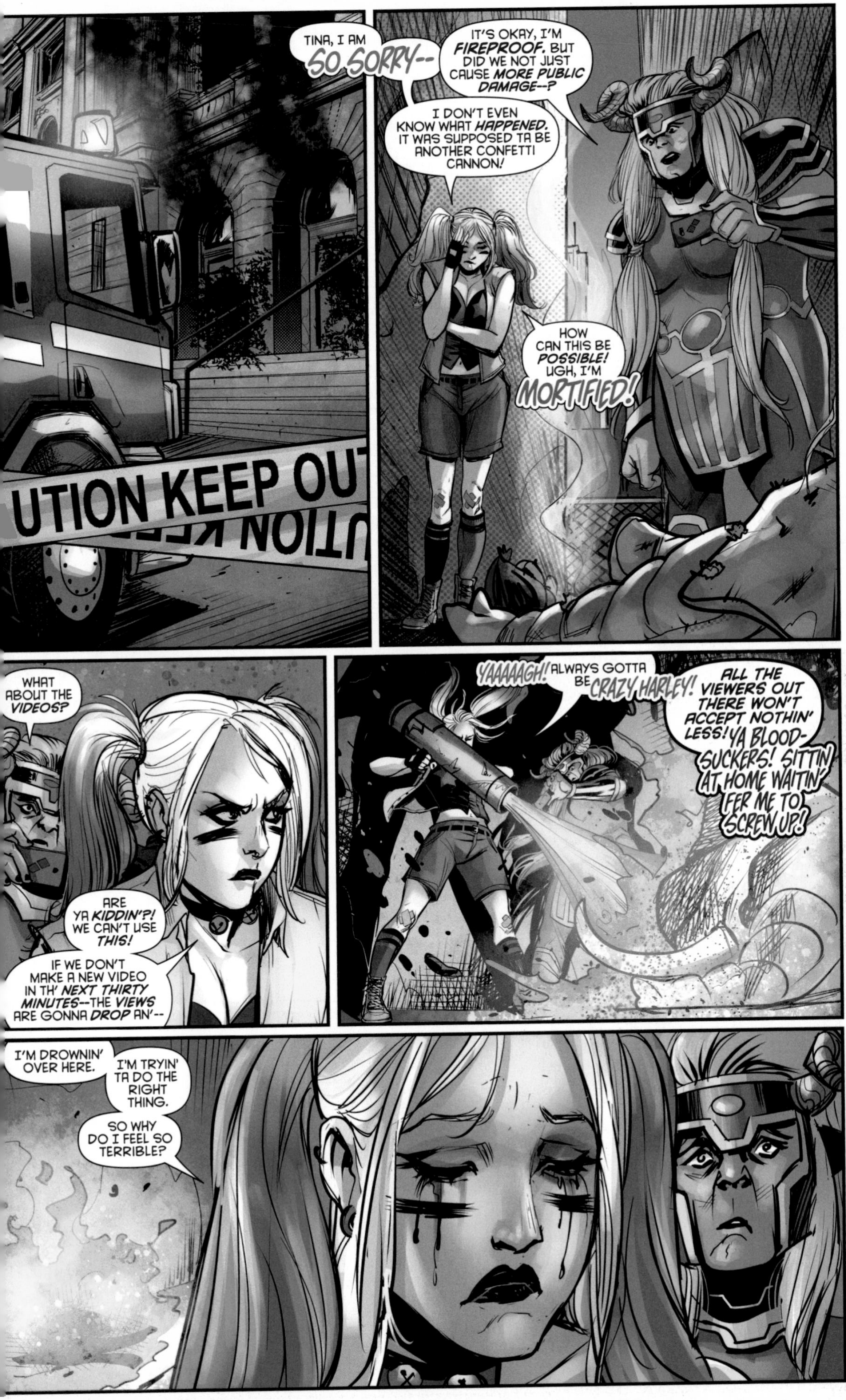
UTION KEEP OUT
TINA, I AM SO SORRY--
IT'S OKAY, I'M FIREPROOF. BUT DID WE NOT JUST CAUSE MORE PUBLIC DAMAGE--?
I DON'T EVEN KNOW WHAT HAPPENED. IT WAS SUPPOSED TA BE ANOTHER CONFETTI CANNON!
HOW CAN THIS BE POSSIBLE! UGH, I'M MORTIFIED!
WHAT ABOUT THE VIDEOS?
ARE YA KIDDIN'?! WE CAN'T USE THIS!
IF WE DON'T MAKE A NEW VIDEO IN TH' NEXT THIRTY MINUTES--THE VIEWS ARE GONNA DROP AN'--
YAAAAAGH!
ALWAYS GOTTA BE CRAZY HARLEY!
ALL THE VIEWERS OUT THERE WON'T ACCEPT NOTHIN' LESS! YA BLOOD-SUCKERS! SITTIN' AT HOME WAITIN' FER ME TO SCREW UP!
I'M DROWNIN' OVER HERE.
I'M TRYIN' TA DO THE RIGHT THING.
SO WHY DO I FEEL SO TERRIBLE?

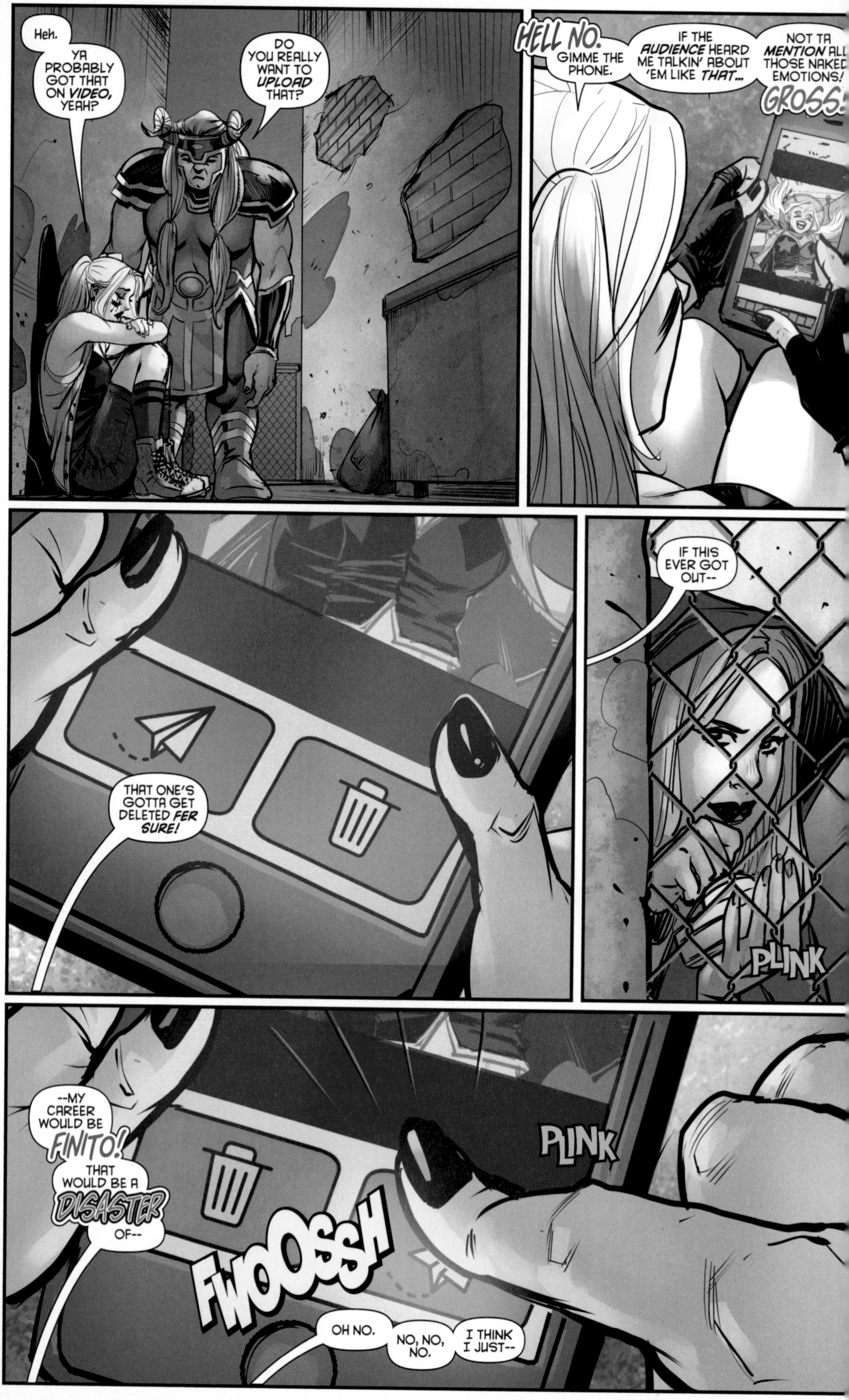
Heh.
YA PROBABLY GOT THAT ON VIDEO, YEAH?
DO YOU REALLY WANT TO UPLOAD THAT?
HELL NO.
GIMME THE PHONE.
IF THE AUDIENCE HEARD ME TALKIN' ABOUT 'EM LIKE THAT...
NOT TA MENTION ALL THOSE NAKED EMOTIONS!
GROSS!
THAT ONE'S GOTTA GET DELETED FER SURE!
IF THIS EVER GOT OUT--
PLINK
--MY CAREER WOULD BE FINITO!
THAT WOULD BE A DISASTER OF--
PLINK
FWOOSSH
OH NO.
NO, NO, NO.
I THINK I JUST--

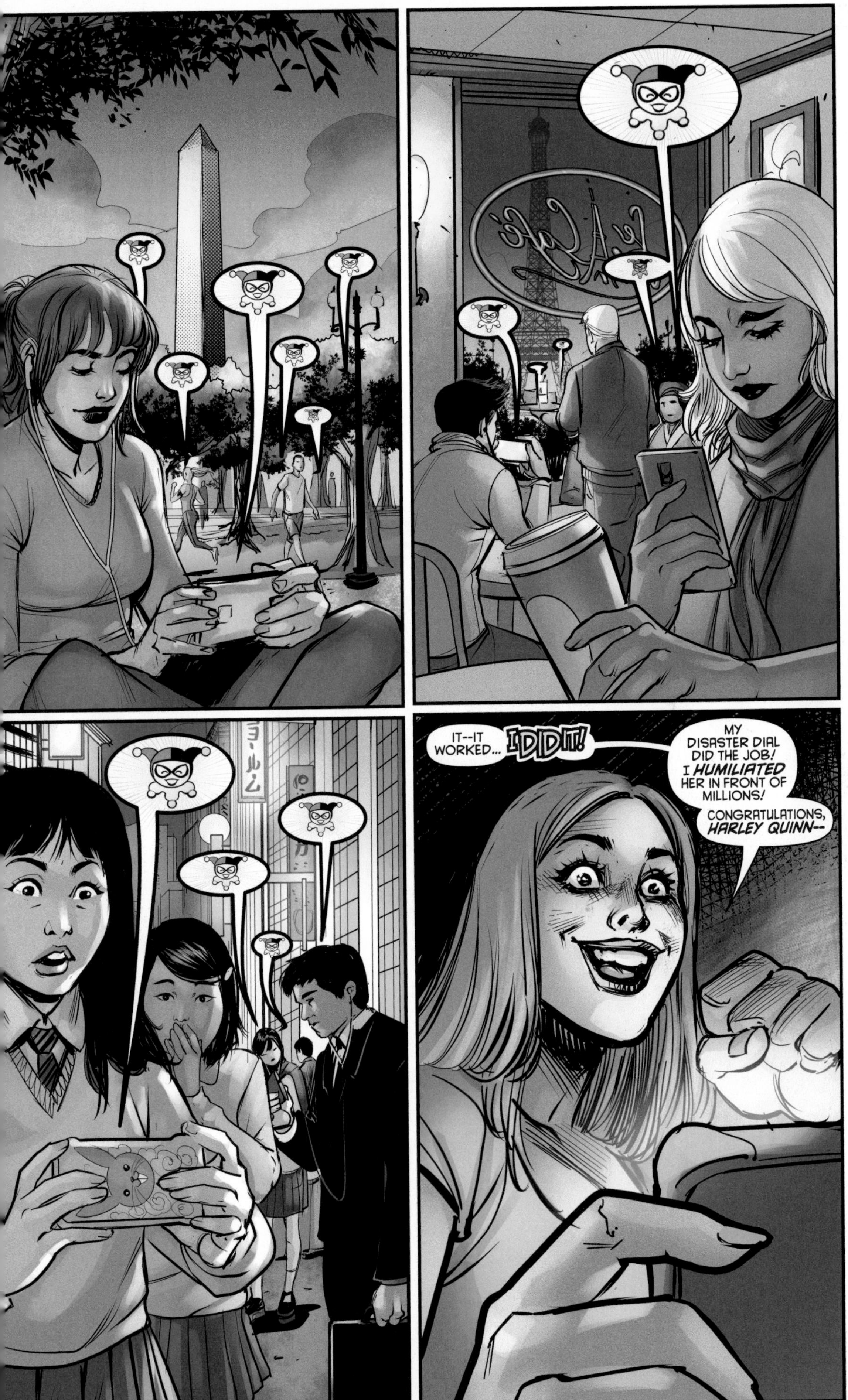
IT--IT WORKED... I DID IT!
MY DISASTER DIAL DID THE JOB! I HUMILIATED HER IN FRONT OF MILLIONS!
CONGRATULATIONS, HARLEY QUINN--

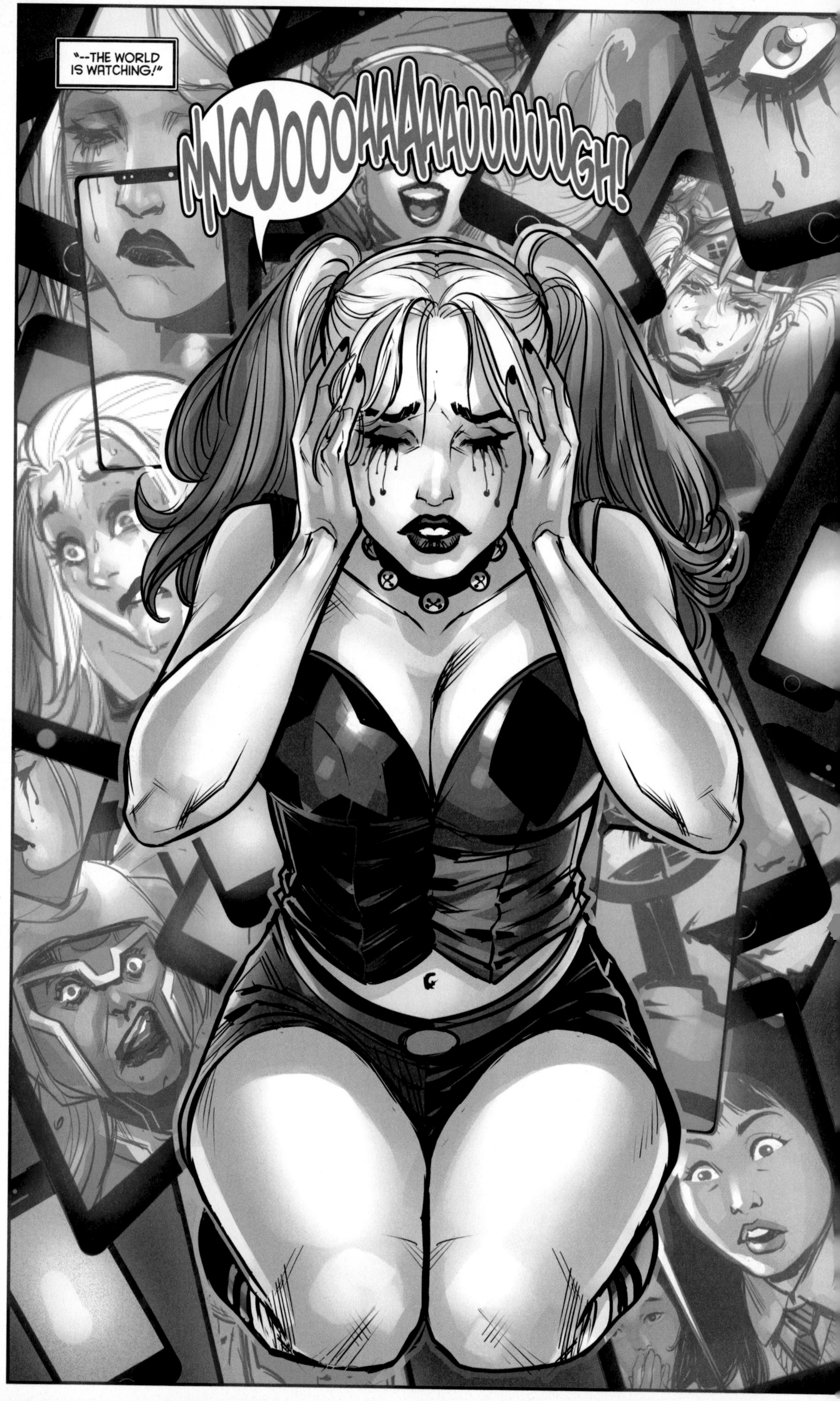
"--THE WORLD IS WATCHING!"
NNOOOOOAAAAAAUUUUUGH!

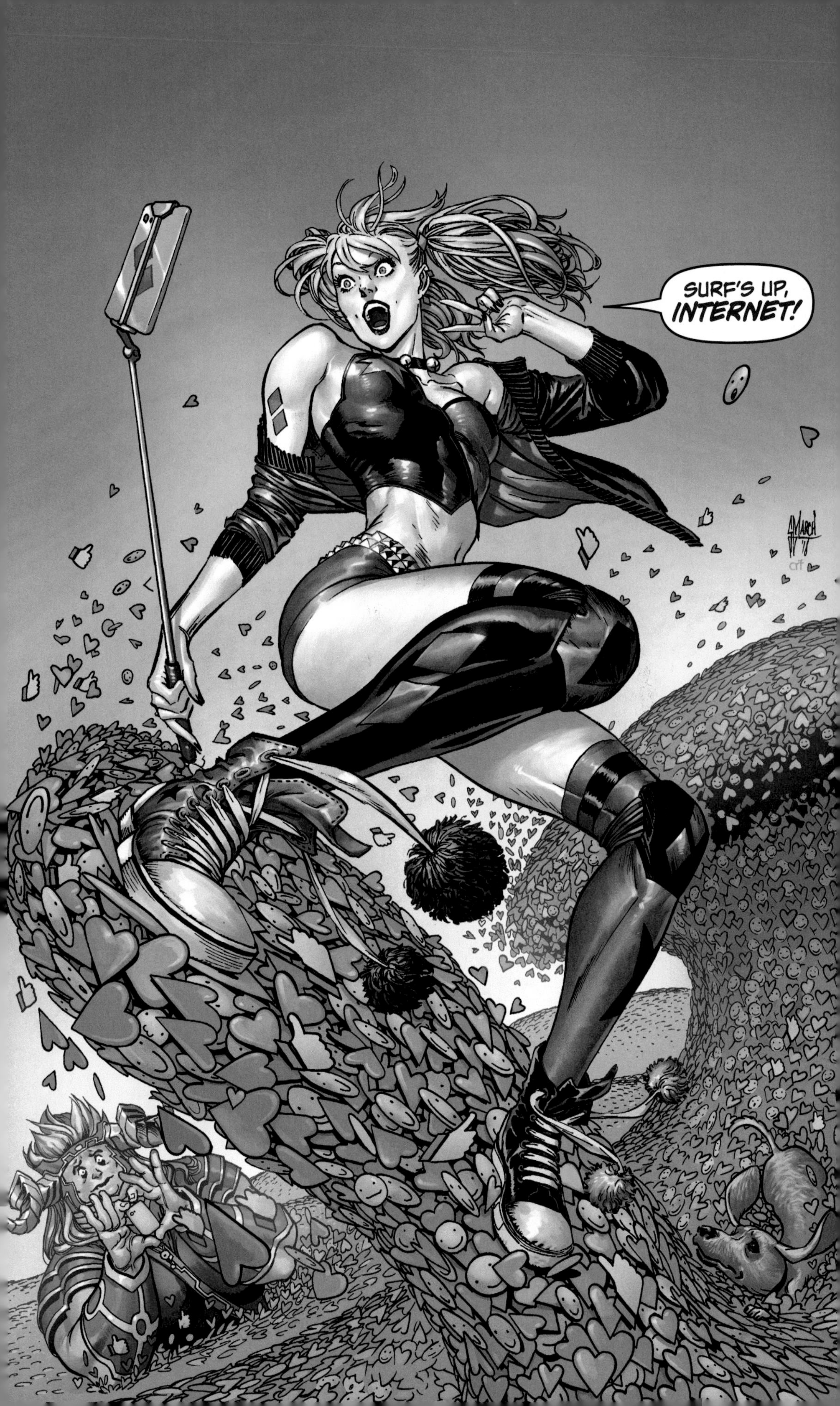
SURF'S UP, INTERNET!

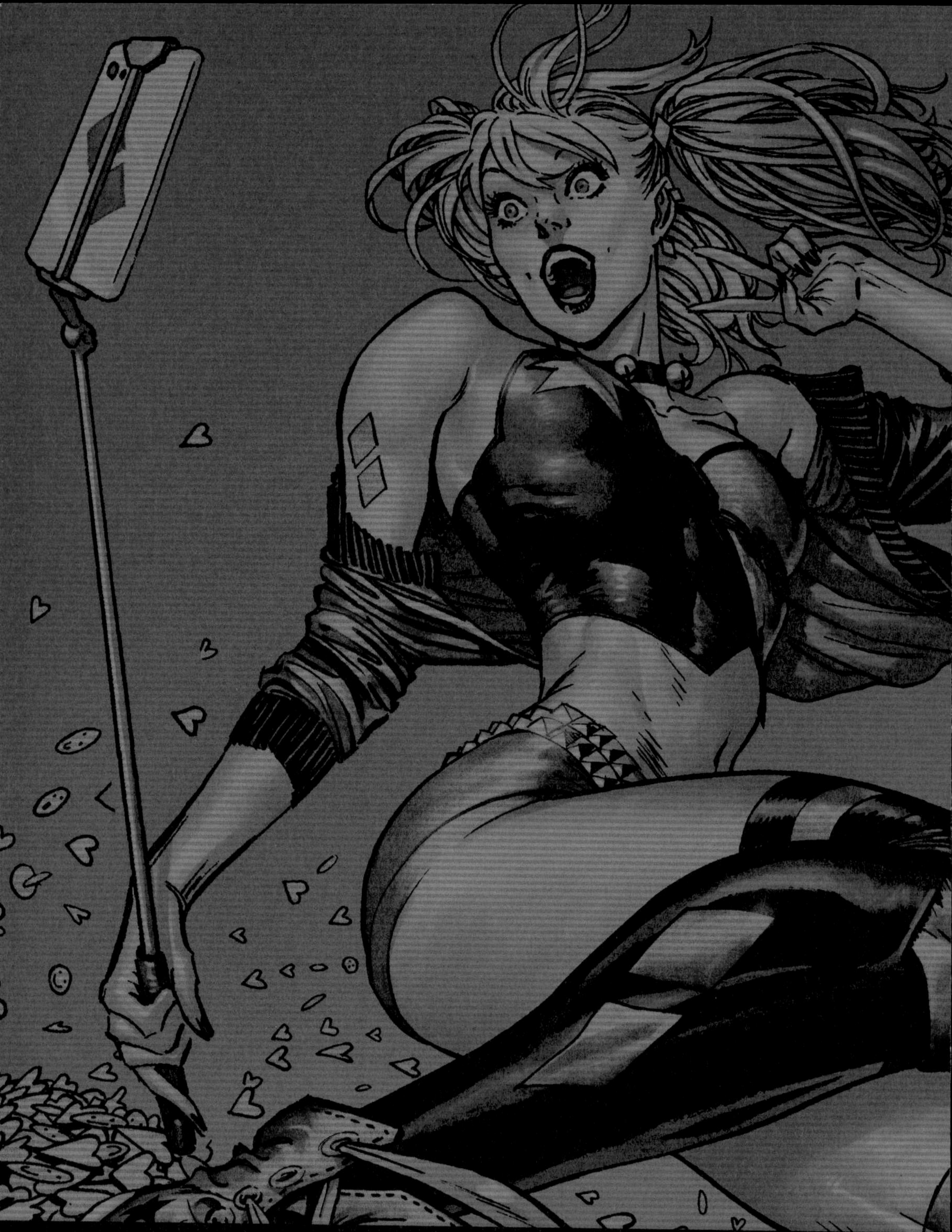

HARLEY QUINN
#54

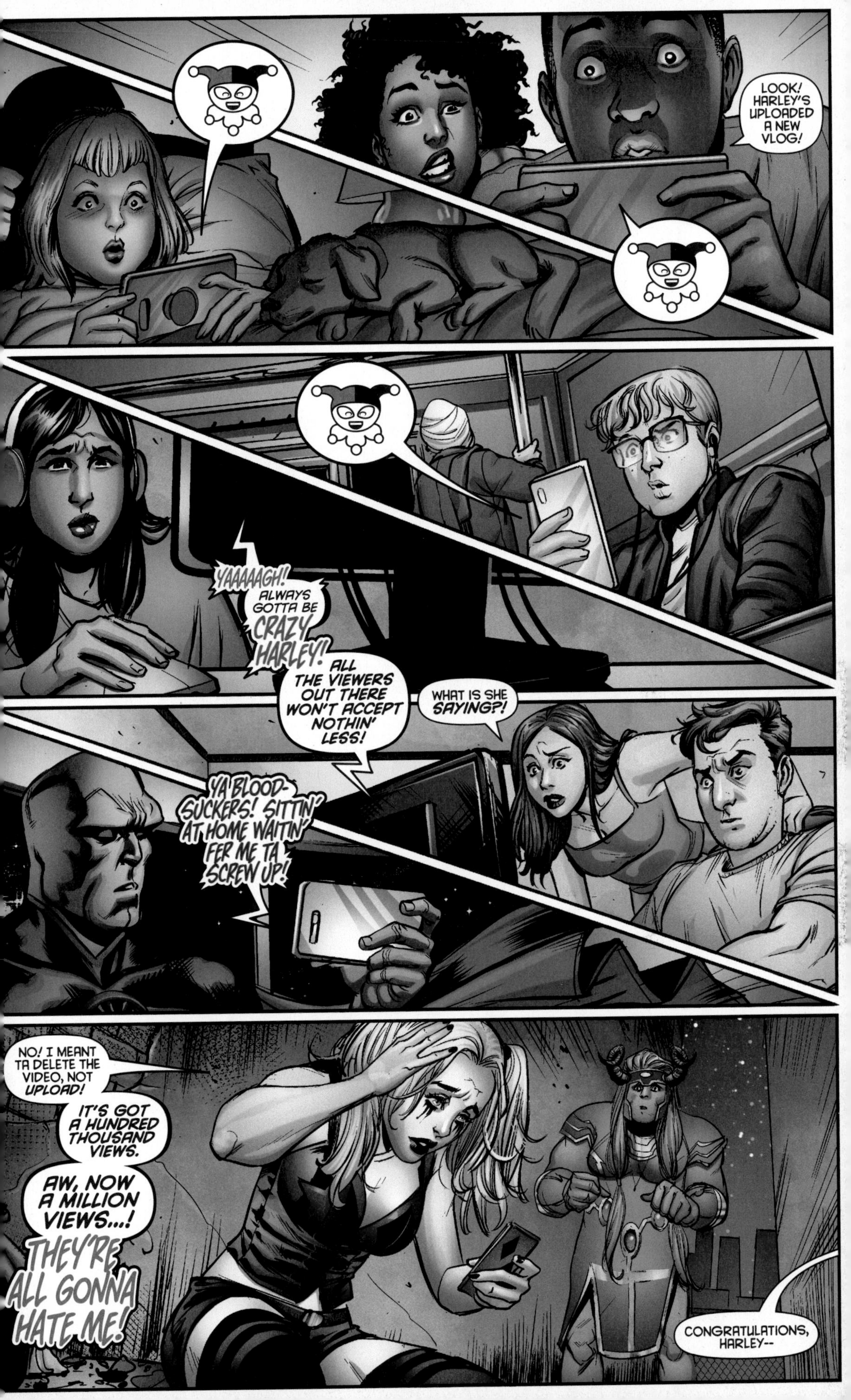

LOOK! HARLEY'S UPLOADED A NEW VLOG!
YAAAAAGH!
ALWAYS GOTTA BE CRAZY HARLEY!
ALL THE VIEWERS OUT THERE WON'T ACCEPT NOTHIN' LESS!
WHAT IS SHE SAYING?!
YA BLOOD-SUCKERS! SITTIN' AT HOME WAITIN' FER ME TA SCREW UP!
NO! I MEANT TA DELETE THE VIDEO, NOT UPLOAD!
IT'S GOT A HUNDRED THOUSAND VIEWS.
AW, NOW A MILLION VIEWS...!
THEY'RE ALL GONNA HATE ME!
CONGRATULATIONS, HARLEY--

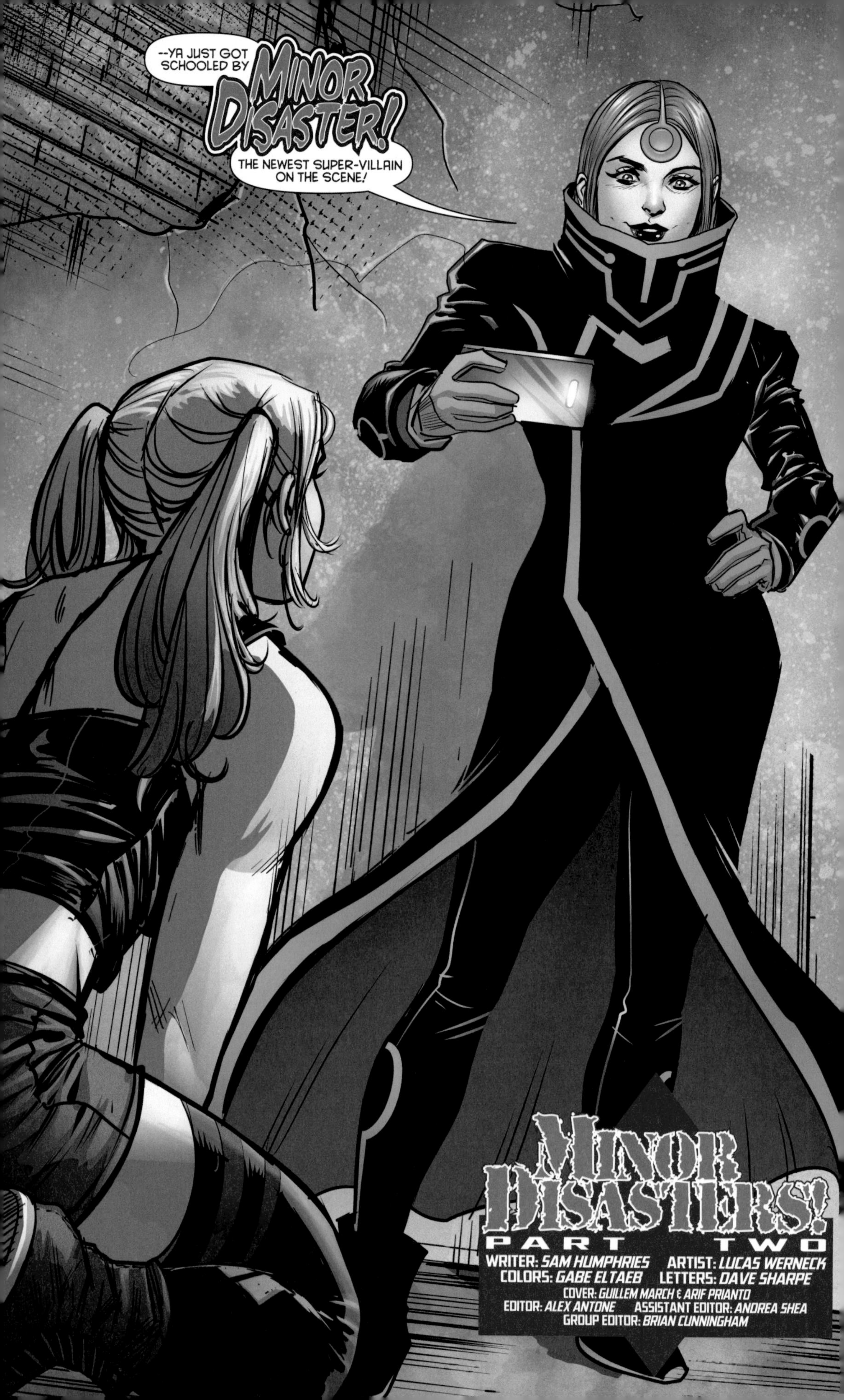
--YA JUST GOT SCHOOLED BY MINOR DISASTER! THE NEWEST SUPER-VILLAIN ON THE SCENE!
MINOR DISASTERS! PART TWO
WRITER: SAM HUMPHRIES ARTIST: LUCAS WERNECK
COLORS: GABE ELTAEB LETTERS: DAVE SHARPE
COVER: GUILLEM MARCH & ARIF PRIANTO
EDITOR: ALEX ANTONE ASSISTANT EDITOR: ANDREA SHEA
GROUP EDITOR: BRIAN CUNNINGHAM

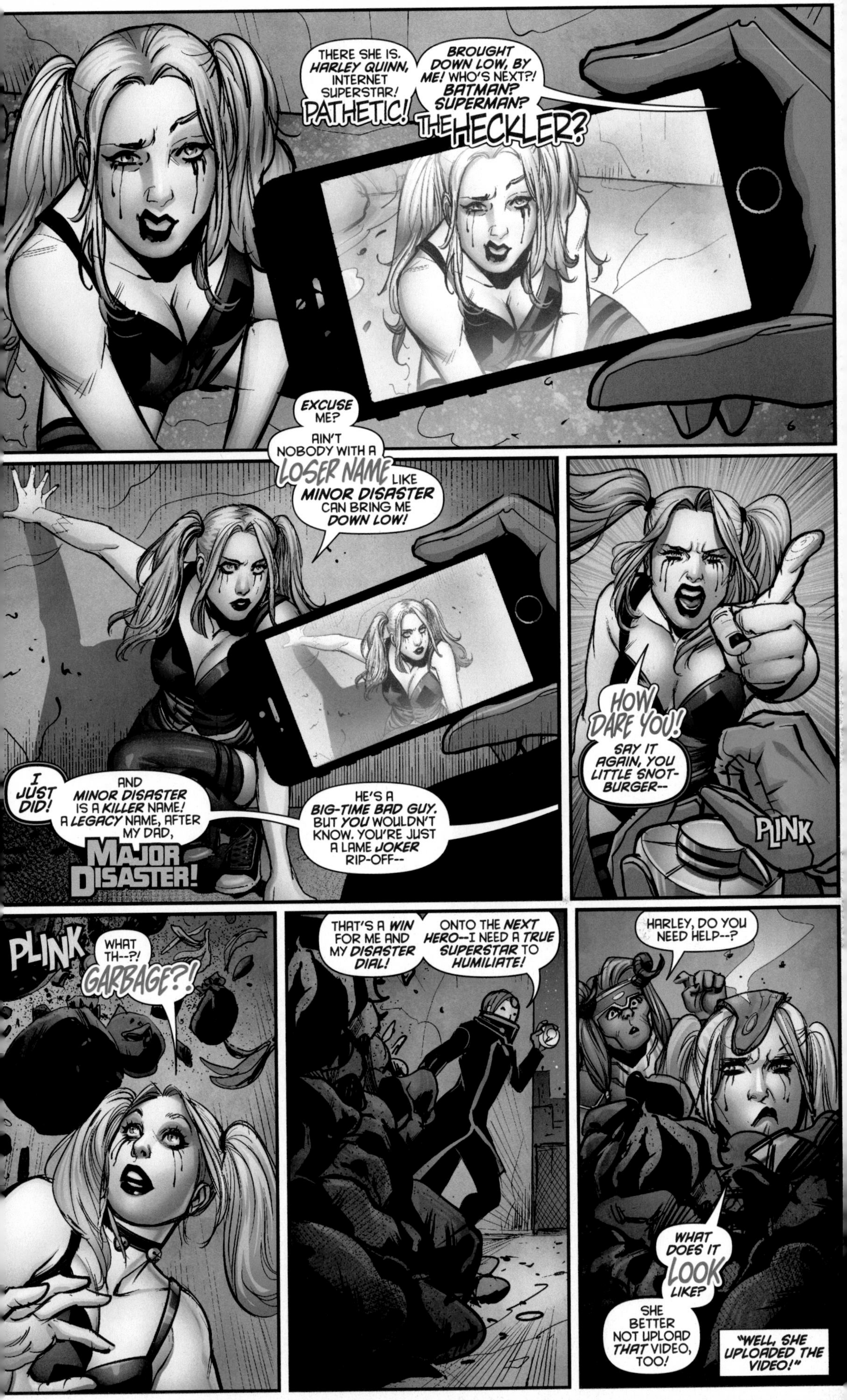
THERE SHE IS. HARLEY QUINN, INTERNET SUPERSTAR! PATHETIC!
BROUGHT DOWN LOW, BY ME! WHO'S NEXT?! BATMAN? SUPERMAN? THE HECKLER?
EXCUSE ME?
AIN'T NOBODY WITH A LOSER NAME LIKE MINOR DISASTER CAN BRING ME DOWN LOW!
HOW DARE YOU!
SAY IT AGAIN, YOU LITTLE SNOT-BURGER--
I JUST DID!
AND MINOR DISASTER IS A KILLER NAME! A LEGACY NAME, AFTER MY DAD, MAJOR DISASTER!
HE'S A BIG-TIME BAD GUY. BUT YOU WOULDN'T KNOW. YOU'RE JUST A LAME JOKER RIP-OFF--
PLINK
PLINK
WHAT TH--?! GARBAGE?!
THAT'S A WIN FOR ME AND MY DISASTER DIAL!
ONTO THE NEXT HERO--I NEED A TRUE SUPERSTAR TO HUMILIATE!
HARLEY, DO YOU NEED HELP--?
WHAT DOES IT LOOK LIKE?
SHE BETTER NOT UPLOAD THAT VIDEO, TOO!
"WELL, SHE UPLOADED THE VIDEO!"

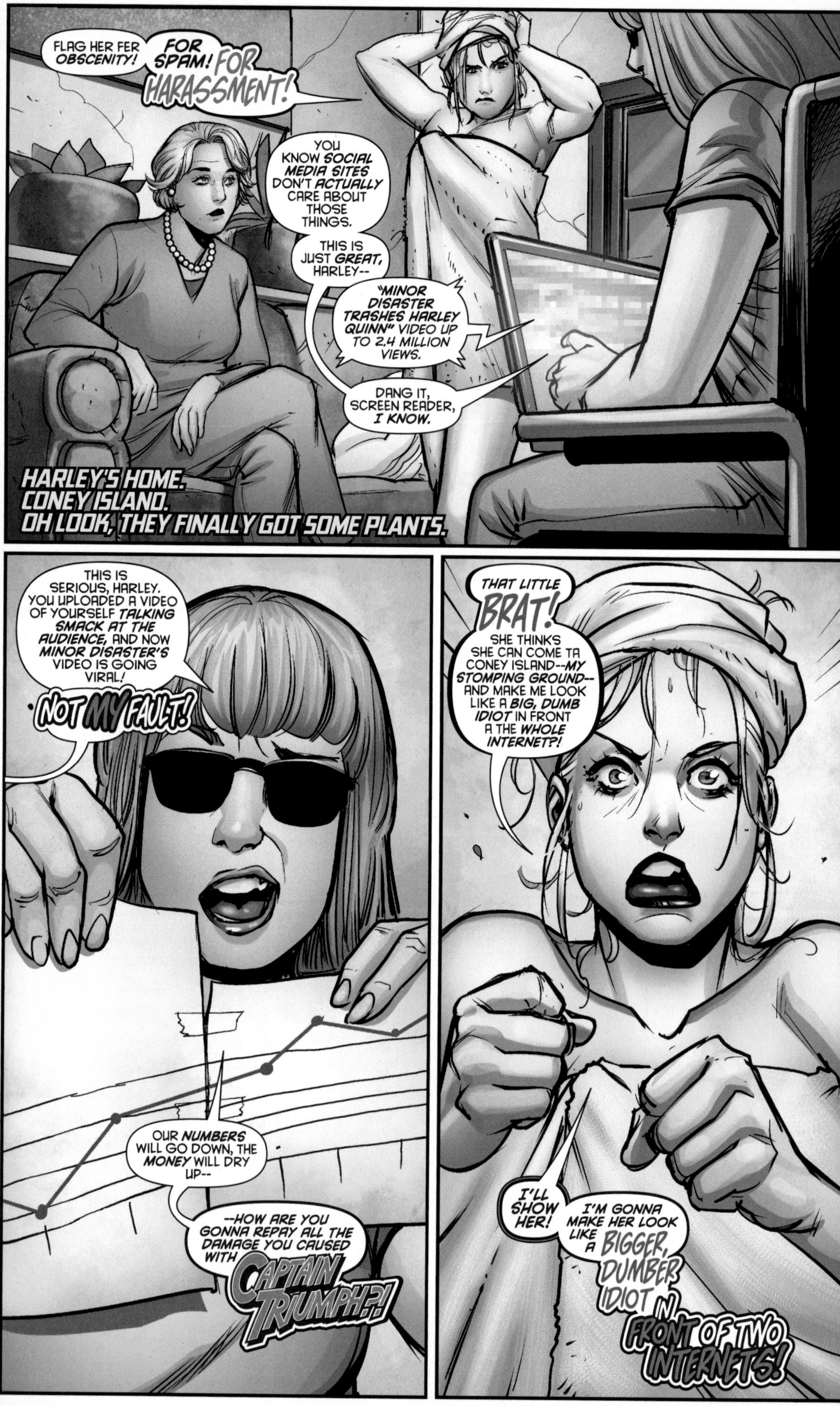

FLAG HER FER OBSCENITY!
FOR SPAM! FOR HARASSMENT!
YOU KNOW SOCIAL MEDIA SITES DON'T ACTUALLY CARE ABOUT THOSE THINGS.
THIS IS JUST GREAT, HARLEY--
"MINOR DISASTER TRASHES HARLEY QUINN" VIDEO UP TO 2.4 MILLION VIEWS.
DANG IT, SCREEN READER, I KNOW.
HARLEY'S HOME.
CONEY ISLAND.
OH LOOK, THEY FINALLY GOT SOME PLANTS.
THIS IS SERIOUS, HARLEY. YOU UPLOADED A VIDEO OF YOURSELF TALKING SMACK AT THE AUDIENCE, AND NOW MINOR DISASTER'S VIDEO IS GOING VIRAL!
NOT MY FAULT!
OUR NUMBERS WILL GO DOWN, THE MONEY WILL DRY UP--
--HOW ARE YOU GONNA REPAY ALL THE DAMAGE YOU CAUSED WITH CAPTAIN TRIUMPH?!
THAT LITTLE BRAT!
SHE THINKS SHE CAN COME TA CONEY ISLAND--MY STOMPING GROUND--AND MAKE ME LOOK LIKE A BIG, DUMB IDIOT IN FRONT A THE WHOLE INTERNET?!
I'LL SHOW HER!
I'M GONNA MAKE HER LOOK LIKE A BIGGER, DUMBER IDIOT IN FRONT OF TWO INTERNETS!

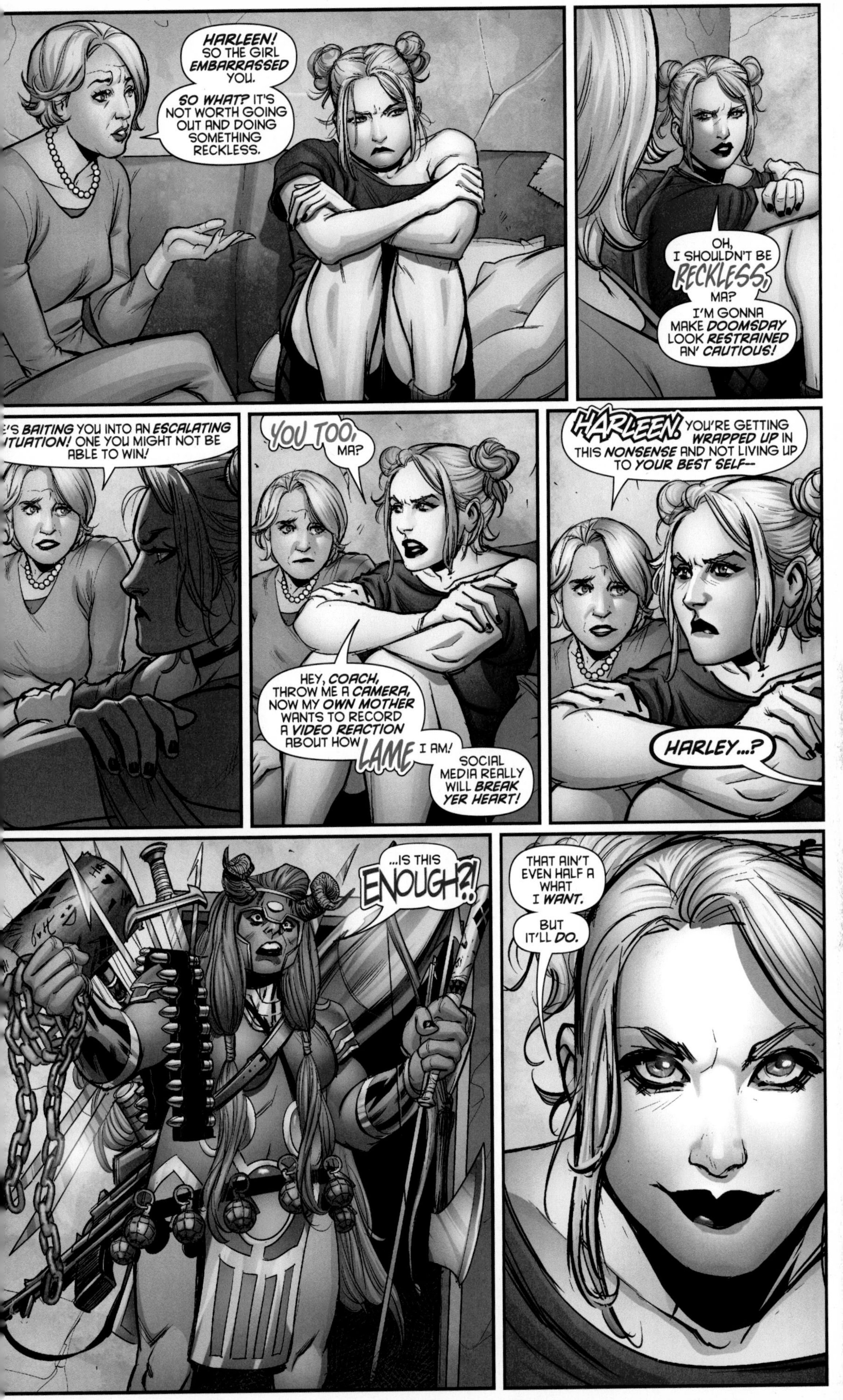

HARLEEN! SO THE GIRL EMBARRASSED YOU.
SO WHAT? IT'S NOT WORTH GOING OUT AND DOING SOMETHING RECKLESS.
OH, I SHOULDN'T BE RECKLESS, MA?
I'M GONNA MAKE DOOMSDAY LOOK RESTRAINED AN' CAUTIOUS!
'S BAITING YOU INTO AN ESCALATING TUATION! ONE YOU MIGHT NOT BE ABLE TO WIN!
YOU TOO, MA?
HEY, COACH, THROW ME A CAMERA, NOW MY OWN MOTHER WANTS TO RECORD A VIDEO REACTION ABOUT HOW LAME I AM!
SOCIAL MEDIA REALLY WILL BREAK YER HEART!
HARLEEN! YOU'RE GETTING WRAPPED UP IN THIS NONSENSE AND NOT LIVING UP TO YOUR BEST SELF--
HARLEY...?
...IS THIS ENOUGH?!
THAT AIN'T EVEN HALF A WHAT I WANT.
BUT IT'LL DO.

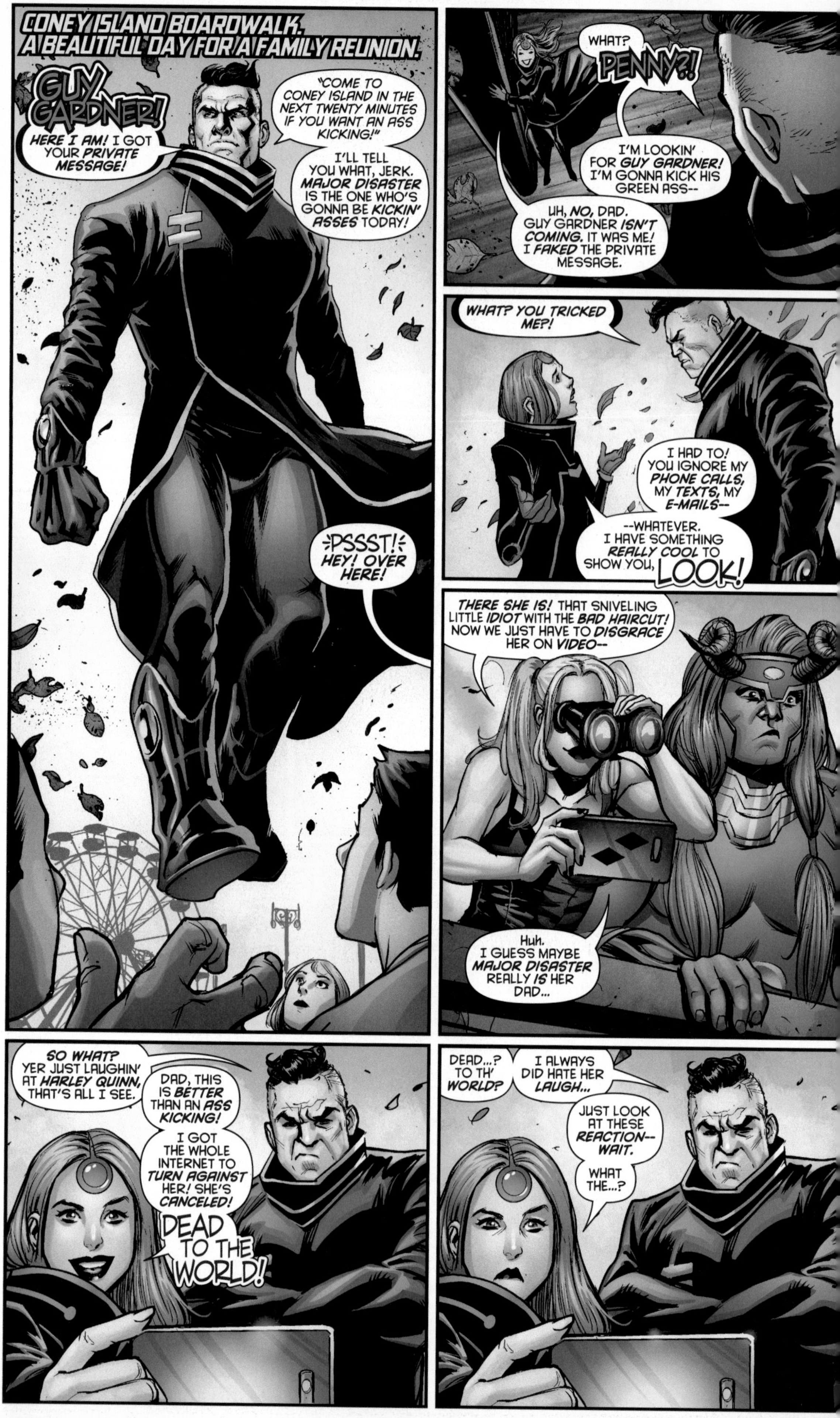
CONEY ISLAND BOARDWALK. A BEAUTIFUL DAY FOR A FAMILY REUNION.
GUY GARDNER! HERE I AM! I GOT YOUR PRIVATE MESSAGE!
"COME TO CONEY ISLAND IN THE NEXT TWENTY MINUTES IF YOU WANT AN ASS KICKING!"
I'LL TELL YOU WHAT, JERK. MAJOR DISASTER IS THE ONE WHO'S GONNA BE KICKIN' ASSES TODAY!
PSSST! HEY! OVER HERE!
WHAT? PENNY?!
I'M LOOKIN' FOR GUY GARDNER! I'M GONNA KICK HIS GREEN ASS--
UH, NO, DAD. GUY GARDNER ISN'T COMING. IT WAS ME! I FAKED THE PRIVATE MESSAGE.
WHAT? YOU TRICKED ME?!
I HAD TO! YOU IGNORE MY PHONE CALLS, MY TEXTS, MY E-MAILS--
--WHATEVER. I HAVE SOMETHING REALLY COOL TO SHOW YOU, LOOK!
THERE SHE IS! THAT SNIVELING LITTLE IDIOT WITH THE BAD HAIRCUT! NOW WE JUST HAVE TO DISGRACE HER ON VIDEO--
Huh. I GUESS MAYBE MAJOR DISASTER REALLY IS HER DAD...
SO WHAT? YER JUST LAUGHIN' AT HARLEY QUINN, THAT'S ALL I SEE.
DAD, THIS IS BETTER THAN AN ASS KICKING!
I GOT THE WHOLE INTERNET TO TURN AGAINST HER! SHE'S CANCELED!
DEAD TO THE WORLD!
DEAD...? TO TH' WORLD?
I ALWAYS DID HATE HER LAUGH...
JUST LOOK AT THESE REACTION-- WAIT.
WHAT THE...?

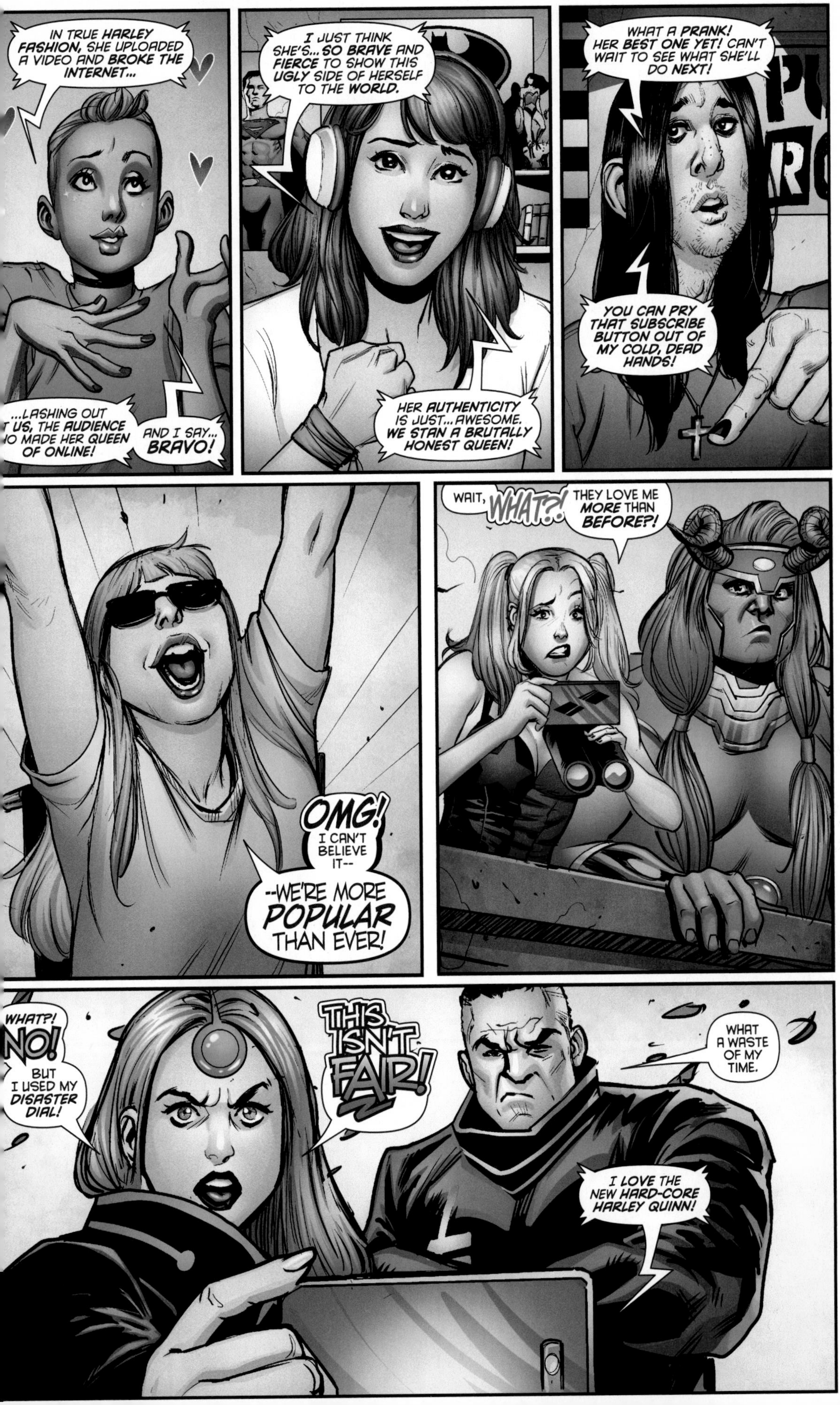
IN TRUE HARLEY FASHION, SHE UPLOADED A VIDEO AND BROKE THE INTERNET...
...LASHING OUT T US, THE AUDIENCE IO MADE HER QUEEN OF ONLINE!
AND I SAY... BRAVO!
I JUST THINK SHE'S... SO BRAVE AND FIERCE TO SHOW THIS UGLY SIDE OF HERSELF TO THE WORLD.
HER AUTHENTICITY IS JUST... AWESOME. WE STAN A BRUTALLY HONEST QUEEN!
WHAT A PRANK! HER BEST ONE YET! CAN'T WAIT TO SEE WHAT SHE'LL DO NEXT!
YOU CAN PRY THAT SUBSCRIBE BUTTON OUT OF MY COLD, DEAD HANDS!
OMG! I CAN'T BELIEVE IT--
--WE'RE MORE POPULAR THAN EVER!
WAIT, WHAT?!
THEY LOVE ME MORE THAN BEFORE?!
WHAT?! NO!
BUT I USED MY DISASTER DIAL!
THIS ISN'T FAIR!
WHAT A WASTE OF MY TIME.
I LOVE THE NEW HARD-CORE HARLEY QUINN!

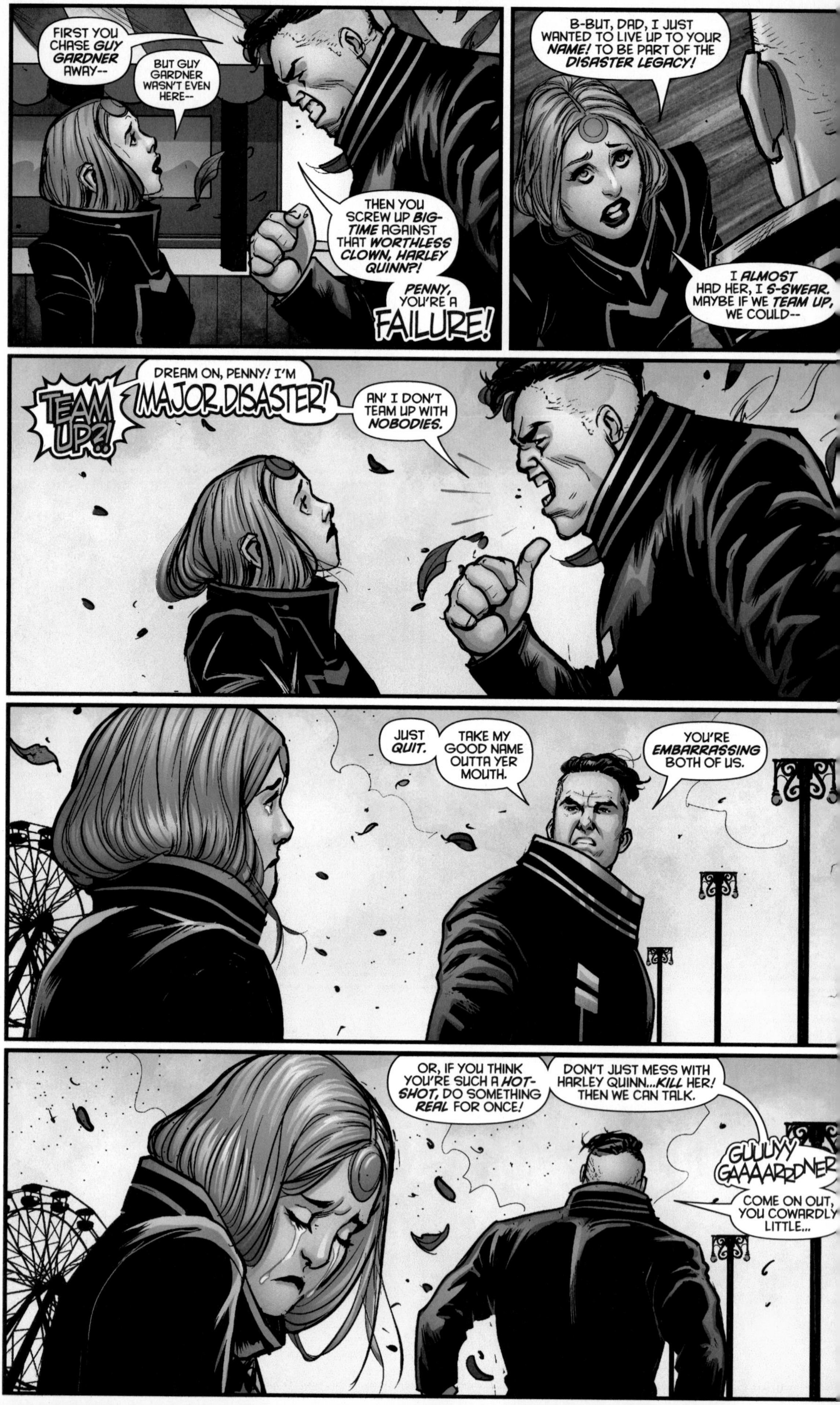
FIRST YOU CHASE GUY GARDNER AWAY--
BUT GUY GARDNER WASN'T EVEN HERE--
THEN YOU SCREW UP BIG-TIME AGAINST THAT WORTHLESS CLOWN, HARLEY QUINN?!
PENNY, YOU'RE A FAILURE!
B-BUT, DAD, I JUST WANTED TO LIVE UP TO YOUR NAME! TO BE PART OF THE DISASTER LEGACY!
I ALMOST HAD HER, I S-SWEAR. MAYBE IF WE TEAM UP, WE COULD--
TEAM UP?!
DREAM ON, PENNY! I'M MAJOR DISASTER!
AN' I DON'T TEAM UP WITH NOBODIES.
JUST QUIT.
TAKE MY GOOD NAME OUTTA YER MOUTH.
YOU'RE EMBARRASSING BOTH OF US.
OR, IF YOU THINK YOU'RE SUCH A HOT-SHOT, DO SOMETHING REAL FOR ONCE!
DON'T JUST MESS WITH HARLEY QUINN...KILL HER! THEN WE CAN TALK.
GUUUYY GAAAARRDNER
COME ON OUT, YOU COWARDLY LITTLE...

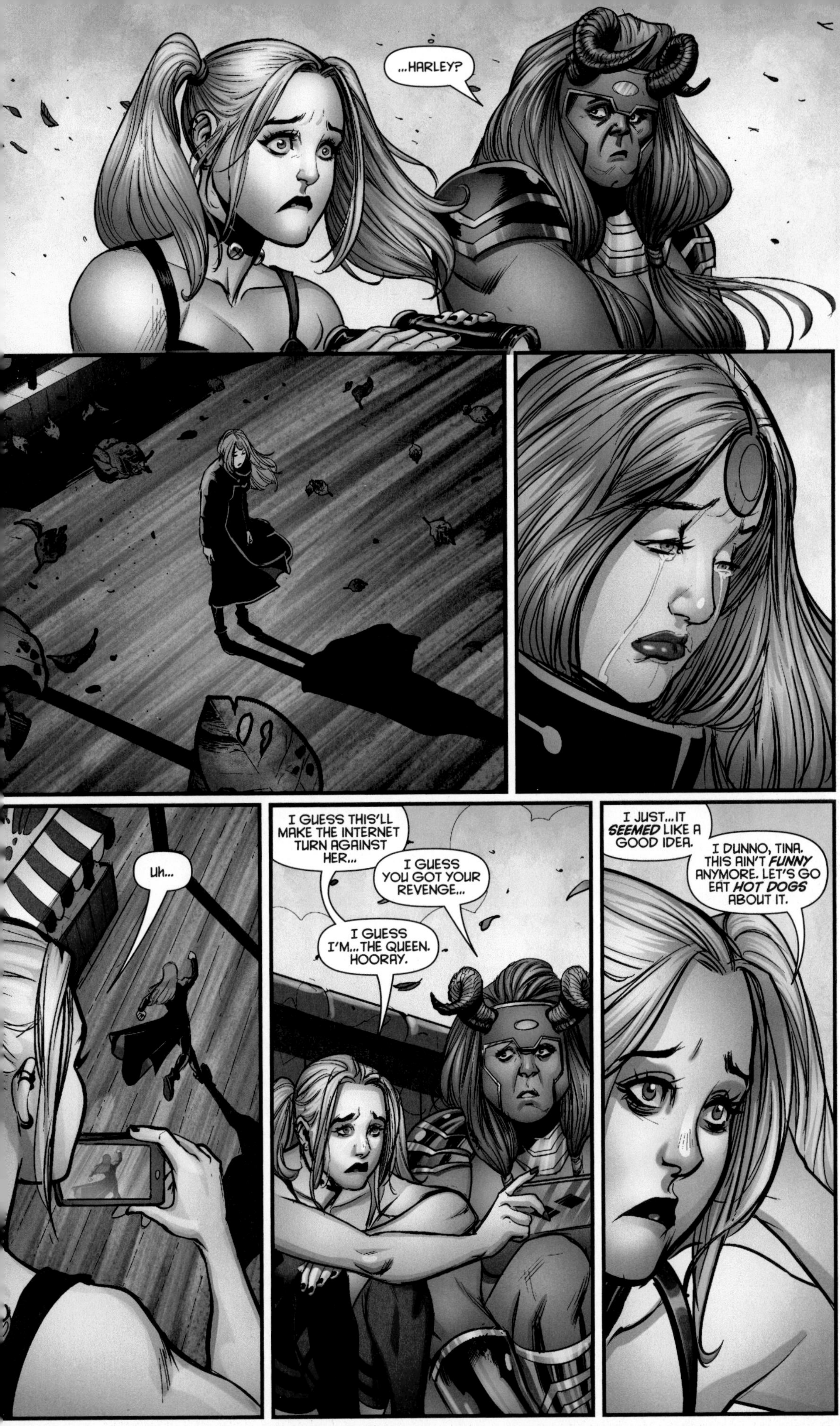
...HARLEY?
Uh...
I GUESS THIS'LL MAKE THE INTERNET TURN AGAINST HER...
I GUESS YOU GOT YOUR REVENGE...
I GUESS I'M... THE QUEEN. HOORAY.
I JUST... IT SEEMED LIKE A GOOD IDEA.
I DUNNO, TINA. THIS AIN'T FUNNY ANYMORE. LET'S GO EAT HOT DOGS ABOUT IT.

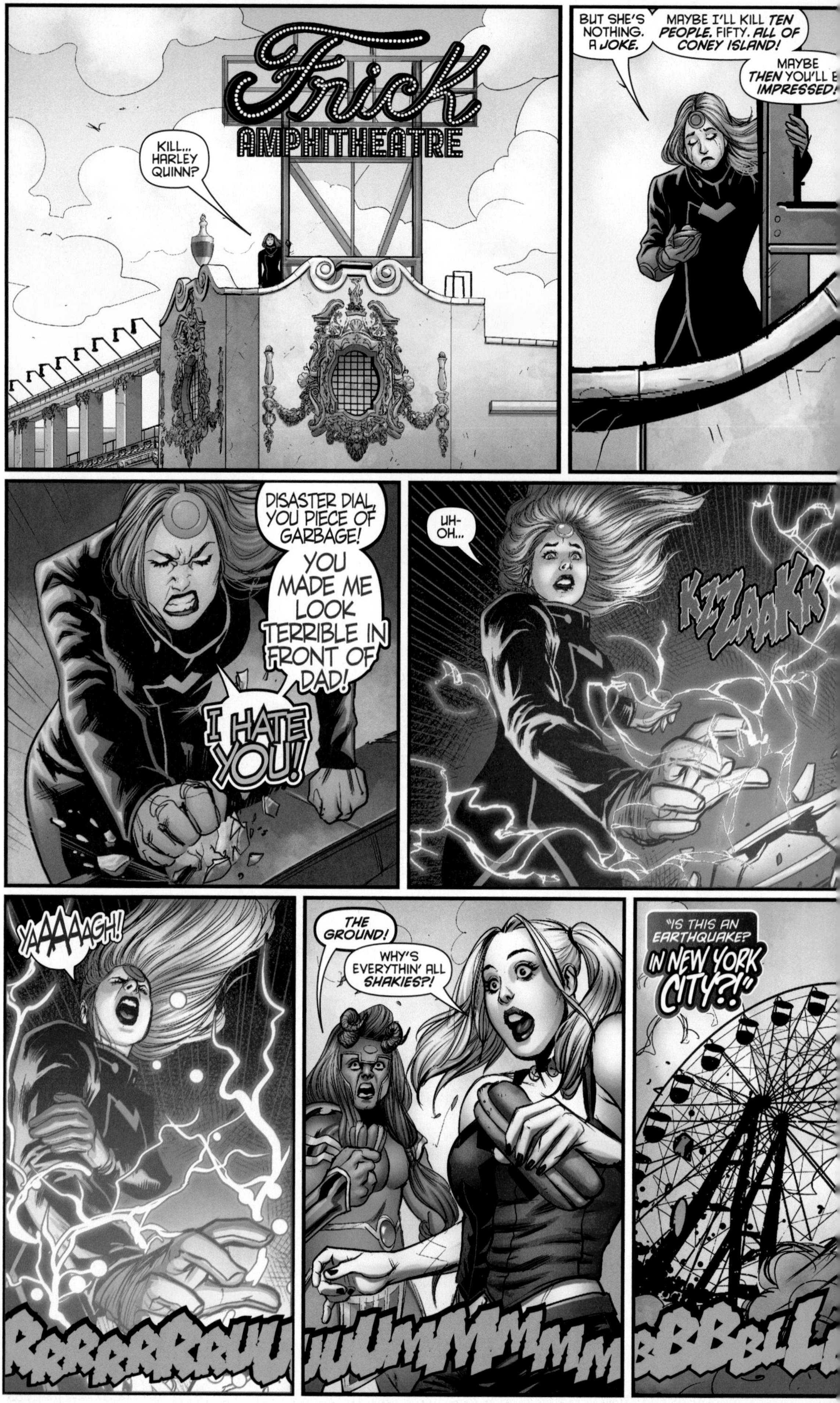
Frick
AMPHITHEATRE
KILL... HARLEY QUINN?
BUT SHE'S NOTHING. A JOKE.
MAYBE I'LL KILL TEN PEOPLE. FIFTY. ALL OF CONEY ISLAND!
MAYBE THEN YOU'LL B IMPRESSED!
DISASTER DIAL, YOU PIECE OF GARBAGE!
YOU MADE ME LOOK TERRIBLE IN FRONT OF DAD!
I HATE YOU!
UH-OH...
KZZAAKK
YAAAAAGH!
THE GROUND!
WHY'S EVERYTHIN' ALL SHAKIES?!
"IS THIS AN EARTHQUAKE? IN NEW YORK CITY?!"
RRRRRRRUUUUUMMMMMMMMBBBLL

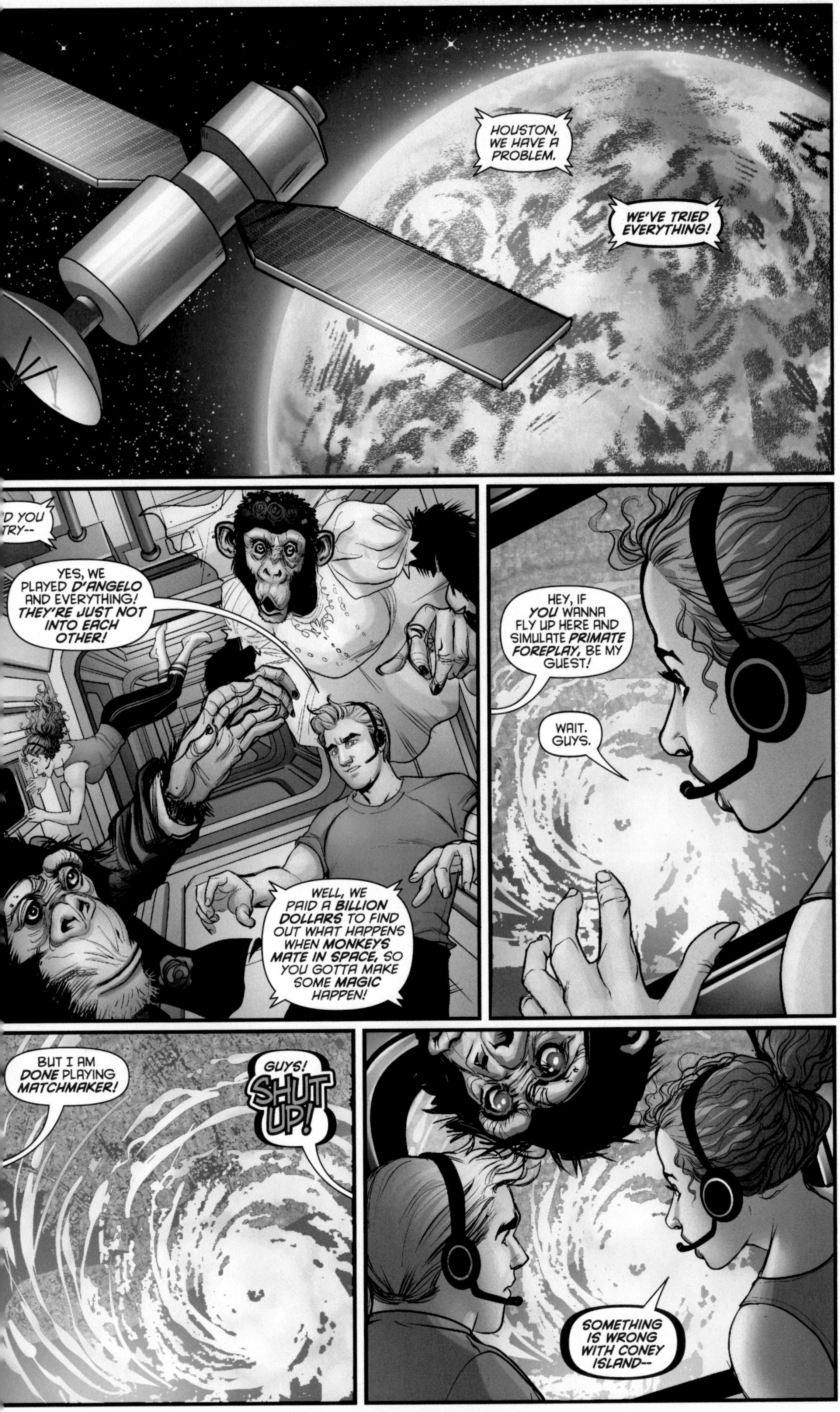
HOUSTON, WE HAVE A PROBLEM.
WE'VE TRIED EVERYTHING!
'D YOU TRY--
YES, WE PLAYED D'ANGELO AND EVERYTHING! THEY'RE JUST NOT INTO EACH OTHER!
WELL, WE PAID A BILLION DOLLARS TO FIND OUT WHAT HAPPENS WHEN MONKEYS MATE IN SPACE, SO YOU GOTTA MAKE SOME MAGIC HAPPEN!
HEY, IF YOU WANNA FLY UP HERE AND SIMULATE PRIMATE FOREPLAY, BE MY GUEST!
WAIT. GUYS.
BUT I AM DONE PLAYING MATCHMAKER!
GUYS!
SHUT UP!
SOMETHING IS WRONG WITH CONEY ISLAND--

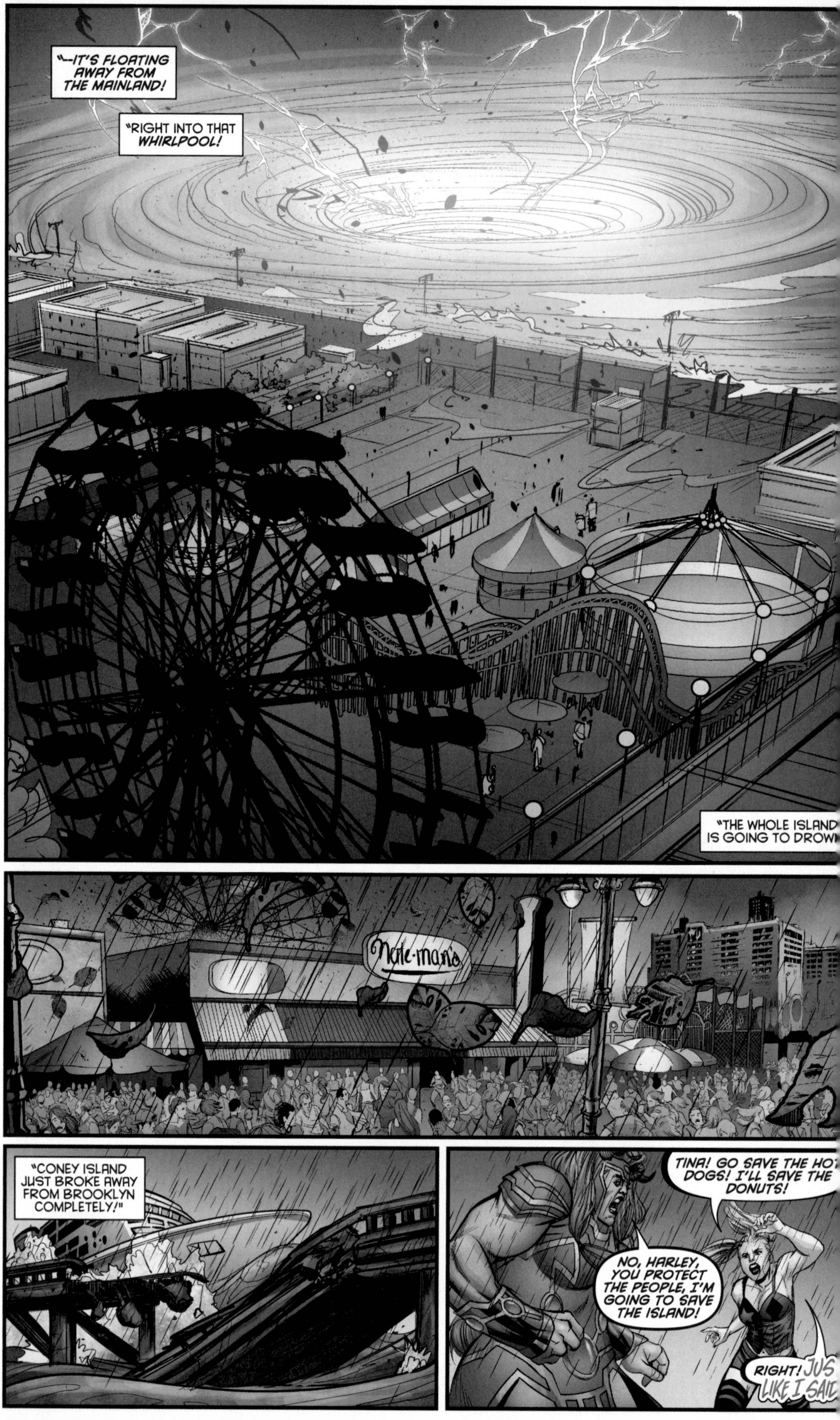
"--IT'S FLOATING AWAY FROM THE MAINLAND!
"RIGHT INTO THAT WHIRLPOOL!
"THE WHOLE ISLAND IS GOING TO DROW
"CONEY ISLAND JUST BROKE AWAY FROM BROOKLYN COMPLETELY!"
TINA! GO SAVE THE HO DOGS! I'LL SAVE THE DONUTS!
NO, HARLEY, YOU PROTECT THE PEOPLE, I'M GOING TO SAVE THE ISLAND!
RIGHT! JUS LIKE I SAI

IF THIS *FORGED CLAW* IS *STRONG* ENOUGH FOR A *GIANT SHIP*--

--PERHAPS IT IS *MIGHTY* ENOUGH TO SAVE AN *ISLAND!*

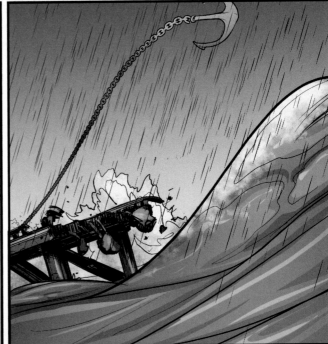

"I'VE *HOOKED* IT TO THE *MAINLAND!*

THAKK

BUT THE *WHIRLPOOL* IS PULLING AT THE ISLAND--WITH THE FORCE OF *GRANNY'S HELL POODLES!* I MUST HOLD *FAST!*

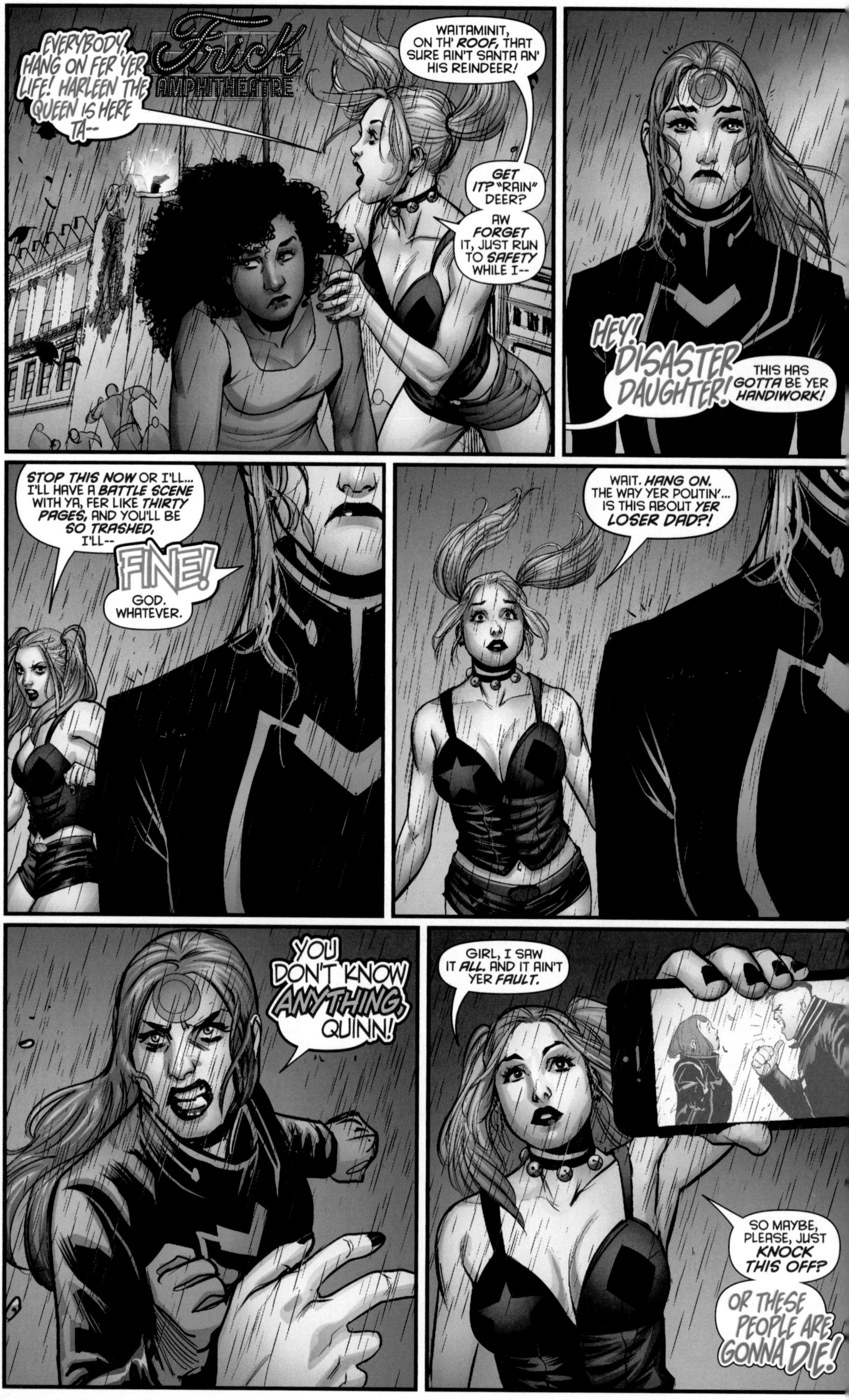
EVERYBODY HANG ON FER YER LIFE! HARLEEN THE QUEEN IS HERE TA--
Frick AMPHITHEATRE
WAITAMINIT, ON TH' ROOF, THAT SURE AIN'T SANTA AN' HIS REINDEER!
GET IT? "RAIN" DEER?
AW FORGET IT, JUST RUN TO SAFETY WHILE I--
HEY! DISASTER DAUGHTER!
THIS HAS GOTTA BE YER HANDIWORK!
STOP THIS NOW OR I'LL... I'LL HAVE A BATTLE SCENE WITH YA, FER LIKE THIRTY PAGES, AND YOU'LL BE SO TRASHED, I'LL--
FINE!
GOD. WHATEVER.
WAIT. HANG ON. THE WAY YER POUTIN'... IS THIS ABOUT YER LOSER DAD?!
YOU DON'T KNOW ANYTHING, QUINN!
GIRL, I SAW IT ALL. AND IT AIN'T YER FAULT.
SO MAYBE, PLEASE, JUST KNOCK THIS OFF?
OR THESE PEOPLE ARE GONNA DIE!

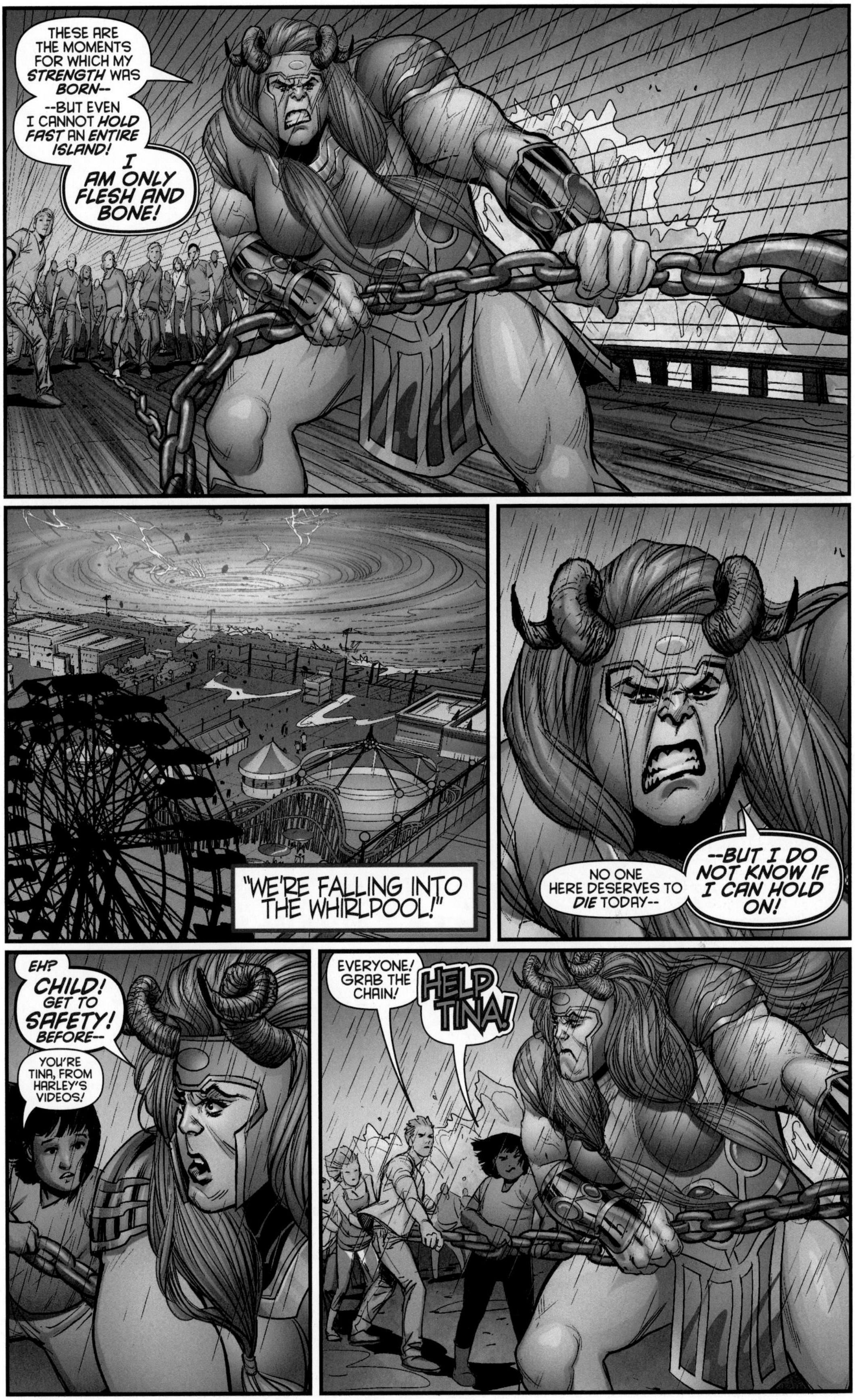
THESE ARE THE MOMENTS FOR WHICH MY STRENGTH WAS BORN--
--BUT EVEN I CANNOT HOLD FAST AN ENTIRE ISLAND!
I AM ONLY FLESH AND BONE!
"WE'RE FALLING INTO THE WHIRLPOOL!"
NO ONE HERE DESERVES TO DIE TODAY--
--BUT I DO NOT KNOW IF I CAN HOLD ON!
EH? CHILD! GET TO SAFETY! BEFORE--
YOU'RE TINA, FROM HARLEY'S VIDEOS!
EVERYONE! GRAB THE CHAIN!
HELP TINA!

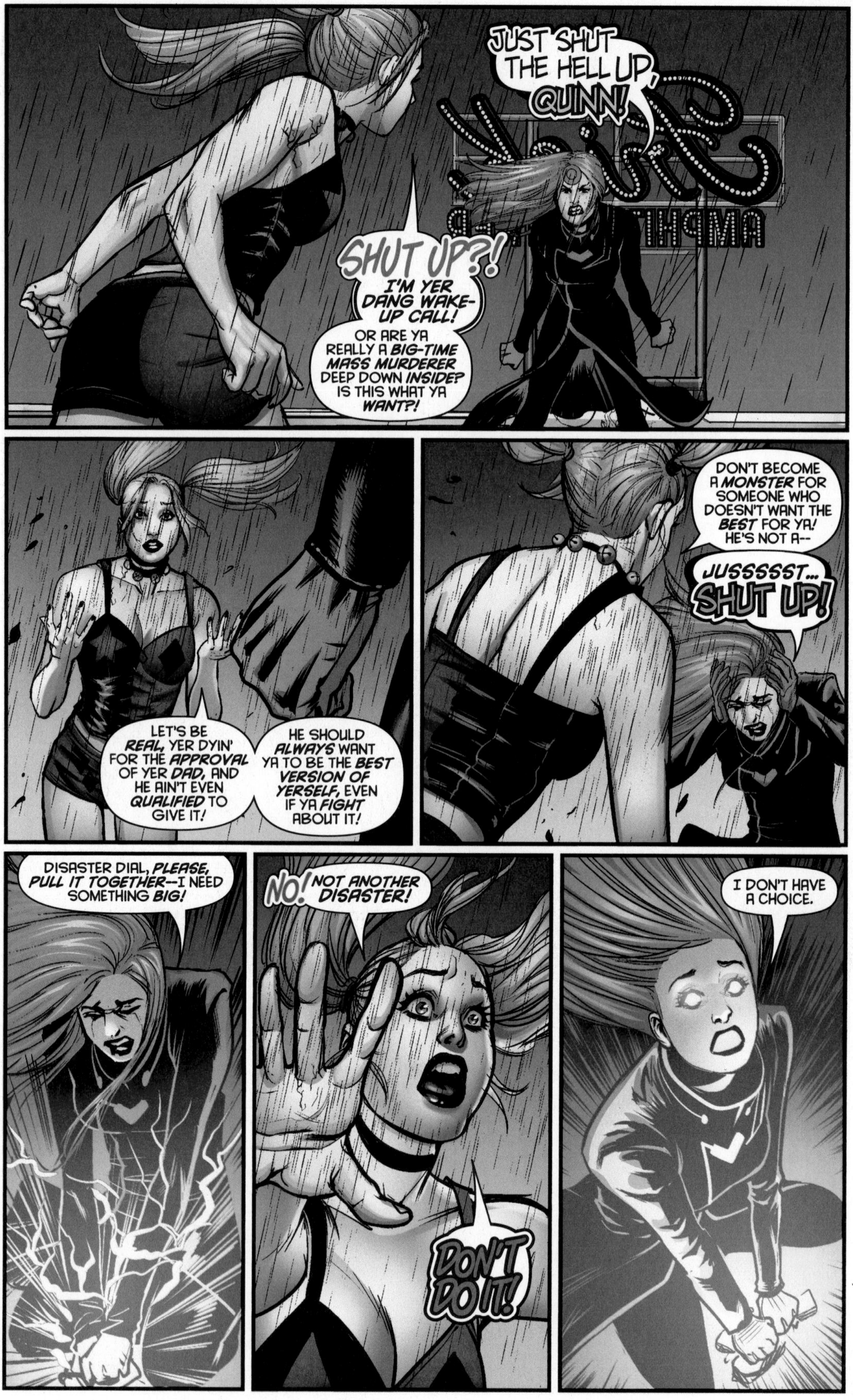
JUST SHUT THE HELL UP, QUINN!
SHUT UP?!
I'M YER DANG WAKE-UP CALL!
OR ARE YA REALLY A BIG-TIME MASS MURDERER DEEP DOWN INSIDE? IS THIS WHAT YA WANT?!
LET'S BE REAL, YER DYIN' FOR THE APPROVAL OF YER DAD, AND HE AIN'T EVEN QUALIFIED TO GIVE IT!
HE SHOULD ALWAYS WANT YA TO BE THE BEST VERSION OF YERSELF, EVEN IF YA FIGHT ABOUT IT!
DON'T BECOME A MONSTER FOR SOMEONE WHO DOESN'T WANT THE BEST FOR YA! HE'S NOT A--
JUSSSSST... SHUT UP!
DISASTER DIAL, PLEASE, PULL IT TOGETHER--I NEED SOMETHING BIG!
NO! NOT ANOTHER DISASTER!
DON'T DO IT!
I DON'T HAVE A CHOICE.

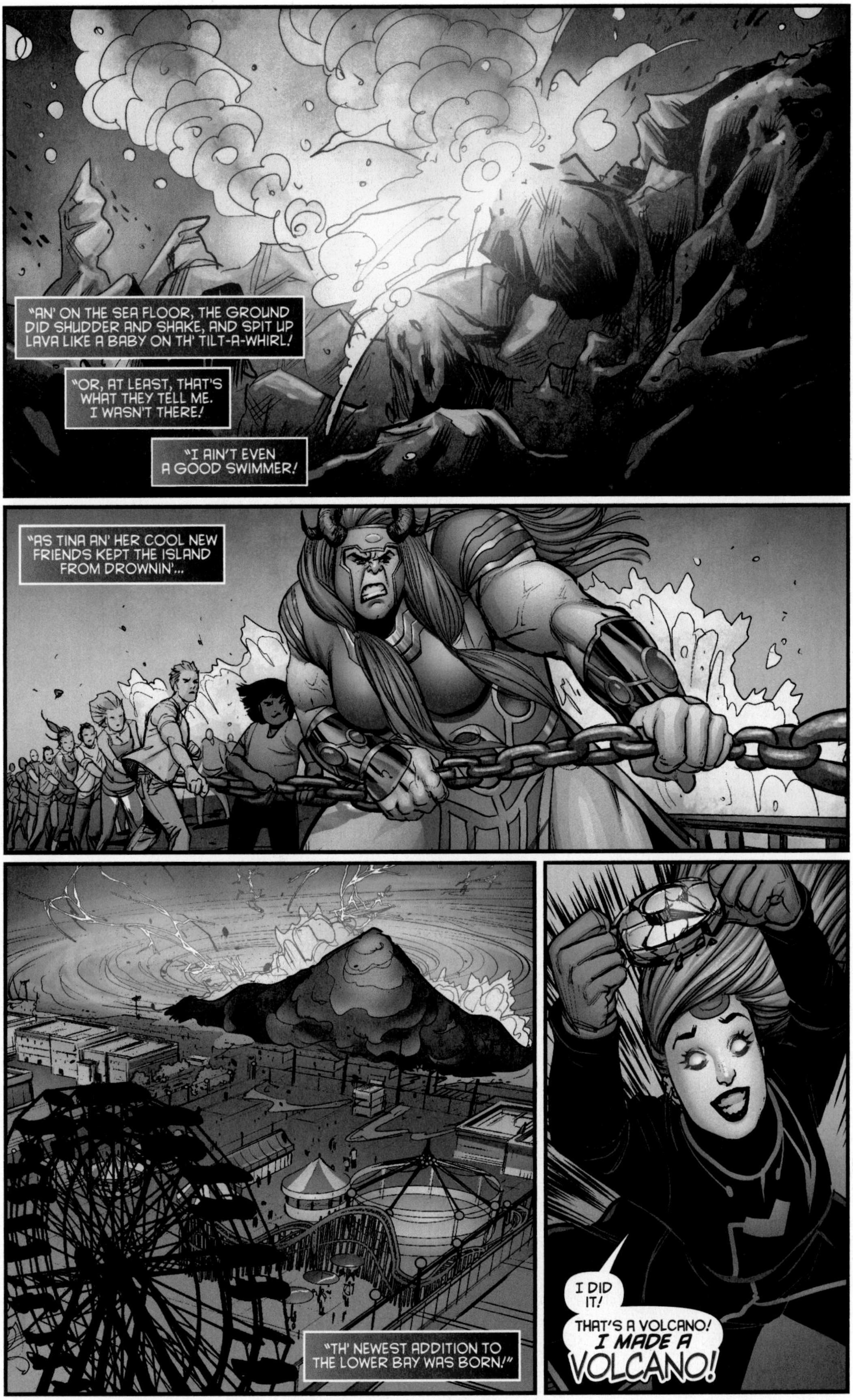
"AN' ON THE SEA FLOOR, THE GROUND DID SHUDDER AND SHAKE, AND SPIT UP LAVA LIKE A BABY ON TH' TILT-A-WHIRL!
"OR, AT LEAST, THAT'S WHAT THEY TELL ME. I WASN'T THERE!
"I AIN'T EVEN A GOOD SWIMMER!
"AS TINA AN' HER COOL NEW FRIENDS KEPT THE ISLAND FROM DROWNIN'...
"TH' NEWEST ADDITION TO THE LOWER BAY WAS BORN!"
I DID IT!
THAT'S A VOLCANO! I MADE A VOLCANO!

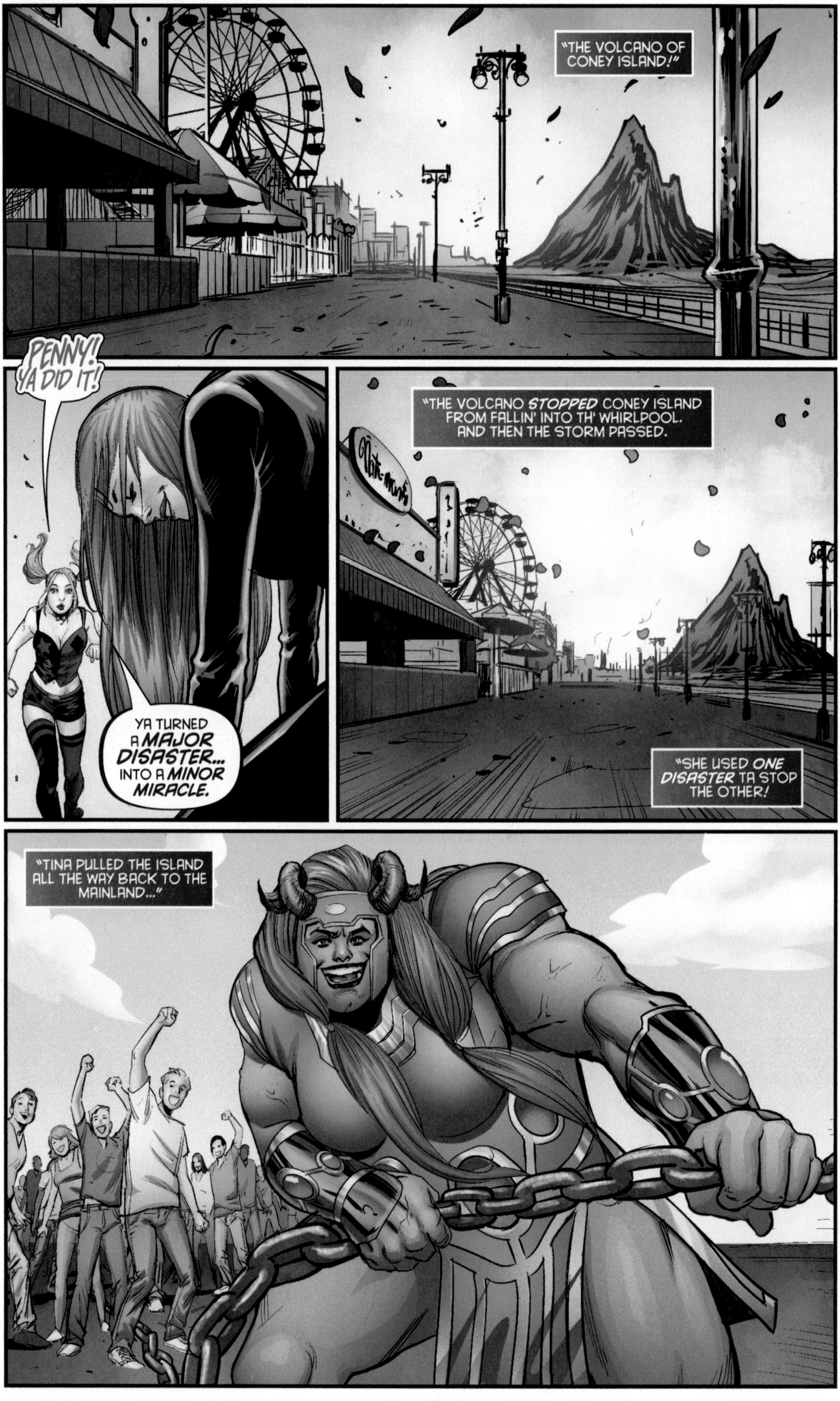
"THE VOLCANO OF CONEY ISLAND!"
PENNY! YA DID IT!
YA TURNED A MAJOR DISASTER... INTO A MINOR MIRACLE.
"THE VOLCANO STOPPED CONEY ISLAND FROM FALLIN' INTO TH' WHIRLPOOL. AND THEN THE STORM PASSED.
"SHE USED ONE DISASTER TA STOP THE OTHER!
"TINA PULLED THE ISLAND ALL THE WAY BACK TO THE MAINLAND..."

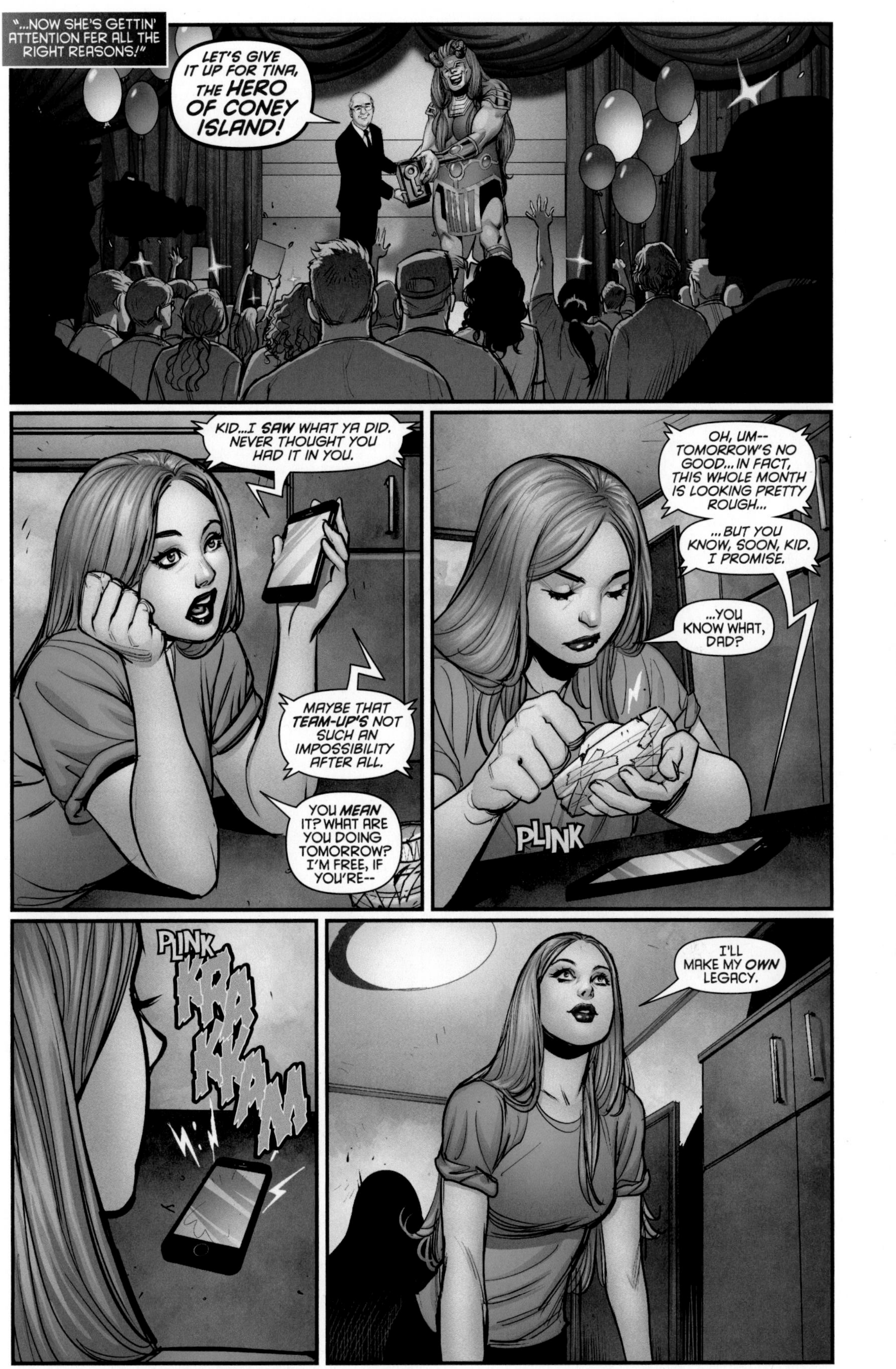
"...NOW SHE'S GETTIN' ATTENTION FER ALL THE RIGHT REASONS!"
LET'S GIVE IT UP FOR TINA, THE HERO OF CONEY ISLAND!
KID...I SAW WHAT YA DID. NEVER THOUGHT YOU HAD IT IN YOU.
MAYBE THAT TEAM-UP'S NOT SUCH AN IMPOSSIBILITY AFTER ALL.
YOU MEAN IT? WHAT ARE YOU DOING TOMORROW? I'M FREE, IF YOU'RE--
OH, UM-- TOMORROW'S NO GOOD...IN FACT, THIS WHOLE MONTH IS LOOKING PRETTY ROUGH...
...BUT YOU KNOW, SOON, KID. I PROMISE.
...YOU KNOW WHAT, DAD?
PLINK
PLINK
KRAKKAM
I'LL MAKE MY OWN LEGACY.

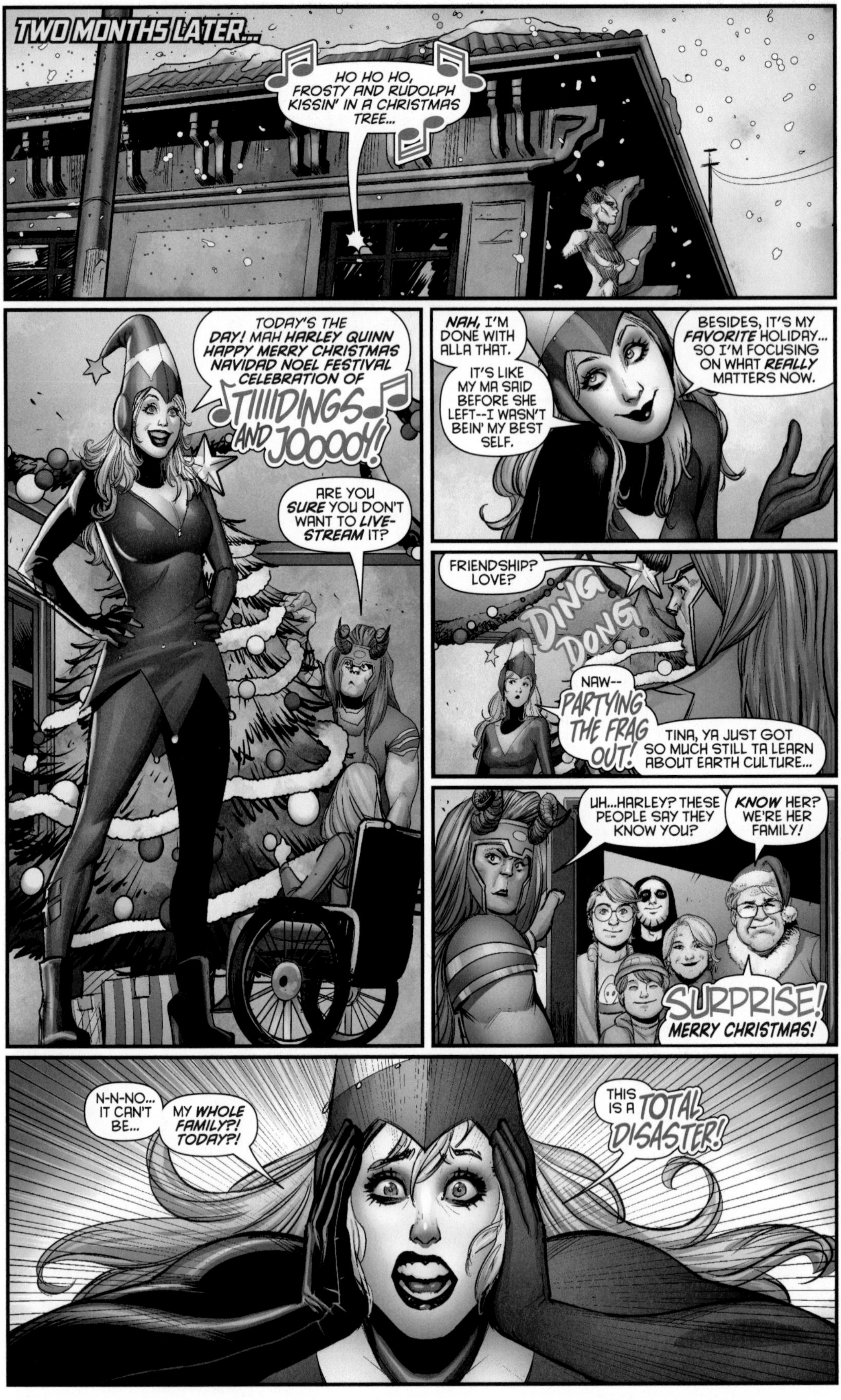

TWO MONTHS LATER...
HO HO HO, FROSTY AND RUDOLPH KISSIN' IN A CHRISTMAS TREE...
TODAY'S THE DAY! MAH HARLEY QUINN HAPPY MERRY CHRISTMAS NAVIDAD NOEL FESTIVAL CELEBRATION OF TIIIIDINGS AND JOOOOY!
ARE YOU SURE YOU DON'T WANT TO LIVE-STREAM IT?
NAH, I'M DONE WITH ALLA THAT.
IT'S LIKE MY MA SAID BEFORE SHE LEFT--I WASN'T BEIN' MY BEST SELF.
BESIDES, IT'S MY FAVORITE HOLIDAY... SO I'M FOCUSING ON WHAT REALLY MATTERS NOW.
FRIENDSHIP? LOVE?
DING DONG
NAW-- PARTYING THE FRAG OUT!
TINA, YA JUST GOT SO MUCH STILL TA LEARN ABOUT EARTH CULTURE...
UH...HARLEY? THESE PEOPLE SAY THEY KNOW YOU?
KNOW HER? WE'RE HER FAMILY!
SURPRISE! MERRY CHRISTMAS!
N-N-NO... IT CAN'T BE...
MY WHOLE FAMILY?! TODAY?!
THIS IS A TOTAL DISASTER!

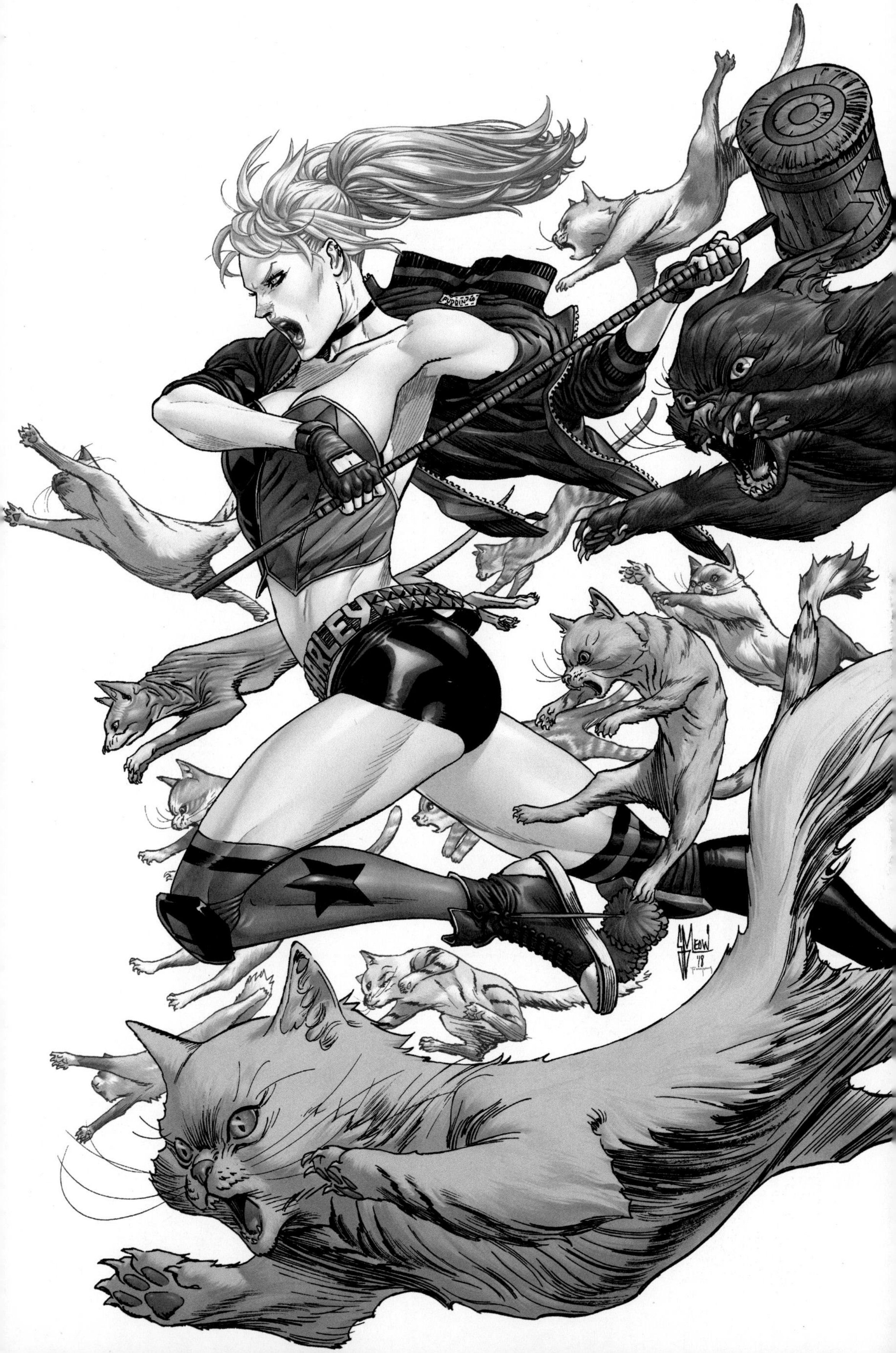

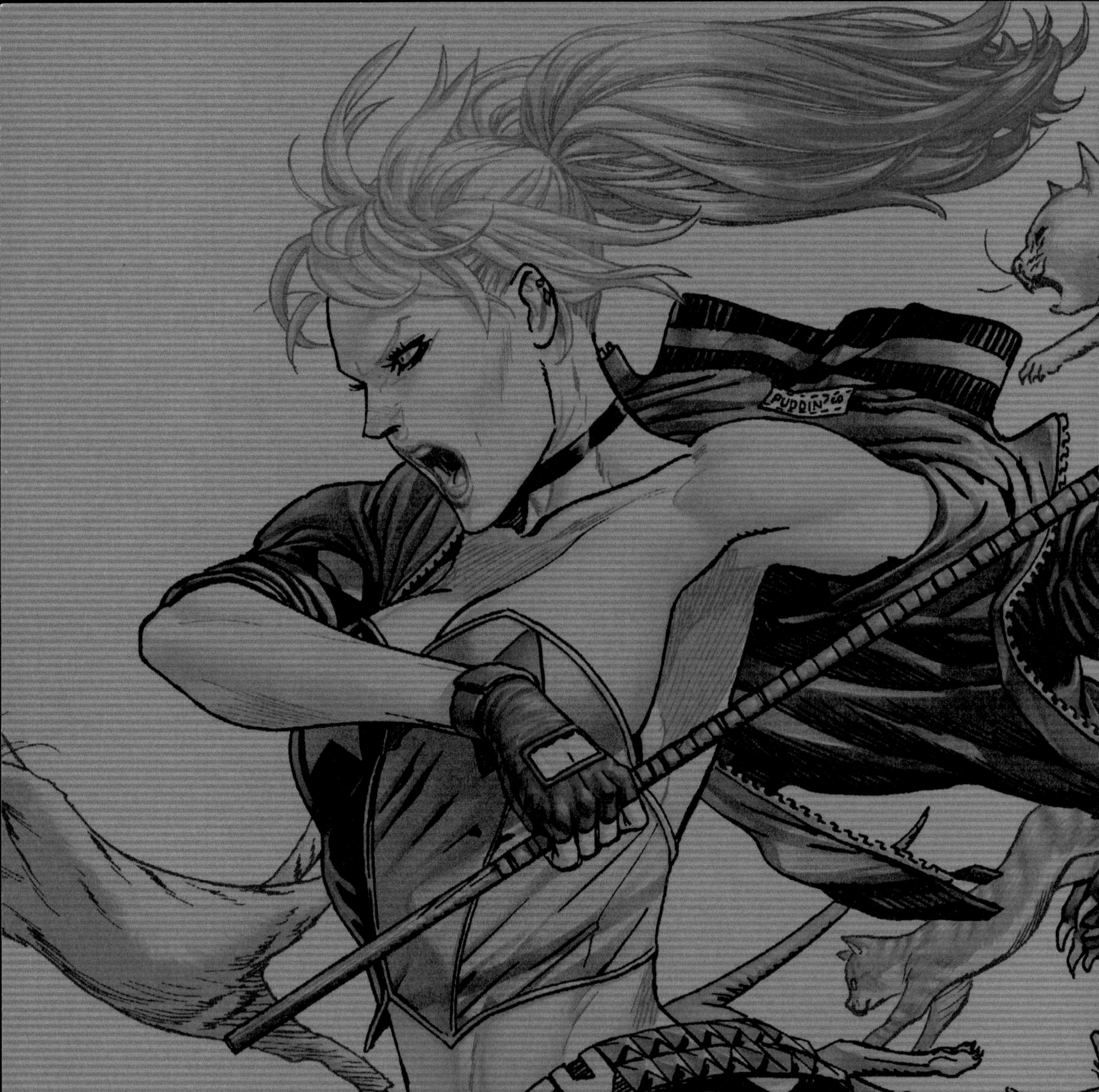

PUDDIN
HARLEY

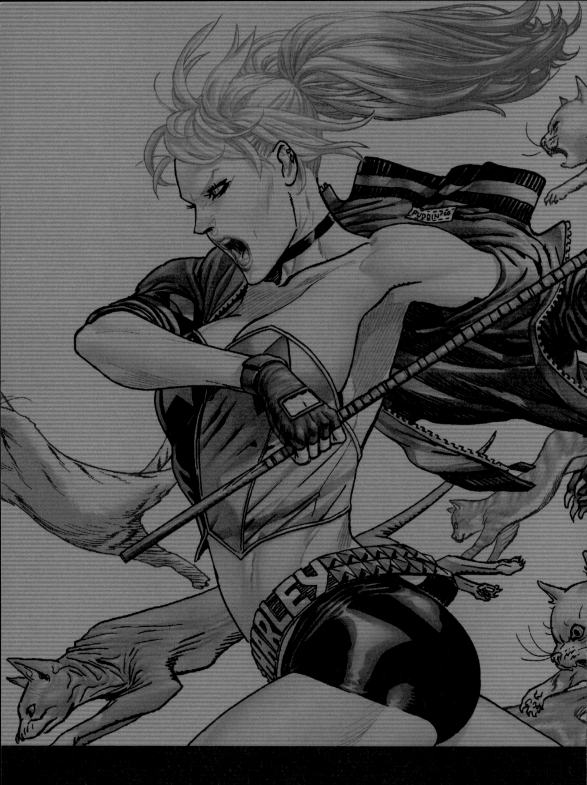

HARLEY QUINN
#56

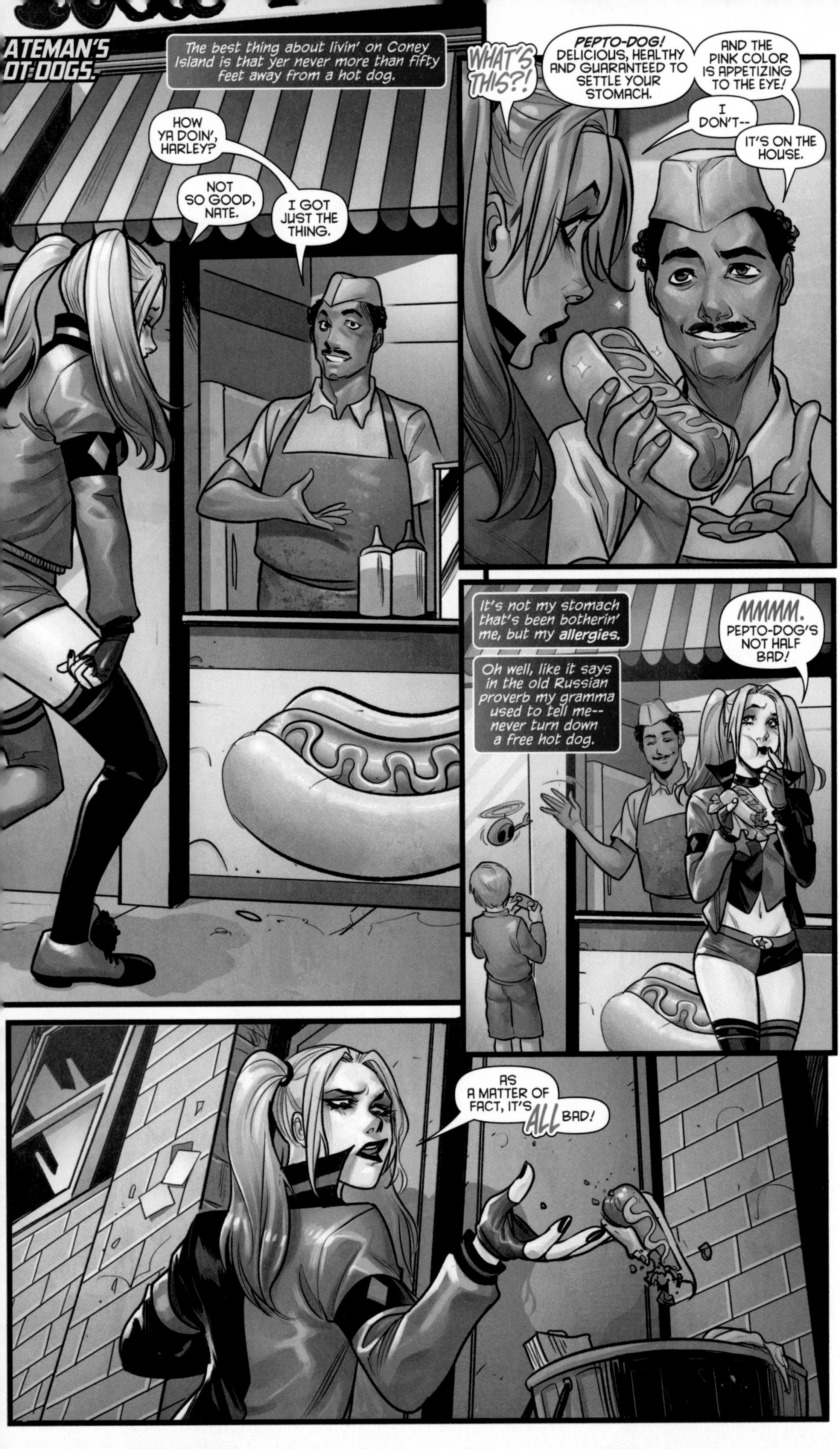

ATEMAN'S
OT-DOGS.
The best thing about livin' on Coney Island is that yer never more than fifty feet away from a hot dog.
HOW YA DOIN', HARLEY?
NOT SO GOOD, NATE.
I GOT JUST THE THING.
WHAT'S THIS?!
PEPTO-DOG! DELICIOUS, HEALTHY AND GUARANTEED TO SETTLE YOUR STOMACH.
AND THE PINK COLOR IS APPETIZING TO THE EYE!
I DON'T--
IT'S ON THE HOUSE.
It's not my stomach that's been botherin' me, but my allergies.
Oh well, like it says in the old Russian proverb my gramma used to tell me-- never turn down a free hot dog.
MMMM. PEPTO-DOG'S NOT HALF BAD!
AS A MATTER OF FACT, IT'S ALL BAD!

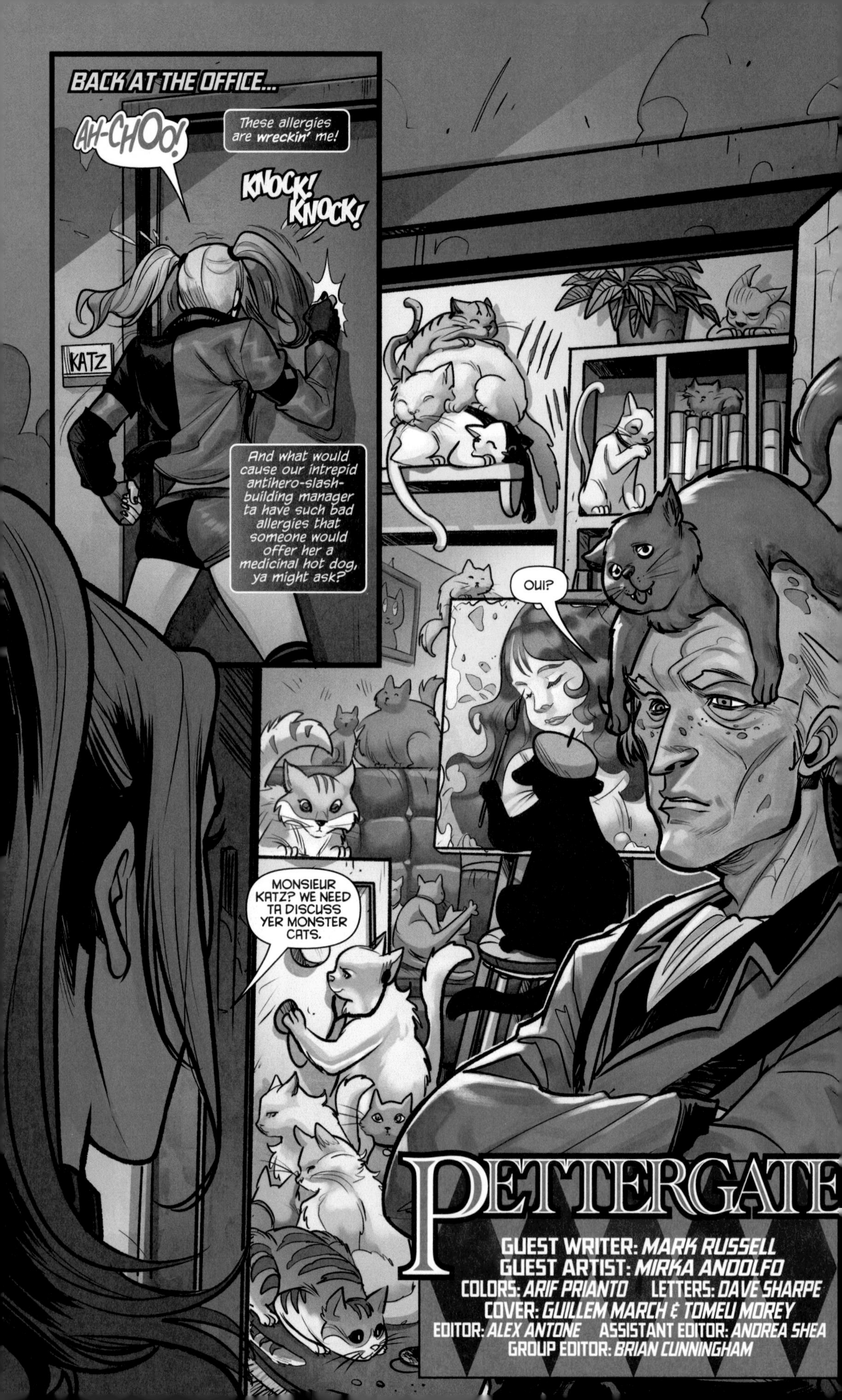
BACK AT THE OFFICE...
AH-CHOO!
These allergies are wreckin' me!
KNOCK! KNOCK!
KATZ
And what would cause our intrepid antihero-slash-building manager ta have such bad allergies that someone would offer her a medicinal hot dog, ya might ask?
OUI?
MONSIEUR KATZ? WE NEED TA DISCUSS YER MONSTER CATS.
PETTERGATE
GUEST WRITER: MARK RUSSELL
GUEST ARTIST: MIRKA ANDOLFO
COLORS: ARIF PRIANTO LETTERS: DAVE SHARPE
COVER: GUILLEM MARCH & TOMEU MOREY
EDITOR: ALEX ANTONE ASSISTANT EDITOR: ANDREA SHEA
GROUP EDITOR: BRIAN CUNNINGHAM

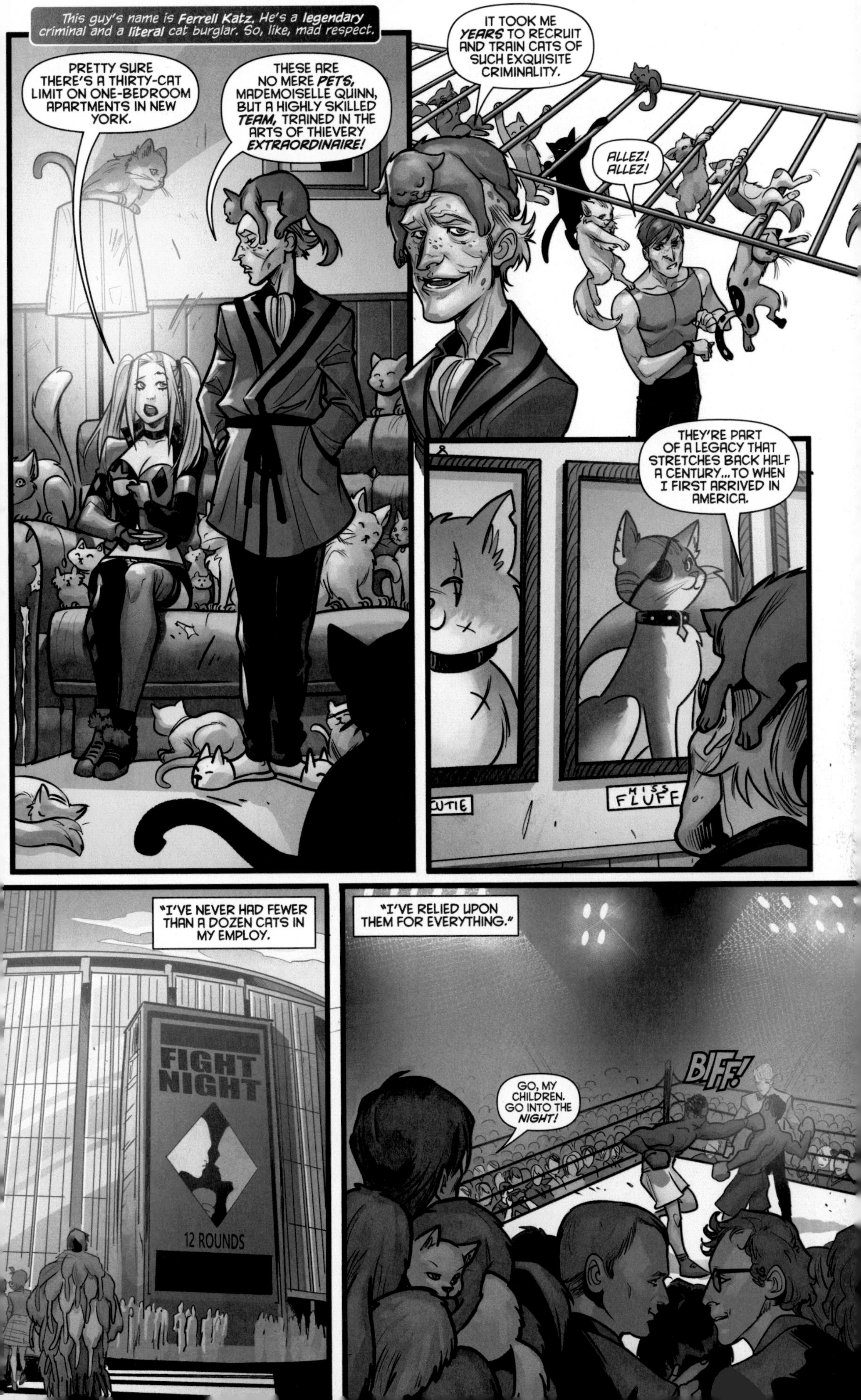

This guy's name is Ferrell Katz. He's a legendary criminal and a literal cat burglar. So, like, mad respect.
PRETTY SURE THERE'S A THIRTY-CAT LIMIT ON ONE-BEDROOM APARTMENTS IN NEW YORK.
THESE ARE NO MERE PETS, MADEMOISELLE QUINN, BUT A HIGHLY SKILLED TEAM, TRAINED IN THE ARTS OF THIEVERY EXTRAORDINAIRE!
IT TOOK ME YEARS TO RECRUIT AND TRAIN CATS OF SUCH EXQUISITE CRIMINALITY.
ALLEZ! ALLEZ!
THEY'RE PART OF A LEGACY THAT STRETCHES BACK HALF A CENTURY... TO WHEN I FIRST ARRIVED IN AMERICA.
CUTIE
MISS FLUFF
"I'VE NEVER HAD FEWER THAN A DOZEN CATS IN MY EMPLOY.
FIGHT NIGHT
12 ROUNDS
"I'VE RELIED UPON THEM FOR EVERYTHING."
BIFF!
GO, MY CHILDREN. GO INTO THE NIGHT!

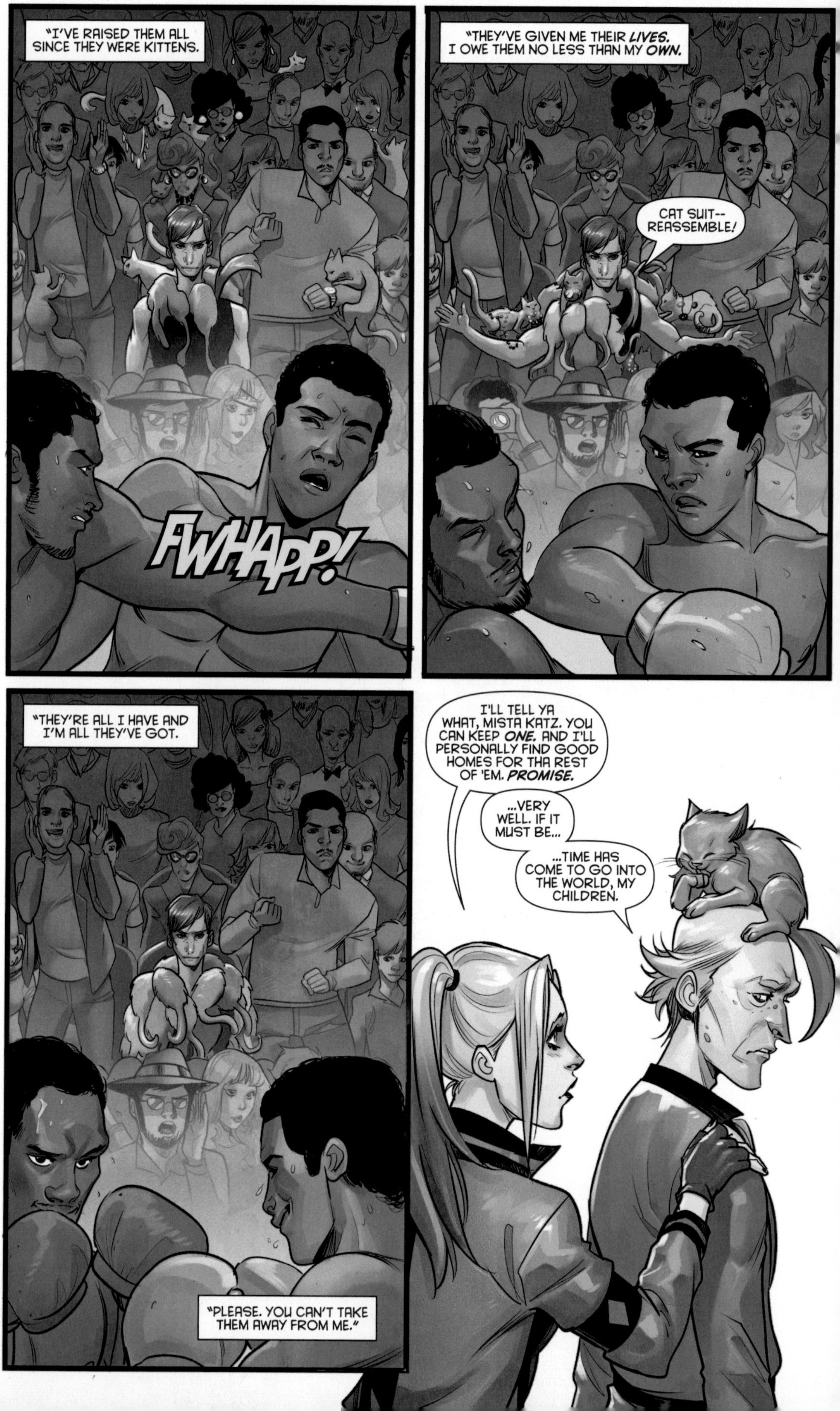
"I'VE RAISED THEM ALL SINCE THEY WERE KITTENS.
FWHAPP!
"THEY'VE GIVEN ME THEIR LIVES. I OWE THEM NO LESS THAN MY OWN.
CAT SUIT-- REASSEMBLE!
"THEY'RE ALL I HAVE AND I'M ALL THEY'VE GOT.
"PLEASE. YOU CAN'T TAKE THEM AWAY FROM ME."
I'LL TELL YA WHAT, MISTA KATZ. YOU CAN KEEP ONE. AND I'LL PERSONALLY FIND GOOD HOMES FOR THA REST OF 'EM. PROMISE.
...VERY WELL. IF IT MUST BE...
...TIME HAS COME TO GO INTO THE WORLD, MY CHILDREN.

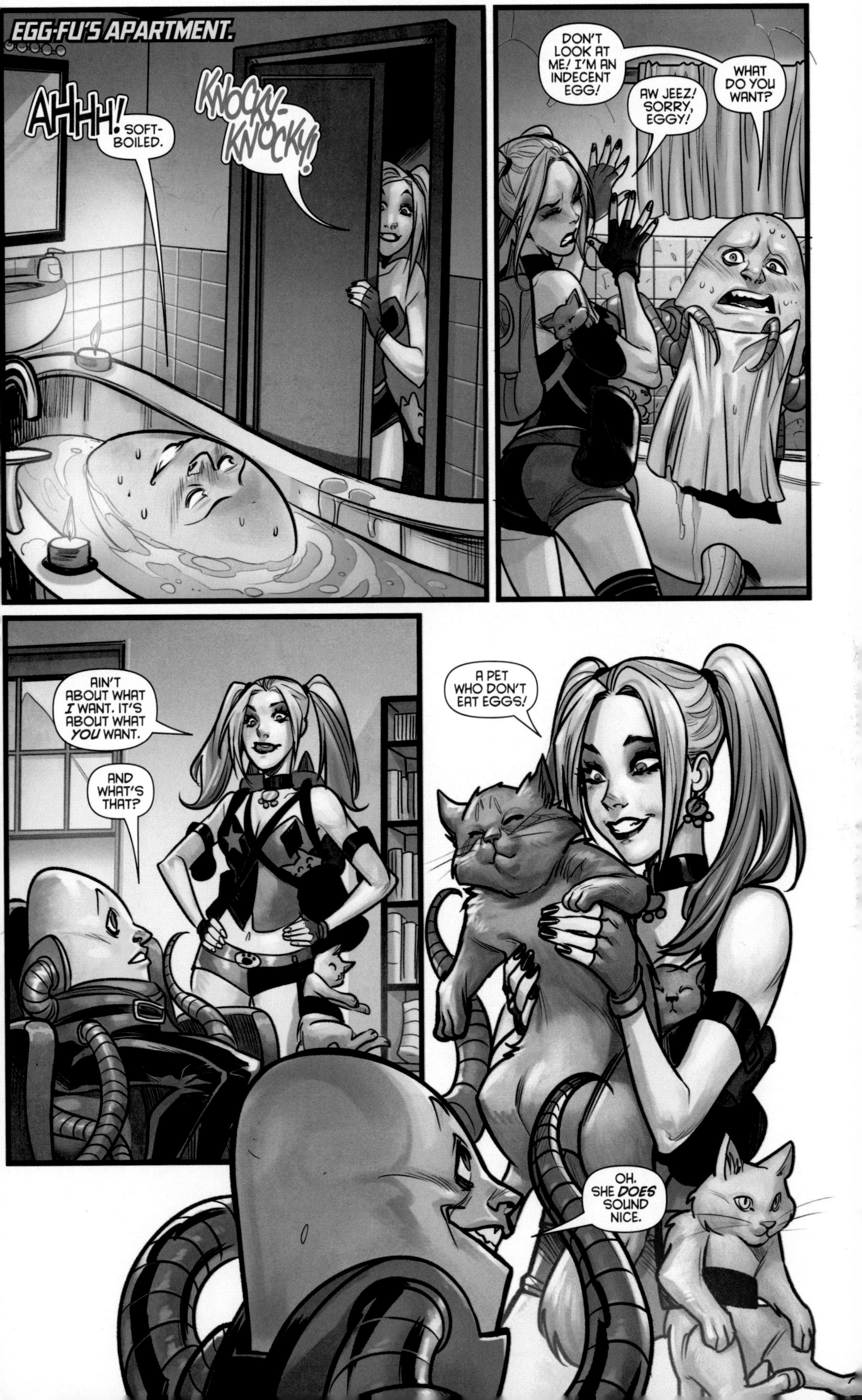
EGG-FU'S APARTMENT.
KNOCKY-KNOCKY!
AHHH! SOFT-BOILED.
DON'T LOOK AT ME! I'M AN INDECENT EGG!
AW JEEZ! SORRY, EGGY!
WHAT DO YOU WANT?
AIN'T ABOUT WHAT I WANT. IT'S ABOUT WHAT YOU WANT.
AND WHAT'S THAT?
A PET WHO DON'T EAT EGGS!
OH. SHE DOES SOUND NICE.

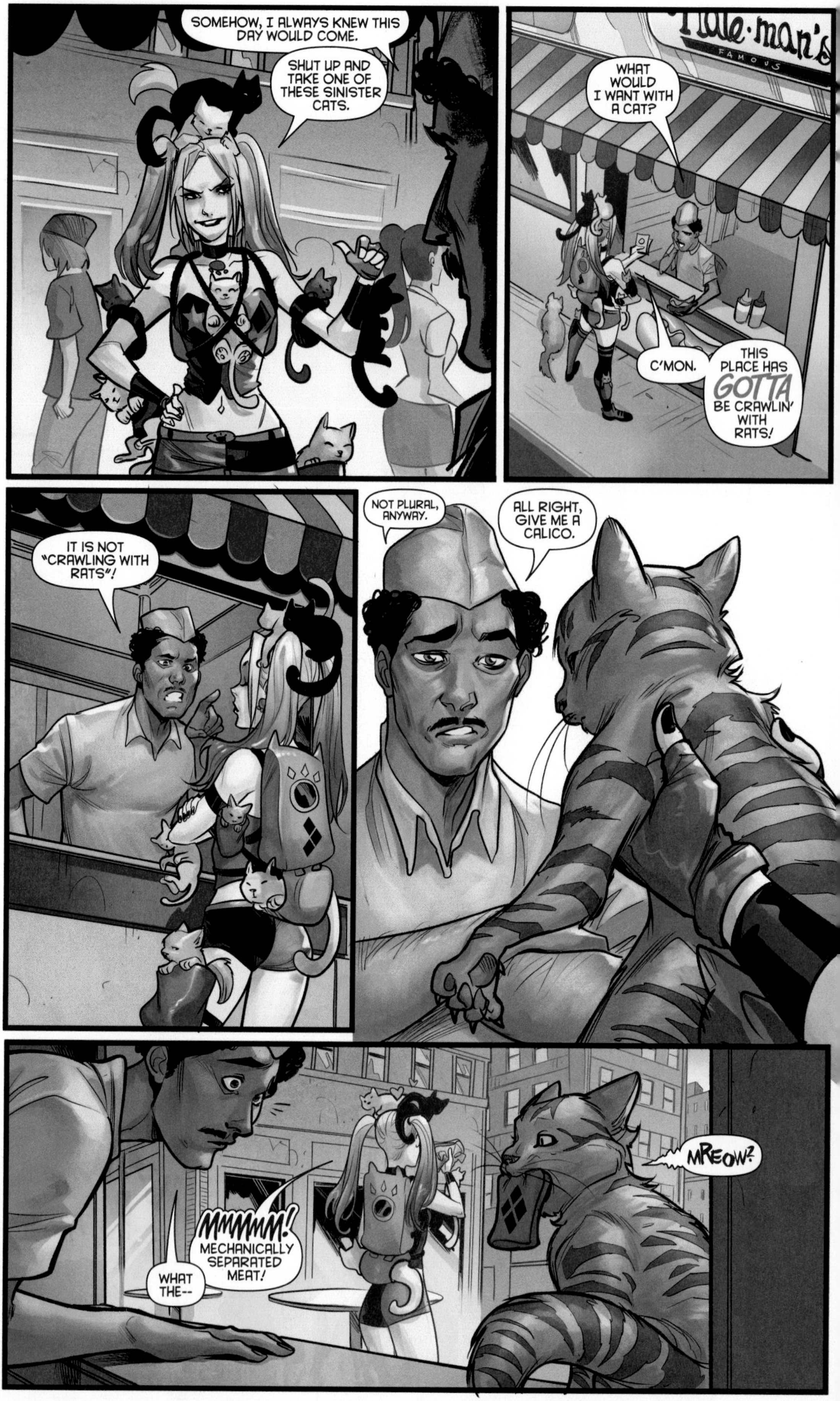

SOMEHOW, I ALWAYS KNEW THIS DAY WOULD COME.
SHUT UP AND TAKE ONE OF THESE SINISTER CATS.
Nate·man's
FAMOUS
WHAT WOULD I WANT WITH A CAT?
C'MON.
THIS PLACE HAS GOTTA BE CRAWLIN' WITH RATS!
IT IS NOT "CRAWLING WITH RATS"!
NOT PLURAL, ANYWAY.
ALL RIGHT, GIVE ME A CALICO.
MREOW?
MMMMM! MECHANICALLY SEPARATED MEAT!
WHAT THE--

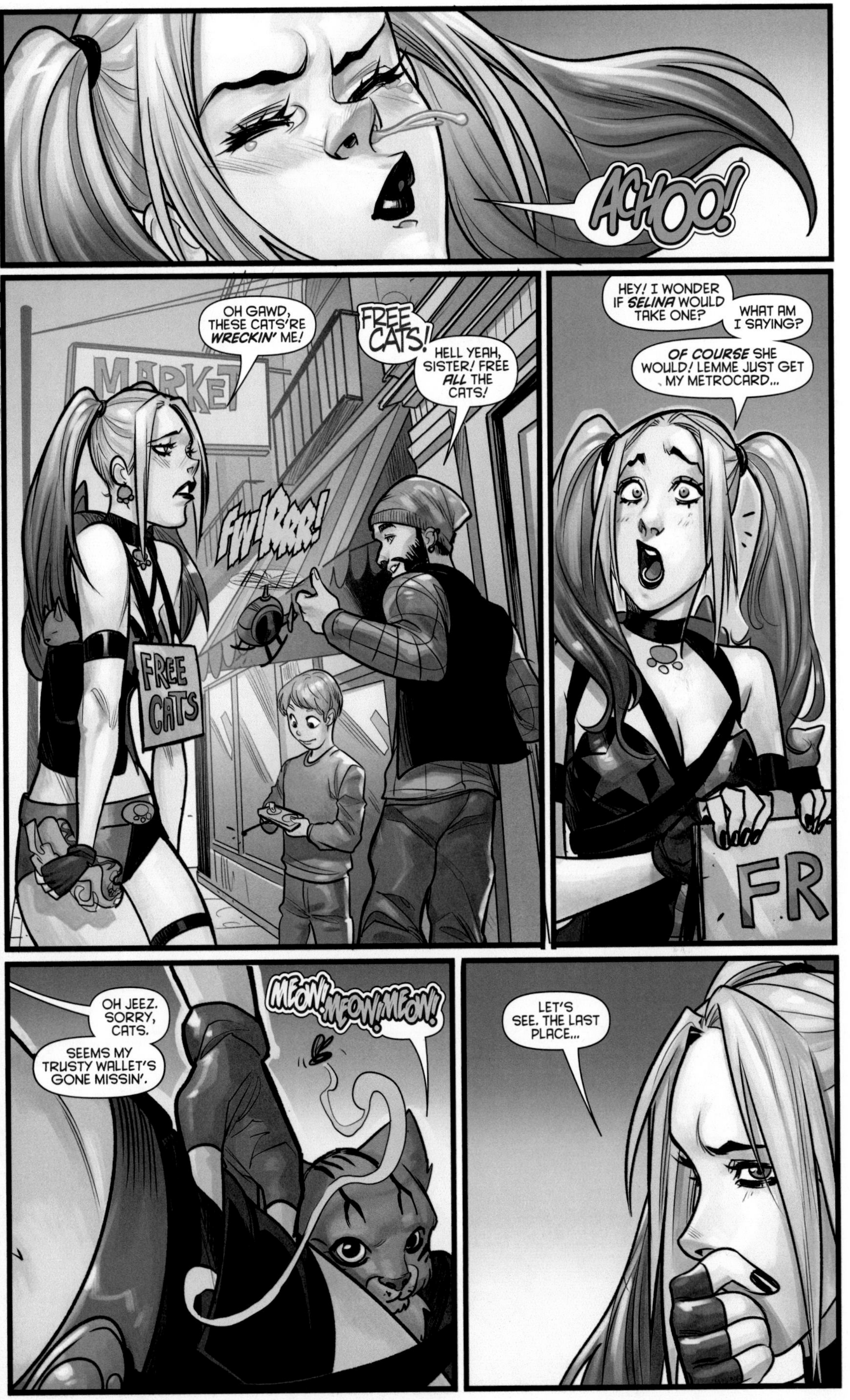
ACHOO!
OH GAWD, THESE CATS'RE WRECKIN' ME!
FREE CATS!
HELL YEAH, SISTER! FREE ALL THE CATS!
FWIRRR!
FREE CATS
HEY! I WONDER IF SELINA WOULD TAKE ONE?
WHAT AM I SAYING?
OF COURSE SHE WOULD! LEMME JUST GET MY METROCARD...
FR
OH JEEZ. SORRY, CATS.
SEEMS MY TRUSTY WALLET'S GONE MISSIN'.
MEOW! MEOW! MEOW!
LET'S SEE. THE LAST PLACE...

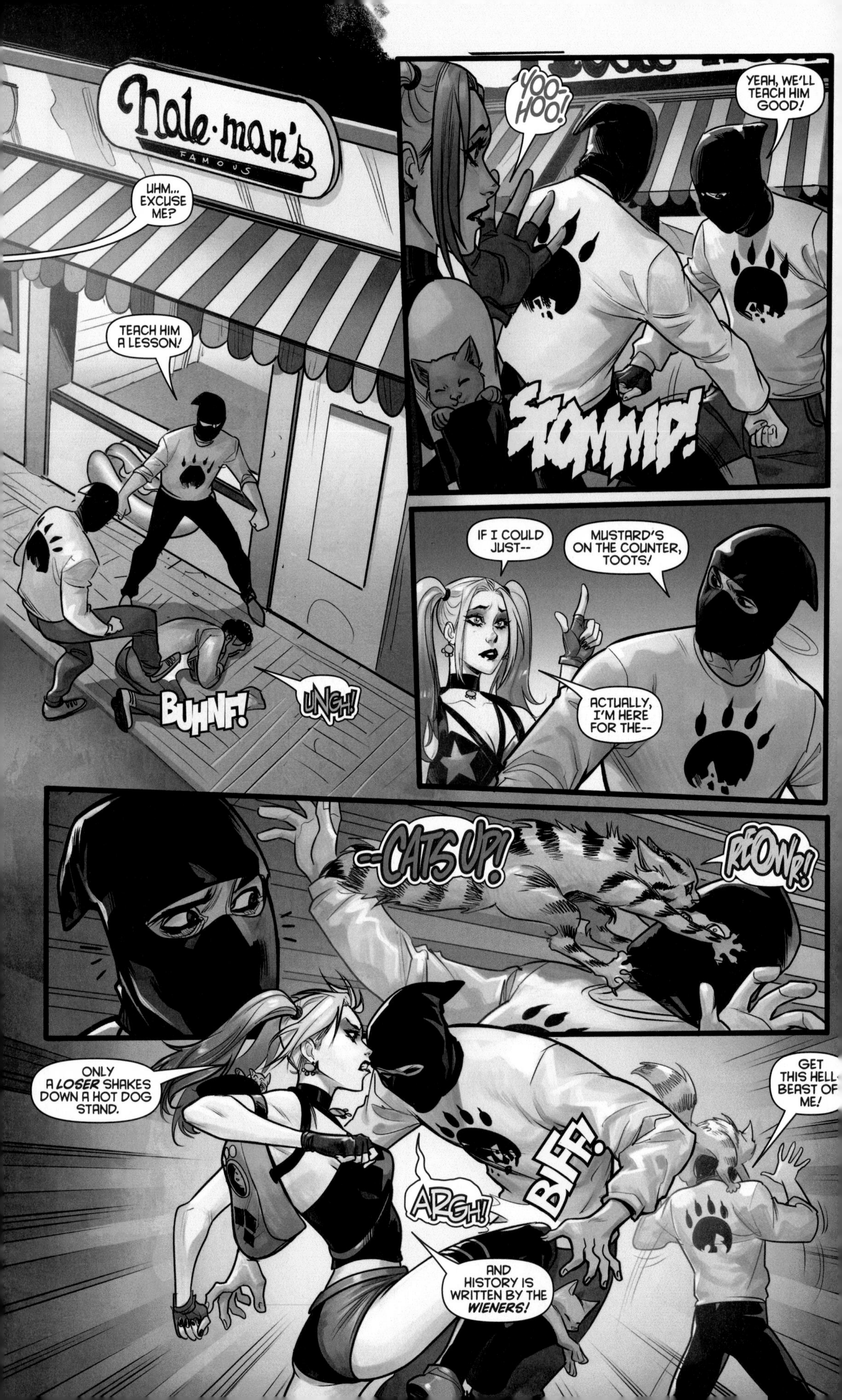
Nate·man's
FAMOUS
UHM... EXCUSE ME?
TEACH HIM A LESSON!
BUHNF!
UNGH!
YOO-HOO!
YEAH, WE'LL TEACH HIM GOOD!
STOMMP!
IF I COULD JUST--
MUSTARD'S ON THE COUNTER, TOOTS!
ACTUALLY, I'M HERE FOR THE--
--CATS UP!
REOWR!
ONLY A LOSER SHAKES DOWN A HOT DOG STAND.
GET THIS HELL BEAST OF ME!
BUFF!
ARGH!
AND HISTORY IS WRITTEN BY THE WIENERS!

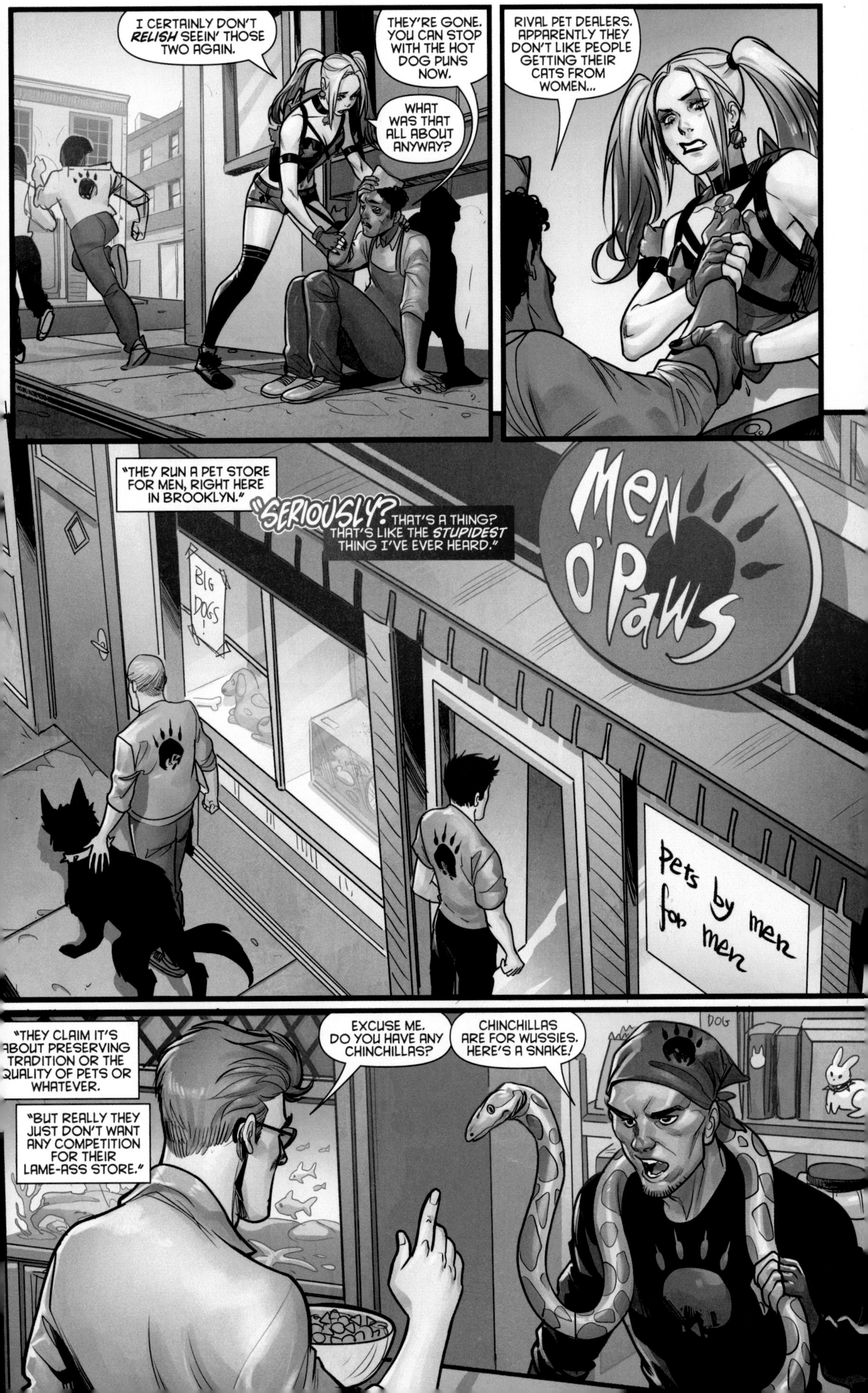

I CERTAINLY DON'T *RELISH* SEEIN' THOSE TWO AGAIN.
THEY'RE GONE. YOU CAN STOP WITH THE HOT DOG PUNS NOW.
WHAT WAS THAT ALL ABOUT ANYWAY?
RIVAL PET DEALERS. APPARENTLY THEY DON'T LIKE PEOPLE GETTING THEIR CATS FROM WOMEN...
"THEY RUN A PET STORE FOR MEN, RIGHT HERE IN BROOKLYN."
"SERIOUSLY? THAT'S A THING? THAT'S LIKE THE *STUPIDEST* THING I'VE EVER HEARD."
MEN O'PAWS
BIG DOGS!
Pets by men for men
"THEY CLAIM IT'S ABOUT PRESERVING TRADITION OR THE QUALITY OF PETS OR WHATEVER.
"BUT REALLY THEY JUST DON'T WANT ANY COMPETITION FOR THEIR LAME-ASS STORE."
EXCUSE ME. DO YOU HAVE ANY CHINCHILLAS?
CHINCHILLAS ARE FOR WUSSIES. HERE'S A SNAKE!
DOG

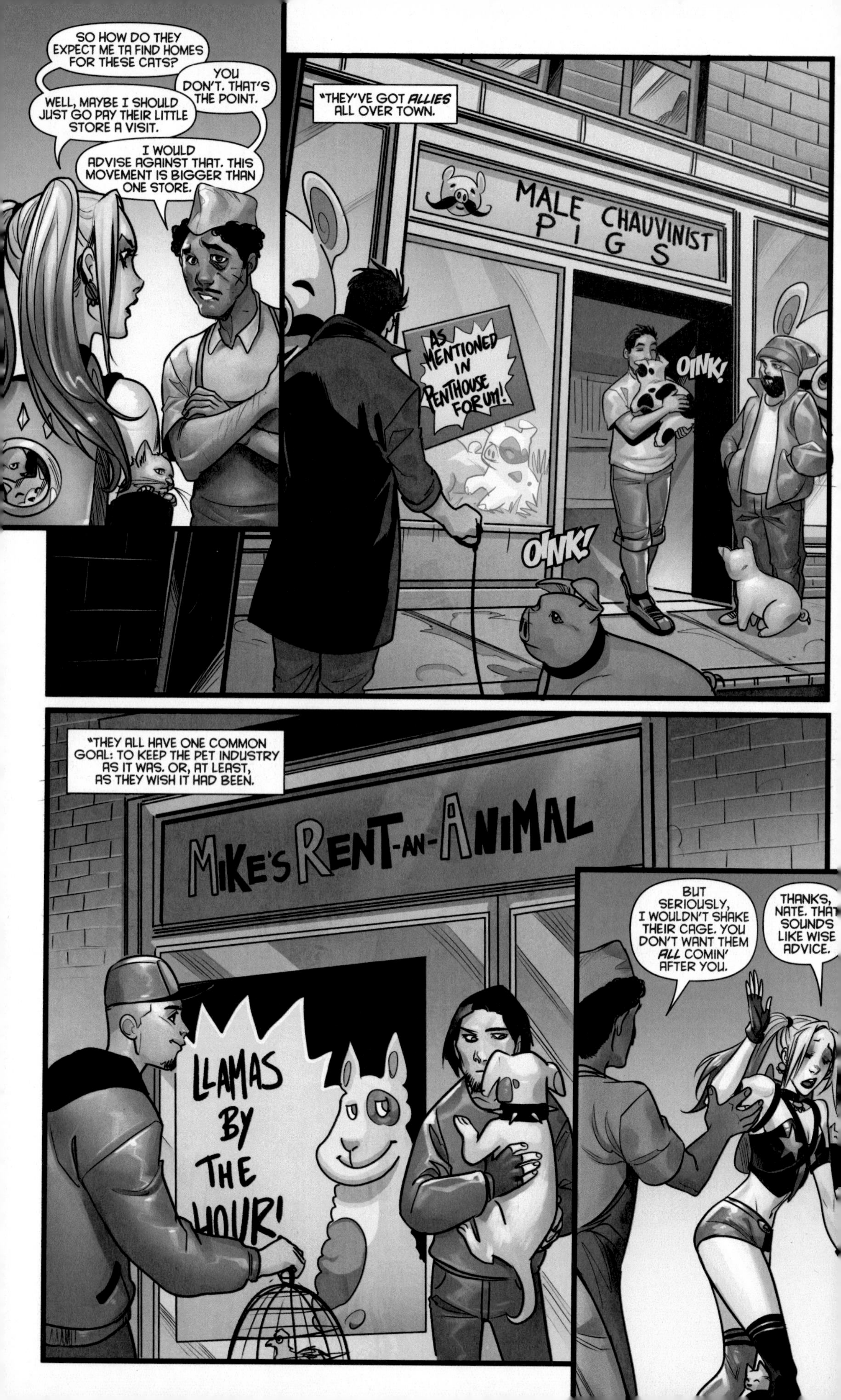
SO HOW DO THEY EXPECT ME TA FIND HOMES FOR THESE CATS?
YOU DON'T. THAT'S THE POINT.
WELL, MAYBE I SHOULD JUST GO PAY THEIR LITTLE STORE A VISIT.
I WOULD ADVISE AGAINST THAT. THIS MOVEMENT IS BIGGER THAN ONE STORE.
"THEY'VE GOT ALLIES ALL OVER TOWN.
MALE CHAUVINIST PIGS
AS MENTIONED IN PENTHOUSE FORUM!
OINK!
OINK!
"THEY ALL HAVE ONE COMMON GOAL: TO KEEP THE PET INDUSTRY AS IT WAS. OR, AT LEAST, AS THEY WISH IT HAD BEEN.
MIKE'S RENT-AN-ANIMAL
LLAMAS BY THE HOUR!
BUT SERIOUSLY, I WOULDN'T SHAKE THEIR CAGE. YOU DON'T WANT THEM ALL COMIN' AFTER YOU.
THANKS, NATE. THAT SOUNDS LIKE WISE ADVICE.

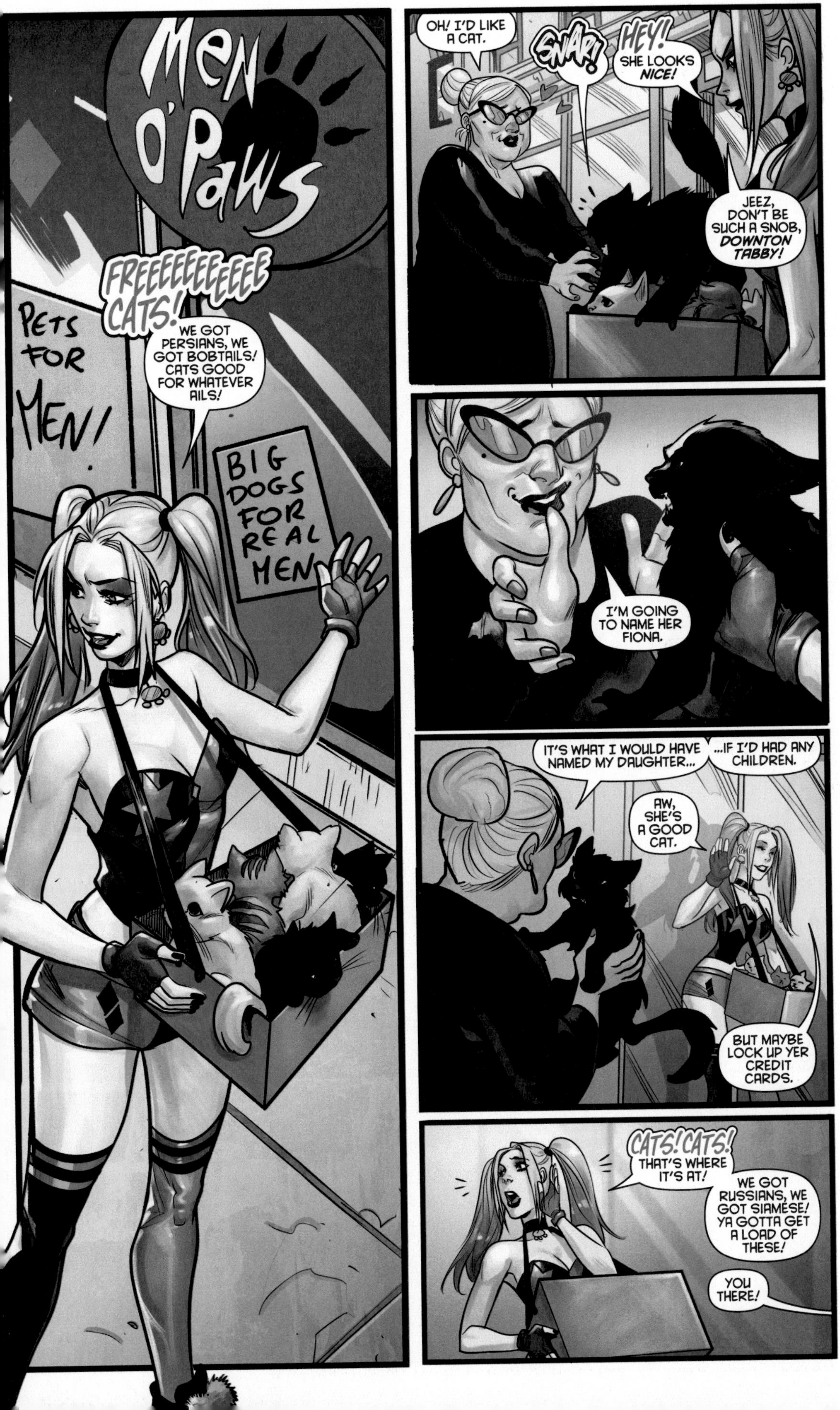
MEN O'PAWS
PETS FOR MEN!
FREEEEEEEEEEEE CATS!
WE GOT PERSIANS, WE GOT BOBTAILS! CATS GOOD FOR WHATEVER AILS!
BIG DOGS FOR REAL MEN
OH! I'D LIKE A CAT.
SNAR!
HEY! SHE LOOKS NICE!
JEEZ, DON'T BE SUCH A SNOB, DOWNTON TABBY!
I'M GOING TO NAME HER FIONA.
IT'S WHAT I WOULD HAVE NAMED MY DAUGHTER...
...IF I'D HAD ANY CHILDREN.
AW, SHE'S A GOOD CAT.
BUT MAYBE LOCK UP YER CREDIT CARDS.
CATS! CATS! THAT'S WHERE IT'S AT!
WE GOT RUSSIANS, WE GOT SIAMESE! YA GOTTA GET A LOAD OF THESE!
YOU THERE!

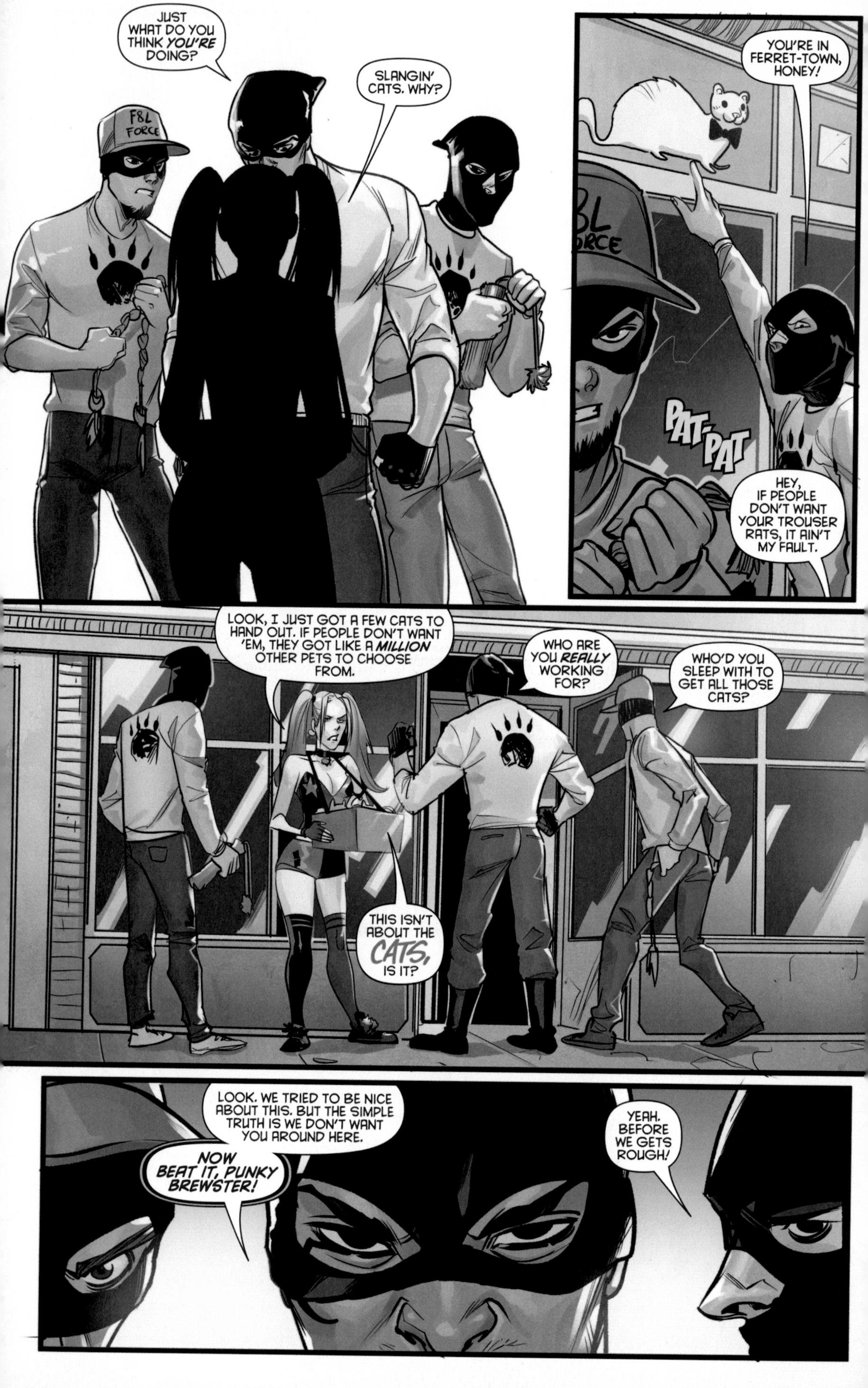
JUST WHAT DO YOU THINK *YOU'RE* DOING?
SLANGIN' CATS. WHY?
F8L FORCE
YOU'RE IN FERRET-TOWN, HONEY!
F8L FORCE
PAT-PAT
HEY, IF PEOPLE DON'T WANT YOUR TROUSER RATS, IT AIN'T MY FAULT.
LOOK, I JUST GOT A FEW CATS TO HAND OUT. IF PEOPLE DON'T WANT 'EM, THEY GOT LIKE A *MILLION* OTHER PETS TO CHOOSE FROM.
WHO ARE YOU *REALLY* WORKING FOR?
WHO'D YOU SLEEP WITH TO GET ALL THOSE CATS?
THIS ISN'T ABOUT THE *CATS,* IS IT?
LOOK. WE TRIED TO BE NICE ABOUT THIS. BUT THE SIMPLE TRUTH IS WE DON'T WANT YOU AROUND HERE.
NOW BEAT IT, PUNKY BREWSTER!
YEAH. BEFORE WE GETS ROUGH!

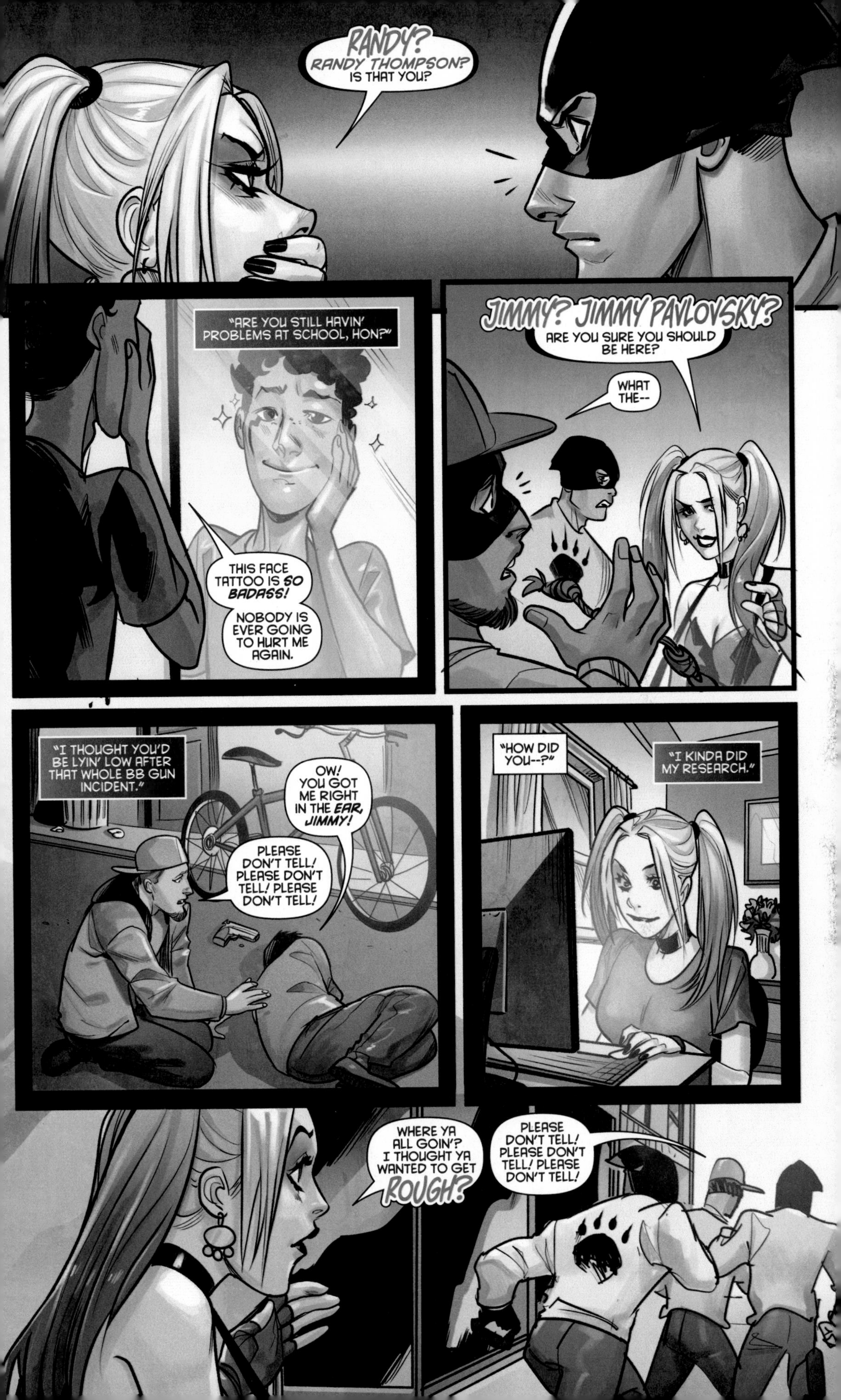
RANDY? RANDY THOMPSON? IS THAT YOU?
"ARE YOU STILL HAVIN' PROBLEMS AT SCHOOL, HON?"
THIS FACE TATTOO IS SO BADASS!
NOBODY IS EVER GOING TO HURT ME AGAIN.
JIMMY? JIMMY PAVLOVSKY? ARE YOU SURE YOU SHOULD BE HERE?
WHAT THE--
"I THOUGHT YOU'D BE LYIN' LOW AFTER THAT WHOLE BB GUN INCIDENT."
OW! YOU GOT ME RIGHT IN THE EAR, JIMMY!
PLEASE DON'T TELL! PLEASE DON'T TELL! PLEASE DON'T TELL!
"HOW DID YOU--?"
"I KINDA DID MY RESEARCH."
WHERE YA ALL GOIN'? I THOUGHT YA WANTED TO GET ROUGH?
PLEASE DON'T TELL! PLEASE DON'T TELL! PLEASE DON'T TELL!

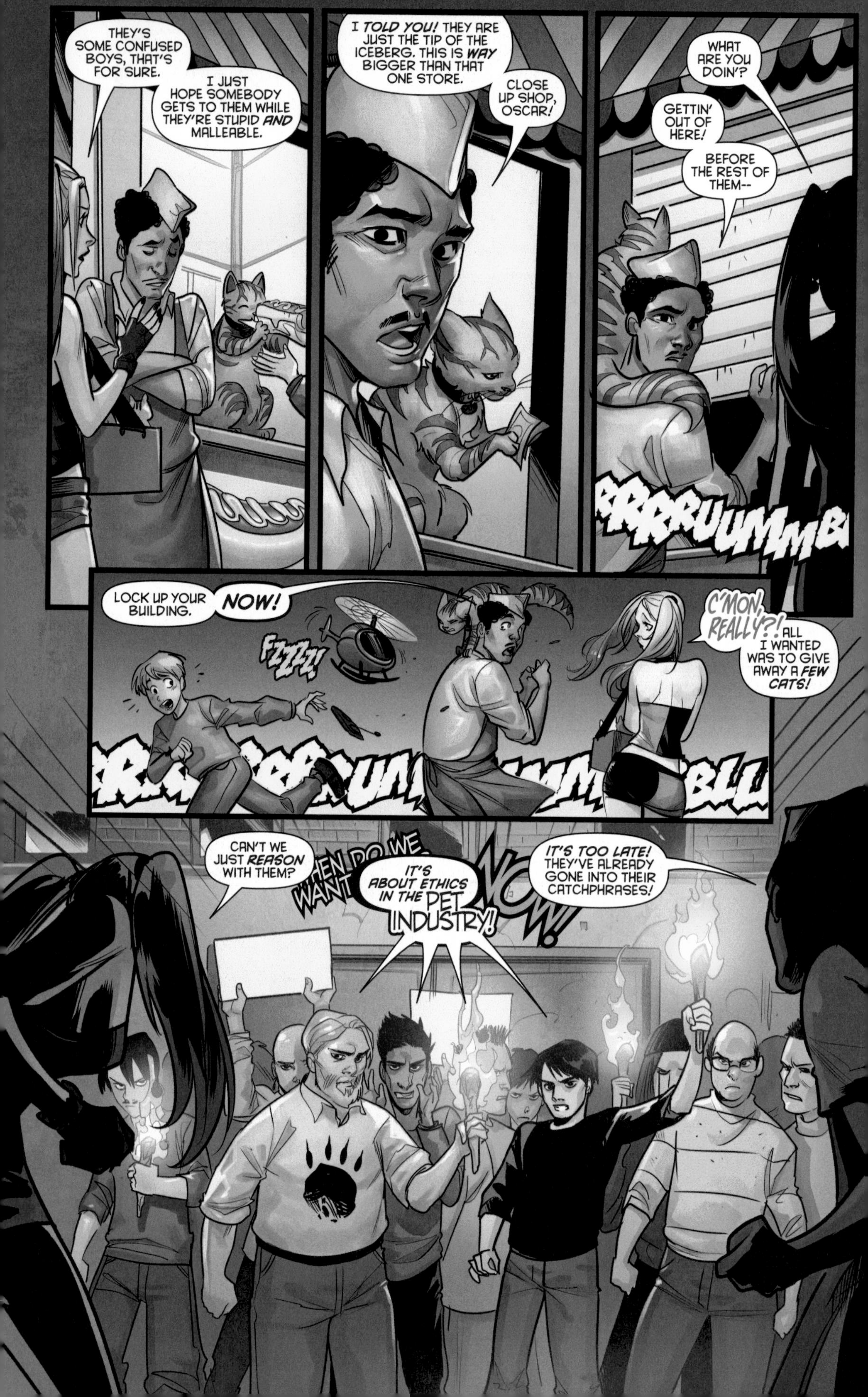
THEY'S SOME CONFUSED BOYS, THAT'S FOR SURE.
I JUST HOPE SOMEBODY GETS TO THEM WHILE THEY'RE STUPID *AND* MALLEABLE.
I *TOLD YOU!* THEY ARE JUST THE TIP OF THE ICEBERG. THIS IS *WAY* BIGGER THAN THAT ONE STORE.
CLOSE UP SHOP, OSCAR!
WHAT ARE YOU DOIN'?
GETTIN' OUT OF HERE!
BEFORE THE REST OF THEM--
RRRRUUMMB
LOCK UP YOUR BUILDING.
NOW!
FZZZZ!
C'MON, REALLY?! ALL I WANTED WAS TO GIVE AWAY A *FEW* CATS!
CAN'T WE JUST *REASON* WITH THEM?
IT'S ABOUT ETHICS IN THE PET INDUSTRY!
NOW!
IT'S TOO LATE! THEY'VE ALREADY GONE INTO THEIR CATCHPHRASES!

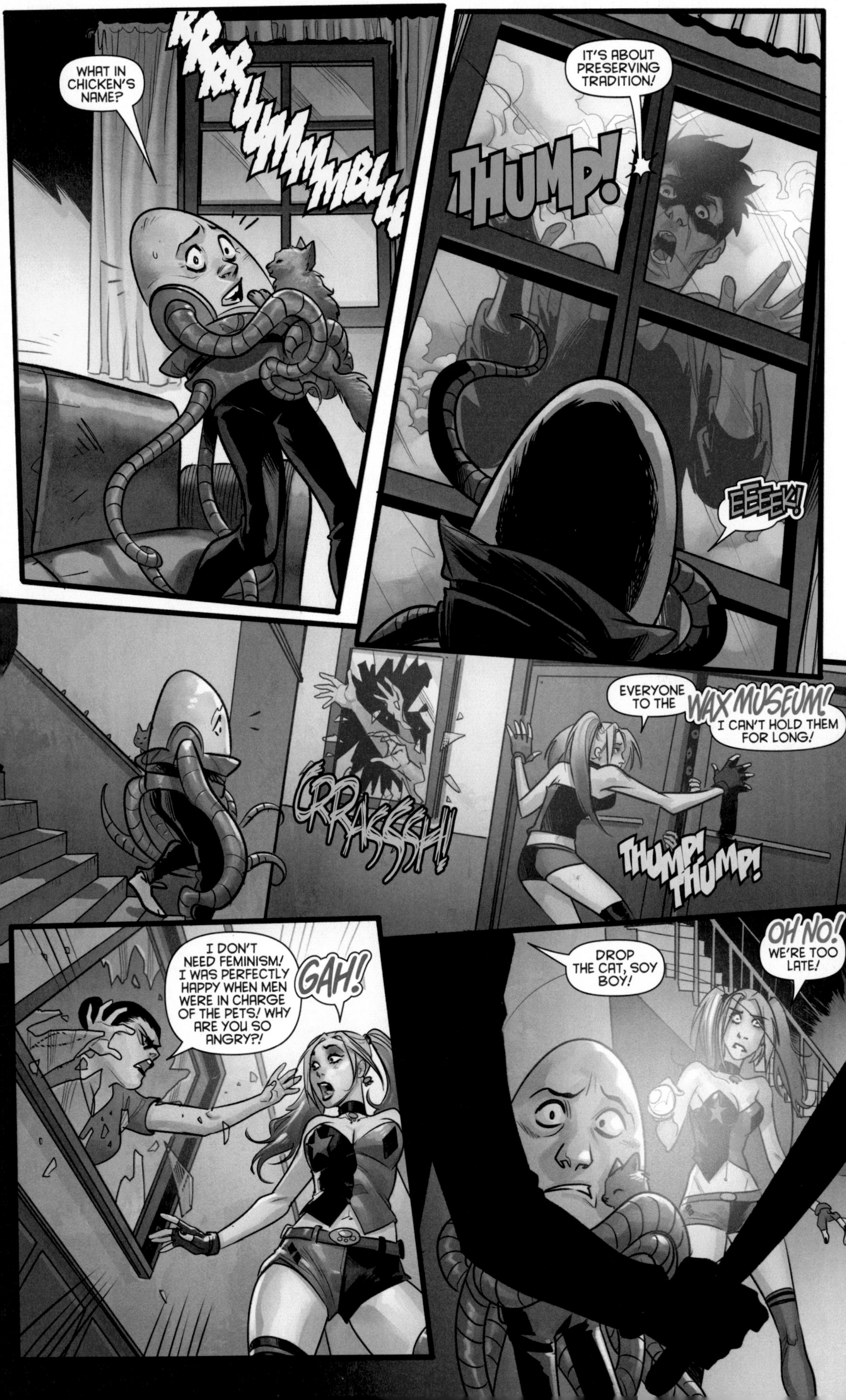
WHAT IN CHICKEN'S NAME?
KRRRUMMMBLLE
IT'S ABOUT PRESERVING TRADITION!
THUMP!
EEEEK!
CRRASSSH!
EVERYONE TO THE WAX MUSEUM! I CAN'T HOLD THEM FOR LONG!
THUMP! THUMP!
I DON'T NEED FEMINISM! I WAS PERFECTLY HAPPY WHEN MEN WERE IN CHARGE OF THE PETS! WHY ARE YOU SO ANGRY?!
GAH!
DROP THE CAT, SOY BOY!
OH NO! WE'RE TOO LATE!

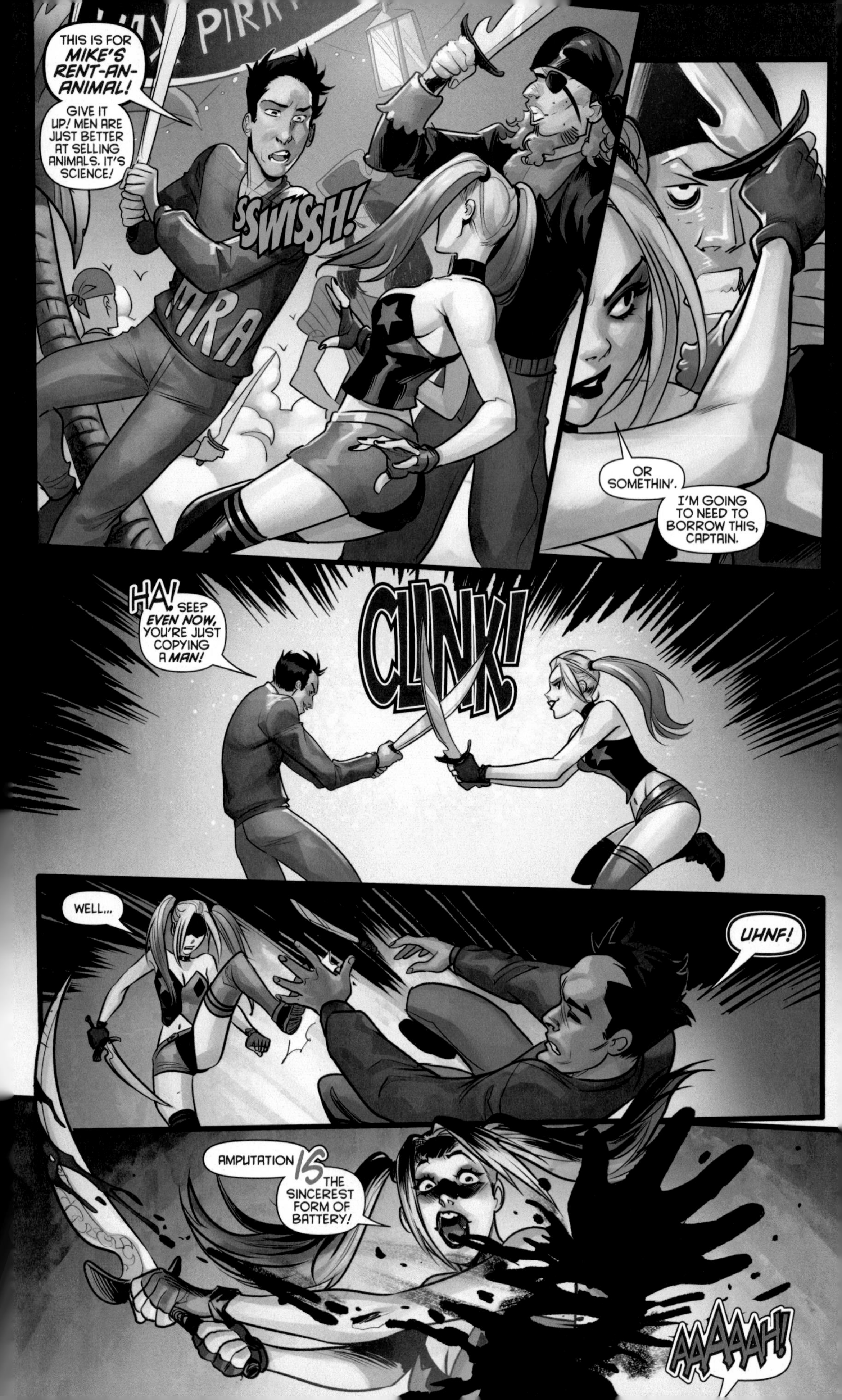

THIS IS FOR *MIKE'S RENT-AN-ANIMAL!*
GIVE IT UP! MEN ARE JUST BETTER AT SELLING ANIMALS. IT'S SCIENCE!
SWISSH!
MRA
OR SOMETHIN'.
I'M GOING TO NEED TO BORROW THIS, CAPTAIN.
HA! SEE? *EVEN NOW,* YOU'RE JUST COPYING A *MAN!*
CLINK!
WELL...
UHNF!
AMPUTATION *IS* THE SINCEREST FORM OF BATTERY!
AAAAAH!

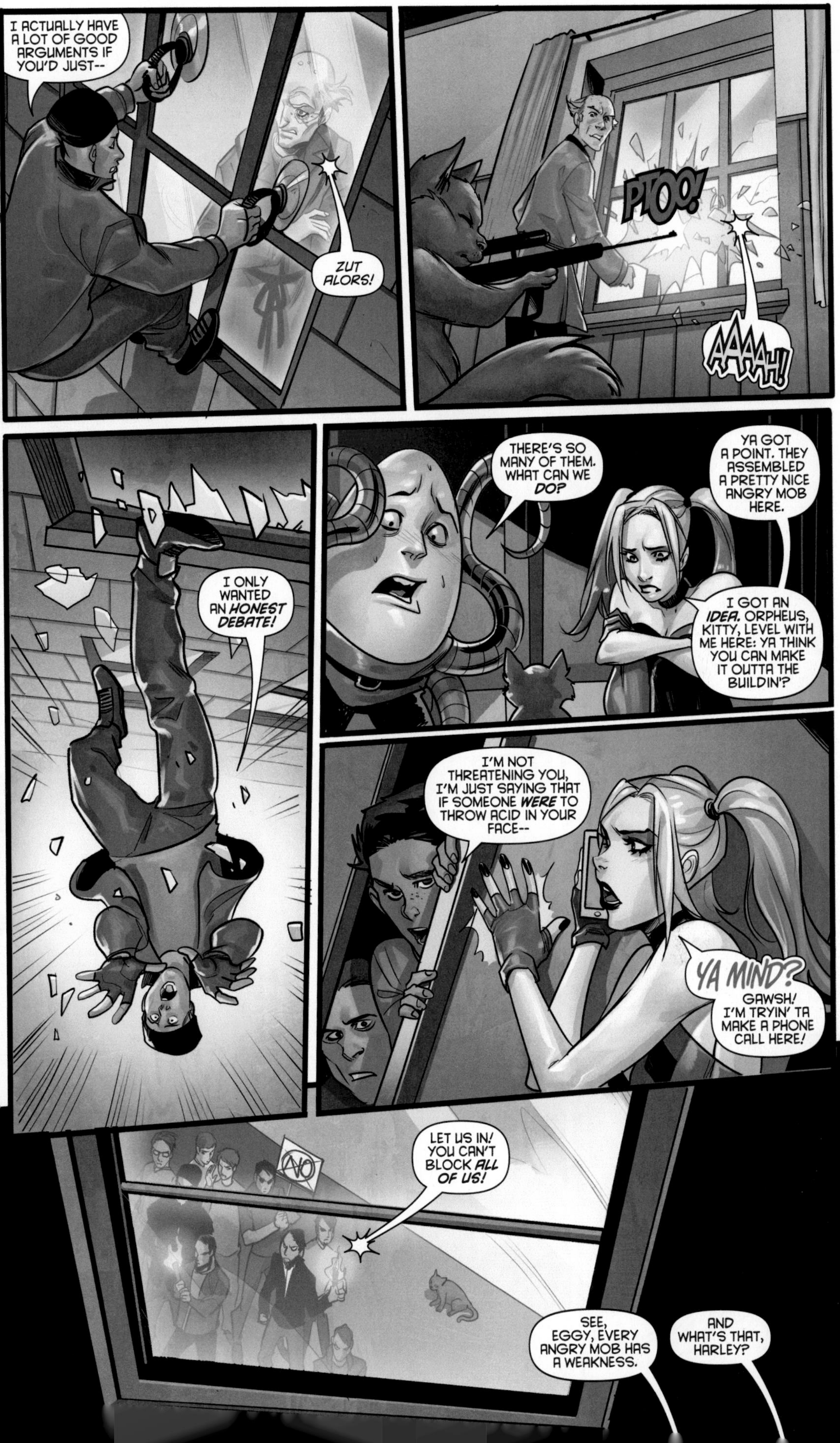
I ACTUALLY HAVE A LOT OF GOOD ARGUMENTS IF YOU'D JUST--
ZUT ALORS!
PTOO!
AAAAH!
I ONLY WANTED AN *HONEST DEBATE!*
THERE'S SO MANY OF THEM. WHAT CAN WE *DO?*
YA GOT A POINT. THEY ASSEMBLED A PRETTY NICE ANGRY MOB HERE.
I GOT AN *IDEA.* ORPHEUS, KITTY, LEVEL WITH ME HERE: YA THINK YOU CAN MAKE IT OUTTA THE BUILDIN'?
I'M NOT THREATENING YOU, I'M JUST SAYING THAT IF SOMEONE *WERE* TO THROW ACID IN YOUR FACE--
YA MIND?
GAWSH! I'M TRYIN' TA MAKE A PHONE CALL HERE!
NO
LET US IN! YOU CAN'T BLOCK *ALL OF US!*
SEE, EGGY, EVERY ANGRY MOB HAS A WEAKNESS.
AND WHAT'S THAT, HARLEY?

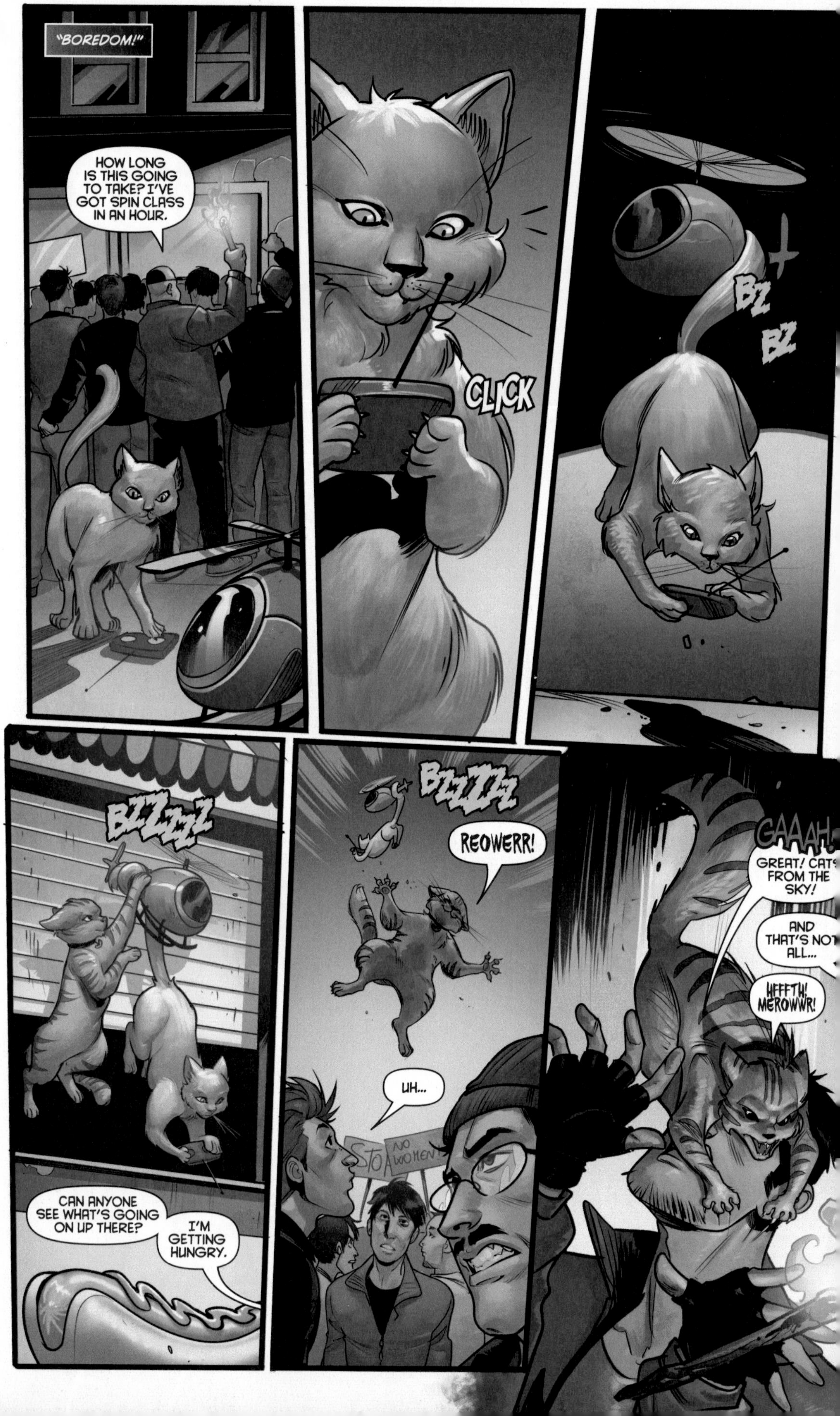
"BOREDOM!"
HOW LONG IS THIS GOING TO TAKE? I'VE GOT SPIN CLASS IN AN HOUR.
CLICK
BZ
BZ
BZZZZZ
CAN ANYONE SEE WHAT'S GOING ON UP THERE?
I'M GETTING HUNGRY.
BZZZZZ
REOWERR!
UH...
GAAAH
GREAT! CATS FROM THE SKY!
AND THAT'S NOT ALL...
HFFFTH! MEROWWR!

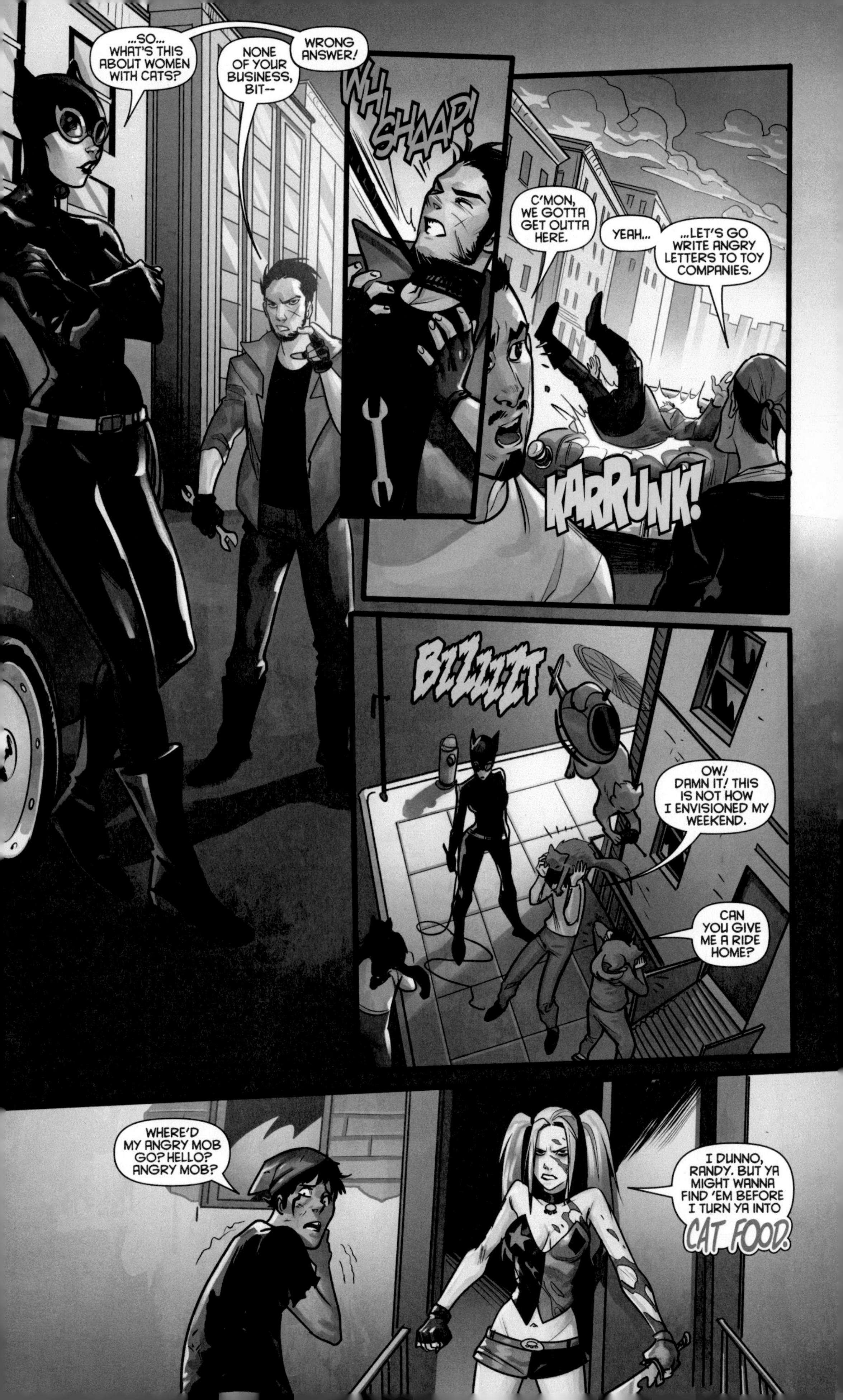
...SO... WHAT'S THIS ABOUT WOMEN WITH CATS?
NONE OF YOUR BUSINESS, BIT--
WRONG ANSWER!
WHHSHAAP!
C'MON, WE GOTTA GET OUTTA HERE.
YEAH...
...LET'S GO WRITE ANGRY LETTERS TO TOY COMPANIES.
KARRUNK!
BZZZZZT
OW! DAMN IT! THIS IS NOT HOW I ENVISIONED MY WEEKEND.
CAN YOU GIVE ME A RIDE HOME?
WHERE'D MY ANGRY MOB GO? HELLO? ANGRY MOB?
I DUNNO, RANDY. BUT YA MIGHT WANNA FIND 'EM BEFORE I TURN YA INTO CAT FOOD.

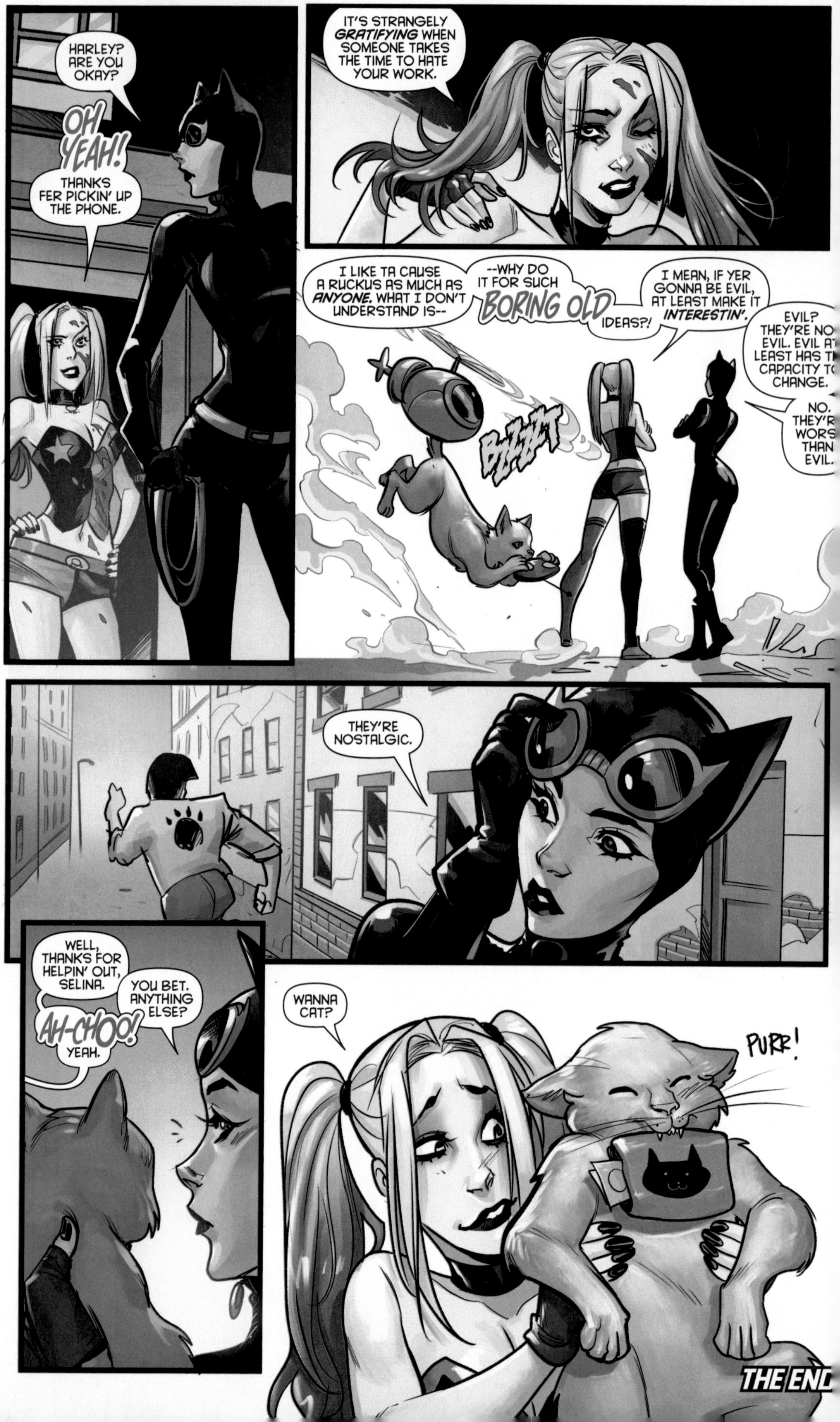
HARLEY? ARE YOU OKAY?
OH YEAH!
THANKS FER PICKIN' UP THE PHONE.
IT'S STRANGELY GRATIFYING WHEN SOMEONE TAKES THE TIME TO HATE YOUR WORK.
I LIKE TA CAUSE A RUCKUS AS MUCH AS ANYONE. WHAT I DON'T UNDERSTAND IS--
--WHY DO IT FOR SUCH BORING OLD IDEAS?!
I MEAN, IF YER GONNA BE EVIL, AT LEAST MAKE IT INTERESTIN'.
BZZZZT
THEY'RE NOSTALGIC.
WELL, THANKS FOR HELPIN' OUT, SELINA.
YOU BET. ANYTHING ELSE?
AH-CHOO! YEAH.
WANNA CAT?
PURR!
THE END

HARLEY QUINN #50 variant cover
by FRANK CHO and SABINE RICH

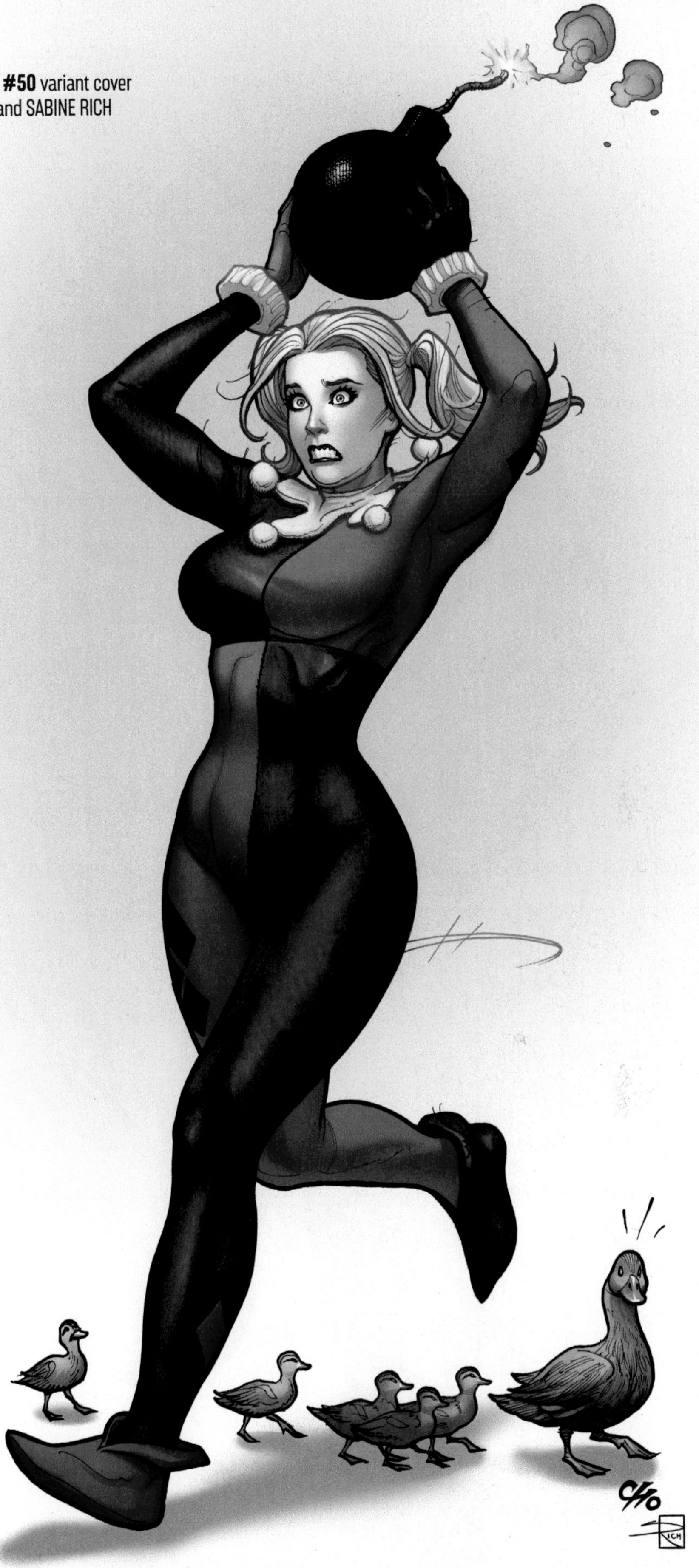
CHO
RICH

HARLEY QUINN #51 variant cover
by FRANK CHO and SABINE RICH

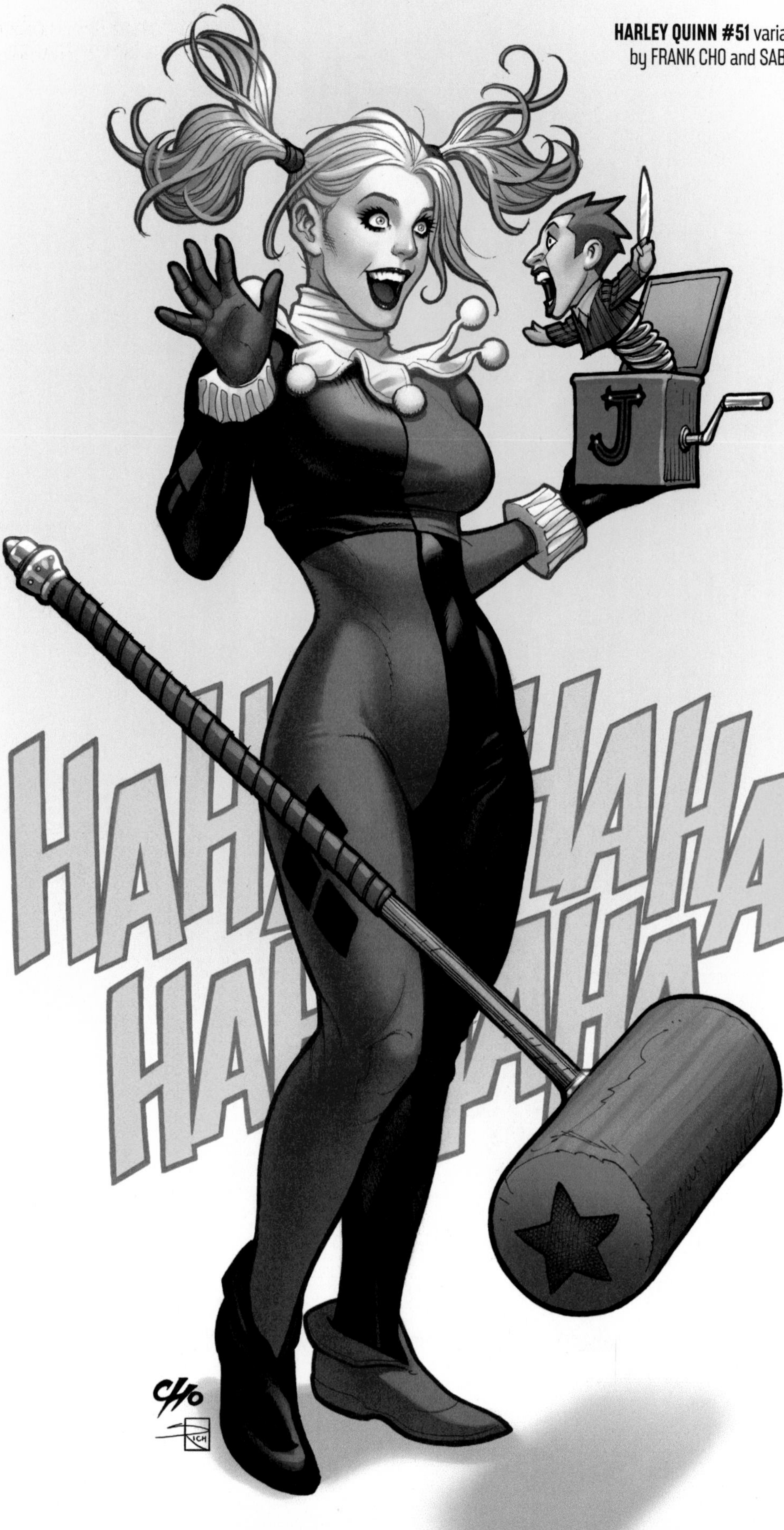

HARLEY QUINN #52 variant cover
by FRANK CHO and SABINE RICH

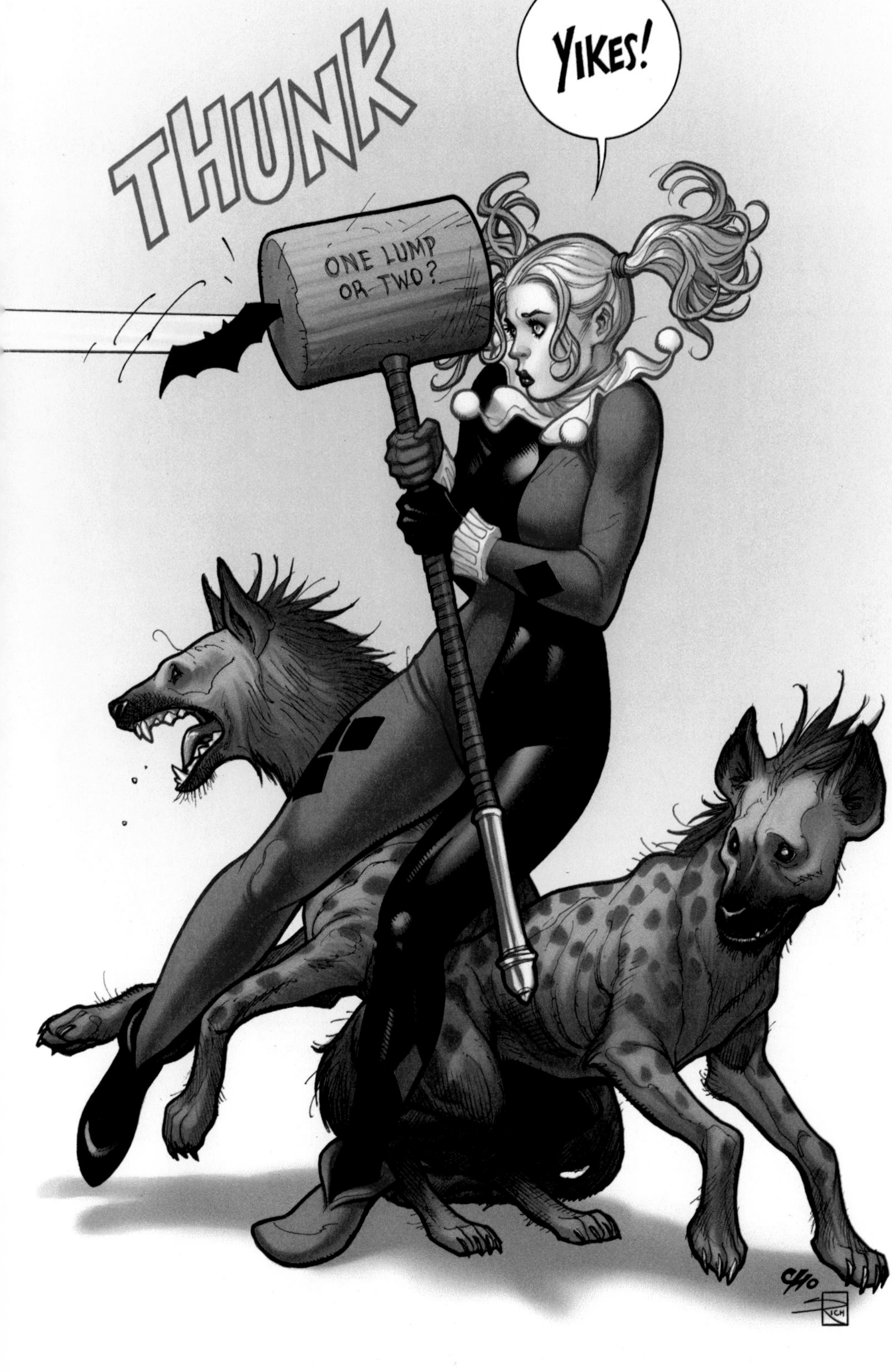
THUNK
YIKES!
ONE LUMP OR TWO?

HARLEY QUINN #53 variant cover
by FRANK CHO and SABINE RICH

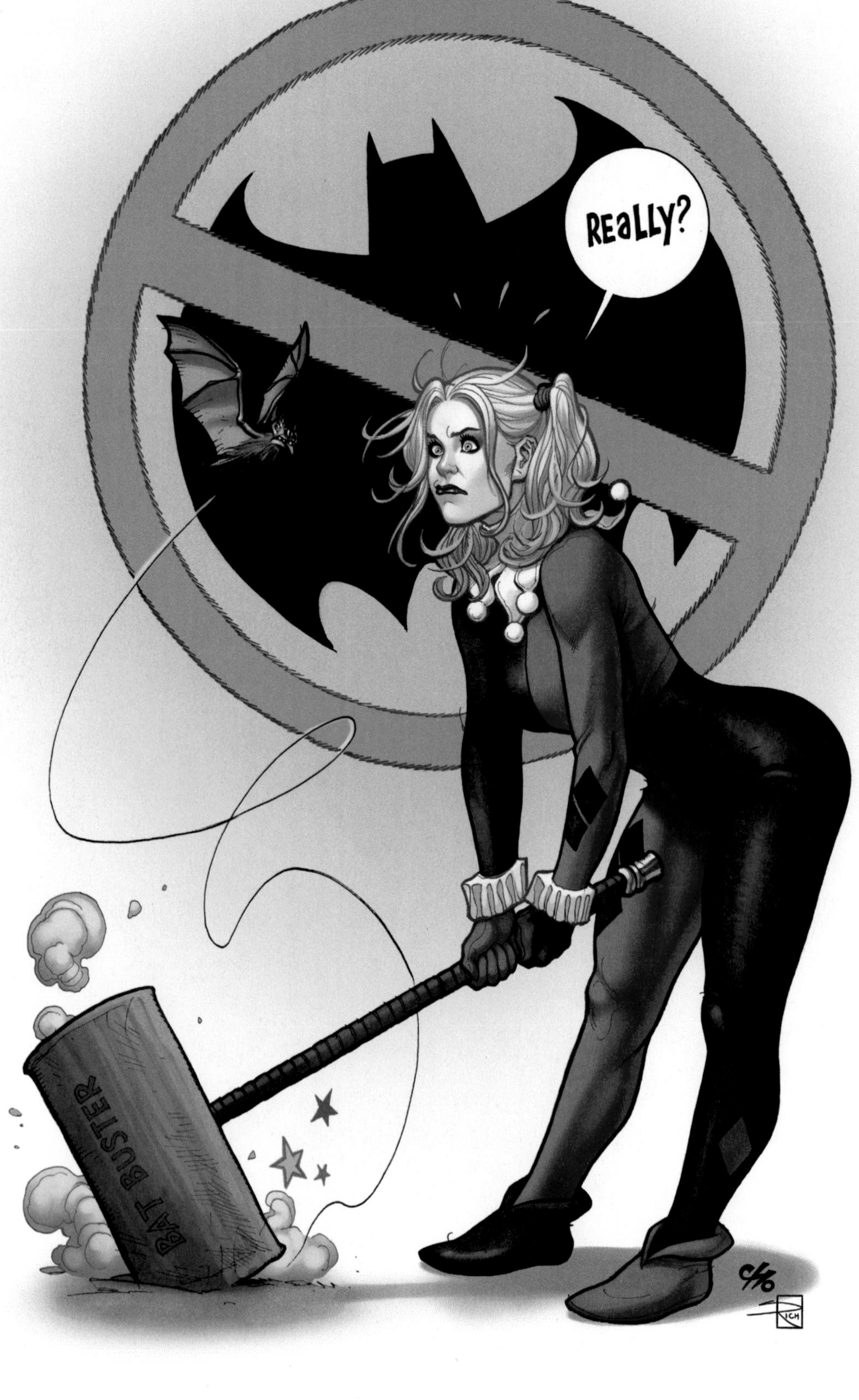
REALLY?
BAT BUSTER

HARLEY QUINN #54 variant cover
by FRANK CHO

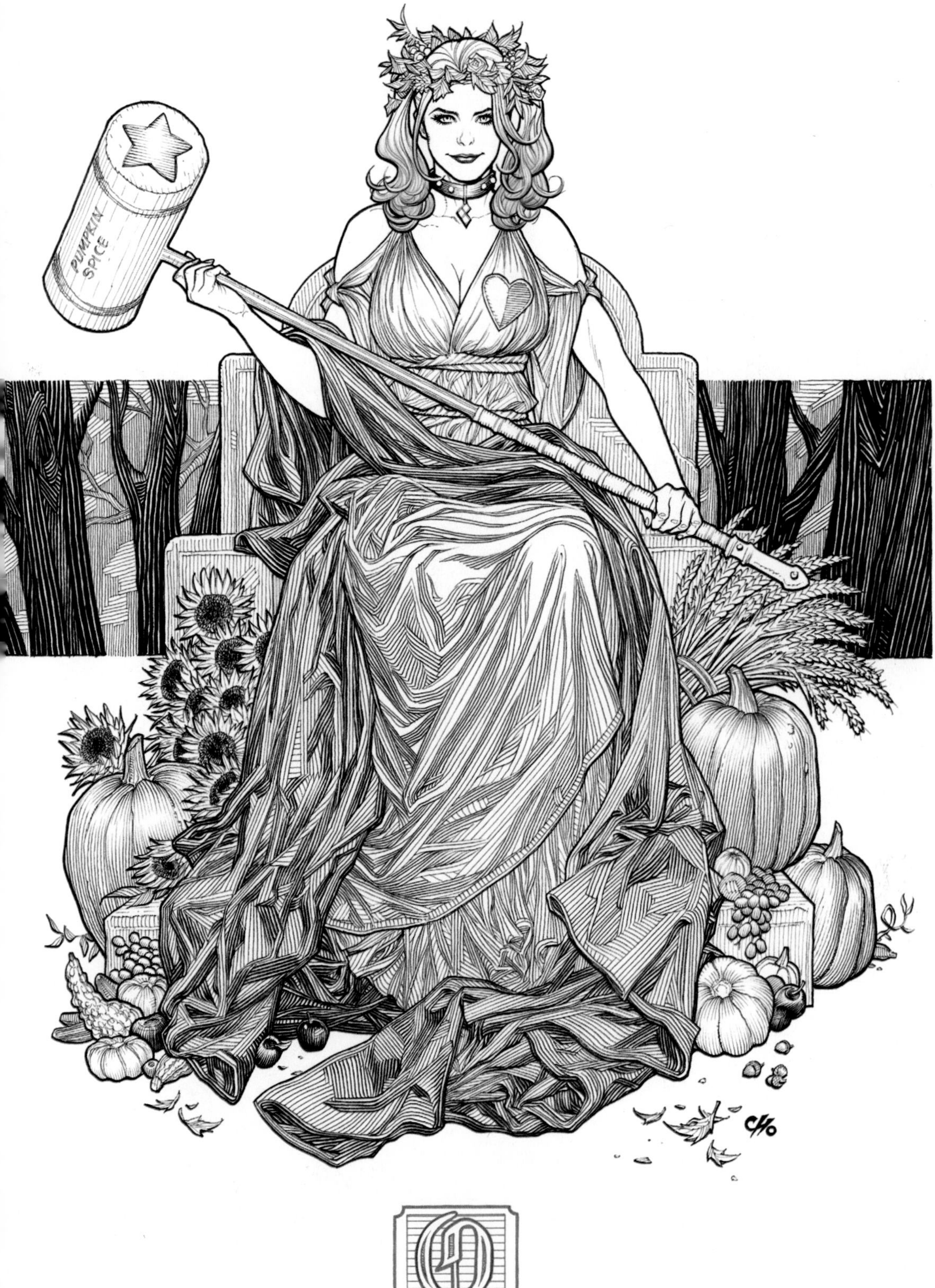
PUMPKIN SPICE
CHO

HARLEY QUINN #56 variant cover
by FRANK CHO and SABINE RICH

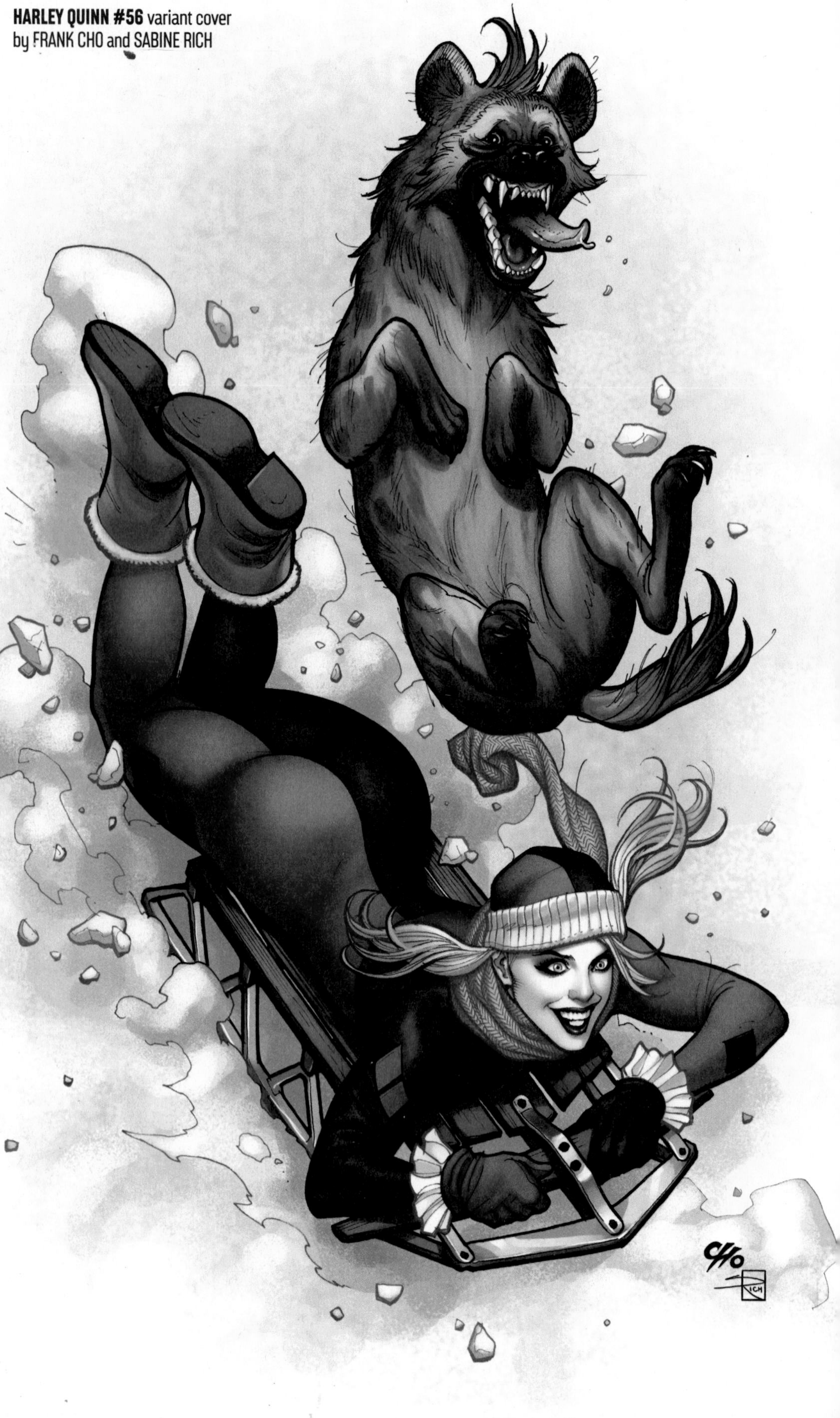
CHO
RICH